THE FORMATION OF COLLEGE ENGLISH

THE FORMATION OF

Rhetoric and Belles

Pittsburgh Series in Composition, Literacy, and Culture

David Bartholomae and Jean Ferguson Carr, Editors

COLLEGE ENGLISH

Lettres in the British Cultural Provinces

Thomas P. Miller

UNIVERSITY OF PITTSBURGH PRESS

Published by the University of Pittsburgh Press, Pittsburgh, Pa. 15261
Copyright © 1997, University of Pittsburgh Press
All rights reserved
Manufactured in the United States of America
Printed on acid-free paper
10 9 8 7 6 5 4 3 2 1

Library of Congress Cataloging-in-Publication Data

Miller, Thomas P.
    The formation of college English : rhetoric and belles lettres in
the British cultural provinces / Thomas P. Miller.
        p.   cm. — (Pittsburgh series in composition, literacy, and culture)
    Includes bibliographical references and index.
    ISBN 0-8229-3970-3 (alk. paper). — ISBN 0-8229-5623-3 (pbk. :
alk. paper)
        1. English philology—Study and teaching (Higher)—Great Britain—
History.   2. English language—Rhetoric—Study and teaching
(Higher—Great Britain—History.   3. English philology—Study and
teaching (Higher)—Ireland—History.   4. Books and reading—Great
Britain—History.   I. Title.   II. Series: Pittsburgh series in composition,
literacy, and culture.
    PE68.G5M55   1997
    420'.71'141—dc21   96-45879

A CIP catalog record for this book is available from the British Library.

Contents

Acknowledgments

The book that you are holding in your hands is very much a collaborative effort. People wrote to support my grant applications for archival research, other colleagues critiqued drafts, editors made my writing more readable, other writers helped me understand the issues I address, and now I hope that what I have written will make sense to you. Lloyd Bitzer, Arthur Quinn, Richard Enos, Richard Sher, Win Horner, and especially Lester Faigley helped me get grants from various sources, especially the National Endowment for the Humanities, which provided summer fellowships for archival research in Scotland and England and a fellowship to complete the revision of this book. I also received support from the Department of English and the College of Liberal Arts at Southern Illinois University and from the Department of English, the College of Humanities, and the vice president for research at the University of Arizona. Others supported my research by reading and commenting on it: Sharon Crowley, Ross Winterowd, Ronald Reid, Peter Medine, Billie Jo Inman, Theresa Enos, John Warnock, and Tilly Warnock. Without the support of Nan Johnson, this book would not have been accepted for publication at the University of Pittsburgh Press, and my editor there, Jean Ferguson Carr, has provided me with needed support and useful criticism from acceptance through publication. I am also indebted to the expert editing of Jane McGarry, which helped me avoid errors and infelicities. I would also like to thank the staff of the libraries that supplied me with a steady flow of dusty manuscripts and forgotten books, often for weeks at a time: those at the University of Dublin, the University of Aberdeen, Glasgow University, the University of Edinburgh, the National Library of Scotland, the British Library, Oxford University, Dr. Williams' Library at the University of London, Princeton University, the University of Philadelphia, the Presbyterian Historical Society in Philadelphia, Harvard University, Yale University, and Brown University, especially to Martha Mitchell, the university archivist there. Finally, I would like to thank my wife and collaborator, Kerstin Sanger Miller, for her support in the years spent working on this book.

I would like to dedicate this book to three professors who have shaped my work and have now retired from theirs: Maxine Hairston, James Kinneavy, and Charles Davis. Professor Hairston has been my mentor ever since I began teaching writing as her assistant at the University of Texas. Professor Kinneavy has shaped my basic understanding of rhetoric, especially the emphasis on civic humanism that is central to this book. And Charles Davis established the composition program that I work in, a program that could not have withstood the pressures arrayed against it if it had not been so expertly designed to empower the teachers who work in it by involving them in ongoing reforms of the curriculum and collaborations on their teaching. As rhetoricians, Professors Hairston, Kinneavy, and Davis may each want to take issue with some of the arguments I make, but I hope that this book honors teaching and civic rhetoric in ways that are consistent with what they have taught me as a student and colleague.

THE FORMATION OF COLLEGE ENGLISH

Introduction

The Teaching of English
in the British Cultural Provinces

> Every time the question of the language surfaces, in one way or an-
> other, it means that a series of other problems are coming to the fore:
> the formation and enlargement of the governing class, the need to es-
> tablish more intimate and secure relationships between the governing
> groups and the national-popular mass, in other words to reorganize
> the cultural hegemony.
>
> —Gramsci, *Cultural Writings*

IN THE MIDDLE of the eighteenth century, the first professorships were
founded to teach composition, rhetoric, and literature in English at the same
time the first concerted efforts were being made to establish standards for
English usage and taste. Over four hundred editions of English grammars
and some two hundred and fifteen editions of English dictionaries were published in the eighteenth century, with five times more new dictionaries and
grammars appearing after 1750 than had been published in the first half of
the century (see Alston; Tompson, "English and English Education"). As the
reading public expanded to include broader classes of readers who had to be
taught to respect the proprieties of the educated culture, Swift's project of
"Correcting, Improving and Ascertaining the English Tongue" (1712) ceased
being the avocation of a few neoclassical scholars and became the vocation of
a whole class of commentators, lexicographers, grammarians, and professors
of English.[1] While such professorships were not established at the centers of
English education until the latter half of the nineteenth century, in the 1750s
and 1760s professorships were founded to teach English throughout the
British cultural provinces, including the Scottish, Irish, and American uni-

versities as well as the academies that dissenters had established when non-Anglicans were exiled from Oxford and Cambridge in 1662. These professorships mark the formation of English as an object of formal study in higher education. To understand that formation, we need to examine how "the question of the language" arose as cheap print literacy expanded the literate culture to include a heterogeneous reading public.

Professorships dedicated to teaching English were established almost simultaneously throughout the British cultural provinces. The first published university lectures on rhetoric and literature delivered in English were John Lawson's *Lectures Concerning Oratory* (1758), but Lawson's neoclassical perspective was soon superseded by approaches that spoke more broadly to the popular interest in polite taste and correct usage. Most important is Hugh Blair's Regius Professorship of Rhetoric and Belles Lettres, founded at Edinburgh in 1762. That same year Priestley began teaching "languages and belles lettres" at Warrington Academy, and in 1768 Hugh Blair's classmate John Witherspoon emigrated to become president of Princeton and the first influential professor in the American colonies to lecture on English composition, rhetoric, and criticism. The dissenting academies actually began teaching English as early as the end of the seventeenth century, but Blair's *Lectures on Rhetoric and Belles Lettres* (1783) swept the emerging field, passing through over one hundred and ten editions to become "a staple of instruction for half the educated English-speaking world" (Schmitz 3). The appearance of professorships and textbooks marks the formation of English as an object of established study in higher education, but histories of the discipline have been hesitant to accept eighteenth-century professors of rhetoric as the founders of college English because they did not establish literary discourse as a specialized area of study.

In Britain rhetoric has been eliminated from the humanities, and in America the most respected English departments have traditionally defined themselves as departments of literature. One can thus understand why rhetoric has not been accepted as part of the history of college English. Historians of rhetoric and composition such as Berlin, Crowley, Horner, and Johnson have argued that the rhetorical theories that appeared in the eighteenth century have shaped the teaching of composition into the present day, but literary critics have generally paid as little attention to such accounts as they have to other scholarship on the teaching of composition. Histories of the discipline have generally begun with the nineteenth century, when historical philology helped professionalize the study of English literature (see, for example, Palmer or McMurty). The best known history of college English studies in America, Graff's *Professing English Literature: An Institutional History* (1987), straightforwardly defined the discipline as "academic literary studies" and explained its history according to what developed in "research-oriented departments of English at major universities" (2, 39). In *Institutionalizing English Literature: The Culture and Politics of Literary Study, 1750–1900* (1992), Court went one step farther and simply appropriated rhetoric as "the oldest form of literary criticism" (176). Unlike Terry Eagleton, whom he quoted on this point, Court ignored the fact that rhetoric treats criticism as a prelude to action rather than as an end in itself because rhetoricians are more concerned with the composition than the reception of discourse.[2]

Rhetoricians were the first professors to teach English literature and composition, but when literary studies became professionalized in the nineteenth century, scholarship on rhetoric began to be marginalized as the discipline came to concentrate on philological studies and a few literary genres—poetry, drama, and fiction. Rather than accepting this division into the scientific and aesthetic, I find the modern conception of *literature* to be a curiously narrow educational paradigm that requires an historical explanation. As Ong has discussed, before the eighteenth century "poetry enjoyed no particular status as an independent academic discipline whereas rhetoric enjoyed enormous academic prestige" (*Rhetoric, Romance, and Technology* 6). English departments inverted this relationship, but their traditional confines are currently being challenged by more political and less belletristic conceptions of cultural studies and by broader utilitarian trends in American universities that are working to reduce the humanities to "gen ed." Thus it may be an opportune time to reassess how rhetoric's broader attention to political discourse and popular values became subordinated to the study of nonutilitarian, nonfactual discourse. To understand how English studies were reduced to literary studies, we need to look beyond the confines of traditional English departments to examine how the modern culture was introduced into higher education as cheap print literacy expanded the educated culture and reorganized cultural hegemony in the latter half of the eighteenth century.

The introduction of English was but the most obvious part of the modern departure from classicism that transformed higher education. That transition can be located in the British provinces by simply noting the changes at the core of the humanities in the trivium of the language arts of rhetoric, logic, and grammar. According to W. S. Howell's influential account, in the eighteenth century deductive forms of reasoning were supplanted by an inductive approach to logic, and a formalistic rhetoric was replaced by a "new" rhetoric defined by the plain style and experiential logic of the sciences. Taking Howell's account for a quick frame of reference, one finds that in Britain the Ciceronian rhetoric was perpetuated almost entirely by those at the centers of English education, while all of the "new" rhetoricians were Scots except for an Irishman and a dissenter. Surprisingly, the same division holds between the defenders of syllogistic reasoning and the advocates of the inductive logic identified with Locke, who received most of his education in a dissenting academy. All of the major British advocates of inductive reasoning identified by Howell were Scots except for a dissenter, Isaac Watts. In the study of grammar as well, a dissenter and a Scot (Joseph Priestley and George Campbell) were the leading advocates of standardizing English by inductively generalizing from actual usage, while the most influential defender of a more prescriptivist position was Robert Lowth, an Anglican bishop and Oxford professor of poetry.[3] Thus, modern conceptions of logical, rhetorical, and grammatical conventions were first formalized and institutionalized not at the educational centers of the learned culture but in the provinces.

While provincial reformers heralded their innovations by repudiating classicism, the centers of the learned culture no doubt had a very different perspective on the introduction of the vernacular. Viewed from such a position, the introduction of English would have looked like a decline in standards that ensued when provincial institutions proved incapable of perpetuating learned languages. From the perspective of traditional academics, the introduction of English marked the beginning of the modern literacy crisis that would move learned languages to the periphery of the curriculum and establish English literature as the classics of the educated culture. Such literacy crises have generally been blamed on the public schools or on admissions policies that fail to keep out the less educated. Viewed from elite institutions today, the decline of established forms of literacy can be seen in the introduction of "basic" writing courses in American universities. Such efforts at remediation occur whenever the relations between higher education and the educated public are being mediated in new ways, with what needs to be taught changing along with broader changes in class relations and forms of literacy. When such changes disrupt the transmission of the educated culture, educators have to develop new ways to justify and explain its conventions. Such ruptures shaped the "new" rhetoric that introduced English studies into higher education in the eighteenth century as well as the "new" rhetoric that has recently reintroduced rhetoric and composition into English departments in America, in both cases in institutions that were more broadly accessible to the educated public.[4]

The first professors of English had to begin by teaching themselves English because they were not English. When the conventions of polite taste and correct usage began to be formally studied and taught to those who had not acquired them as part of their natural upbringing within the dominant culture, culture itself ceased to seem so natural. It began to be examined both as a specific domain set apart from the "common" experience and as the process of enculturation that provincials experienced as they became assimilated into the dominant culture. As provincials refashioned their own language and sensibility, they became aware of differences in cultural conventions, but teachers generally maintained that the dominant culture had a natural authority because they wanted to believe that it was based in their common nature, rather than simply being imposed upon outsiders such as themselves. Like the other texts that were first used to teach the modern culture in universities, Henry Home's influential *Elements of Criticism* (1762) carefully mapped out a domain between nature and convention where "culture" could be cultivated through the process of personal "refinement":

> A taste for these arts is a plant that grows naturally in many soils; but, without culture, scarce to perfection in any soil; it is susceptible of much refinement, and is, by proper care, greatly improved. In this respect, a taste in the fine arts goes hand in hand with the moral sense, to which indeed it is nearly allied: both of them discover what is right and what is wrong; fashion, temper, and education, have an influence to vitiate both, or to preserve them pure and untainted; neither of them are arbitrary nor local, being rooted in human nature, and governed by principles common to all men. (6)

Home's text was widely used to teach students that "culture" was a matter of "taste," a natural faculty, but one that could be refined through careful enculturation to eradicate "local" customs and prejudices. "Taste" was the pivotal concept for the educational reorientation from the production to the reception of discourse that occurred when rhetoric was first translated into the study of English.

Like previous accounts of the history of college English studies, my view of the field is shaped by where I work within it. Rhetoric has been eliminated from the curriculum in British and elite American universities, but in more broadly accessible American universities and colleges, rhetoric has recently become reestablished as an area of scholarly inquiry in the humanities, almost exactly two centuries after rhetoricians first introduced the study of English into higher education. In the 1960s and 1970s when more open admissions policies brought broader classes of students into many colleges and universities, American teachers of composition rediscovered rhetoric, and research and graduate studies in rhetoric and composition began to become established in English departments. Composition programs grew to become the largest and least respected parts of most English departments, and specialists in rhetoric and composition like myself were hired to direct them. Like others in my area, my work is not confined to my individual research and teaching. My research ranges from Aristotle to business writing, and I work all around the borders of the academy—teaching entering students how to write and read academic discourse, training graduate students to work in the classroom, and collaborating on recruitment and outreach with high schools and community literacy programs. While also serving broader purposes and constituencies, composition programs function within English departments to introduce students to academic writing before they go on to study the classics of English literature. English departments tend to define rhetoric by this service function, but rhetoric is difficult to contain within such functions because it is both an interdisciplinary study and a political art.

Rather than defining the discipline by the history of ideas contained within it, I try to establish a more rhetorical perspective on the formation of college English—a perspective defined by rhetoric's traditional concern for assessing how discourse is used in specific contexts to accomplish particular purposes. Rhetoric's traditional emphasis on contexts and the transactions between audiences and orators or writers is at odds with the emphasis on textual interpretation that characterizes modern literary studies (see Tompkins; Eagleton, *Function of Criticism*). A rhetorical concern for purpose as the controlling element in discursive transactions requires a broader examination of what purposes were served by the formation of college English. The fact that English was first introduced outside the centers of English education challenges the tendency of disciplinary histories to assume that change begins at the top among major theorists in elite universities and is then transmitted down to be taught in less influential institutions. This trickle-down conception of the history of ideas is understandable because the scholars who write histories want to think that scholarship guides trends in the field. However, it may be that changes in language studies are more like changes in language than we imagine, with change coming not from the elite but from those at the boundaries of the language community who develop a dialectical awareness of the cultural and social differences marked by those boundaries through contact with groups who are not contained within them. I believe that those who teach and study in such "contact zones" influence the history and future of the discipline far more than has been recognized.

Rhetoric has historically concentrated on the pragmatics of exercising power over public audiences, and it has always been denigrated by academics for being more concerned with popular opinions than with Truth. The domain of rhetoric lies between what can be assumed and what cannot be argued in public—between what need not be said and what is beyond question. This domain is also demarcated by the assumption that the educated are themselves above rhetoric because it is the art of speaking to the ignorant in ways that they can understand. In this domain between the popular experience and the educated culture, rhetoric has been defined as the art of celebrating public values, resolving legal conflicts, and deliberating over political policies and actions. As the art of drawing on popular values to persuade the public about what it ought to do, rhetoric has historically been associated with the ethical and political concerns of moral philosophy. This relationship was lost when ethics and aesthetics became conflated as matters of personal sentiment and the production of purposeful discourse became subordinated to belletristic criticism concerned with instilling those sentiments. I want to examine how such developments redefined the domain of rhetoric when it was translated into English because I am interested in how the humanities can prepare students to become productively involved in political debates over popular values in practical action.

While such civic concerns are a well-recognized part of the history of rhetoric, modern rhetoric and composition courses have largely concentrated on moving students from the domain of personal experience to the conventions of academic essays, with public issues often providing a convenient backdrop for that transition. Students have traditionally been taught to treat "both sides" of issues and maintain the disinterested stance deemed appropriate with educated audiences, but teachers have recently begun to question such academic ploys and have worked to develop more explicitly politicized ways to approach sites of conflict. I believe that such efforts are an integral part of the general expansion of rhetoric and composition beyond the confines of academic discourse. I hope that this movement will converge with work on community literacies and cultural studies to revitalize and broaden rhetoric's traditional concern for how people draw on popular values to resolve conflicts and deliberate on shared problems.[5] To contribute to this project and establish a context for my own historical analyses, I begin with a critical examination of the civic domain, where rhetoric concerns itself with popular values in political action. I hope to show that rhetoric's traditional involvement with public discourse explains both why it was rhetoricians who introduced the language of public life into higher education, and why rhetoric was then excised from the humanities as disciplines such as literature and science adapted themselves to the modern mission of educating a more heterogeneous public by claiming to speak disinterestedly for it.

Some Guiding Assumptions About the Domain of Rhetoric

The rhetoricians who introduced the study of English into provincial colleges were the first to lecture on modern culture in the public idiom because rhetoric had broader public engagements that made it an important site for the reorganization of cultural hegemony. Traditionally defined as the art of speaking to the public, rhetoric was historically connected with moral philosophy by a shared concern for popular values and public politics. Into the eighteenth century, rhetoric and moral philosophy were broadly influenced by the same two civic humanists, Aristotle and Cicero. Civic humanists treated rhetoric as a political art that the educated use to resolve political conflicts, but as the public sphere expanded to include a heterogeneous reading public, new classes of readers needed to be taught to respect the proprieties of polite society. This need was met by the emphasis on taste in the classrooms and self-improvement literature of the mid-eighteenth century. While civic humanism provides the historical point of departure for considering rhetoric's traditional involvement in the political sphere, modern rhetoric has been defined by the development of civil society ever since Adam Smith and his colleagues first began to teach English to adapt higher education to the needs of "commercial society." As higher education expanded its frame of reference to address broader classes of students, the perspective of the humanities began to shift from the political agent to the disinterested spectator or critical observer. The subordination of rhetoric to belletristic criticism was part of this broader transition.

Within the civic humanist tradition, rhetoric and moral philosophy shared a concern for questions about how traditional values can be made to speak to practical conflicts. Moral philosophers have tended to be concerned with practical morality, and those who were too exhortative and unsystematic tend to be dismissed by modern academics for being too "rhetorical"— mere defenders of the faith or popular moralists.[6] From a rhetorical perspective, moral philosophy is a crucial area for studying the educational transmission of the dominant culture, because moral philosophy is charged with teaching and preaching to the public about how to put received values into practical action, whether it be in the form of a political statement, an act of private devotion, or the process of introspection involved in internalizing received beliefs. In its more exhortative forms, moral philosophy becomes rhetorical precisely because it is concerned with persuading people to adopt a set of values, values that in practice will tend to define who can speak and what is beyond question. Moral philosophy also tends to be rhetorical in another sense as well, for like rhetoric, moral philosophy has traditionally been involved in projecting the authority of the educated into the public domain —the domain where questions about moral authority and personal identity take on practical political significance. Through their involvement with practical values in social action, rhetoric and moral philosophy are the historical domain of philosophies of social praxis.[7] In this domain intellectual inquiry becomes practically involved with the popular experience, though that involvement has generally maintained rather than challenged the authority of the dominant culture.

The historical ties between rhetoric and moral philosophy are evident in the fact that Adam Smith and other professors of moral philosophy such as John Witherspoon taught some of the first university courses in English on rhetoric (see also Irvine). Smith lectured to his private class on rhetoric and belles lettres at Glasgow in the 1750s and 1760s at the same time that he was broadening his public course on moral philosophy to include the "science" of political economy. Like other belletrists such as Hugh Blair, Smith gave less emphasis to composition and oratory than to stylistic criticism, and in the lectures on moral philosophy that formed the basis of his *Wealth of Nations,* he identified "the power of persuasion" with the natural "disposition to barter," rather than with the sphere of popular politics (*Lectures on Jurisprudence* 493–94). As I discuss, the institutional origins of such social sciences as political economy and psychology are connected to the formation of college English through the traditional continuities between rhetoric and moral philosophy. In the chapter on Smith, I examine how the effort to reduce politics to a science helped reorient rhetoric away from the classical focus on public discourse to center on the mental processes of the isolated individual. While classical rhetoric was concerned with drawing on shared assumptions to speak to public problems, the psychology of the individual auditor became the definitive concern of the "new" rhetoric, including Hugh Blair and other belletrists concerned with taste as well as George Campbell, Joseph Priestley, and others who programmatically redefined rhetoric according to what Hume had termed "the science of man" or the "science of human nature" (Hume, *Treatise* 43, *Inquiry* 15; see also Campbell, *Philosophy of Rhetoric* lxvii).

As I argue more fully in later chapters, the introduction of the modern culture into higher education was influenced by two trends that shaped the formation of college English as well as the modern conception of the arts and sciences as two distinct spheres of experience, a distinction that only became established in the eighteenth century (see *OED*). The civic concerns of moral philosophy and rhetoric were redefined by a belletristic tendency to treat ethics and aesthetics as matters of personal sentiment or taste, as Henry Home did in the passage already quoted. At the same time, moral philosophers and rhetoricians set out to apply the "experimental" method to create a science of political economy with a laissez-faire view of politics. As Olson has discussed in *Science Deified and Science Defied* (1982), the works of Smith and other Scottish moral philosophers mark "the first stages in the popular and relatively unsophisticated attempt to appropriate the methods and authority of empiricist natural science" to establish a science of politics (72–73). When the humanities evolved into what C. P. Snow has termed the "two cultures" of the arts and sciences, rhetoric was left betwixt and between—too situated and self-interested to be scientific and too calculated, political, and utilitarian to be literary. Belletrism subordinated composition to criticism as a means to instill taste and maintain the proprieties of civil society, while the trend toward scientism moved moral philosophy toward the social sciences and away from a practical involvement in political conflicts.[8] The trends toward belletrism and scientism converged on a critical stance better oriented to making disinterested appraisals of the moral and political "economy" than to speaking to public conflicts—the stance of the impartial spectator.

Adam Smith's "impartial spectator" is central to my argument because the perspective of the disinterested observer aptly suited belletristic critics and social scientists but was antithetical to rhetoric's classical engagement with politics. The "great inmate," "the demigod within the breast" internalized the perspective of the detached observer in the form of a second self who judges every thought and deed according to the proprieties of polite society and approves of actions and reactions if they are not self-interested (Smith, *Theory of Moral Sentiments* 146, 131). Smith's reflections on how morés are internalized are an important site to examine how the relations of intellectual reflection and practical action were refigured as the educated public expanded beyond a stable elite with a well-defined set of shared values. To establish a reliable point of reference to judge changing morés, Smith turned inward to reflect on how individuals develop sympathy for others in daily life, and his examinations of sympathetic responses to other individuals modeled the process of introjection by which individuals were to internalize a more refined second self to monitor their own reactions. Smith's *Theory of Moral Sentiments* was popular with the reading public because the "impartial spectator" aptly characterized the position of provincials who stood at a distance from the centers of political conflict and wanted to have someone tell them how to speak and respond appropriately. As I discuss, provincials learned to assume the detached perspective of the impartial spectator in English classes and literary societies dedicated to studying the refined style and rhetorical stance of essays of taste and manners such as those of the *Spectator,* which may in fact have been the source of Smith's term. Through such studies, readers learned to internalize the stance of the impartial spectator, "voluntarily" acceding to the hegemony of the dominant culture by accepting it as a model for their experience in the manner discussed by Antonio Gramsci (see *Prison Notebooks* 12).

Several of Gramsci's key terms are central to my analysis of the formation of college English. Gramsci's conception of *civil society* provides a model for my understanding of Smith's laissez-faire effort to free "commercial society" from politics. Gramsci distinguished the domains of civil and political society with the shorthand equation of "state = political society + civil society, in other words hegemony protected by the armor of coercion" (263). Political society is under the control of the state, while civil society includes socioeconomic transactions and cultural relations not directly controlled by political authorities. Like the carefully depoliticized domain of civil society, commercial society was conceived to be public but not political, a distinction inconceivable to civic humanists, who equated the public with the *polis* and relegated economics to matters of personal business and household finance.[9] In the classical period, the humanities had centered on rhetoric in order to prepare a narrow citizenry to exercise public power. When the public became an empire and then a "republic of letters," rhetoric helped to maintain the boundaries of the educated culture by emphasizing the stylistic proprieties that limited access to those who had mastered the refinements of learned languages. Such boundaries were difficult to maintain when the learned culture was translated into the common idiom, especially when the borders between the polite culture and the popular experience were being blurred by cheap print literacy and social diversification. Like a modern consumer society, a reading public by definition treats its members as consumers and not producers of discourse, and this stance was reproduced within the academy by emphasizing reception and concentrating on a narrow range of nonutilitarian and nonpolitical texts.

Another of Gramsci's concepts, *cosmopolitanism,* aptly characterizes a function that college English studies served first in the British provinces and then throughout the colonies of the English-speaking world, a function still served whenever educated usage, critical detachment, and literary tastes are taught as decontextualized ideals rather than as conventions shaped by the exercise of power through discourse. As Gramsci has discussed, as a metropolitan culture expands its sphere of influence, ambitious individuals from marginal groups learn to identify themselves with the dominant culture and become alienated from their social experience and cultural traditions.[10] As we shall see, the cosmopolitan culture popularized by the *Spectator* and its provincial imitators was avidly studied in the literary societies that spread polite taste throughout the provinces and helped establish the study of English in higher education. Cosmopolitanism is but the obverse of provincialism. Out of a provincial anxiety about maintaining proprieties, Scots, Irish, and Americans eradicated provincial variations from English usage while simultaneously romanticizing the primitive genius of the oral traditions that were being eliminated by the stifling emphasis on correctness. The best historical example of this provincial synthesis of proprieties and primitivism is Hugh Blair, who subordinated the teaching of composition to stylistic criticism at the same time that he was celebrating a fabricated Gaelic bard as the native genius of Scotland. The alienation of provincials from the language and traditions of their own societies becomes directly relevant to contemporary English studies when one considers that E. D. Hirsch has hailed Hugh Blair as "an early, perhaps the first, definer of cultural literacy for the English national language" (85).

Gramsci's distinction between "organic" and "traditional" intellectuals provides another point of reference for my overall argument. As long as intellectuals maintain an organic involvement with the work and needs of the social group they come from, they can articulate the shared experience of the group so that it can understand its historical development and act toward shared goals. Organic intellectuals are frequently appropriated by the dominant culture and taught to work within established norms and institutions. Traditional intellectuals such as preachers and teachers may claim to speak autonomously for the common good, but they speak from institutional positions that serve to maintain the stability of the prevailing class system. I use the distinction between traditional and organic intellectuals as a way to relate rhetoricians to broader social groups and to examine how articulate individuals from marginal groups are taught to identify themselves with cosmopolitan tastes. Almost all of the first professors of English were clergy, but some worked to integrate the provinces into the dominant political system, while others challenged political authorities and popularized theories and practices that had revolutionary potential. The best example of the former is the party of "Moderate" clergy led by Hugh Blair and William Robertson who integrated the Scottish church into the British patronage system, and the best examples of the latter are liberal dissenters such as Joseph Priestley who taught middle-class students how to speak from a critical understanding of received traditions to challenge established political and religious authorities.

Cosmopolitanism, civil society, and organic and traditional intellectuals provide a framework for analyzing the cultural ideology, discursive domain, and political relations among social groups and intellectuals that defined the formation of college English. The introduction of the modern culture into higher education was an integral part of the expansion and standardization of the educated culture that occurred with the emergence of the modern public sphere. According to Habermas's *The Structural Transformation of the Public Sphere* (1989), in the eighteenth century the modern public sphere emerged as the reading public arose out of the "private sphere" or "civil society in the narrower sense, that is to say, the realm of commodity exchange and of social labor" (30). While Gramsci characterized civil society as a carefully depoliticized sphere, Habermas has treated it as a discursive domain for liberal debate and critical self-reflection. Both conceptions of civil society challenge us to examine how the teaching of criticism and composition contribute to critiques of prevailing values and practical action that produce political change. As a rhetorician, I believe that such action needs to be situated in local contexts and informed by a practical assessment of the purposes that are possible in those contexts. While the expansion of the educated public presented possibilities for political transformation, those possibilities were contained by efforts to standardize educated discourse and by discursive forms that carefully divorced critical reflection from political action, most notably the essay of taste and manners that situated readers as disinterested observers within civil society.

Blurred Boundaries and Genres

At the same time that the reading public was expanding to include broader classes of readers, English was being formalized and institutionalized as an object of study—a "centripetal" reaction to the "centrifugal" expansion that blurred the boundaries of the literate culture (Bakhtin 270). While England's population had risen only about seven percent in the first half of the century to around six and a half million, the population grew five times faster from 1750 to 1800, reaching nine million by 1801 and ten million a decade later (Adamson 11). Faced with such unprecedented growth in the number of students who had to be taught to respect the educated culture, educational institutions had difficulty perpetuating the authority of learned languages and classical models. Population growth meant more readers as well as more students. The circulation of the periodical press increased from 2,250,000 in 1711, to 7,000,000 in 1753, to 12,230,000 in 1776, almost doubling again by 1811 (Williams, *Long Revolution* 185). Much of this growth came outside the metropolitan center of the culture, with the number of presses in the provinces tripling in the latter half of the century (Colley 101). Paper became a disposable commodity, the press became a steam-driven technology, and the newspaper became a mass medium. Such developments created a need for mapmakers to chart the borders of the reading public and teachers to explain its laws to those who wanted to enter it. Critics surveyed and anthologized the educated culture to make it accessible to those not born within it, and such efforts expanded the authority of the dominant culture by reducing its conventions to rules that could be taught to outsiders.

Cheap print literacy transformed the relations of rhetoric, composition, and literature. In his review of Howell's *British Logic and Rhetoric*, Ong notes that "by the close of the eighteenth century orality as a way of life was in effect ended, and with it the old-time world of oratory, or, to give oratory its Greek

name rhetoric" (641). According to one of the literature professors who occupied the chair of rhetoric and belles lettres established for Hugh Blair, Blair
was the first to recognize that "'Rhetoric' in modern times really means 'Criticism'" (Saintsbury 463). Rhetoric and composition began to be subsumed
into literary criticism at the same time that the modern sense of *literature* was
emerging (see Terry). As one can see from the *Oxford English Dictionary,* literature had been defined in a broad and now "*obsolescent*" way as all "'letters'
or books; polite or humane learning; literary culture." In the eighteenth century, literature was reconceived as "literary work or production; the activity
or profession of a man of letters," and it moved toward the modern "restricted sense, applied to writing which has claim to consideration on the
ground of beauty of form or emotional effect." Literature became understood
as the work of a particular "profession" as professional critics and teachers
began to teach readers to think of literature not as something that they themselves might compose but as something to be consumed at leisure for a pleasing "emotional effect." Ironically, composition was becoming subordinated to
criticism, and literature was becoming narrowed to imaginative works oriented to aesthetic effects at the same time that authorship was actually expanding. From a survey of the authors included in the *Oxford Introduction to
English Literature,* Williams has concluded that beginning in the eighteenth
century fewer "literary" writers were coming from the upper classes than
from the middle classes. For the first time, a majority had not received a classical education, and an unprecedented number were women (see *Long Revolution*). Classically educated upper-class males lost unchallenged hegemony
in the literary culture as it became a domain of public commerce, and at just
this juncture professors and critics appeared to teach the public how to read
with taste and understand literature as part of what one early professor of literature termed the "culture of the heart" (Maurice, *Sketches of Contemporary
Authors* [1828] 118).

Conceptions of literature were narrowing just as the boundaries of the literate culture were becoming blurred. Print was praised by Priestley and other
liberal reformers for bringing "the learned and unlearned into more familiar
intercourse," but traditionalists were not sure they wanted to have "familiar
intercourse" with the public (Priestley, *Works* 24: 17). Conservatives such as
the Oxford don Vicesimus Knox believed that literacy disturbed social subservience but could also establish it on a more enlightened foundation:

> Men by reading were led to reflect, and by reflection discovered that they had
> been under an error when they looked up to their governors as to a Superior
> Order of Beings; but at the same time they learned the happiness of living
> under a well regulated constitution, the duty of obedience in return for pro-
> tection, and the political necessity of subordination. (*Essays* 1: 373)

Traditional intellectuals like Knox hoped that literacy would teach people to realize that the "necessity of subordination" was part of a "well regulated constitution." Through literate "reflection," people would learn to transfer their submission from their traditional "governors" to a rationalized system of "subordination." According to Knox, the Puritan era had shown that print could also be a "means of encouraging licentiousness, of animating sedition, and kindling the flames of civil war" (*Essays* 1: 375). To ensure that literacy maintained "the duty of obedience," the reading public had to be shown that English taste and usage followed laws that were consistent with other constituted systems of subordination.

As discussed more fully in the first chapter, the first attempts to "regulate" English were made by traditional intellectuals such as Jonathan Swift who called for their courtly patrons to establish a central academy that would simply dictate correct usage. When the reading public grew beyond the control of its traditional "governors," critics looked to the logic of print itself to formalize the conventions of English. In 1755 Johnson compiled a dictionary of printed authorities that systematically distinguished literate usage from common speech. A host of grammars soon appeared to make literate discourse as methodical as print itself. These grammars formalized correct usage into a rule-governed system that was absurdly logical in its consistency, as evident for example in the rule that two negatives equal a positive. Of all these grammars the "most cited, most praised, and most imitated" was Bishop Lowth's *Short Introduction to English Grammar* (1762) (Cohen, *Sensible Words* 82). Lowth's grammar went through at least twenty-two editions and countless printings, and the standard for American usage was set by works modeled on Lowth such as Lindley Murray's *English Grammar* (1795), which went through over six hundred printings through the next century (Downey xv). A more liberal and methodologically self-reflexive approach was taken by Joseph Priestley's *Rudiments of English Grammar* (1761) and George Campbell's *Philosophy of Rhetoric* (1776). Along with Campbell, Priestley established a "scientific school" of grammar that determined correct usage by inductively generalizing from existing conventions (Leonard 32; see also Baugh and Cable).

The standardization of educated usage was but the most obvious example of how English became constituted as an object of formal study according to the logic of a "well-regulated constitution." The model of language as a law-governed system, which grammarians but observed and codified, reproduced the basic conception of the reading public as a discursive space open to all—a "competitive marketplace" of ideas that was governed by natural laws that were intrinsic to the system or "economy," rather than imposed by external authorities. In fact the reading public was limited to those who had the price of a book and the ability to read it, but such limitations were consistent with the logic of liberal political economy, within which one was free to operate as long as one had goods or services to exchange. The reading public, laissez-faire political economy, and the "science of man" were governed by the same self-regulating logic. Free from the imposed authority of courtly patrons, state controls, or classical authorities, the individual was a free agent, as long as he (or even she) operated within the logic of the system—preserving polite proprieties, dealing but not stealing, and maintaining tasteful self-restraint. The individual thus became free insofar as he or she internalized Knox's view that a "well-regulated constitution" rested on the "political necessity of subordination" (*Essays* 1: 375). The print economy expanded its domain by teaching people its systems of self-control and self-expression, not only in classes dedicated to teaching polite taste but also through the literature of polite self-improvement.

A primary vehicle for instilling the virtues of self-improvement was the essay of taste and manners. The essay is a dialogical form that contains centripetal and centrifugal forces—a "blurred genre" that had predecessors in both the popular press and the high culture.[11] While Montaigne and Bacon are generally cited as the founders of the genre, the essay was popularized by the party politics that fueled the periodical press in the eighteenth century. While the polemics of Defoe and Swift do not fit neatly within modern conceptions of the essay, the essays of taste and manners from belletristic journals such as the *Spectator, Idler,* and *Rambler* are consistent with the view that the essay is a free-form genre that is characterized by the personal style of its individual author. According to one of its historians, the essay differs from "the standard prose form" of previous centuries, the classical oration, because the essay "does not seek to do anything, and it has no standard method even for doing nothing" (Hardison 13, 15). Rather than being defined as a means to do something in the world, the essay is characterized by the perspective of the observing subject. The essay embodies a conception of authorship as the publication of a private self, "a private experiment carried out in public" (Sanders 36). The essay of taste and manners combines introspective reflections on the logic of its own experience with surveys of prevailing norms or "manners"—the codes of conduct, expression, and deportment through which individuals express their personal character, or their lack of it.

The perspective for the essay of taste and manners was set by the *Spectator*. Joseph Addison and Richard Steele presented their periodical as the personal journal of a narrator who characterized himself and his literary club as impartial observers of public affairs. Studiously maintaining his public anonymity, the "Spectator" moved silently through society observing how individuals reveal their character in the ways they speak, act, and react, and then he retired to his private chambers to write out his impressions as the essays of the *Spectator*. The *Spectator*'s attention to the "inward Disposition of the Mind made visible" through facial expressions and off-handed gestures drew on rhetorical theories of "delivery" or "action" (1:366). The *Spectator* itself became a popular source for the introspective examinations of sympathetic responses that redefined the shared concerns of rhetoric and moral philosophy. With such commentaries as a common point of reference, elocutionists devoted whole volumes to codifying "natural" intonations and gestures, and moral philosophers defined ethics and aesthetics as matters of personal sentiment rather than purposeful action. The *Spectator* and its predecessor the *Tatler* were imitated by belletristic periodicals that ranged from the *Northern Tatler* (1710) to the *Female Spectator* (1744–1746), and the Spectator Club provided the model for the literary societies where provincials gathered to imitate the refined style and cosmopolitan sensibility of the *Spectator*'s essays of taste and manners.

The first university professors to teach English taught the English of the *Spectator*. Belletristic rhetoricians such as Blair gave more detailed attention to the essay of taste and manners than to any traditional rhetorical form. When grammarians and rhetoricians set the standard for politeness, they set it by essays from journals such as the *Spectator*. Unlike the plethora of party organs of the time, the *Spectator* excluded explicit political commentary from its pages in order to distance itself from the factionalized rhetoric that fueled the popular press. The *Spectator* claimed to speak for the common interest by speaking for no interest at all. Essayists such as Samuel Johnson looked to the *Spectator* as a model precisely because it taught readers to distance themselves from political controversies and concentrate on polite self-improvement. By excluding party politics from civil society, the *Spectator* presented middle-class readers with a more refined sense of their social situation and cultural aspirations (see Eagleton, *Function of Criticism*). As readers painstakingly imitated the stylistic proprieties of such belletristic essays, they learned to step back from party politics and internalize a stable authorial voice that spoke for the dispassionate sensibility of the impartial spectator. From the formation of college English, the essay has been taught as part of what Trimbur has termed the "rhetoric of deproduction"—an approach that divorces texts from the social conditions and political purposes that shaped their composition and reception in order to represent them as autonomous and disinterested. In short, a "rhetoric" that is arhetorical.

Before examining the provincial traditions that brought English into higher education, I should perhaps justify grouping them together under the phrase *British cultural provinces* (see also Clive and Bailyn). While Scotland became a British province in 1707 with the Union of Parliaments, America and Ireland were actually colonial dependencies, and dissenters tended to come from the urban middle classes.[12] A sense of who was deemed provincial is provided by Thomas Sheridan's *Dissertation on the Causes of the Difficulties which Occur in Learning the English Tongue* (1762). Sheridan defined his "provincial" readers in terms that clearly placed them at the borders of civil society: "By Provincials here meant all British Subjects whether inhabitants of Scotland, Ireland, Wales, the several counties of England, or the city of London, who speak a corrupt dialect of the English tongue" (2 n). Like the other leading elocutionist of the time, John Walker, Sheridan was himself an outsider who knew that a "corrupt dialect" marked one as "provincial." As a loyal Irishman, Sheridan argued that the British Empire would not become truly unified until English was founded "upon certain principles" that were "capable of being taught by rule" (*British Education* 160). To teach by rule, elocutionists reduced speech to written laws and taught provincials how to eliminate every idiom and gesture that violated those laws. The elocutionists are but the best example of how early English teachers worked to unify the nation by eradicating the dialectical differences that distinguished provincials.[13]

Now as then, an accent or grammatical impropriety is only one of the more obvious ways to distinguish an outsider, for the religious and cultural differences that are common in any complex society present many ways to distinguish outsiders, if such distinctions need to be made. Dissenters such as Priestley who did not worship the king's religion were ostracized as descendents of Puritan regicides when the Restoration established the Church of England as part of the national constitution. With the Test Acts of 1662, dissenters were forced out of the English universities and forbidden to vote or hold posts in the government and military. The academies founded by dissenters transformed higher education because they taught students who were more likely to work in trade and business than to retire to a country estate or parish. Because of their differing social positions, dissenters took a practical interest in English as the language of politics and business, while the Scots and Irish taught English as a means to cultural assimilation. However, whether the first professors and students of English were set apart by political restrictions or cultural differences, they shared a dialectical identity as both Britons *and* dissenters, Irish or Scots, and they studied English because they were not accepted as English.

We need detailed descriptions of what and who were taught if we are to understand how college English studies have since their formation served the modern need of assimilating a heterogeneous public into the educated culture. Educational institutions are the reproductive system of a culture. A close attention to changes in student populations, curricula, and pedagogy can document broader changes in class relations, the boundaries between politics and culture, and prevailing conceptions of how to apply learning to life. Educational archives record the intimate workings of cultural hegemony because the classroom is where intellectual elites reproduce themselves, in times of social change by enlisting organic intellectuals from emerging classes. While Gramsci assumed that "every relationship of 'hegemony' is necessarily an educational relationship," the dynamics of cultural hegemony are perhaps most evident in classes where students are taught how to express themselves (*Prison Notebooks* 350). If one attends to such rhetorical processes and domains, one can understand why rhetoric was central to the formation of college English and was then effaced from that formation. When a discipline becomes institutionalized, it can deny that it is a rhetorical response to a particular social problem or cultural need because it has become authoritative enough to establish its purposes and positions as autonomous categories such as "science" or "literature." The conventions that constitute such categories become accepted as natural parts of the field of inquiry, not rhetorical strategies aimed at persuading audiences to assume a particular stance on issues that have been called into question. In many respects, the arhetorical conception of academic disciplines as self-contained traditions exemplifies the "cosmopolitan" tendency to set off the "world of ideas" as a civil society distinct from the rhetorical domain where class relations and material conditions are publicly contested.

The Formation of College English

The introduction of the modern culture is one of the most important and least studied developments in the history of higher education. In subsequent chapters, I examine the provincial traditions that introduced modern history, politics, rhetoric, literature, and science into the college curriculum as case studies of how the teaching of culture functions as a means of social reproduction and transformation. In the first chapter I examine the centripetal and centrifugal trends that expanded and standardized educated discourse, and in chapter 2 I review how the centers of English education continued to reproduce traditional intellectuals in a traditional way—by confining the learned culture within learned languages and highly formalized modes of expression and reasoning. As discussed in the third chapter, the dissenting academies provide a case for studying how the introduction of English was shaped by the practical needs of middle-class students, whom academies depended upon to survive. In chapter 4, I examine the colonial purposes served by the teaching of English in Ireland. Rhetoric and belles lettres did not become well established in Ireland's Anglican university because the Anglo-Irish were too attached to English institutions and too alienated from the Irish public to look beyond the classical curriculum and examine the public experience. The modern culture first became part of the university curriculum in Scotland. Rhetoricians began to lecture on English literature and composition at the same time that moral philosophers began studying contemporary social and cultural affairs. Scottish reforms were avidly studied by Americans such as Jefferson and Franklin, who were concerned with using education to advance knowledge and create a national culture, and Scottish ideas and immigrants helped expand American higher education through their influence on newly established colleges such as those founded at Princeton and Philadelphia by religious and secular critics of Harvard and Yale.

The English universities provide an opportunity to examine how an antiquarian emphasis on ancient languages and classical literature served to preserve the cultural authority of traditional intellectuals. Oxford and Cambridge remained aloof from the Whig politics and commercial sensibility that were undermining traditional hierarchies. Aristotelian logic and Ciceronian rhetoric provided highly formalized systems of reasoning and expression, while the tutorial system of instruction was comparatively informal and nonsystematic, much like the apprenticeship methods of instruction common in scribal cultures. Such tacit methods of instruction preserved the cultural authority of the learned by not calling received knowledge into question. The antiquarian perspective of classicism served the same purpose. Students concentrated on mastering dead languages, ritualized disputations, and sacred texts as they moved through a curriculum that had been purposefully designed to resist change, which could only be seen as corruption by those who believed in the timeless authority of the ancients. The confines of the classical curriculum suited the traditional elite, with the eighteenth century one of the most elitist eras in the history of Oxford and Cambridge. The number of middle and lower-class students decreased steadily through the century as "public" grammar schools became the private enclaves of the upper classes (see Stone "Size and Composition"). In the next century classical languages were made an important part of the civil service exams required for admission to the imperial bureaucracy, not because a clerk would need Latin in Bombay, but because requiring a knowledge of Latin helped to ascertain that an applicant was a graduate of an English university and had thus been taught to think as an English gentleman.

The English universities provide the first opportunity to examine how educational institutions stagnate when teaching is not valued and received traditions are not assessed against the changing needs of students. In part because of the restricted access to higher education, the English cultural elite was narrower than the Scottish, as is evident in Hans's analysis of the social backgrounds of the Scots and English included in the *Dictionary of National Biography*. In England, those from the upper classes (peers and gentry) were two and a half times more likely to be listed than those from the lower classes (farmers, craftsmen, workers). However, Scottish farmers, for example, were just as likely to be listed as the Scottish gentry or clergy (Hans 28–30). One reason that poorer people were able to accomplish more in Scotland is that higher education was more accessible, cost less, and admitted younger students who were less prepared in learned languages because few had studied in grammar schools. Scottish universities were nonresident institutions, with many students able to attend a university in their home town, unlike in England where the universities were removed from the burgeoning population centers. While the Scottish universities were well situated to contribute to the needs of the middle classes in a commercial society, the English universities helped maintain the cultural authority of the gentry and their clerics. According to Gramsci, in England "the new social grouping that grew up on the basis of modern industrialism shows a remarkable economic-corporate development but advances only gropingly in the intellectual-political field." In this "higher sphere we find that the old land-owning class preserves its position of virtual monopoly. It loses its economic supremacy but maintains for a long time a politico-intellectual supremacy and is assimilated as 'traditional intellectuals'" (*Prison Notebooks* 18). The traditionalism of the English universities was integral to this historical development.

In the third chapter I look beyond the centers of English education to the academies established by non-Anglicans when they were exiled from the classical curriculum. Rather than swear the Oaths of Supremacy imposed by the Test Acts in 1662, "nonconformists" left the English universities. The dissenting academies evolved away from the classical tradition through several generations of educators, and English rose in significance along with the teaching of modern science, politics, and culture. The most important educator of the first generation was Charles Morton, who taught English literature and composition and a comparatively wide range of subjects completely in English to such important dissenters as Daniel Defoe. In 1686 Morton emigrated to escape being prosecuted for violating the laws against dissenting academies, and in 1692 he became vice president of Harvard, where he introduced experimental studies of science. The next generation was dominated by Isaac

Watts and Philip Doddridge. Watts was the most widely influential advocate of Lockean logic and epistemology in the eighteenth century, while Doddridge helped to translate the new learning into a new pedagogy by establishing a comparative method of instruction that institutionalized a dialectical awareness of the contested nature of established beliefs. Opposing views were studied, researched, and argued in compositions in order to teach students how to debate the religious and political restrictions imposed upon them. Such methods of instruction fostered a liberal faith in "free inquiry" in the generation that succeeded Watts and Doddridge, most notably in Joseph Priestley, the dissenter who made the best recognized contributions to the teaching of English. In 1762 Priestley began teaching "Languages and Belles Lettres" at Warrington Academy, one of the most innovative educational institutions of the century. Priestley was later succeeded by William Enfield, whose elocutionary text *The Speaker* (1774) became "the most widely used of all school anthologies" in English courses (Michael 186).

Because the dissenters founded new educational institutions that directly depended on the economic support of the middle classes, the dissenting tradition provides a case study of how changes in political relations and material conditions shaped the introduction of English into higher education. The dissenters followed the Puritans in supporting popular literacy as a means to provide individual access to the Word. According to Harvey Graff, Puritan communities had been "the most education-conscious and literate centers in England" (162). The dissenters' educational reforms were intended to serve students who would work in trade and manufacture as well as those who would preach against restrictions on dissent. Dissenters developed a utilitarian approach to the teaching of English that stressed composition but deemphasized literary refinements. Students were taught to speak and write about controversial issues of public significance because dissenters believed that "free inquiry" and critical literacy promoted reasonable reform. Priestley was one of the most controversial practicing rhetoricians of the era, but even comparatively radical reformers such as Priestley advocated laissez-faire liberalism in the assumption that charity would only make the poor less industrious and more numerous. Priestley is an influential example of the sort of individuals produced by dissenting academies, individuals who were critically aware of historical developments and had the practical expertise needed to advance liberal reform, scientific research, and economic modernization—in short, the "organic intellectuals" of the urban bourgeoisie.

As in my chapters on the dissenting academies and the English universities, when I discuss English studies in Ireland, I try to examine what students learned as well as what professors taught. The first university professor to publish lectures on rhetoric and literature that had been delivered in English was John Lawson, professor of oratory and history at Trinity College, Dublin, from 1750 to 1758. Ireland's Anglican university was subservient to English institutions, and even notable professors of rhetoric such as Lawson concentrated on classical and religious literature and ignored political discourse. However, if the history of the discipline is not limited to the teaching of professors, then a different picture emerges. Beyond Trinity's lecture halls in the debating societies established by students such as Edmund Burke, the political controversies of the day influenced what students studied if not what professors taught. The Irish colonial experience had a broad impact on college English through the writings of Lawson's student Thomas Sheridan, the elocutionist who was one of the most popular advocates of English studies in the eighteenth century. Sheridan claimed that the lack of instruction in English had created a national orality crisis, and he toured the country advocating the creation of a discipline to teach the British English. At Edinburgh in 1761 the Irish elocutionist lectured the Scots on how to speak like the English, thus helping to popularize the studies that Blair was introducing into the curriculum. Sheridan and the elocutionary movement provide the first occasion to examine how the expansion of the English reading public colonized the oral traditions of the provinces. While elocutionists valorized the natural genius of speech, they were systematically scripting oral discourse by written laws to eliminate the idioms that provincials naturally spoke.

In the American colonies as elsewhere in the provinces, higher education was changing: students created literary and debating societies to teach themselves English, professors began lecturing on English, and syllogistic disputations in Latin were superseded by forensic debates and orations in English. As in Britain, these developments had some of their most propitious beginnings in less established colleges, particularly those with close ties to the Scots and dissenters. Most notable were the colleges at Philadelphia and Princeton led by Scottish immigrants. The college that Franklin helped establish at Philadelphia was a major conduit for Scottish moral philosophy and reportedly included the first professorship of English in America (see William Riley Parker; Norton, "Hutcheson in America"; and Miller, "Formation"). The college at Princeton was headed by the most important professor of rhetoric and moral philosophy in colonial America, John Witherspoon, as I have discussed in my edition of his writings.[14] Such institutions were less bound to the classical tradition because they were founded as practical or religious alternatives to Harvard and Yale. While Oxford and Cambridge retained their monopoly on higher education in England through the eighteenth century, eleven American colleges were established within the half century following the

"Great Awakening" of anti-establishmentarian evangelism in the 1740s. Because these social and educational changes are too complex to be adequately discussed in a chapter or two, I plan to examine the development of rhetorical theory and practice in America in a companion volume to this book.

As in America, the origins of English studies in Scotland were shaped by rhetoric's traditional relations with moral philosophy. In the civic humanist tradition that remained influential into the eighteenth century, rhetoric and moral philosophy shared a practical engagement with public controversies. Civic humanism exercised a formative influence on early eighteenth-century Scottish moral philosophers, who included the first university professors in Britain to lecture in the public idiom—George Turnbull, David Fordyce, John Pringle, and Francis Hutcheson, the teacher of Adam Smith. At the same time that he was broadening moral philosophy to include the issues addressed in his popular *Theory of Moral Sentiments* (1759) and *Wealth of Nations* (1776), Smith created one of the first university courses on English literature, composition, and rhetoric.[15] The works of Smith and other Scottish moral philosophers such as David Hume and Thomas Reid mapped out the discursive domain within which English was first constituted as an object of study in the university. From Hutcheson through Hume and Smith, morality and aesthetics became conflated by the idealization of polite sensibility, with practical political action given less attention than the reactions of the sympathetic but impartial spectator. The transition from the perspective of the political agent to the critical observer enabled moral philosophers to claim to be social scientists who stood above the self-interest that motivates action, but it made disinterestedly observing political economy and personal sentiments more important than engaging in the political debates that had been the civic locus of rhetoric and moral philosophy.

In the last chapter, I briefly examine how nineteenth-century Utilitarians carried on the reforms of the Scots and dissenters to establish the first professorship of English literature, which was created as part of the college that a coalition of dissenters and Utilitarians founded at London in 1828. Such professorships became a standard part of the colleges that were opened for women and working people in the middle of the nineteenth century. As literature became established as a subject of study unto itself, the practical attention to composition became marginalized, and the belletristic theories of the rhetoricians who founded college English were superseded by works that demarcated the literary from the rhetorical. The teaching of literature was set in direct opposition to the "provincial" utilitarian values that had founded college English studies by influential figures such as Matthew Arnold. The broader opposition of the two cultures of the arts and sciences emerged in

Arnold's argument with Thomas Huxley over whether education should center on science or literature. As that opposition became institutionalized in the modern university, rhetoric and other political arts fell into the chasm that opened between political philosophy and political science as they moved to opposite sides of the academy, and the humanities lost the practical engagement with popular controversies that had been maintained by rhetoric and moral philosophy. Literary critics moved beyond studying texts against their purposes and effects in order to make disinterested appraisals of literature as a subject unto itself—a domain that shrank considerably when the study of English was reduced to the study of nonutilitarian nonfactual discourse.

Conclusion: The Dialectical Differences Contained Within the Formation of College English

It is as unsurprising as it is important that provincials who had to teach themselves English taste and usage were the first to introduce English into higher education. Those at the boundaries of the dominant culture tend to be intensely aware of the differences marked by those boundaries.[16] Joseph Priestley, for example, was from Yorkshire, which was often caricatured for having the crudest dialect, and hence the most uncultured sensibility, in England (see Rothblatt 93). Priestley also had a speech impediment, as did the leading professor of rhetoric in colonial America, John Witherspoon, as well as such ancient rhetoricians as Demosthenes and Isocrates. Demosthenes overcame his problem by practicing speaking with pebbles in his mouth, but even though Isocrates was perhaps the most influential teacher of oratory in Periclean Greece, he did not deliver his own "orations" but circulated them as manuscript pamphlets. The personal handicaps that motivate students and teachers are part of what gets excluded from histories of ideas contained within disciplines. Few English professors want to believe that their discipline began with a stutter, or that it was founded by provincials motivated by insecurities about their own speech and culture. Rather than acknowledging that the history of college English began in marginal institutions with students who were too poorly prepared to use learned languages, histories have generally begun in the nineteenth century when respectable institutions established research methods and professional priorities that look like the discipline we know. What gets left out of such histories are the dialectical forces that were contested and contained at the boundaries of the field as it became a well demarcated area of study. In short, what gets left out of such histories are students.

Lowland Scots were particularly aware of the differences that separated them from both the English and the Highlanders. Literati like Smith who had studied and traveled in the south knew what sort of reactions to expect when their Scottish dialect was heard by the English, and they studiously refashioned their speech and manners to get more "sympathetic" responses. Reflecting on such experiences, Smith formulated the concept of the "impartial spectator." The impartial spectator internalizes the outsider's dialectical awareness of cultural differences in the form of a second self who monitors every thought and word against the proprieties of civil society, enabling one to identify with those proprieties, and also perpetuating their authority by demonstrating that they are second nature, as those with a refined nature will recognize from their own experience. While the dialectical process of reflecting on social interactions can generate a critical awareness of the contested nature of cultural conventions, the "impartial spectator" taught individuals to step back from social conflicts in order to maintain the polite decorum of civil society. Civil society, as Gramsci has discussed, is where hegemony is instilled in "subaltern" groups such as provincials. "Subaltern classes, by definition, are not unified and cannot unite until they are able to become a 'State': their history, therefore, is intertwined with that of civil society" (*Prison Notebooks* 52). Also "intertwined" with the history of civil society is the history of college English, which was first established to "unite" educated Britons by teaching them to eliminate their dialectical differences.

As the boundaries around the educated culture became blurred by the decline of learned languages and the admission of broader classes of students, higher education was called upon to explain historical changes and cultural differences—matters that only needed explanation when the ancients lost their timeless authority and students entered the classroom who had not been inculcated into the learned culture by years of studying learned languages. Explanations were provided by the "science of man," which was institutionalized at the same point in the curriculum in the dissenting academies and Scottish universities. As part of its traditional attention to natural religion, moral philosophy included the study of "pneumatology"—the "science" of "spirits or spiritual beings," including "the doctrine of God as known by natural reason, of angels and demons, and of the human soul" (*OED*). In the dissenting academies and Scottish universities, "pneumatology" began to include more psychology and less cosmology as moral philosophers set out to apply the methods of the natural sciences to the study of human nature. This epistemological orientation defined the "new" logic and rhetoric by the mental processes of the individual auditor. The "science of man" also provided a unifying logic that could be used to explain the sociological and psychological processes involved in economic modernization, social diversification, and cultural assimilation. Moral philosophers studied the proliferating accounts of foreign cultures as "experiments" in human nature that verified that "man is every where the same" by demonstrating "that the untutored Indian and the civilized European have acted upon the same principles" (Millar iii).

The movement of moral philosophy toward the human sciences was part of the modern project of using "the scientific conquest of nature for the scientific conquest of man" (Marcuse xiv). According to Foucault, "man is only a recent invention, a figure not yet two centuries old" who "will disappear again" with the waning of modernism (*Order* xxiii). Foucault's *On the Order of Things* argued that at the end of the eighteenth century, "the tradition of general grammar was replaced by an essentially historical philology; natural classifications were ordered according to the analyses of comparative anatomy; and a political economy was founded whose main themes were labour and production" (xii). The formation of college English was an integral part of these developments. As in the "science of man," the vantage point of the autonomous individual became the source and end of discourse, and discourse itself became defined as a logical system whose laws could be determined through historical studies in the same way that a science of political economy was formed from researching the modes of production. The traditional relations of moral philosophy and rhetoric provide a broader frame of reference for assessing how such developments transformed the teaching of language and culture. This frame of reference is not only broader than the discursive domain that would be included within college English studies, it is also more situated in social praxis because moral philosophy and rhetoric had an engagement with popular values and political debates that would be lost when the field of study became confined to nonutilitarian nonfactual discourse.

In the ancient as well as the modern periods, rhetoricians from the provinces transformed the humanities by introducing an awareness of cultural differences and the power of discourse to construct "shared" values. Rhetoric was originally introduced into the Western tradition by Sophists from provincial city states who came to Athens to teach rhetoric along with a relativistic moral philosophy (see Jaeger; Enos). Rhetoricians established the liberal arts upon the philosophy that a broad education in the shared traditions of the culture would enable citizens to speak with practical wisdom to public problems (see chapter 6). In the eighteenth century, provincials who came from outside the dominant culture and had consciously taught themselves its conventions introduced a "new" rhetoric and logic as part of an effort to redefine liberal education in more utilitarian terms to suit a more heterogeneous public. From their experiences as outsiders, Sophists came to view prevailing values and political hierarchies as social constructions that were founded on convention and not nature. The founders of English studies were also interested in how values are socially constructed and internalized, but they were no Sophists. In reaction to Hume's view that morality and knowledge were founded on social conventions and acquired associations, provincials formalized common sense and the polite sensibility according to the laws of human nature. The moral philosophers and rhetoricians who introduced the modern culture into higher education redirected the liberal arts away from classical texts toward the methods of science because they spoke for a broad reading public who lacked a set of shared beliefs from which one could deduce answers to public problems, but who did share a common ambition to gain advancement by mastering the proprieties of civil society and the laws of economic progress.

Two centuries after rhetoricians first introduced English studies into British higher education, in America rhetoric is becoming the newest as well as the oldest area of study in the humanities as undergraduate courses and majors in rhetoric are reestablished in English departments. Composition courses and writing across the curriculum programs are also developing a more rhetorical concern for the values and political purposes that constitute disciplines and publics, and the basic dichotomies of learning and teaching and service and research are being redefined by efforts to learn from students' experience and break down the borders of the academy to become more involved with civic issues. Rhetoricians in English departments in America seem to be on the verge of expanding their field of study beyond academic discourse, and I believe that this trend would benefit from a critical reassessment of rhetoric and moral philosophy's shared involvement with public debates over popular values and political problems. While the classical continuities between rhetoric and moral philosophy have been well recognized, their modern relations are little studied because political scientists and philosophers are disdainful of rhetoric, and rhetoricians in English departments have studied literature far more than politics and ethics. As rhetoric and composition expand their work beyond academic discourse, the area could become a point of convergence for work on cultural studies, community literacies, and critical pedagogy concerned with "teaching the conflicts," including not just those contained within the discipline but those it has worked to exclude since it was first established. I would like to contribute to this trend by expanding the historical frame of reference beyond histories of ideas about rhetoric, and beyond the histories of college English that begin when it was reduced to the study of literature.

As the art of drawing on popular values to address public audiences, rhetoric should be of central importance to anyone who wants to understand and teach the art of exercising power through discourse. Its pragmatic concerns for purpose, audience, and the situational nature of discursive transactions make rhetoric an important area for studying how authors claim authority, position their audiences, and adapt the conventions of discourse to suit changing purposes and relations (see Berlin, "Revisionary History"). Situating rhetoric within its traditional relations with moral philosophy can help relate such concerns to the value systems and political practices that establish who has the authority to speak and who should remain silent. Rhetoric and moral philosophy have traditionally been situated in the domain where the learned culture made contact with the popular experience. Provincials working and living in this domain were the first to introduce the modern culture into higher education, and the teaching of English, particularly in broad-based institutions and in lower division courses, has been an area where the conventions of academic discourse and the learned culture still come into contact with those who have not been taught to respect them. Such sites have recently been widely characterized as "contact zones," and Pratt's term provides a particularly apt way to situate the historical formation of college English.[17] As Pratt has discussed, the dominant culture is itself transformed by such contacts through the dialectic process of "transculturation." In this process, "subordinated or marginal groups" reform their language and mores to incorporate "materials transmitted to them by a dominant or metropolitan culture," and the dominant culture is itself transformed through its contact with those who do not accept it as natural and unproblematic (6). In subsequent chapters, I try to show that the formation of college English was a product of "transculturation," and that such dialectical processes make what gets taught and learned in marginal courses and institutions central to the ongoing development of the discipline.

The Expansion of the Reading Public,

the Standardization of Educated Taste and Usage,

and the Essay as Blurred Genre

> Unitary language constitutes the theoretical expression of the historical processes of linguistic unification and centralization, an expression of the centripetal forces of language. A unitary language is not something given but is always in essence posited—and at every moment of its linguistic life it is opposed to the realities of heteroglossia. But at the same time it makes its real presence felt as a force for overcoming this heteroglossia, imposing specific limits to it, guaranteeing a certain maximum of mutual understanding and crystallizing into a real, although still relative, unity—the unity of the reigning conversational and literary language, "correct language."
>
> —Bakhtin, *Dialogic Imagination*

EARLY IN THE eighteenth century, neoclassical writers like Dryden and Swift complained that English was a language without a grammar, but by the end of the century no one could complain about a shortage of English grammars. While only two had been published in the sixteenth century and seventeen in the seventeenth century, thirty-five were published in the first half of the eighteenth century, with over five times more in the latter half of the century.[1] These works formalized the conventions of educated usage and established "the unity of the reigning conversational and literary language, 'correct language.'" With the publication of authorities for judging what common idioms meant and which ones were too common to be correct, standards were established for English. At just this time professors of rhetoric were also institutionalizing English in higher education.[2]

The "unification and centralization" of English came at the same time that

changes in technology and literacy were expanding the reading public beyond the confines that had been maintained by learned languages, courtly
patronage, and the high cost of books. Bookmaking had been one of the first
crafts to be transformed by technology, and pamphleteering had been a major
force in the Puritan Revolution, but not until the eighteenth century was the
public sphere transformed by print. Parliamentary debates became published
as the news of the day; the end of the perpetual copyright made polite literature a popular commodity; and literary forms like the novel and essay
blurred the boundaries between personal refinement and the public experience. In such an era, it is easy to understand why English became important
enough to be widely studied and problematic enough to need to be formally
taught. Print both dispersed knowledge and provided a paradigm for its standardization (see Eisenstein, and Febvre and Martin). Such dialectical developments have been discussed by Bakhtin in terms of the "centrifugal" and
"centripetal" forces in discourse—with the movement outward to include
more diverse groups in the cultural dialogue resulting in efforts to consolidate the authority of the dominant culture. Bakhtin stresses that a language
is "heteroglot from top to bottom" because it contains "socio-ideological
contradictions between the present and the past, . . . between different
socio-ideological groups in the present, between tendencies, schools, circles
and so forth" (291).

In the eighteenth century these contradictions expanded and intensified.
England's union with Scotland in 1707 and Ireland in 1799 expanded the cultural authority of English and increased pressures for linguistic unification.
English and French were replacing Latin as languages of international relations, and cheap books and periodicals were circulating the educated culture
to broader classes of readers who had not been formally taught to respect the
proprieties of educated taste and usage. The spread of literacy created a demand for encyclopedias, grammars, digests, and dictionaries to organize and
explain educated discourse and the educated culture, promising to make
them as accessible and systematic as print itself. Histories, anthologies, and
critical treatises formalized English literature, while dictionaries and grammars intensified the awareness of the dialectical variations within English, including the provincial idioms that the first professors of English worked to
eradicate.

The rhetoricians who introduced college English studies assumed that few
of their provincial students would speak from positions of public authority
but all would need taste to be accepted into civil society (see Blair, "Lectures,"
1: 8). The emphasis on taste was consistent with the view that consumption is
the driving force in commercial society. According to the first great theorist

of consumer society, Adam Smith, "consumption is the sole end and purpose of all production; and the interest of the producer ought to be attended to, only so far as it may be necessary for promoting that of the consumer" (*Wealth of Nations* 660). In "commercial society," as Smith conceived it, the individual is not a political so much as an economic agent: "when the division of labour has been once thoroughly established. . . . Every man thus lives by exchanging, or becomes in some measure a merchant, and the society itself grows to be what is properly a commercial society" (37). Smith was instrumental in establishing a laissez-faire conception of the public sphere that divorced civil society from the domain of party politics, and from practical political arts such as rhetoric. Civil society had to be kept free from factional interests and political enthusiasms if people were to be able to "essay" experience from a disinterested perspective and thus learn to respect the natural laws that maintained the balance of self-interest and the common good within the individual consciousness and the general political economy.

The subordination of composition to criticism in the formation of college English was consistent with the nature of the reading public as a consumer society. Eagleton has argued that "the modern concept of literary criticism is closely tied to the rise of the liberal, bourgeois public sphere in the early eighteenth century" (*Function of Criticism* 10). Habermas's *Structural Transformation of the Public Sphere* has further argued that the "bourgeois reading public of the eighteenth century" is where modern conceptions of the public sphere began to develop out of traditional definitions of the "public" as "the critics of art and literature" (85, 32). According to both these accounts, the reading public provided a domain where the middle classes could develop a critical understanding of their social experience. Rather than equating critical reflection with political action, I want to examine how criticism became a means to instill taste as the reading public expanded beyond the traditional elite, and readers began to conceive of literature not as all "eloquent" discourse—discourse that they themselves might compose—but rather as the literary work or production of a particular class of writers gifted with productive genius. While *criticism* and *composition* are both abstractions from actions, the actions are quite different. Criticism implies passing judgment (*censurer*), while composition means putting (*poser*) together (*com*). While the former is concerned with making distinctions, the latter is synthetic and treats critical analysis as a prelude to action. The dichotomy of production and reception provides a convenient, if ultimately reductivist, point of reference for examining how the critical stance of the disinterested spectator dislocated readers from becoming more productively engaged with political action.

In this chapter I sketch out how cheap print literacy publicized the educated culture and blurred distinctions between polite arts and popular forms of leisure, creating the need for the first histories and critical treatises on English literature. Next I review how such blurred boundaries led to attempts to standardize literate usage, beginning with neoclassicists' calls for a courtly academy and concluding with the dictionaries and grammars that formalized the conventions of published writers in order to demarcate the world of print from the idioms of common people. The attempt to reason inductively from literate usage to the laws that governed educated discourse was part of the project of redefining the language arts according to the grammatical laws, experiential logic, and unadorned rhetoric authorized by the "science of man," a project that was most systematically undertaken by George Campbell. While the first professors of English were rhetoricians, they modeled taste and usage not on traditional oratorical forms but on the essay of taste and manners, especially the essays of the *Spectator*. While it was to become institutionalized as the model of academic discourse, the essay is a "blurred genre" that had predecessors in the popular press as well as the learned culture. To divorce themselves from the party politics that fueled the periodical press, belletristic essayists assumed the cosmopolitan perspective of the disinterested observer of public controversies.

Such stances served to maintain the proprieties of civil society as revolutionary ideas were spread among the working classes by the cheap pamphlets and correspondence societies that gave reading and writing practical political significance. In order to assume the stance of the impartial spectator as a means to self-improvement, "organic" intellectuals had to distance themselves from provincial idioms and class conflicts, and as a result became alienated from the experiences of those at the margins of the educated culture. As the educated public became more diversified, higher education took up the modern mission of teaching broader classes of students to respect the cosmopolitan tastes of the dominant culture—a mission that only became important as higher education expanded beyond classically educated upper-class males.

Publicizing the Literate Culture

Not until the beginning of the nineteenth century does the reading public begin to include the majority of the public, but in the eighteenth century the secular book-buying public grew to include better educated, more prosperous crafts and trades workers (see Graff, *Legacies* 230–48). About half the families in England were still living at subsistence levels at the beginning of the century (see Porter), and until almost the end books remained too expensive for the lower classes. Literacy among adult English men apparently rose from over 50 to around 65 percent, with approximately two-thirds that rate for women.[3] Literacy did not increase as dramatically as in the Puritan era, partially because unprecedented population growth put tremendous strain on educational institutions, but also because the Anglican establishment tended to associate popular literacy with the public unrest of the previous century.[4] As discussed in chapter 3, dissenters helped foster critical literacy by founding academies that were more broadly accessible and practically engaged than the English universities and grammar schools. Dissenters were largely from the middle classes, who generally enjoyed almost universal literacy. Of course, statistics on literacy provide only the broadest outlines of the reading public, with some of the best known authorities disagreeing over whether it extended beyond the middle classes (see, for example, Altick and Neuburg). The existing scholarship does suggest that the expansion of literacy was more qualitative than quantitative, a matter of refining reading tastes and writing styles rather than simply teaching basic skills.

While it is difficult to know who read what, the records of who wrote for the reading public suggest that authors increasingly came from the middle classes as literature became commercialized by the print economy. From his analysis of the social backgrounds of the writers included in the *Oxford Introduction to English Literature,* Williams has concluded that authorship expanded to include the middle classes as courtly patrons lost influence to the exigencies of the marketplace.[5] For the first time, fewer British writers came from the nobility and gentry than from backgrounds in trades, merchandizing, and crafts. Also for the first time, the majority had not received a classical education at Oxford and Cambridge. Women began to publish increasing numbers of works, including the over five hundred novels noted in Spender's *Mothers of the Novel,* most of which did not become part of the canon of "English literature." "The present age," according to Johnson, "may be styled, with great propriety, *The Age of Authors;* for, perhaps, there never was a time in which men of all degrees of ability, of every kind of education, of every profession and employment, were posting with ardour so general to the press." Kernan has contrasted the attitudes of Johnson's generation with that of Pope, whose *Dunciad* describes "Printing as a scourge for the Sins of the Learned," with paper "so cheap, and printers so numerous, that a deluge of authors cover'd the land" (qtd. 74, 11). This "deluge" swept away barriers around the literate culture, creating anxieties among those who had depended on courtly patrons, but opportunities for those who hoped to earn a living by teaching the public a taste for politeness.

In the eighteenth century print transformed reading and writing. Spelling became standardized, and prose styles became simplified and more accessible as people began to read more widely and less intensively than they had when books were precious possessions.[6] Books on cooking, gardening, and other leisure activities became popular genres, as did literature for children. Books were serialized and excerpted to fill the pages of journals that combined political broadsides, ads for personal products, and cultural commentary aimed at self-improvement. Those who could not afford to buy even penny installments of books could borrow them from libraries. One of the first libraries was Allan Ramsay's in Edinburgh, which opened in about 1725, but by 1800 London alone had 122 circulating libraries, with 268 more in the rest of England (Houston 174–75). Johnson claimed that England had become a "nation of readers," and he noted that "he who writes otherwise than for money is a fool" (qtd. Prior 1: 70). The boundaries between the "low" and "high" cultures became even more blurred when the perpetual copyright was finally eliminated in 1774 and innovative booksellers made polite literature into a popular pastime. The classics of English literature were reprinted in cheap series that sold for around a shilling a volume, series like Bell's British Theatre (21 volumes, 1776 to around 1778) and the Poets of Great Britain (109 volumes, 1776 to around 1792). The mechanical reproduction of literature publicized and hence demystified the elite culture (see Benjamin). Whole classes of readers now had to be taught to distinguish the truly polite from the merely popular.

Johnson, the son of a lower-middle-class bookseller, was a leader of the generation of critics who taught the public how to appreciate "English" literature. When he could not afford to complete his education at Oxford, Johnson turned to selling his writing to booksellers. He wrote essays for popular journals like the *Gentleman's Magazine* that appealed to those who turned to magazines for quick summaries, abstracts, and criticisms of popular periodicals and books to gain easy access to the culture of "gentlemen" (see Kaminski). A consortium of booksellers who recognized the market for works of taste hired Johnson to survey the emerging canon of British literature in his *Prefaces, Biographical and Critical, to the Works of the English Poets* (10 volumes, 1779–1781). As I discuss in the next section, Johnson's *Dictionary* was the consummate work of print, for it was an index of literate usage that used published authors to systematically distinguish the written language from common speech. His edition of Shakespeare was also a product of the print economy, for it was the first edition to collate published editions to reconstruct the intentions of the authorial subject (see Kernan 93, 171).

The commercialization of authorship and the commodification of literature are but two examples of how the print economy publicized the educated culture. While pamphlets and broadsides had mobilized popular opinion in the Puritan era, print did not transform the public sphere until the eighteenth century because periodicals were virtually nonexistent and books tended to be expensive and largely confined to religious and scholarly domains.[7] At the same time that the reading public was expanding, other public outlets for polite culture began to appear. In the seventeenth century even London had been without a public opera, ballet, music festival, or concert hall, but in the eighteenth century theaters and concert halls became common throughout Britain. In provincial towns, assembly rooms were built on a subscription basis so that the middle classes could attend the concerts and balls that had been reserved for the salons of the gentry. Such rooms were often used for the sort of lectures on taste and elocution delivered by Sheridan, Smith, and Blair that are discussed in subsequent chapters. As the audience for the theater grew, the number of new plays almost doubled from 1,095 in the first half of the eighteenth century to 2,117 in the second (Plumb 279, 276). While the music of the high culture had generally been reserved for sacred occasions or state celebrations, a "concert going public" arose that was an integral part of the bourgeois reading public (Habermas, *Structural Transformation* 39). Plays and musical scores became best-selling books, and print helped to professionalize the theater and other forms of popular entertainment by providing access to national audiences, in the process bringing the provinces into the increasingly unified national culture.

The popularization of classical music, literature, and theater was part of the general commercialization of leisure that accompanied the rise of a consumer society. According to McKendrick, a "consumer boom" reached "revolutionary proportions" by the last quarter of the eighteenth century (9). Per capita consumption increased fifteenfold during the century, with the sales of excised goods like tea and tobacco growing at twice the increase in population in the last decade alone. More people were buying more goods, which were becoming valued for their style rather than just their utility or durability. As the public began to emulate the tastes of the leisured classes, traditionalists became anxious about maintaining the subservience necessary to social order. Such anxieties were fostered by Mandeville's widely popular *Fable of the Bees* (1714), which satirized the traditional view that public order depended on private economy. Mandeville cynically noted that "Luxury Employ'd a Million of the Poor, And odious Pride a Million More: Envy it self, and Vanity, Were Ministers of Industry; Their darling Folly, Fickleness, In Diet, Furniture and Dress, That strange ridic'lous Vice, was made The very Wheel that turn'd the Trade" (1: 25).[8] In 1776 the birth of a consumer society was heralded in less provocative and more scientific terms by Adam Smith's

Wealth of Nations. After Smith's generation, the classical opposition of private luxury and civic virtue broke down as self-interest became accepted as not just natural but actually conducive to public prosperity.

As conservatives had feared, traditional hierarchies were undermined as refined tastes spread beyond the leisured classes. Wealth began to lose its traditional association with land and became reconceived as a transferable commodity. The circulation of wealth became understood as an abstract system or "economy" distinct from, and perhaps even opposed to, traditional hierarchies. And individuals began to be defined not by their positions in those hierarchies but by how effectively they had mastered the logic of the market economy. That logic was seen as intrinsic to the system, rather than as arbitrarily imposed by the power of the state or the authority of tradition. According to Habermas, "a liberalized market economy" was a "precondition" for the bourgeois public not simply because that economy provided economic opportunities for social advancement but also because liberal political economy provided the logic in which the middle classes came to understand themselves as possessing a social identity and "natural" power apart from their subservient positions within the class system of the time (*Structural Transformation* 11). In the context of the liberal political economy, culture became "a commodity" and evolved into "something that pretended to exist merely for its own sake" (29). Literature became a popular leisure—a relief from the demands of the marketplace within which it circulated. Writers and critics of imaginative literature developed, according to Eisenstein, "a vested interest in idleness, in promoting the value of pleasure-seeking and leisure, in cultivating consumption of the 'finer' things of life" (1: 156). To teach the public a taste for leisural refinement, critics presented the psychological reactions of enculturated readers as models of appropriate responses, and essays of taste and manners taught readers to assume perspectives that were consistent with the natural laws that governed liberal political economy.

To bring order to the print economy, efforts were made to chart the boundaries of all the polite arts in the middle of the century. According to Lipking's *Ordering of the Arts in Eighteenth-Century England* (1970), music, painting, and poetry were each formalized by an array of critical treatises that provided authoritative histories, standards, and models of appropriate responses. The first histories of English literature included such works as Thomas Percy's *Reliques of Ancient Poetry* (1765), V. J. Peyton's *The History of the English Language* (1771), and the first book-length history of English literature, Thomas Warton's *History of English Poetry* (1774–1781). The modern sense of *literature* as nonutilitarian and generally nonfactual discourse oriented to achieving an aesthetic effect emerged in the latter half of the eighteenth century, though *poetry* and *belles lettres* had previously been used in this sense upon occasion, and like *literature* continued to be used in the broader sense of all "polite letters" or "works of taste" (see Terry). Ironically, as Eagleton has discussed, "the birth of aesthetics as an intellectual discourse coincides with the period when cultural production is beginning to suffer the miseries and indignities of commodification" (*Ideology of the Aesthetic* 64). While commentators on English literature claimed to speak disinterestedly for the values of the aesthetic experience, those values need to be situated in the economy in which they circulated to understand the purposes they served. As leisure became commercialized, polite literature had to be demarcated from popular cultural forms if its commentators and consumers were to be able to claim it was a means to self-improvement and social advancement.[9] Just as the distinction of polite literature from popular entertainments enabled educated readers to distinguish themselves by their refined tastes, the conventions of educated usage had to be formalized if correct usage was to be employed to distinguish the formally educated from the merely literate.

Formalizing English

In this section, I briefly review how efforts to standardize educated usage intensified as the reading public expanded beyond the confines maintained by learned languages, courtly patrons, and the high cost of books. In a letter to the *Tatler* in 1710 Swift first proposed establishing a courtly academy to establish standards for the republic of letters. The initial proposals to "fix" English were shaped by the classical backgrounds of traditional intellectuals (Swift, *Works* 9: 33). As a dead language, Latin was impervious to change, and scholars of Swift's perspective hoped to create a universal grammar with the same timeless authority. While Swift assumed a royal academy could simply dictate correctness, Johnson recognized that the reading public had grown beyond the control of traditional authorities. To distinguish the written language from the speech of common people, he compiled a dictionary of the language of printed authors. Following Johnson, Priestley and Campbell established principles for scientifically determining correct usage by compiling and systematizing the conventions of authoritative writers. Once grammarians and lexicographers had established "the unity of the reigning conversational and literary language," college professors took up the project of teaching it to provincials who hoped to gain acceptance in polite society by mastering its conventions (Bakhtin 270).

While Swift's idea that a handful of people could dictate the language of the educated may seem absurd today, Swift and other neoclassicists did not view discourse as a freely circulating commodity. Of course the French did establish such an academy, and the English might well have done so if Queen Anne had not died. The failure to do so was noted with regret a century later by Matthew Arnold in "The Literary Influence of Academies." Arnold felt that the lack of an academy had left English infected with a "provinciality" that prevented the development of "classical prose, prose of the centre" (*Works* 3: 245). The question for Swift, as for Arnold, was who would have the authority to regulate taste and usage. Of course Swift's "Proposal" for an academy and related works such as *The Battel . . . Between the "Antient" and the "Modern" Books* (1704) were not disinterested speculations but purposeful responses to particular conflicts within the patronage system.[10] Swift maintained that English "offends against every part of grammar" because he assumed that a *grammar* was by definition a rational and thus universal system (*Works* 11: 6). Later conservatives such as Bishop Lowth cited Swift as an authority for their efforts to prescribe correct usage, concluding that Swift's views had "never yet been questioned" (*Grammar* iv). More empirically oriented grammarians such as Campbell found Swift's position to be not unquestionable but unintelligible (*Philosophy of Rhetoric* 140–41). Campbell could not understand how English could systematically violate its own grammar because he defined grammar as a systematic description of the observable features of a language, noting that "there cannot be such a thing as an universal grammar, unless there were such a thing as an universal language" (34).

Johnson's *Dictionary* documents the developments that had made the conception of a universal grammar unintelligible to empiricists such as Campbell. When Johnson "took the first survey of my undertaking, I found our speech copious without order, and energetick without rules" (*Dictionary* ix). Like Swift, Johnson was a neoclassicist who defined change as corruption. Swift had hoped that if English "were once refined to a certain standard, perhaps there might be ways found out to fix it for ever" (Swift, *Works* 11: 9). In his initial *Plan* for the *Dictionary,* Johnson also set out to "fix the English language," but by the time he completed the work, he came to realize that English could not be "fixed" (*Plan* 11). Instead, he set standards for judging change by providing an index to published writers of "classical reputation or acknowledged authority" (*Dictionary* ix). While he continued to view variations as dangerous "spots of barbarity," he ridiculed his initial plans to "embalm" the language (*Dictionary* x, xxiii). Johnson had changed other positions as well. He refused the patronage he had previously sought from Lord Chesterfield, a former patron of Pope. Johnson claimed autonomy as a freely employed author in a famous letter to Chesterfield that is a noted transitional point in the shift from courtly patronage to a print economy governed by the exigencies of the marketplace (see Kernan 198–203).

The *Dictionary* was itself a product of that economy, for as Ong has stressed, "dictionaries are essentially printed constructs, their totally alphabetized reference economy being virtually inoperable in a nontypographic script culture" (*Interfaces* 21). Johnson straightforwardly rejected the very idea that literate usage ought "to comply with the corruption of oral utterance" (*Dictionary* x). He compiled authorities from the printed record in order to prevent the literate idiom from becoming as mutable as he perceived the dialects of spoken English to be. Johnson particularly proscribed the language of "the laborious and merchantile part of the people." Their "fugitive cant, which is always in a state of increase or decay, cannot be regarded as any part of the durable materials of a language, and therefore must be suffered to perish with other things unworthy of preservation" (xxii). As a person of lower-middle-class background, Johnson was quick to distinguish himself from the "common people," but his distaste for the "corruption of oral utterance" is more than class anxiety, though it is obviously that as well. For Johnson, the literate culture possesses the permanence of books, while the common experience is as quickly forgotten as an exchange in the marketplace. As Ong has noted of such perspectives, "away from print, all was chaos, for away from print, 'corruption was likely or even sure to set in'" (*Interfaces* 21–22).

Johnson's was but the most influential of the numerous dictionaries that reduced English to an orderly system. While only seven dictionaries of English had appeared before 1700, ten were published between 1700 and 1750, and over forty appeared in the latter half of the century, reproduced in over two hundred total editions (see Alston). These dictionaries, and the numerous grammars that accompanied them, methodically distinguished educated usage from the idioms of common speech. Formalizing conventions can make them easier to explain to outsiders, but the systematic distinction of literate English from common usage can also limit less educated people's ability to express themselves in print (see Olivia Smith). Textbooks often propounded complex rules that were more systematic than helpful. For example, Lowth defined irregular verbs using the suffix *en* in this way: "The irregulars of the third class form the past time by changing the vowel or diphthong of the present; and the participle perfect and passive, by adding the termination *en*, beside for the most part, the change of the vowel or diphthong. These also derive their formation in both parts from the Saxon" (50). Many familiar grammatical laws were first codified in this period, for example the absurdly logical principle that two negatives equal a positive and the systematic distinction of *shall* and *will* and *between* and *among*.

Lowth felt that the problem with English was not that it lacked a grammar but that it was not studied enough: "were the Language less easy and simple, we should find ourselves under a necessity of studying it with more care and

attention" (see Baugh and Cable 276–77). By providing an elaborate codification of the laws of English, Lowth helped ensure that it would have to be
studied with "more care and attention" if it was to be used correctly. Viola-
tions of the rules marked one not only as ignorant but also as morally corrupt
and even politically suspect because illiteracy, immorality, and rebelliousness
were commonly compounded. According to Johnson, a writer may gain
"publick infatuation" who does not know "the original import of words," but
such a writer "will use them with colloquial licentiousness, confound distinction, and forget propriety" (*Dictionary* xxiv). Even grammarians such as
Priestley who assumed that they were merely compiling "prevailing custom"
advised writers to avoid the idioms of spoken English because of the "danger
of debasing their style, by vulgar words and phrases, or such as have been
long associated with, and, in a manner appropriated to, vulgar and mean
ideas" (Priestley, *Theory of Language* 184; *Rudiments* 56). Such advice became
a mainstay of the teaching of composition (see Glau).

Johnson based his standard on authors of "classical reputation," but
Priestley and Campbell claimed authority for a broader class of writers, including provincials such as themselves. Campbell defined standard usage as
that which is *reputable, national,* and *current,* a definition that maintained its
authority into the twentieth century. This definition mapped out the boundaries of the reading public by granting authority to writers throughout
Britain who maintained the proprieties of civil society. Campbell was quite
precise about who was to be excluded as disreputable:

> The far greater part of mankind, perhaps ninety-nine of a hundred, are, by
> reason of poverty and other circumstances, deprived of the advantages of ed-
> ucation, and condemned to toil for bread, almost incessantly, in some nar-
> row occupation. . . . As the ideas which occupy their minds are few, the
> portion of the language known to them must be very scanty. (*Philosophy of
> Rhetoric* 142)

Liberal grammarians like Campbell and Priestley were no less class-oriented
than prescriptivists. Liberals simply defined their class in broader terms because they lived farther from the cosmopolitan center of the culture than a
more conservative commentator such as Johnson. Like Johnson, they formalized the conventions judged appropriate by their class—that language "found
current, especially in the upper and the middle ranks, over the whole British
Empire" (Campbell, *Philosophy of Rhetoric* 145). They granted authority
to writers from the provinces as well as the capital of the reading public
but treated most readers as essentially mute, or at best with but a "scanty"
vocabulary.

Campbell and Priestley did depart from traditional intellectuals in claim-

ing the authority not of a classical or neoclassical tradition but of an empirical investigation of the natural laws of language itself. Priestley was most explicit about the scientific nature of the new grammar:

> *Grammar* may be compared to a treatise of *Natural Philosophy;* the one con-
> sisting of observations on the various changes, combinations, and mutual
> affections of words; and the other of the parts of nature: and were the language
> of men as uniform as the works of nature, the *grammar of language* would be
> as indisputable in its principles as the *grammar of nature.* (*Rudiments* vi)

However, it was Campbell who developed a methodical set of strategies for
eliminating variations in usage. Grammarians were to observe the language
of reputable writers, systematically codify it, eliminate all inconsistencies, and
then teach it to those "comdemned to toil for bread" who had a "scanty" vocabulary and hence few ideas of their own. Because Priestley and Campbell
took a descriptive approach concerned with reasoning inductively from literate usage, they have been hailed as the most progressive grammarians of the
eighteenth century.[11] Their application of the scientific method to grammar
was part of the broader project of founding the laws of discourse upon the
"science of man" developed by Locke, Hume, and others who looked inward
to discover the laws that govern human experience. As discussed in later
chapters, the "science of man" provided a reliable methodology and point
of reference for reformulating the three language arts—logic, rhetoric, and
grammar—according to experiential modes of reasoning, dispassionate
forms of exposition, and unadorned style that were consistent with the emerging sciences of political economy and psychology. This reformulation of the
language arts mirrored the conception of a liberal political economy in which
discourse circulated free of externally imposed authorities governed only by
the natural laws of the system itself, leaving individuals free to operate within
the system as long as they internalized its logic and respected its laws.

Once the laws governing English had been systematically compiled and
codified, the public had to be taught to obey them. According to Murray
Cohen, "to most later-eighteenth-century linguists, the ostensible categories
and capacities of language seemed settled" (78). Cohen examined how pedagogical concerns gradually gained priority over theoretical speculations,
which became confined to passing references to more scholarly works that
were increasingly removed from the educational project. Earlier proposals for
universal grammars and academies came to be seen as arcane speculations
that were irrelevant to teaching students to obey the rules. Webster noted that
"it is the business of grammar to inform the student, not how a language
might have been originally constructed, but how it is constructed" (*Dictio-*

nary 3). Lindley Murray's popular *English Grammar* (1795) ran through over sixty-five editions and six hundred printings, and he claimed to supply nothing original, just an accessible survey of established rules with "common" words conveniently listed to be methodically eliminated (Murray 5; Downey xv). English schools gained popularity, and traditional grammar schools were criticized for only teaching English indirectly through translation and ignoring "English classics" (Priestley, *Rudiments* viii–ix). The authority of the classical tradition itself was directly challenged by popular texts such as James Buchanan's *A Plan of an English Grammar-School Education. With an Introductory Inquiry, Whether by the English Language alone, without the Embarrassment of Latin and Greek, the British Youth, in general, Cannot be Thoroughly Accomplished in Every Part of Useful and Polite Literature, and Qualified to Make a More Early, Advantageous, and Elegant Figure in Life* (1770) and Butler's *An Essay upon Education Intended to shew that the Common Method is Defective in Religion, Morality, Our Own Language, History, Geography, and that the Custom of Teaching Dead Languages, When Little or no Advantage can be Expected from them is Absurd . . .* (1753).

More utilitarian and less classically oriented schools became common from the 1740s onward, resulting in a 250 percent increase in endowed nonclassical schools during the century. Such schools helped fuel the explosion of grammars, dictionaries, and rhetorics that began a decade later (see Tompson, "English and English Education"). In these schools, as elsewhere, English was taught as a means to mold character.[12] Students were taught to assume a detached perspective and eliminate provincial idioms that might identify them as outsiders. Reasoning from the assumption that language was but a window on the mind, style was studied as an index to sensibility, readers were taught to conduct experiments upon themselves to assess whether they responded appropriately to experience, and criticism turned from classical authorities to psychological concepts like sympathy and sublimity that could be used to model appropriate responses. Every system of discourse establishes positions from which one can speak and works to silence those who do not follow its laws, but epistemologically oriented rhetoricians, grammarians, and critics were especially systematic in their effort to found the laws of discourse upon a scientific study of human psychology. The whole formation of English as a logically consistent system was centered on the project of teaching people to internalize a tasteful self-restraint and a disinterested perspective on experience. The essay of taste and manners was a perfect vehicle for instilling polite tastes because it divorced itself and its readers from the political rhetoric of the party press that had popularized the essay.

The Essay as Blurred Genre

The interaction of the polite culture and the popular experience shaped the formation of the novel as well as other novelistic forms of discourse such as the essay. The novel is better recognized for being a blurred genre—a hybrid form that evolved from courtly romances and vulgar tales of adventure that had traditionally been confined to chapbooks aimed at the marginally educated (see, for example, Watt; Rogers, *Literature and Popular Culture*). The novel is one of the most studied genres in English departments, but what such departments produce is the essay, not only in the composition courses that initiate students into academic discourse, but also in the classes where students write about literature and in the journals where professors demonstrate their professional expertise.[13] The genre is commonly traced back to Bacon's *Essays* (1597) and Montaigne's *Essai* (1590), which apparently coined the term *essay* from *essayer,* to try, taste, or test the fitness of a thing or idea. Like the novel, the essay had predecessors in the popular press, and it is characterized by the intermingling of fact and fiction that was common before journalism became distinguished from literature, and literature became limited to nonutilitarian nonfactual genres. While the novel and the essay have evolved over the last two centuries, English classes have maintained a narrow concentration on the proprieties of syntax and sensibility with such success that the student essays written today are not too removed from the compositions that were written in the first university classes on English, as discussed in chapter 5. Such uniformity is striking when one considers the dialectical nature of the genre.

The style and content of Bacon's and Montaigne's essays are so different that it is hard to understand how they are read as the sources of the same genre. However, the essay has always contained conflicting purposes and voices in a manner that is typical of novelistic discourse. Montaigne was the first to emphasize the essay's self-expressive purpose and highly personalized conversational style, while Bacon provided the model for essays that represented experience in simple unadorned language that did not call attention to itself. These somewhat conflicting views of language and experience have been dynamic parts of the essay since its origins. According to Good's *The Observing Self,* "the essayist's authority is not his learning, but his experience," with the essay providing the occasion "where self and object reciprocally clarify and define each other" (7, 8). With both Montaigne and Bacon, the observer claims to stand outside of traditional hierarchies and received ways of knowing to speak in an unmediated way from the immediate experience. Both assume that an "informal" style provides a clear window on experience, though Montaigne expresses a personalized experience and Bacon conveys empirical experience from an "objective" perspective that purports to make the event directly available to be experienced by the reader. Despite their differing purposes, Bacon and Montaigne are often read the same because both are read as literature. While Montaigne is unproblematically literary in the modern sense of the term, Bacon's essays helped define the conventions of scientific literature. When read as literature, the essay became self-contained and decontextualized from the rhetorical contexts and purposes that shaped its production, reception, and reproduction. This mode of reading is enacted in essays themselves when essayists distance themselves from received traditions in order to speak freely from unmediated experience (see Trimbur).

The continuities from Montaigne to belletristic essayists such as Addison and from Bacon to the plain style advocated by the Royal Society are so well established that little attention tends to be paid to how the rhetorical functions of the essay changed as it became popularized. Bacon and Montaigne wrote for an elite audience who could afford expensive folios, with Bacon spending the last years of his life translating all his works into Latin because he believed that "these modern languages will . . . play the bankrupts with books" (qtd. Baugh and Cable 259). In the eighteenth century essays became a staple of the print economy sold in cheap pamphlets on street corners, often to promote the politics of the party in power. Essayists such as Swift, Steele, and Defoe were political rhetoricians, publicists paid to legitimize the political positions of the day, though that is not how they were read by the critics who first canonized them or by the professors who taught students to imitate them. When the essay is situated in the party politics that popularized it, then such decontextualized readings become even more problematic, for they reproduce the tendency of the essay to deny its rhetorical nature as a purposeful response to a less than disinterested situation. Essays have often been characterized and taught as free-form expressions of personal feelings or as mere representations of the facts themselves. When romanticized or upheld as a transparent genre for reporting information, the essay becomes a model for the cosmopolitan perspective that positions individuals outside of traditional hierarchies in order to enable them to speak freely from experience in a disinterested fashion.

The essay, like the novel, had predecessors in the popular culture as well as the literary tradition. From courtly romances and chapbook tales of adventure and romance, the novel evolved into a form that included domestic affairs, personal experience, and the adventures of realistically portrayed individuals. Newspapers and novels often used quite similar strategies to claim verisimilitude, with the former often reporting more fantastic stories than the latter and occasionally adopting a dialogue form to "converse" with representative readers about party politics. The very terms *novel* and *news* still referred to overlapping domains that included reports of novel events and news of daily life because fact and fiction were just beginning to diverge into distinct discursive categories (see *OED* and Davis's "Social History of Fact and Fiction"). The first newspaper was established in 1665 to publish government-sanctioned news, but the official voice of the government lost its legal monopoly with the lapse of traditional licensing requirements in 1695. The first daily appeared in 1702, and from 1711 to 1753 the newspaper press grew from two and a quarter million to seven million copies, doubling again by 1780 (Harris 83; Bond 10; Williams, *Long Revolution* 184). In the process periodicals were transformed from a printer's sideline into stock corporations that shaped public opinion. Early newspapers and magazines fed the popular taste for news with a pastiche of voices, forms, and topics, combining commentary on polite improvement and public executions, reports on bankrupts and miracles, and accounts of affairs in the House of Lords and the bedrooms of prime ministers.

The heteroglossia of the popular essay is dramatically evident in the journal that gave Johnson his first job as an essayist, the *Gentleman's Magazine* (founded 1731). Magazines "essayed" the expanding domain of print by publishing an inexpensive collage of excerpts, summaries, and criticisms of diverse periodicals and books. The motto of the *Gentleman's Magazine* was "more in Quantity, and greater Variety, than any Book of the Kind and Price." Essays from various periodicals were reprinted in a section labeled "A View of the Weekly Essays and Controversies." The essays included in the first issue were summarized on the title page as "Q. *Elizabeth;* Ministers; Treaties; Liberty of the Press; Riot Act; Armies; Traytors; Patriots; Reason; Criticism; Versifying; Ridicule; Humours; Love; Prostitutes; Music; Pawn brokers; Surgery; Law." The *Gentleman's Magazine* treated the essay as a vehicle of popular controversy that respected few proprieties, with queens and prostitutes both appropriate subjects, and criticism and poetry situated amid riots and pawnbrokers. The essays themselves include polemics on political and religious controversies that ridicule each other as well as the powers that be. The various essays are distilled and reprinted free of explicit editorial commentary to fit them into little five-paragraph snippets that can be conveniently read before moving on to the other sections of the magazine—"*Domestick* Occurrences," "Poetry," "Remarkable *Advertisements*," "Prices of Goods and Stocks, and a List of Bankrupts," as well as articles on topics ranging from gardening to witchcraft. This packaging of the essay helped to make it readily accessible to readers but also dislocated it from the party journals that were abstracted by the anonymous editors of the *Gentleman's Magazine*.

While the *Gentleman's Magazine* anthologized essays that took an openly rhetorical stance on the controversies of the week and the news of the day, the growth of the periodical press gave rise to journals that concentrated entirely on social commentary aimed at self-improvement. These journals popularized the essay of taste and manners that would become a key element of the formation of college English. In a manner that embodied the centrifugal and centripetal forces that expanded the educated public and standardized educated taste and usage, the essay of taste and manners refined the novelistic dynamics of the essay to combine commentaries on social conventions with a unifying authorial voice that spoke for tasteful self-restraint. The essay of taste and manners is characterized by the disinterested perspective of the critical commentator whose personal character is revealed in a polished style, restrained sense of polite decorum, and critical attention to how gestures and expressions reveal individuals' sensibility. The narrative voices of belletristic journals such as the *Spectator, Rambler, Idler,* or *Loiterer* represented a coherent and stable authorial perspective that provided a perfect model for the experiential modes of reasoning and belletristic sensibility that were taught by the first professors of English. Outside as well as inside the classroom, essays of taste and manners were widely used to initiate new classes of readers into the proprieties of civil society. Such essays were reprinted in self-improvement manuals like Moore's *Young Gentleman and Lady's Monitor* to teach the polite code of conduct under headings such as "Sobriety," "Cleanliness," "Genteel Carriage," and "Elegance of Expression."[14] Those who needed further instruction on "elegance of expression" could turn to works like William Scott's *Lessons in Elocution* (1779), which went through over thirty-five editions in America before 1820. Scott provided extracts from belletristic essays, along with excerpts from the elocutionary textbooks of John Walker and James Burgh, to teach provincials to speak with the voice of the *Idler* or *Spectator*.

When such essays are situated in the context of the popular press, one can see that the essay of taste and manners popularized a rhetorical stance that served clearly defined political purposes. According to Addison, reading the essays of the *Spectator* "draws Mens Minds off from the Bitterness of Party and furnishes them with Subjects of Discourse that may be treated without Warmth or Passion." Addison noted that "the first Design" of the Royal Society had also been to distract the public from "Politicks" (*Spectator* 2: 519). As discussed in the next section, Johnson also identified the *Spectator* and the Royal Society with the common purpose of diverting the public from politics to self-improvement. While the essays of the popular press were often unabashed polemics, the *Spectator* distanced itself from the politics of the day in order to preserve the proprieties of civil society. The essay of taste and manners helped to constitute a discursive space at the boundaries of the political and the private. Manners were understood to be public enactments of personal character, and a person of taste had the self-restraint to avoid discussing politics and religion in public. When readers were taught to parse the style and sentiments of the *Spectator* in the first university courses on English, the political contexts and rhetorical purposes of the essay were placed outside the realm of critical analysis, and it became established as literature, in the modern sense of that term. The political purposes served by this arhetorical stance can be traced back to the rhetorical context that gave rise to the essays that were canonized by the first professors of English.

Readers as Spectators in Civil Society

From their initial publication between 1709 and 1715, an edition of the *Spectator* or its predecessor, the *Tatler,* was published about once a year throughout the eighteenth century (see Winton 30). While other journals were also widely anthologized and reprinted, the *Spectator* set the standards for taste and usage that were taught by belletristic rhetoricians such as Hugh Blair. An issue of the *Spectator* was a single essay of about twenty-five hundred words printed in double columns on a single sheet. The purported author of the essays characterized himself in the first issue as a disinterested "Spectator" of public affairs, and in the second issue he began the commentary on his private club that set the context for later essays. The Spectator Club included a carefully balanced cross-section of the journal's intended readers. Prominence was given to a country gentleman, Roger de Coverly, whose perspective was balanced by the character of Sir Andrew Freeport, a wealthy merchant who spoke for the free-trade interests of the Whigs. The other members were represented in ways that distanced their personal characters from public controversies—a clergyman with no set theological orientation, a captain whose modesty led him to prefer a private life to public office, and a law student who is "disinterested and agreeable" because "few of his Thoughts are drawn from Business" (1: 9–13). Also included is a thrifty merchant who maintained that "A Penny saved is a Penny got," a sentiment that Franklin took to heart when he joined countless other provincials in refining his style by parsing the sentences of the *Spectator* (*Autobiography* 11). The Spectator pointedly emphasized that he always maintained "exact neutrality" in politics, never entering "into the Commerce of Discourse with any but my particular Friends, and

not in Publick even with them" (1: 5, 19). He can "discern the Errors in the Oeconomy, Business, and Diversion of others better than those who are engaged
in them" because he is a silent and uninvolved "Spectator of Mankind" who
does not become involved in "any Practical Part in Life" (1: 4, 5). Studiously
maintaining a public anonymity as a disinterested "Looker-on," the Spectator
retired to his chambers and composed his private thoughts to "Print my self
out" in the essays of the *Spectator* (1: 5).

The *Spectator* thus modeled a disinterested rhetorical stance for readers,
showing them how to step back from public debates and confine their political opinions to personal essays. The Spectator Club became a popular model
for the literary societies where provincials gathered to imitate the style and
sensibility of English essayists. These literary societies routinely proscribed
discussions of public controversies that might disturb the decorum of "conversible society." In them provincials could rise above political and religious
divisions and develop a unifying commitment to cultural assimilation as a
means to social progress. In groups like the Select Society and the Aberdeen
Philosophical Society, Smith, Blair, and Campbell discussed philosophy and
taste and corrected each other's compositions, including drafts of the works
that introduced English studies into the university. These societies provide an
archival site to examine the cosmopolitanism that linked college English
studies and the trends in public discourse that popularized the essay of taste
and manners. With Smith and his colleagues, the impartial spectator became
institutionalized as the perspective of the critic, the social scientist, and the
personalized author who has internalized the dominant culture in the form
of a second self, Smith's famous "inmate within our breast." This second self
served as a means to internalize self-restraint in a "commercial society" where
social mobility and economic change were undermining established hierarchies and traditional values.[15]

The *Spectator* became one of the best-selling publications of the eighteenth century because the essay of taste and manners provided accessible
commentary on polite self-improvement that served the needs of a society
that felt threatened by increasing social diversification. The essays' original
audience was small compared to the generations of students who would be
taught to imitate its style and stance. Addison made the "modest computa-
tion" that twenty people read each of the three thousand copies of the *Spectator* (1: 44), and he may not have been overly immodest because its essays
were passed from hand to hand in coffeehouses, of which there were some
two thousand in London (Plumb 269–70). Coffeehouses and private literary
societies provided a place apart from established forums and hierarchies
where intellectuals, shopkeepers, and the gentry could meet as equals. The

Spectator provided standards of taste for those who wanted to distinguish themselves from the workers who might be sitting at the next table listening to a literate colleague read the news, a common practice that spread the values and voices of the print culture even among the illiterate. Readers interested in self-improvement valued the *Spectator*'s commentary on how to distinguish between the merely popular and truly polite, and by helping readers to make such distinctions, the *Spectator* strengthened the popular authority of the polite culture. As Ketcham discusses, the essays of the *Spectator* "do not test conventions" to explore "their inadequacies or hidden potentials," instead the essays "create conventions which will, in turn create a self-confirming system of values" (5).

The essay of taste and manners popularized by the *Spectator* created a "self-confirming" set of values by modeling how tasteful self-restraint is conveyed through a studious attention to appropriate manners, keeping the code of conduct as informal as the conventions of the essay itself. The *Spectator* silently and dispassionately viewed urban society as a theater of human nature where one can observe from a critical distance how people converse in the street, how the sexes communicate their desires with veiled gestures, and how individuals with taste exercise self-control to preserve a sense of decorum. From a self-detached perspective, the *Spectator* represented individuals revealing their personal character through their modes of expression and behavior, providing details on the polite code of conduct while unmasking the pretenses of those who attempt to play the part of a gentleman or lady but do not have the taste to master the nuances of the role. Such details were dutifully studied by readers who had not inherited a position in polite society but hoped to earn one by improving their manners. Essays often digressed into personal observations on a chance encounter or conversation that convey an ironic awareness of social conventions, while at the same time effacing the essay's own formal conventions and rhetorical purposes behind an apparent indirectness and artlessness that is common in essayistic discourse. With space for personal narrative and endless digression but not explicit argumentation, the essay of taste and manners enacted the conventions of civility without explicitly explicating them, preserving the sense of decorum by not saying too much. An incident can be narrated, but the convention it dramatized need not be explicated because taste is a matter of sympathy, not system—an experience as natural and unmediated as the essay of taste and manners itself.

The essay of taste and manners depends on the readers' sympathetic identification with the personal character of the critical observer who has the sensitivity to pick up on the nuances of gesture and tone. The doctrines of sympathy popularized by the *Spectator* arose out of a rhetorical awareness of how speakers express their character when they deliver a speech, but the effectiveness of the rhetorical stance of the *Spectator* depended on its appearing to be a disinterested position divorced from public controversies. The assumption that "every passion gives a particular Cast to the Countenance, and is apt to discover itself in some Feature or other" was drawn from rhetorical theories of "delivery" (1: 365). For a sense of "the inward Disposition of the Mind made visible" the *Spectator* cited Cicero as a point of reference, and according to Ketcham, Addison's specific source may have been a 1699 translation of Cicero's *De officiis* that included a chapter titled "Outward Carriage discovers the inward Dispositions of the Mind" (*Spectator* 1: 366; Ketcham 31–32). Classical theories of delivery also influenced Hume's and Smith's sense of how hearers sympathize with speakers by feeling the emotions written on their faces. Cicero's *De oratore* is cited by Potkay as a source for Hume's observation that "when I see the *effects* of passion in the voice and gesture of any person, my mind immediately passes from these effects to their causes, and forms such a lively idea of the passion as is presently converted into the passion itself" (46). Hume's conception of the "lively idea" had a major impact on George Campbell's effort to redefine rhetoric by the "science of man," and such sources also influenced the elocutionists' efforts to make gestures, facial expressions, tones, and pauses into a formal sign system that would script speech according to the laws of human nature. Commentators on taste and manners turned to rhetoric for analyses of how gestures and facial expressions influenced audiences' responses, but the essay of taste and manners was represented as an arhetorical form that remained aloof from the politics of the day in order to speak disinterestedly for the virtues of self-restraint.

The essay of taste and manners encouraged readers to look inward and refine their responses and attitudes according to the manners deemed appropriate in polite society. These essays provided perfect models for studying style as the expression of character, for the very form of the essay was understood to be an enactment of the author's personal experience. Belletrists' commentary in the *Spectator* had a broad impact on the introspective turn of rhetoric and moral philosophy later in the century, particularly the tendency to conflate ethics and aesthetics in terms of the refinement of personal sentiment. The four essays in the *Spectator* on the "Pleasures of the Imagination" are one of the first attempts to give a psychological account of the effects of literature on readers, and they formed the point of departure for many later accounts, including the first publications of the moral-sense philosopher Francis Hutcheson—Adam Smith's teacher and predecessor as professor of moral philosophy at Glasgow. The psychological effects of imaginative literature would be widely studied by moral philosophers such as Hutcheson and

Smith who turned to the sympathetic imagination to maintain civility in an increasingly diversified society. In a fashion that was consistent with the introspective turn of later belletristic critics and commentators on moral sentiments, the *Spectator* set out to enter "into the Passions of Mankind, and to correct those depraved Sentiments that give Birth to all those little Extravagancies which appear in their outward Dress and Behaviour" (1: 70). The refinement of taste was valued because the tastes of the leisured classes were spreading beyond the confines of the educated culture and broader classes of readers had to be taught to exercise self-restraint and respect traditional hierarchies.

The essay of taste and manners was a very effective media for instilling cosmopolitan tastes in broader classes of readers. According to *Spectator* 411 and many later belletristic accounts, the "Pleasures of the Imagination" are confined to leisure hours and serve the purposes of self-improvement. When appropriately refined, the imagination provides not "criminal" but "idle and innocent" pleasures, unlike the leisure activities individuals often resort to when they "step out of business." A refined imagination enables a person to take as much pleasure in observing as "another does in the possession. It gives him indeed, a kind of property in everything he sees" and enables "him" to discover "in it a multitude of charms that conceal themselves from the generality of mankind" (qtd. Blair, *Lectures on Rhetoric* 1: 423–26). Such sentiments were highly valued by belletristic critics such as Hugh Blair, who devoted four of the lectures of the first volume of his *Lectures on Rhetoric and Belles Lettres* to explicating these essays as a model of style that has "no labor, no stiffness, or affectation" (1: 424). As I discuss in chapter 8, Blair confined his critical analysis to explicating Addison's unlabored style and had his students labor over essays imitating it, but he did not look beyond the level of syntax to explicate the ideas or forms of the essay of taste and manners because he found them to be as natural and free from controversy as the style he taught his students to internalize. Such instruction was part of what Eagleton has termed the "process of refashioning the human subject from the inside," or what Gramsci has called simply "hegemony" (Eagleton, *Ideology of the Aesthetic* 43).

Perhaps the most distinctive aspect of the essay of taste and manners, especially when compared to the rest of the periodical press of the time, is how studiously it avoided any explicit commentary on political controversies. The *Spectator* did occasionally dramatize political themes in images that suited the tastes and interests of middle-class readers, but it did not openly take a stand on political issues. For example, in the third issue, a member of The Club visits a bank and then dreams of a beautiful virgin on a golden throne, "Publick Credit," whose chamber is piled high with money and lined with various symbols of British freedom like the Magna Carta. Suddenly, pairs of horrible phantoms burst in: "Tyranny and Anarchy," "Bigotry and Atheism," "the Genius of Common-Wealth," and Charles the Jacobite Pretender. In the presence of such political extremes, the heaps of money begin to shrink. The vision disappears and is replaced by another: "Liberty, with Monarchy at her right Hand"; "Moderation leading in Religion"; and a third person who had never been seen before, Prince George, who had yet to visit England. Upon his entrance, the money bags swell to their former size (1: 15–17). Easy credit was of dramatic significance to the *Spectator*'s readers. It contributed to the rise of the mercantile class whose "moveable" wealth challenged the classical conceptions of property that made the landed gentry the voice of civic virtue because only they had a permanent stake in the public good. However, when one considers the polemics of the popular press, such political imagery is as restrained as the ideals it promoted. Within the essay of taste and manners and the polite society it helped popularize, "man" is defined as a "Sociable Animal" who joins together in clubs, "knit together, by a Love of Society, not a Spirit of Faction" (*Spectator* 1: 39, 42). This ideology and the groups modeled upon it helped to translate the ambitions of provincials into the language of civility, a language that maintained the decorum of civil society by popularizing a cosmopolitan sensibility that was carefully divorced from the civic rhetoric of party politics.

The distinctiveness of the essay of taste and manners was recognized at the time by one of its most important practitioners, Samuel Johnson. According to Johnson's "Life of Addison," the *Tatler* and *Spectator* had made the essay a popular form and used it to divert public attention from politics to politeness in a time of social unrest. The essay had first become popular during

> the Civil War, when it was much the interest of either party to raise and fix the prejudices of the people. . . . ; but hitherto nothing had been conveyed to the people, in this commodious manner, but controversy relating to the Church or State, of which they taught many to talk whom they could not teach to judge. . . . It has been suggested that the Royal Society was instituted soon after the Restoration to divert the attention of the people from public discontent. The *Tatler* and *Spectator* had the same tendency. (*Lives* 1: 334–35)

Johnson valued the essays of the *Spectator* precisely because they moved the genre out of the domain of popular politics and made it a means to teach readers to remain silent and learn the virtues of self-improvement. Following Addison's own reference to the Royal Society, which I already quoted, Johnson echoed Sprat's comment in his *History of the Royal Society* that that group had also sought to persuade the public to renounce factions and concentrate on "*calm* and *indifferent* things, especially *Experiments.*" Conflicting parties could then learn to coexist "with the same peacableness as men of different

Trades live one by another in the same *Street*" (Sprat 426–27; see also Ward, *Lives* 1: x).

In his comments on how to divert public opinion from politics to progress, Sprat modeled the commerce of discourse according to economic transactions in civil society, much as Adam Smith would do in his theories of rhetoric and political economy. Like Smith, Sprat followed Bacon in assuming that political rhetoric should be excised from civil society. According to Sprat, "eloquence ought to be banish'd out of all civil Societies, as a thing fatal to Peace and good Manners" (111). As has often been noted, the Royal Society advanced very persuasive arguments against persuasion and the general "luxury and redundance of speech" because Sprat and his colleagues hoped to make language as objective and disinterested as the scientific method was understood to be (111). What is less noted is that this criticism was a rhetorical response to a specific political situation, and it was recognized as such by essayists such as Addison and Johnson. As a Royalist, Sprat had witnessed popular orators promoting public unrest in the Commonwealth era, "when the greatest affairs" had been "manag'd by the violence of popular assemblies and those govern'd by the most plausible speakers" (22). Since Sprat, the "plain style" has been identified with the "rise of science," but the language of science was from the outset defined in opposition to the heated oratory of political assemblies and the highly figured style that was used by popular orators to inflame the passions. Sprat and other advocates of the "progress of reason" viewed science as a better subject for public study, and he looked to the relations of independent economic agents as a model for depoliticized social relations, as would later advocates of the science of political economy such as Adam Smith.

According to Johnson, the essay had originally served as a historical distraction to "minds heated with political contest" (*Lives* 1: 335), and in the eighteenth century, the polite diversions of essayists established a domain of civil discourse well suited to teaching readers to mind their manners:

> Before the "Tatler" and "Spectator," if the writers for the theatre are excepted, England had no masters of common life. No writers had yet undertaken to reform either the savageness of neglect or the impertinence of civility, to show when to speak or to be silent, how to refuse or how to comply. We had many books to teach us our more important duties, and to settle opinions in philosophy and politics; but an *arbiter elegantiarum*—a judge of propriety— was yet wanting, who would survey the track of daily conversation, and free it from thorns and prickles. (*Lives* 1: 334)

The essay of taste and manners directed public attention to a middle ground between "savageness" and "civility," a space apart from politics where "masters of common life" taught readers how to speak and when to remain silent.

This was the domain of civil society, and the essay of taste and manners helped maintain its boundaries by teaching readers a tasteful self-restraint and a well-mannered aversion to politics and religion as inappropriate topics for polite conversation. At a more subtle level, the essay of taste and manners itself inscribed such boundaries by representing a discursive domain free of traditional hierarchies, political divisions, and arbitrary authorities—a domain accessible to any individual who had internalized its logic and values as a natural part of his or her experience.

In the decades following the appearance of the *Spectator,* the print economy spread cosmopolitan tastes throughout the provinces of the English empire. A separate department of the post office was set up in 1787 to mail newspapers free of charge to the provinces, with four and a half million being mailed from London by 1790, over four times as many as a quarter-century earlier (Asquith 101; Black 299). At least thirty-six towns also had newspapers of their own (Jackson 3). The essay of taste and manners was a popular filler for newspapers in the provinces, and not simply because provincials wanted to imitate cosmopolitan tastes. Printers and booksellers outside metropolitan markets needed to appear impartial to avoid alienating factions within their limited audiences (see Asquith 105). Polite diversions from political differences were also welcome because armed rebellions continued to divide educated society up to the middle of the century in Scotland, and through the next century in Steele's own homeland, Ireland. The *Spectator* and its imitators spread a unifying commitment to personal refinement as a means to social progress through cultural assimilation. The essay of taste and manners was the perfect vehicle for teaching provincials to respect the proprieties of civil society, because it spoke directly to their anxieties and ambitions in an accessible style that was as natural as speech (once they had studiously eliminated all the idioms of their own society) and as disinterested as science (once they had learned to divorce themselves from the political conflicts of the time). In literary societies and in the works composed in them, provincials learned to assume the cosmopolitan perspective of the impartial spectator who has internalized the polite decorum of civil society in the form of a second self who monitors the propriety of every thought, word, and deed.

Conclusion: Reading Publics and Politics

The formation of college English was shaped by the centrifugal and centripetal forces that expanded the literate culture and standardized literate usage. Print provided both the means for expanding the reading public and a model for its standardization. The print economy came to be viewed as a domain for the free commerce of discourse that was governed by its own natural laws, rather than by political hierarchies or ancient authorities. Critics, grammarians, and rhetoricians took up the task of formalizing those laws by reasoning inductively from the conventions of educated discourse, while at the same time the "natural laws" of political economy were being formalized into a science by the moral philosophers who helped introduce English into higher education, most notably the great theorist of consumer society, Adam Smith. Essays of taste and manners were the perfect vehicle for spreading cosmopolitanism. They provided accessible surveys of the conventions of civil society and reinforced the authority of those who possessed the natural faculty of taste. By setting themselves outside traditional hierarchies and factional divisions, essayists represented civil society as a discursive domain open to all—all who had internalized its cosmopolitan sensibility and disinterested perspective on political controversies.

In the reading public of the eighteenth century, "public opinion battled with public power" according to Habermas (51). To understand the domain where those battles were waged, one must complicate Habermas's views of the early modern public sphere as a domain for social critique with Gramsci's conception of civil society as a depoliticized discursive domain where individuals are taught to internalize the hegemony of the dominant culture. The subordination of rhetoric to belletristic criticism within the formation of college English was consistent with the view that conversible society was distinct from political society, and that taste could bring advancement in the former even if one lacked the power to speak in the latter. Hume's "Of Civil Liberty," for example, argued that political freedom is not necessary to cultural advancement, with France the historical exemplar of a tyrannical society that had refined belles lettres as part of the general "*Arte de Vivre*, the art of society and conversation" (*Essays* 91). Hume, like Smith and other provincials, spoke from the experience of cultural provincials who had little access to political power but were beginning to gain influence as commentators on the conventions of taste and manners.[16]

The political limitations of the reading public become clear when one considers those who were excluded from civil society—the vast numbers of the public who lacked civility. For the reading public, the poor were generally objects but not agents of discourse. Whether writers advocated paternalistic acts of charity or greater severity in punishing the indolent, the urban working classes were generally discussed but not addressed. Nonetheless, as print expanded beyond the confines of civil society, literacy helped laboring people become aware of their shared history and problems, and the working class became constituted as a "social and cultural formation" (Thompson 11). Class consciousness, according to Thompson, was developed in workers' improvement clubs that differed quite significantly from literary societies. Rather than assuming that politics and religion were inappropriate topics of discussion, workers' groups routinely combined discussions of self-improvement and political reform in the belief that collective action was necessary to gain real progress. Correspondence societies shared the costs of printing radical tracts in revolutionary numbers, with sixty thousand copies of Price's *Observations on the Nature of Civil Liberty* (1776) sold in six months, and sales of as high as one and a half million for the second part of the *Rights of Man* (1792) (see Altick 71). Such workers' groups fostered critical reflection as a prelude to practical action and often had close ties with liberal reformers in the dissenting academy tradition discussed in the third chapter. The political crises of the time not only kept the presses running, they shaped how people read, as is clear in the emphasis that corresponding societies and debating clubs placed on critical literacy—the ability to read texts against their intended purposes and compose texts to accomplish one's own purposes, a very different sort of relationship among readers, texts, and purposes than that formalized by the essay of taste and manners.

As political opposition spread among the working classes, the state responded in 1799 by imposing anticombination, censorship, and sedition laws specifically aimed at containing print literacy. Revolutionary writings were banned, booksellers were imprisoned for selling cheap radical tracts to the public, and laws were passed against the correspondence societies, where working people came together to read the news and write about how to organize. Conservatives congratulated themselves on having been right that public literacy led to public unrest, and liberals and evangelicals redoubled their efforts to teach the public to read with propriety. Conservatives and liberals shared the basic assumption that the purpose of education was to create a more stable and productive society; they only differed on whether literacy made the poor more industrious or more presumptuous (see Neuberg 1–2). The most effective efforts to dissuade the working classes from reading radical political tracts were made by the Wesleyans. Hannah More imitated the popular chapbooks that preceded the novel to compose a series of Cheap Repository Tracts that promised sensational tales of romance and adventure but delivered the familiar moral lesson that industrious self-improvement was best for one and all. More's works reportedly sold some two million copies in 1795 alone (Lawson and Silver 232). "When it was impossible to prevent our reading something," Priestley's student William Hazlitt wrote, "the fear of . . . a *Reading Public* . . . made the Church and State anxious to provide us with that sort of food for our stomachs, which they thought best" (qtd. Altick 73).

As revolutions abroad led to unrest at home, the state openly intervened in civil society to reestablish the controls on public opinion traditionally maintained by a deference to educated proprieties. As Gramsci has discussed, only at times when the hegemony of the elite is directly threatened does one see the "apparatus of state coercive power" openly exercise its authority in this way (see *Prison Notebooks* 12). When systems of cultural reproduction such as schools and the literature of self-improvement are fulfilling their purposes, individuals are taught to assume appropriate positions and fulfill their duties. In the latter half of the eighteenth century, such systems of cultural reproduction were put under great strain by unprecedented population growth and changes in technology and economic relations. These changes have been broadly surveyed in this chapter: the spread of cheap print literacy, the expansion of the educated culture beyond the confines of learned languages, and the resultant blurring of the boundaries between the educated and popular cultures that gave rise to such blurred genres as the essay and novel. In response to these centrifugal trends, efforts were made to contain the educated culture by formalizing the conventions of correct expression, standardizing appropriate modes of response, and modeling the process by which individuals were to internalize "a spectator within the breast" to judge changing morés with tasteful self-restraint. These centripetal and centrifugal forces created the awareness of cultural differences and the need to explain them away that led to English first becoming established as an object of formal study in higher education.

Of course how one interprets the politics of the reading public will depend upon how one views the politics of reading and writing. Such views need to be carefully assessed against the material conditions and political relations of the time, more carefully than I have been able to do in this chapter. For example, I have suggested that the reading public was a consumer society that was taught to concentrate its attention on the reception rather than the production of discourse. The subordination of composition to criticism could be explained by the simple empirical fact that it took much longer to teach the public to write than to read. A teacher of the time estimated that he could teach reading in a year, while writing tended to take three to four times as long. Since the average student only attended his working-class school for thirteen months, few of his students would have become fluent writers (Schofield, "Measurement" 317). The material conditions of reading and writing tend to be ignored by even the best studies of the reading public. In my analyses, I have several times cited Altick's history of "the reading public as a social phenomenon." Altick has argued that "the democracy of print" was a "revolutionary social concept" that was instrumental in the "democratizing of reading" (8). Much like Habermas, Altick has concluded that "the history of the mass reading audience is, in fact, the history of English democracy seen from a new angle" (1–3). Such conclusions depend on the modern tendency to equate literacy with democracy and prosperity. However, the equation of literacy and progress has been challenged by research on literacy's contributions to industrialization, the historical test case of the modern experience. Schofield and other researchers have argued that industrialization did not depend on literacy and may actually have suppressed it, with early industrial towns often having lower levels of literacy than more rural communities, especially those where land ownership was dispersed and trades and crafts workers were organized (Schofield, "Dimensions of Illiteracy" 211–13).

Such historical facts call into question the assumption that literacy expanded along with increased individual opportunities to create a reading public that provided access to critical debate and political reform. The culture of literacy had a complex historical relationship with industrialization. It is a commonplace that ears attuned to the school bell are more likely to obey the factory whistle because children who have been taught to accept a routine of unfulfilling labor with promises of self-improvement will grow up to accept assembly lines and savings plans. The culture of literacy also changed relations between less and better educated workers, including those with the abilities and aspirations to make improvements in themselves or their communities, the sort of potential leaders Gramsci termed "organic intellectuals." According to Lacquer, "by the late eighteenth century, reading among the most articulate elements of the working class was no longer just another leisure activity, or a means for functioning more effectively in everyday life," but a "process of individual self-improvement." Literacy came to distinguish "the respectable from the nonrespectable poor, the washed from the unwashed . . . a division which was far less clear" earlier in the century (268). As a result, those who spoke, or rather wrote, from the working-class experience "became powerfully attached to bourgeois forms of reason and reasonableness; they fundamentally accepted bourgeois definitions of improvement and of the parameters of political action" (275). For those at the boundaries of the reading public, including middle-class provincials as well as the working classes, the culture of literacy maintained the existing hegemony by teaching organic intellectuals from marginal social groups to assume the perspective of a refined member of civil society, a perspective internalized as a second self in the form of the impartial spectator. Print itself facilitated this process by restructuring consciousness to separate "the knower from the external universe and then from himself" and thus creating "alienation within the human lifeworld" (Ong, *Interfaces* 17–18). The essay of taste and manners mediated this alienation by representing experience in a "conversational" style that was accessible to all who had internalized the tasteful self-restraint and polite proprieties of the literate culture.

The conventions of English were charted to map out the boundaries of the literate culture, but as literacy expanded and the working classes became politicized, more attention needed to be paid to teaching the public to obey the laws of correct usage and polite taste. As discussed in the next chapter, Oxford and Cambridge remained aloof from broader changes within the literate culture and continued to reproduce traditional intellectuals in the traditional way—by perpetuating the authority of the ancient languages and formalistic modes of reasoning that had long preserved the boundaries of the learned culture. Beyond the centers of the educated culture, provincial colleges began to take up the modern mission of public education because the Scottish universities and dissenting academies were more accessible and hence more responsive to the middle classes. Of course efforts to regulate language will inevitably concentrate on the margins of the dominant discourse because that is where boundaries are drawn and the awareness of cultural differences is most intense. The fact that English was introduced into provincial academies and universities over a century earlier than at the centers of English education challenges the view that educational change begins at the top, among influential theorists at elite institutions. Such a view cannot account either for the institutionalization of the modern culture by rhetoricians in the eighteenth century or for the reintroduction of rhetoric into the humanities in public universities in America two centuries later. To understand such developments, we need to pay more attention to the rhetorical strategies involved in formalizing and transmitting disciplinary knowledge, and the rhetorical situations to which such strategies responded.

The discursive relations that constitute an academic discipline only make sense within a well-defined economy that has been demarcated as a system of values and methods, including formalized modes of evaluation and reference and institutionalized positions of authorship. As traditionally understood, an academic discipline is essentially a print construct that tends to be defined by the research published in the field, not by the teaching practices, funding sources, and other practical activities that situate intellectuals in the work of institutions and the general political economy. The disciplining of discourse is a highly rhetorical process, but rhetoric becomes effaced when a discipline establishes its modes of inquiry, reference, and authority as natural parts of work in the field, rather than as the purposeful responses of a particular group to a specific social situation. While the first professors to translate the humanities into English were rhetoricians, they deemphasized the composition of public discourse and concentrated on teaching taste to adapt higher education to the mission of instilling a common culture in the reading public, a mission higher education had not had to concern itself with when the educated culture was demarcated by learned languages, ancient authorities, and highly formalized modes of reasoning and expression. The belletristic perspective that first defined the formation of college English ended up making the study of English synonymous with the study of literary discourse, eliminating rhetoric as a domain of scholarly study in the humanities in Britain if not completely in America. While rhetoric's engagement with political controversies had traditionally served to preserve the public authority of the educated, such associations threatened to politicize class relations within the heterogeneous reading public, which was precisely what the cosmopolitan sensibility fostered by the essay of taste and manners worked to avoid. In the academy, as in civil society, rhetoric had to be effaced for the culture of literacy to be able to claim authority as a disinterested critical enterprise.

2

The Antiquarianism of the

English Universities

Every culture has its speculative and religious moment, which coincides with the period of complete hegemony of the social group of which it is the expression and perhaps coincides exactly with the moment in which the real hegemony disintegrates at the base, molecularly: but precisely because of this disintegration, and to react against it, the system of thought perfects itself as dogma and becomes a transcendental "faith." For this reason one can observe that every so-called decadent epoch (in which a disintegration of the old world takes place) is characterized by a refined and highly "speculative" form of thought.

—Gramsci, *Prison Notebooks*

The moment antiquarian history is no longer inspired and quickened by the vigorous life of the present, it degenerates.

—Nietzsche, "History in the Service and Disservice of Life"

THE EIGHTEENTH CENTURY has long been noted as one of the most decadent eras in the history of Oxford and Cambridge. Classicism had become mere antiquarianism.[1] Aristotelianism continued to define both what was studied and how it was taught, with the emphasis on syllogistic disputations paralleled by a Ciceronian rhetoric more concerned with stylistic elaborations of commonplaces than with Cicero's civic ideals. These highly formalized modes of reasoning and expression were transmitted through an uncritical method of instruction that worked to prevent their being called into question against the contemporary experience. This moribund classicism apparently suited the narrow student population. With the decline of the tradition of the poor scholar, the English universities had become "a preserve for the idle and the rich" (Barnard 24). The antiquarianism of the English universities was also consistent with their positions as bastions of the Church of England. From the exile of dissenters in 1662 until their readmission two centuries later, the English universities preserved "ramparts of conventional religious observances and traditional divinity" (Greaves 5: 401). The English universities were openly hostile to the expansion of commercial society and maintained the High Church doctrines and Tory politics that aligned the clerisy with the squirearchy. Precisely because dead languages and sacred texts effectively preserved the authority of the gentry and their clerics, the curriculum remained all but unchanged through the eighteenth century. Such change as did occur, most notably the imposition of more rigorous examinations, actually strengthened the authority of the ancients.

The English universities are thus central to assessing how higher education was shaped by the centripetal forces discussed in the last chapter. Over the centuries, the language, literature, and logic of the learned culture had become divorced from public life. As Ong has discussed, "Learned Latin was a literary medium in a specialized, distanced sense," a literary medium that placed whole domains of social and cultural experience beyond educated inquiry (*Interfaces* 37). The boundaries of the educated culture were also protected by explicit restrictions on access to education. Only those who would swear allegiance to the established church could gain admission to the centers of English education, and graduates had to swear the Stamford Oath that they would not challenge the universities' monopoly on learned knowledge by lecturing in public. Additional restrictions included laws against the sort of academies established by dissenters when they were forced out of the universities. Because they lacked the rich endowments of Oxford and Cambridge, dissenting academies (like the Scottish universities) had to depend on the support of their students, and their students were much more diverse than those of the English universities. Faced with limited access to positions in the military, learned professions, and government, dissenters tended to go into manufacture and commerce. In response to such students, the dissenting academies and Scottish universities expanded higher education to include modern politics, science, literature, ethics, and rhetoric. Because of their differing social functions, the centers of English education did not really begin to teach the modern culture until the end of the nineteenth century, a century after the Scots and about two centuries after the dissenters.

While an antiquarian approach to culture helped preserve the centers of English education against change, their hegemony began to disintegrate "at the base, molecularly." The educational base of the universities was the grammar school, which preserved the boundaries of the learned culture by confining learning to the learned languages. In the eighteenth century, the charitable foundations and preparatory purposes of grammar schools diverged, with many schools taking on broader educational missions and leaving the "public" grammar schools as the private enclaves of the elite. At an even more basic level, within the universities themselves, the learned culture's involvement with learning and teaching also disintegrated. While the learned culture was demarcated by highly formalized modes of expression and reasoning, they were transmitted in an informal fashion from masters to novices in the manner common in an oral or scribal culture. In the tutorial system, initiates recited in ancient languages on sacred truths in the private chambers of their masters and then performed ritualistic disputations to exhibit their mastery of syllogistic forms of reasoning. Similar to apprenticeships, such "implicit" modes of instruction are, according to Bourdieu, effective at "transmitting traditional, undifferentiated, 'total' knowledge" such as the "assimilation of styles" and the internalization of forms of behavior and reasoning. The immersion in the tacit mastery of particulars enabled "the possessors of the prerequisite capital to continue to monopolize that capital" (47). Such didacticism and formalism protected the learned culture against change, preserving its authority but also stifling its development. Students bring change into the classroom, but when the classroom ceases to be a place for dialogue, the learned culture ceases to learn and is "no longer inspired and quickened by the vigorous life of the present." At least partially because they only had to lecture and not really to teach, the professors of poetry and rhetoric discussed later in this chapter were antiquarians who divorced the learned tradition from the needs of contemporary learners.

A Classical Education Suitable for a Gentleman

Many historians of England's oldest universities have commented on the "Euthanasia of the Eighteenth Century" (Godley 5). Reports from the time support such assessments. In his first year at Oxford in 1740, Adam Smith wrote "it will be his own fault if anyone should endanger his health at Oxford by excessive study" (*Correspondence* 1). Like other provincial students sent south to study, Smith did benefit from the opportunity to learn the speech and manners of the English. Because he spoke English better than most of the Edinburgh literati, he was selected to deliver the public lectures on rhetoric and belles lettres that led to his gaining a professorship at Glasgow. In *Wealth of Nations*, Smith noted that at Oxford "the greater part of the public professors have for these many years given up altogether even the pretence of teaching." He attributed the perpetuation of "nonsense" in a "dead language" to the fact that the English system, unlike the Scottish system, did not reward professors for teaching what students needed to learn (761–63).[2] Most professorships were treated as sinecures, and none relied on student fees in the way that Scottish professors did (see Godley 60). Smith's assessment is supported by Gibbon's comments on the fellows he met at Oxford in 1752: "from the toil of reading or thinking, or writing they had absolved their conscience," and "their conversation stagnated in a round of College business, Tory politics, personal stories and private scandal" (*Memoirs* 52–53). Rather than a "liberal knowledge of Philosophy and literature," instruction was generally confined to "some tattered shreds of the old Logic and Metaphysics," a state of affairs that led Gibbon to conclude that "these venerable bodies are sufficiently old to partake of all the prejudices and infirmities of age" (50).

Even defenders of classicism criticized the moribund curriculum and methods of instruction. For example, the ex-fellow and grammar school headmaster Vicesimus Knox upheld the values of classical studies, but he had to conclude that reforms were needed if the universities were to compare with the teaching available in Scotland or elsewhere. Knox's *Liberal Education* (1781) criticized the limited curriculum and noted that professorships were "perfect sinecures" granted without any regard for applicants' abilities to teach (2: 230; see also Winstanley 6). He cited testimonies to the lack of lectures and the reigning pedantry at both Oxford and Cambridge (2: 126, 169). Critics were often especially harsh on disputations and examinations, which served little function beyond perpetuating the empty forms of scholasticism. Knox provides a detailed account of ritualistic disputations that had remained unchanged for centuries, becoming but an empty exercise in formal display—"an *ethico-logico-physico-metaphysico-theological drama*." Disputations were little more than "a formal repetition of a set of syllogisms upon some ridiculous question in logic" that had been learned by rote. "Strings" of these syllogisms were passed down by generations of students along with crib books called "schemes" (*Liberal Education* 2: 127–34). According to most historians, this examination system "remained for too long archaic in theory and in practice a farce," and students' letters document their frustration with being subjected to such rituals (Godley 12; see also Sutherland, "Curriculum" 469; Evans 143).

As in grammar schools, the confines of the university curriculum were preserved by statutes that maintained the authority of the ancients against change. The program of studies at Oxford was laid out by the Laudian Statutes of 1636, which remained in place well into the nineteenth century. The statutes were specifically designed to prevent reform, and they were largely responsible for perpetuating a curriculum that had become "hopelessly out of touch with the needs of the time" (Sutherland, *University* 16). The first year was supposed to be devoted to grammar and rhetoric (Priscian and Aristotle, Cicero, and Quintilian), and the second year was to include logic and Aristotle's ethics and politics, with the last two years continuing the studies of logic and ethics as well as geometry and Greek. Aristotle remained the official authority, though the rising emphasis on mathematics at Cambridge continued the challenges to his preeminence that had been posed by Ramism and Cartesianism. Some effort was made to advance the research of Bacon and Newton, but scientific studies markedly declined in the eighteenth century.[3] While the curriculum was restricted by formal statutes, little emphasis was given to teaching even the limited requirements. One disgruntled father wrote his son at Oxford in 1778 complaining about the "modes of education there; if indeed those may be called modes of education, where no mode—no plan—not even a book, beyond a logic or ethic compend is recommended. From the *genius* of the place, the emotions it inspires, the connections that may be formed, the opportunities of libraries; &c. much may be expected from a lad of spirit—but from tutors, I verily believe, *nothing*" (Evans 53).

Such comments on what an Oxford education really offered its students are especially notable because the quality of instruction depended almost entirely on how committed to teaching tutors were. An undergraduate depended almost entirely for direction and instruction on his individual tutor or "fellow" (generally a masters student or junior scholar). As is still all too common, masters students received no instruction on how to teach because learning was treated as mere mastery of information and not as a generative process of critical reflection on received knowledge. When a culture is tacitly transmitted rather than formally taught, the cultural capital of the educated is preserved in several ways. First, if conventions are merely memorized and not discussed, they are not raised to the level of conscious examination where they can be called into question. Also, the memorization of complex forms takes considerable time, and the lengthy process of initiation bonds the educated to the conventions of the educated culture, particularly when the process is marked by rituals and disciplines that force individuals to invest themselves in those conventions. Finally, what has not been formally learned cannot easily be taught except through rote repetition, thus preserving the value of the knowledge by limiting its broader circulation among the uninitiated. Any criticism of received beliefs was shared behind closed doors without challenging the institutionalized cultural ideology. The whole system of instruction may have been well suited to initiating disciples into a well-demarcated canon but was poorly suited to advancing the "new learning," not just because of the reverence for classical authorities but also because there was no attention to the process of learning from experience that was formalized by the experiential modes of reasoning of the "new" logic.

The antiquarianism of the English universities was most evident in the Aristotelian logic that predominated as both an object and a means of study. English university professors were the leading defenders of Aristotelianism against Lockean empiricism. All of the major eighteenth-century spokesmen for the Peripatetic tradition in Britain cited by Howell's *Eighteenth-Century British Logic and Rhetoric* were associated with the English universities, while all of the advocates of the inductive logic of Locke were Scots except for one, Isaac Watts, who was a dissenter. The reasons are clear. While the Scots and dissenters were expanding education to include empirically oriented studies of the contemporary experience, the English universities remained bound to a classical tradition embodied in a well-defined corpus of texts from which one could deduce all that was worth knowing.[4] Locke was read by a few tutors at Oxford and Cambridge as early as 1697, and even after his logic was formally censured in 1703, it was studied by tutors interested in the new learning. Nonetheless, Aristotelianism continued to dominate the curriculum into the nineteenth century, despite the fact that the "logic of Schools" was condemned even by defenders of the English universities. Johnson called it the "mere Art of Wrangling," and Knox found it as barren as the metaphysics upon which it was founded (qtd. Yolton 5: 576; Knox, *Essays* 2: 169).

The antiquarian counterpart to the Aristotelian logic was a Ciceronian rhetoric more concerned with mastering the nuances of Cicero's style than with his guiding concern for public issues. Here too the English universities were bastions of classicism, and the "new" rhetoric, according to Howell, was developed by professors in the cultural provinces, primarily Scotland. Later in this chapter, I examine the most important of the neoclassical rhetoricians, John Ward, who lectured at Gresham College, a stepchild of Oxford and Cambridge that was traditionally staffed by their graduates. Ward himself was educated in a dissenting academy, and his lectures will provide a transition from the classicism of the English universities to the educational tradition that the dissenters established. The dissenting tradition took a practical approach to rhetoric and composition, as is evident both in the popular notoriety of the rhetorical practices of dissenters such as Priestley and Price, and in the dissenters' pedagogical practice of contrasting various views of controversies and then having students compose their own positions on them. At the centers of English education, rhetoric had become merely a subject of antiquarian scholarship, for Ciceronianism had lost the civic humanist concern for speaking persuasively to public controversies and had become devoted to the stylistic refinements that distinguished the truly learned from the merely literate. While the full corpus of civic humanism—most notably the rhetoric and moral philosophy of Aristotle and Cicero—was a mainstay of classicism, civic humanism had been too long confined to the library, leaving Oxford and Cambridge "dumb in the study of eloquence" according to the *Spectator* (#483, 4: 214).

Into the next century, the English universities resisted public attempts to make them more relevant to the contemporary experience. In an effort to better educate civil servants and the teachers of the gentry, the Bishop of London got King George I to sponsor professorships in modern history at both universities in 1724. Despite the support of the king himself, "the traditional systems of study had become so ossified that no room could be found for these new subjects, and if professors started by giving lectures they soon stopped because nobody went to hear them" (Lawson and Silver 212). The first professor at Cambridge lectured once in Latin in 1725 and never lectured again until his death in 1733. Despite public complaints, his successors made no pretence of lecturing until 1771, when John Symonds delivered a poorly attended series of lectures on the history of Europe from the fall of Rome (see Winstanley 154–61). Symonds's lectures were praised by Jebb's *Remarks upon the Present Mode of Education in the University of Cambridge* (1773). Jebb suggested awards for Latin and English compositions, and he recommended including an attention to "the Law of Nature and of Nations" and "Philosophy natural and moral" (12–14).

While such concerns remained peripheral to English universities, natural rights doctrines and the methods of natural philosophy were central to the reformation of moral philosophy in the cultural provinces, and to the transitions in rhetoric and logic that were closely associated with it. Into the next century, defenders of the English universities upheld classicism against change by arguing that universities should concentrate on transmitting "what is thoroughly approved" rather than on discovering new knowledge (*A Reply to the Calumnies of the Edinburgh Review* 151). The defenders of classicism maintained that moral philosophy should be confined to the ancients, with contemporary moral questions left to the established church: "The scheme of Revelation we think is closed, and we expect no new light on earth to break in upon us" (152). In sharp contrast with this position, dissenters believed that research on the book of nature would provide new evidence of divine Providence, and that revelation was not a "closed" event in history but an individual experience to be observed and recorded to demonstrate one's personal membership in the elect.[5]

What the English universities offered was a place where one could retire from the world, develop connections with gentlemen, and refine one's understanding of classical literature. After all, even Locke assumed that a classical education was "absolutely necessary to a gentleman" (119–20). Classical languages could have been valued for providing access to an international tradition that included two thousand years of scholarship in areas as diverse as history, astronomy, physiology, and architecture. However, influential works like Walker's *Of Education, Especially of Young Gentlemen* (1673), Blackwall's *Introduction to the Classics* (1718), Rollin's *Method of Teaching and Studying the Belles Lettres* (translated 1734), and Knox's "Classical Learning Vindicated" (in *Essays,* 1778) defended classical languages primarily as a means to instill the character of a gentleman, rather than as an entrance to a broad domain of knowledge. Contemporary learning was excluded not simply because it was inferior but because it was so accessible that it corrupted students: "it requires no pains on their parts and presents only roses without thorns" and thus will give them a "distaste" for classical studies, "which as they are more difficult and less agreeable, so they are infinitely more useful and important" (Rollin 332). Well into the next century, classical languages would be defended in exclusionary terms as a way to discipline the mind and inculcate character. For such purposes, making the learned culture easy to learn was actually counterproductive. Students should have to memorize canonical texts by rote precisely because it was "more difficult and less agreeable" and would thus instill discipline.

At the same time that higher education in the provinces was responding to the needs of middle-class students by broadening the curriculum to include modern cultural and scientific studies, the English universities became increasingly confined to the children of the gentry and their clerics, and such changes as occurred were consistent with a traditional understanding of how to form a gentleman. The universities were themselves highly stratified societies, with each student's social class "distinguished by the gown and cap he wore, by the fees he paid, the privileges he enjoyed, the table at which he sat in hall and by the place he occupied in chapel" (Green 5: 317). Noblemen were not obligated even to attend upon a tutor or participate in exercises and could receive a degree by requesting one, while "servitors" had an increasingly difficult time even getting into the centers of English education. One reason for their declining numbers was that the emphasis on classical studies actually increased during the eighteenth century, and the imposition of more rigorous examinations in the last decades of the century made the English universities even more exclusive by raising the standards of classical study (see Sutherland, "Curriculum"). A systematic program of English studies was not introduced until the end of the nineteenth century at either Oxford or

Cambridge.[6] A major reason why English studies were introduced over a century later in the English universities than in the provinces was the difference in student populations.

Public Change and "Public" Schools

Enrollment in the Scottish universities more than quadrupled between 1700 and 1820, rising from around 1,000 to 4,400 (Houston 82). Despite dramatic increases in population, the English universities steadily declined, with a peak reached in the first half of the seventeenth century that was not surpassed until the latter half of the nineteenth century. At Oxford, undergraduates decreased from 460 in the 1660s, to 310 by the 1690s, to as few as 200 in the 1750s, before an upturn to around 250 at the end of the century (Green 5: 309). At midcentury, twelve Oxford colleges had fewer than ten students, and the numbers of graduate students also declined (Sutherland, "Curriculum" 4). From his analysis of enrollments, Stone has concluded that in periods of expansion higher education tended to "move to the center of the new developments of the day, whether in humanist scholarship, religion, political thought, or natural science." On the other hand, when enrollment at the English universities went into decline, they became "introverted, and withdrawn from the center of affairs, cut off from the vital flow of young men and from the interchange of ideas and values they brought with them" ("Size" 4, 5). Stone provides some of the best documentary evidence of how teaching and learning can foster change by involving the educated culture in a dialogue with the less educated. Educational change occurred where an expanding generation was being educated, but at the educational centers of the learned culture, learning was less of a dialogue than a monologue, confined to rote recitations, ritual disputations, and notorious "wall" lectures where professors droned on in a dead language to empty halls.

In addition to declines in enrollment, the student population became increasingly restricted to the upper classes. After the Restoration, education became a less accessible path to advancement as the Church of England became securely established and the clergy evolved into a self-perpetuating class that was less open to the sons of farmers and laborers who lacked the connections needed to secure a decent parish. Though the term was changing in meaning, students from "plebian" backgrounds decreased from over half the population at seventeenth-century Oxford to 27 percent in 1711, to 17 percent in 1760, and to around 1 percent in 1810 (Stone, "Size" 20). In the eighteenth century, richer students began to claim the scholarships that had enabled poorer students to matriculate. Knox complained that students were swearing the oaths that they had less than five pounds a year even if it had "ten times that value" (*Liberal Education* 2: 121). Scholarships had enabled poorer students to attend grammar schools to learn the classical languages needed for college studies, but the eighteenth century saw a split between grammar schools' charitable foundations and their functions as preparatory schools for the elite (see Tompson, *Classics and Charity*). Fifty percent of students entering Oxford in 1640 came from local grammar schools, but in 1700 only 30 percent came from such schools, a decline that deepened through the century as the numbers of poor scholars decreased (Stone, "Size" 40). Students increasingly came from prestigious grammar schools such as Eton, Harrow, and the seven other elite boarding schools that were later designated "public" schools by Parliament.[7]

In "public" schools and other well-endowed grammar schools, masters taught their students that classical learning "contributes more to form the true Gentleman, than the substituted ornaments of modern affectation" (Knox, *Essays* 2: 14). According to a popular educational guide, the classics are "the *Fountain-head* of true Sense and Sublimity." The contemporary idiom is too "unsettled and changeable" to be worth study because "that which was written in English two hundred Years ago is now scarce intelligible; and few *Authors* of one hundred Years standing can by this refin'd Age be read with Patience" (Blackwall 134). These lessons had been taught for centuries, but the context of such instruction was changing. While generations of foundationers had sat alongside gentlemen in local grammar schools, eighteenth-century "public" schools were the private preserves of the upper classes. Within these enclaves, upper-class males were sequestered for years of disciplined study concerned with mastering the sacred texts and dead languages of the ancients.[8] The rituals and hazings that were a routine part of such rites of passage inculcated a common culture that helped to perpetuate the traditional elite's sense of class superiority through the changes brought by industrialization. Even today in England the right school tie remains an essential emblem of a proper gentleman, and old school boys share a network of experiences and associations with considerable power. According to Stone, "today England is the most highly stratified of all modern western societies, an important cause and consequence being its highly elitist educational pattern" ("Literacy" 71).

While centripetal forces limited the curriculum and the student populations of traditional grammar schools, centrifugal forces widened the gap between these elite schools and the local schools that expanded their curricula to meet the needs of more diverse student populations. One of the best examples was a Hull grammar school run by John Clarke (1687–1734). In opposition to classicists' arguments that ancient languages were more difficult and hence more useful in instilling discipline, Clarke's *Essay Upon Education* (1720) and his *Essay on Study* (1731) reasoned that languages that "have been dead for many Ages" are less useful to study than English (*Essay on Study* 178). English was also taught in "English schools" and other "private" academies that provided business and technical instruction to the expanding middle class. Works on English produced by such academies included *An Essay Towards a Practical English Grammar* (1711) by James Greenwood and *The Principles of English Language* (1765) by James Elphinston, an Edinburgh graduate who became a noted advocate of reducing English orthography to a logical system to facilitate the spread of English throughout the British Empire. *The Plan of Education at Mr. Elphinston's Academy* (1760) shows that such private academies could include traditional learned subjects as well as experimental science, modern history, and English (14–15). Thus, while the stratification of the educational system maintained the authority of classical studies within a narrow "learned" domain, the modern culture was being introduced in institutions that taught broader classes of students, most notably the dissenting academies discussed in the next chapter.[9]

The English universities were only able to perpetuate the cultural authority of the ancients because grammar schools had already taught students to believe that learned languages were a prerequisite for all learning. To students already versed in the classics, Oxford and Cambridge offered an intensely literary education, with students spending their time mastering the classics, imitating their style, and internalizing their cultural sensibility. To gain the literary awards that could lead to fellowships or livings, students practiced their composing skills in literary societies. As discussed in later chapters, provincial students gathered in literary societies to study English taste and usage, but Oxford students prided themselves on burlesques of polite sentiments known as "waggery" and published their best satires of popular tastes in journals and collections like *The Oxford Sausage; or Select Poetical Pieces* (1764) edited by Thomas Warton. The best-known piece of waggery was the periodical *The Connoisseur* (1754–1756), which satirized essays of taste and manners from journals such as the *Spectator* that provincials looked to as models of sensibility (see Fairer 5: 794–95). Awards were offered by a few colleges for English compositions (see Godley 139; Clarke, "Classical" 5: 518). Even in such cases, students learned English indirectly by translating and composing works in Latin and Greek. This antiquarian approach to culture placed more emphasis on mastering the commonplaces and decorum of the ancients than on communicating with one's contemporaries about public issues. Because the language and culture of modern life were not valued, the study of classical literature was not brought into a dialectical relationship with the modern experience.

The reigning antiquarianism is evident in such Oxford professors of poetry as Thomas Warton. Warton is a prominent example of the men of letters that the English universities produced. The son of a clergyman and Oxford professor, Warton entered Oxford in 1744, became a fellow in 1750, held the professorship in poetry for the standard two terms from 1756 to 1766, and became the professor of history in 1785. He first gained the recognition that led to preferment with *The Triumph of Isis* (1749), an idyllic poem defending Oxford against charges of reactionary Jacobitism leveled by a Whig student's poem. Like some of his other early poems, Warton's "The Progress of Discontent" (1750) was composed in Latin for an exercise and then translated at the encouragement of his instructor (see Mant xxii–xxiii). After graduation, Warton continued to write poetry, contributed to Johnson's *Idler* and other belletristic journals, and even became poet laureate in 1785. His poetry was studiously neoclassical but given to a taste for melancholy that led to his being categorized as a nascent Romantic of the graveyard school. Warton was most important as a literary critic. Warton's *Observations on the Faerie Queene of Spenser* (1754) has been called "the first important piece of modern historical criticism" because it attempted to situate literary texts within their historical contexts (Rinaker 38). Wellek has even claimed that Warton's *History of English Poetry* (four volumes, 1774–1781) "determined the whole future development of English literary history," a claim that has interesting implications when one considers Warton's antiquarian sensibility (vi).

Most important here, while Warton and other Oxford professors of poetry made noted contributions to English criticism, they did not teach English. Established in 1708 by a bequest of a former fellow, the professorship required several lectures and two ceremonial orations annually for a five-year term, which could be repeated but once. Professors had to lecture to be paid, so the professorship did not become yet another sinecure, though professors were often nonresident (see Mackail). An unsuccessful effort was made to integrate the professorship into the curriculum by adding training in rhetoric to the responsibilities of the chair (see Pittock, "Warton" 16), but the professorship remained a largely ceremonial position. Until almost the end of the century, lectures were confined to classical literature, with perhaps a passing reference to English classics like Shakespeare. The Oxford professors of poetry took an antiquarian approach to teaching literature that represented a centripetal reaction to the expansion of the reading public. While two of the Oxford professors of poetry made significant contributions to English criticism, they did not connect what they wrote with what they taught because, like many traditional academics, they did not feel the need to relate their teaching to what was going on outside the lecture hall. The reigning classicism and the lack of commitment to teaching also limited the scope of reference and practical usefulness of the professorship of rhetoric held by John Ward that I examine later in this chapter.

Thomas Warton and the Oxford Professorship of Poetry

I have attempted to establish that the English universities preserved the boundaries of the learned culture by confining learning to a tacit method of instruction, ritualistic disputations, and the ossified forms of Aristotelianism and Ciceronianism. This antiquarianism helped maintain the universities' position as bastions of the traditional elite by ensuring that only those who had mastered ancient languages and forms of reasoning would be accepted as learned. The learned culture was not brought into a dialogue with the contemporary experience because modern life and letters were viewed to be too corrupt and mutable to be worth studying. While a professor might make a passing comment on the "classics" of English literature, the general attitude was that the contemporary experience and popular culture were not just unworthy of study but a threat to the authority of classical literature. The antiquarianism of the Oxford professors of poetry worked to contain the contemporary implications of literary studies in a fashion that was consistent with the formalism and elitism that characterized the centers of English education. The limitations of this antiquarian approach are evident in the positions taken by several of the most noted professors: Joseph Trapp (1708–1718), Robert Lowth (1741–1751), Thomas Warton (1756–1766), and James Hurdis (1793–1801).[10]

The first Oxford professor of poetry, Joseph Trapp, formalized the study of poetry by merely reiterating the doctrines of the reigning authority, Aristotle. In the first of his translated and published lectures, *Lectures on Poetry* (1742), Trapp stated that he was entering "a Province unattempted by others," a statement that could only be made and accepted if one completely ignored the popular interest in the study of literature at the time. Rejecting the idea that poetry has too "unbounded a Nature to submit to the Regulation of Precept," Trapp reduced the art to a set of "rules" drawn from the doctrines of "our Master *Aristotle*, who has accurately treated of the other Sciences, and whose Authority we follow in them all" (3). Trapp provided his students and readers with a survey of classical aesthetics, with passing references to "Moderns" such as Spenser and Milton, who are judged to be original geniuses despite their "inferior" language (351). Trapp felt the need to restate the doctrines of Aristotle because he feared that people were no longer absorbing classical culture through the process of dutifully imitating the ancients (3–4). Trapp complained that people of "coarse Materials" lacked the "Capacity" for such studies and were dissuading others from them. With an almost complete indifference to the literary commentary of the contemporary reading public, Trapp spoke for the classical laws of poetry in order to defend the virtues of classical literature against "obscene Writers" and "Pretenders" (6–7).

Trapp saw his task as beginning scholarly lectures on poetry, but Lowth's translated *Lectures on the Sacred Poetry of the Hebrews* (1787) began by congratulating Oxford for providing a retreat from public life where scholars can "discover and relish those delicate touches of grace and elegance, that lie beyond the reach of vulgar apprehension" (1: 5). The diverse cultures contained within classicism are evident in Lowth's use of Greek aesthetics to lecture the English in Latin on Hebrew poetry. The dialogical possibilities of Lowth's polyglot situation are inscribed in his basic argument that the "sacred poetry" of the Hebrews has a "parabolic" nature that uses parables drawn from everyday life to express the most elevated truths, creating "the most perfect union between perspicuity and sublimity" (1: 154, 1: 144). The idea that poetry is the natural language of uncultured peoples obviously had democratic implications, but Lowth attempted to prevent his conclusions from being broadly applied to the popular culture by stressing that poetry is "totally different from common language" (*Lectures* 1: 75).[11] This emphasis would seem to be inconsistent with his overall argument that the Hebrew's "sacred poetry" achieved sublimity and perspicuity by drawing on "familiar objects" and "the most generally understood" imagery (1: 144). Lowth attempted to contain the contemporary relevance of his argument by setting the ancient world apart as an idyllic space, an "uncultivated (or rather uncorrupted) state of life" (1: 146). Unlike modern societies, the Hebrews were "not at all addicted to commerce," and everyone enjoyed the "same equal liberty" from "an equality of lineage and rank" (1: 145).

Some of the strategies that Lowth used to set "sacred poetry" off in an idyllic historical space apart from contemporary society would commonly be used to canonize the classics of English literature and demarcate them from the debasements of the popular culture. Lowth stressed that the voice of poetry is "far remote from vulgar use," and he sharply distinguished classical literary forms from popular corruptions (*Lectures* 1: 37, 1: 26–27). Lowth complained that grammarians had not distinguished "between poetical and common language," but his *English Grammar* would solve this problem by formalizing elaborate laws for educated usage that made it less accessible to the common person (*Lectures* 1: 75). In a similar way, Lowth situated classical literature on a higher plane in order to maintain its authority over the "common" culture. Lowth taught his students to assume the standpoint of the ancients: "In one word, we must see all things with their eyes, estimate all things by their opinions: we must endeavour as much as possible to read Hebrew as the Hebrews would read it" (*Lectures* 1: 113). Such comments show that an awareness of historical differences was penetrating even into concepts of the classical literature and sacred languages. At its best, an antiquarian veneration for the past can contribute to a dialectical understanding of one's own historical situation, but as Nietzsche discussed, such understanding becomes stifling when "the historical sense no longer preserves life but embalms it" within a moribund tradition (101).

The conflicting potentials and limitations of antiquarianism are most pronounced in the critical theories of Lowth's student, Thomas Warton. While Warton confined his lectures to the history of ancient literature, he was the first to write a book-length history of English literature. In his published criticism, Warton explicated English authors' debts to their contemporaries as a means to situate them in the cultural sensibility of their age. Samuel Johnson recognized the significance of this historically oriented criticism when it first appeared in Warton's *Observations on the Faerie Queene of Spenser* (1754). In a letter to Warton, Johnson praised him for advancing scholarship on "the literature of our native country" by showing that "our ancient authors" should be read against their historical context (qtd. Mant xxvii). Following this line of analysis, Warton's *History of English Poetry* (1774–1781) goes well beyond previous dictionaries of poets and fragmentary classifications of the schools of English literature. Wellek treats Warton as the founder of "literary history as a distinct discipline," which "arose only when biography and criticism coalesced and when, under the influence of political historiography, the narrative form began to be used" (1). Wellek's claim is interesting because Warton's *History* is itself an undisciplined hodgepodge of forms that blends antiquarian catalogue, criticism, and anthology with history and biography. Warton's guiding assumptions are also eclectic, even contradictory. While he valued the sensibility of Gothic architecture and the melancholy evoked by the ruins of grand cathedrals, Warton also intently traced the progress of reason (see Mant and Rinaker).

The conflicting assumptions of Warton's antiquarian sensibility are evident from the outset of his *History,* which opens with two essays: "On the Introduction of Learning into England" heralded the advance of knowledge through the coolly rational "North," while "On the Origins of Romantic Fiction in Europe" valorized the romantic imagination that originated in the

Orient. Warton's history purported to show "the gradual improvements of our poetry, at the same time that it uniformly represents the progression of our language," but he also celebrated the uncultured imagination of a lost age of fancy (1: 5). One particularly rich passage in the *History* documents the conflicts between romance and reason that echo throughout his history of English literature:

> the customs, institutions, traditions, and religion of the middle ages were favourable to poetry. Their pageants, processions, spectacles and ceremonies were friendly to imagery, to personification and allegory. Ignorance and superstition, so opposite to the real interests of human society, are the parents of imagination. . . . Romantic poetry gave way to the force of reason and inquiry; as its own inchanted palaces and gardens instantaneously vanished, when the Christian champion displayed the shield of truth, and baffled the charm of the necromancer. The study of the classics, together with a colder magic and a tamer mythology, introduced method into composition: and the faultless models of Greece and Rome, produced that bane of invention, Imitation. Erudition was made to act upon genius. Fancy was weakened by reflection and philosophy. The fashion of treating every thing scientifically applied speculation and theory to the arts of writing. Judgement was advanced above imagination, and rules of criticism were established. The brave eccentricities of original genius, and the daring hardiness of native thought, were intimidated by metaphysical sentiments of perfection and refinement. . . . [T]he lover of true poetry will ask, what have we gained by this revolution? It may be answered, much good sense, good taste, and good criticism. But in the mean time, we have lost a set of manners and a system of machinery more suitable to the purposes of poetry than those which have been adopted in their place. We have parted with extravagancies that are above propriety, with incredulities that are more acceptable than truth, and with fictions that are more valuable than reality. (*History* 4: 21–22)

The conflicts contained in this passage are complex enough to be read in quite contrary ways, but what I see here is the antiquarian sensibility of a traditional intellectual caught between a nostalgia for a lost age of "Romantic poetry" and a classical faith in reason that was being destablized by the increasing tendency to treat "every thing scientifically." However one reads Warton's published criticism, it is clearly a rich site for assessing how cultural theories evolved as the awareness of historical change and cultural differences deepened.

As a teacher Warton was much less notable. During his years as a poetry professor, his lectures and criticism were generally limited to classical scholarship. According to Fairer, "Warton's contemporary fame was as a classical scholar, and in this he represented the Oxford establishment" (5: 797). Warton was known for his love of leisured reflection and was little interested in teaching the classics, or anything else for that matter. According to Ker, Warton's typical approach to students was "simply and openly to discourage their attendance at lectures" (1). Each term he reportedly called his students to his chambers to tell them to pursue their studies and leave him to his. When he became professor of history, he gave an initial lecture surveying the assigned field of study, then left the "rostrum to grow cold" (Mant lxxxiv). Of course, he was merely following the custom of the time. No history professor had bothered to lecture from 1725 to 1771, and about two-thirds of all professors failed to lecture (Curtis 135–36). Such customs were consistent with the assumption that a university was a monastic retreat from the world, not an institution charged with advancing knowledge and teaching students how to promote social and economic progress. The very concept of progress was antithetical to the timeless authority of the ancient traditions of Oxbridge. Only outside the educational centers of classicism were universities beginning to be considered by whether they made "productive" contributions to the political economy.

The last poetry professor of the eighteenth century, James Hurdis (1793–1801), opened his first lecture by pronouncing that he would lecture in English on English: "That my Lectures may not be obscured by quotation from any dead language, I shall draw every example that illustrates my remarks from the POETS OF GREAT BRITAIN" (2). Unfortunately, the medium of instruction is far more noteworthy than what was actually taught. The lectures are merely snippets from poems and plays that are stitched together with a line or two of critical commentary drawn from the commonplaces of the classical tradition, including Hurdis's guiding assumption that "the chief design of the Poet . . . is *to hold the mirror up to Nature*" (1). Rather than teaching his students how to read literature or write criticism, Hurdis merely grouped passages from Shakespeare, Milton, Thompson, and Addison together in a sort of commonplace book according to the objects of imitation —the seasons, the times of day, landscapes. This format followed in the tradition of school books reaching back to John Bodenham's *Politeuphuia: Wit's Common Wealth* (1597) and Francis Mere's *Palladis Tamia: Wit's Treasury* (1598) that grouped short passages under thematic headings to provide models and materials for students' compositions. By the last decades of the eighteenth century such commonplace collections had evolved into the first anthologies that presented complete texts for private study, if not for classroom teaching (see Michael). Hurdis's approach is thus less advanced than the school books of his day, for he used English literature in the traditional manner of classical commonplaces. More importantly for the institutionalization of college English studies, Hurdis was an isolated case: the custom of lecturing in Latin was resumed after Hurdis and was continued up until Matthew Arnold took the chair in 1857 and even from then by some of his successors.

Oxford professors of poetry were antiquarians who did not make the modern culture an object of formal study. Their antiquarianism is evident in Trapp's belief that Aristotle still provided the only precepts for poetry, in Lowth's attempt to demarcate sacred poetry from the common experience, in Warton's romantic depiction of a prescientific age of fancy, and in Hurdis's commonplace compilation of passages from English classics. Lowth, Warton, and their colleagues maintained the cultural sensibility and social exclusiveness of an education dedicated to perpetuating the authority of an ancient culture in a dead language. The professors of poetry themselves tended to be Tories and even nostalgic Jacobites. Like many of his colleagues and successors, Trapp spoke for church and university against the Whig politics and utilitarian reforms of his day (see *Character . . . of Whigs* 5). As to Warton, Rinaker dryly notes that "the line of progress in religion and politics did not lie in . . . a return to medievalism" (164). Fairer seems right to conclude that "to the literary world of the eighteenth century Oxford represented primarily two things: the past and the fancy, each in its own way unconnected with the world" (5: 579). The centripetal forces that disconnected the English universities from the public sphere are clearly evident in the lectures of the Oxford professors of poetry. A quite similar antiquarianism can also be seen in the professorship of rhetoric at Gresham College. Here too antiquarianism divorced the learned culture not just from historical change and the broader social experience but also at a basic level from learning and teaching themselves.

John Ward and the Professorship of Rhetoric at Gresham College

Gresham College was an unusual educational institution that is best known as the original home of the Royal Society. Many Gresham professors were members of the society, which was founded in 1663 and generally held its meetings in Gresham until 1710. Gresham College was originally founded in 1597 by a bequest of Thomas Gresham, a wealthy merchant who was a close financial advisor to Queen Elizabeth and a founder of the Royal Exchange, which provided the income for the college. Conflicts with Oxford and Cambridge were avoided by selecting the faculty from among their graduates, with three professors originally from each and a seventh with degrees from both. According to Gresham's will, rents from the Exchange were to be used to pay professors to lecture weekly on seven subjects: divinity, astronomy, music, geometry, law, "physic," and rhetoric. Thus the "college" did not teach logic, the central discipline of a university education, but did include areas that were outside the English university curriculum, including both professional studies (medicine) and the polite arts (music). George Buck's "The Third Universitie of England" (1615) portrayed Gresham as part of a "Universitie of London," but Buck's description actually suggests that Gresham was more like a cathedral school or courtly academy (see 965–66). According to historians, Gresham College was meant to provide the middle classes with access to university-level instruction, "but being academically dependent on Oxford and Cambridge, whose vested interests were involved, it had little chance of becoming much more than an extramural college" (Lawson and Silver 132). Gresham College did not register students or grant degrees and never became anything more than a foundation for public lectures.

From the outset, tensions developed between the scholarly backgrounds of the faculty and the public nature of the institution. Despite repeated injunctions passed in 1597, lectures did not begin until the next year, perhaps because of debates over the requirement that professors lecture in English as well as Latin (see Ward, *Lives* 1: ix, and Burgon 2: 516). Ward's own *Lives of the Professors of Gresham College* (1740) details the history of the institution. Ward included two statutes defending the requirement that lectures be in English as well as Latin. Eight justifications were offered for lecturing in English, with most following from the first: "The good, that will ensue wilbee more publique," though the "publique" is qualified to exclude "the ruder sort" of citizens (2: 21–22). The intended audience included the "Young gentlemen of the innes of court, and such like," who might not have studied Latin since grammar school (2: 22). The fourth reason is also notable: "It wilbee lesse offensive and dammageable to the universities, if they be read in the English tongue" (2: 22). The use of English at Gresham and in educated societies like the Royal Society and its numerous imitators shows that English was becoming a language of learned inquiry outside the centers of English education at the end of the seventeenth century, though those who were using English to teach learned topics were concerned about infringing on the monopoly of the universities by doing so.

Gresham College was suspended after the fire of London in 1666, and salaries were discontinued from 1669 to 1706, when public petitions led to a resumption of lectures. Complaints about the professors' failure to lecture, continuing financial problems, and divisive legal conflicts continued up until 1768, when the college building was sold and lectures were continued on a much smaller scale in a room in the Exchange (Burgon 2: 495). Ward's lectures as the thirteenth professor of rhetoric from 1720 until his death in 1758 thus come near the end of the college. Ward was best known as an antiquarian who served as a vice president of the Royal Society and helped found the British Museum in 1753. While Ward published widely on British antiquities and other topics during his years as professor of rhetoric, he did not publish anything directly related to his area of study before being appointed, suggesting that he may have gotten the position not because of his expertise but because the poor state of the college and the uncertain wages had attracted no more acceptable applicants (see Ehninger, "John Ward"). While all but one of Ward's predecessors were Oxford and Cambridge men, he was a dissenter who had studied in John Ker's academy and had even opened his own academy in 1710 (see Ward, *Lives* 2: 301–28). Like many dissenters, Ward had Scottish ties, most notably with William Wishart, who as principal of Edinburgh University granted Ward a doctorate in 1751. In 1747, Wishart wrote to Ward to provide a letter of introduction to John Stevenson, who was perhaps the first university professor to teach English literature, criticism, and composition (British Library Mss 6211.f161; see also chapter 5).

Despite his contacts with the dissenters and Scots who were introducing the modern culture into higher education, Ward faithfully maintained a classical conception of rhetoric. His *System of Oratory* (published posthumously in 1759) is the fullest and most popular restatement of classical rhetoric published in the eighteenth century (see Howell). After an inaugural lecture in Latin, Ward lectured in English on the classical precepts of the art. While his lectures made those precepts accessible to a broad readership who did not have the opportunity to study ancient languages or classical authorities, Ward did not reinterpret classical theories against changes in rhetorical practices and forums—a striking omission given the emphasis in classical theory on the situated nature of rhetoric. While he lectured to more diverse students than those of the English universities, Ward paid less attention to applying rhetoric to contemporary public discourse than to reviewing historical facts, definitions of terms, and commonplace precepts. Ward's failure to reexamine the practical relevance of classical doctrines is particularly striking when one considers that he was lecturing in the home of the Royal Society. However, Ward was lecturing in a moribund educational institution on a subject that was peripheral to his own intellectual interests. While one might have expected that a public audience would have prompted a more practical approach, professors at Gresham had as little incentive to teach as professors at Oxford and Cambridge. While Ward lectured in English, he did not lecture on English. Without any attention to public discourse or any effort to teach the composition of such discourse, rhetoric was little more than a subject of antiquarian interest studied for its status in the classical tradition but with little concern for applying classical concepts to contemporary rhetorical situations. Given his background and situation, Ward is a particularly stark example of how antiquarianism sets in when teachers fail to attend to the practical needs of their students.

Ward's *System of Oratory* was published at almost the same time as Lawson's posthumous *Lectures Concerning Oratory* (1758), which also dutifully translated the classical tradition into English. Lawson was a professor of oratory and history at Trinity College, Dublin, and is discussed in chapter 4. The parallels between Ward's and Lawson's situations are worth noting here because both taught in institutions that were too closely tied to the English universities to break from classicism. Ireland's Anglican university actually maintained a higher standard of classical scholarship than Oxford and Cambridge. As I discuss, the subjugation of Ireland's national language and culture did have an effect on rhetorical studies at Trinity, though mostly in the student societies rather than in the classroom. At Trinity as at Gresham, rhetoric was translated into English, but the public idiom was not itself taught. The rhetoric professorships at Gresham and Trinity (like the poetry professorship at Oxford) are important precisely because they mark out the boundaries of the reigning classicism. While the time had clearly come for a reassessment of the relevance of an education confined to the ancients, the conclusion of the eighteenth century saw classicism even more securely in place at the English universities. The centers of English education were able to remain aloof from the modern departure from classicism because an antiquarian emphasis on ancient languages and formalistic modes of reasoning and expression functioned quite effectively to maintain the boundaries of the learned culture and preserve the authority of the traditional elite within them.

Conclusion: "That unprosperous race of men commonly called men of letters"

Beginning with the quote from Gramsci that opens this chapter, I have tried to show how the classical curriculum embodied "a refined and highly 'speculative' form of thought." Gramsci also claimed that such refinements of the dominant culture coincide "with the moment in which the real hegemony disintegrates at the base, molecularly." I have maintained that the antiquarianism of the English universities divorced the teaching of culture not just from the "new learning" but from the basic learning process itself because teaching was not valued. The centers of English education were under little social pressure to change because they educated an increasingly elitist student population that was well served by the status quo. The limitations on education and the educated were reinforced at an elemental level as "public" schools became the private enclaves of the upper classes. As Bourdieu discussed, in times of social change, "the most privileged individuals . . . remain most attached to the former state of affairs" and are the "slowest to understand the need to change" (24). Bourdieu also maintained that traditional elites thus "fall victim to their own privilege," but this did not really occur in the case of the English upper classes. Much more than comparable elites elsewhere in Europe, the English gentry was able to preserve its cultural authority even after its economic and political power was eroded by the expansion of commercial society and liberal reform, in part because of how effectively it preserved its ties with traditional intellectuals (see Gramsci, *Prison Notebooks* 18). The English universities helped maintain the hegemony of the gentry by continuing to produce traditional intellectuals in a traditional way, but at a molecular or material level, Oxbridge made comparatively few productive contributions to the origins of modern education in the eighteenth century.

According to Adam Smith's discussion of productive and nonproductive forms of labor, "that unprosperous race of men commonly called men of letters" had increased beyond demand because they had been supplied at public expense to preach and teach (*Wealth of Nations* 148). "Before the invention of the art of printing, the only employment by which a man of letters could make any thing by his talents, was that of a publick or private teacher," but in his era many were becoming writers (148). The transition from teacher to writer as a means for employing the educated marks a historical transformation in the economics of learning and the learned. Teachers, who were often preachers as well, were charged with transmitting the values and conventions of the dominant culture to succeeding generations. As print reached into domains that had been above or behind the public sphere, writers began to teach the public how to understand the high culture and their private lives. Print was a technology for transmitting knowledge, and it inevitably transformed how knowledge was created and reproduced, in classrooms as well as in the "marketplace of ideas" formed by the expansion of the reading public beyond the formally educated. Through vernacular print literacy, one could learn about the educated culture without being formally taught to respect its proprieties, which is why there was so much attention given to how to read with taste. The traditional product of higher education, men of letters, changed in value as market relations and modes of production changed, and teaching took on broader importance as the learned culture expanded to include broader classes of readers and students and domains of experience that had been beyond the sphere of learned languages.

Through this expansion, the "new learning" helped transform social relations, material conditions, and the economic functions of education and the educated. As noted in the last chapter, the numbers of writers of English literature who had a classical education markedly declined in the eighteenth century. The English universities also produced a decreasing percentage of recognized "men of science." From an analysis of the *Dictionary of National Biography,* Hans has shown that among those who made recognized contributions to the sciences, the percentage of Oxford and Cambridge graduates declined from 67 percent in the seventeenth century to 16 percent in the eighteenth century. The number who had attended a "public" grammar school similarly declined from 58 percent to 16 percent, while the number who had been educated in Scotland and abroad rose from 10 to 23 percent (Hans 34). While the majority of seventeenth-century scientists were sons of the gentry (52 percent), the eighteenth century marks a shift downward to the children of merchants (20 percent) and even the lower classes (28 percent), many of whom were self-educated or had studied outside England (Hans 34–35). The number of patents increased over 800 percent from 1680 to 1780, and the types of inventions being patented changed. While gentlemen scientists had tended to invent "impractical devices designed to satisfy intellectual curiosity," eighteenth-century scientists were more intent on developing technical innovations that aided economic advancement (Hans 13). Such documentary evidence becomes all the more impressive when one considers that national biographies and literary anthologies inevitably have a class bias and will acknowledge the contributions of the upper-class graduates of the educational centers of the dominant culture more readily than those from the provinces and lower classes who do not have backgrounds that demand recognition. Hans's analysis shows that Oxford and Cambridge contributed comparatively little not just to the production of scientists but also to other professions that contributed to the rise of the modern intelligentsia, for the English universities did not play a major role in the professionalization of knowledge that begins to become evident at the end of the eighteenth century in areas like medicine (see also Rothblatt 29).

The changes that helped professionalize the sciences and other studies of utilitarian value were also beginning to transform the values of a liberal education. In a passage quoted more fully in the opening of the next chapter, Joseph Priestley stated that because the dissenting academies were "formed in a more enlightened age," they "are more liberal, and therefore better calculated to answer the purpose of a truly liberal education" (*Works* 19: 128). Priestley's use of the term *liberal* challenged the confinement of liberal arts to the "humane" studies suitable for a gentlemen, as opposed to the "servile" or "mechanical" arts needed by those who must work for a living. The latter oppositions are evident in Johnson's *Dictionary* definition of *liberal* as "not mean; not low in birth; not low in mind." Priestley's use of the term is defined by a different set of oppositions. He uses *liberal* in the modern sense of free from traditional prejudices, and his *Essay on a Course of Liberal Education for Civil and Active Life* (1765) advanced a philosophy of liberal education with a utilitarian concern for economic advancement and political reform. This philosophy of the liberal arts first emerged in the dissenting academy tradition that departed from classicism to teach modern politics, science, ethics, and rhetoric. The English universities helped to perpetuate an antiquarian philosophy of the humanities that maintained the elitist view that a liberal education was suitable only for gentlemen because only they had the discipline and leisure to learn its language and literature.

The dissenters' utilitarian approach to higher education sharply departed from the educational philosophy and economic functions of the traditional literary education, most notably by defining liberal education in terms of economic progress, terms that were antithetical to the timeless authority of classicism. To find the origins of the conception of liberal education that would become institutionalized in modern research universities, one must look to those provincial colleges that first taught experimental science and capitalist political economy as well as the language and literature of the contemporary culture. While the centers of English education did not have a pedagogical engagement with the "new learning" and remained aloof from the economic trends that shaped the origins of modern education, the dissenting academies were instrumental in translating the "new learning" into a new pedagogy because they believed that free inquiry would advance liberal reform, economic progress, and rational religion. For these reasons, if one wants to understand the social, cultural, and institutional trends that contributed to the introduction of the modern culture into higher education, one must look beyond the centers of English education to those institutions that were more broadly responsive to the modern expansion of the public sphere and public education.

Liberal Education in the

Dissenting Academies

By thus shutting the door of the Universities against all sectaries, and keeping the means to yourselves, you may think to keep us in ignorance, and therefore less able to give you disturbance. But ... driven to the expedient of providing, at a great expense, for scientific education among ourselves, we have had this advantage, that our institutions, being formed in a more enlightened age, are more liberal, and therefore better calculated to answer the purpose of a truly liberal education. Thus while your Universities resemble pools of *stagnant water* secured by damns and mounds, ours are like *rivers,* which, taking their natural course, fertilize a whole country.

—Priestley, *Letter to Mr. Pitt*

AFTER BEING DISLOCATED from the English universities by the imposition of religious tests in 1662, the dissenters reformed liberal education according to their understanding of an enlightened age. They taught the "natural laws" of science, politics, and history, and they took a more critical and less didactic approach to received traditions. In the comparative method of instruction, conflicting views of controversial issues were presented, and then students researched and composed essays arguing their positions. This method was consistent with the dissenters' belief that free inquiry would advance political reform and economic and moral improvement. The dissenting academy tradition provides some of the best evidence for Habermas's argument that the eighteenth-century expansion of the reading public created a public sphere where the middle classes began to develop a critical awareness of their shared needs and aspirations. The dissenters' middle-class background encouraged them to take a particular interest in practical subjects related to trade and industry, including experimental science and English composition. After moving far beyond the classical curriculum, the dissenting academy tradition came to an end in 1828 with the opening of London University, which included the first recognized professorship of English literature. Dissenters were instrumental in founding the university, which was free of religious tests. The dissenting academy tradition also influenced the other practically oriented "red-brick" universities that opened up English higher education in the nineteenth century. The academies were thus instrumental in introducing the modern culture and in making higher education more accessible to the public.[1]

Most important here is the fact that the dissenters were the first to teach English literature, composition, and rhetoric to college-level students in any systematic and concerted fashion. In this chapter I discuss how the teaching of English developed through several generations of dissenters. Charles Morton (1627–1698) lectured entirely in English on contemporary science, politics, and culture, according to his student, Daniel Defoe. Like other dissenters, Morton taught English as a "tool" subject—as a means to speak to the political and economic needs of the prosperous but disenfranchised dissenters. The most significant educators of the second generation were Isaac Watts (1674–1748) and Philip Doddridge (1702–1751). Watts and Doddridge developed the new learning into a new pedagogy. Doddridge developed a comparative method of instruction in order to foster critical inquiry and open debate in the classroom, and Watts wrote accessible textbooks on reading and writing as well as a logic textbook that introduced generations of British and American students to the inductive logic identified with Locke (see Howell 331–45). The third generation of dissenting educators included the best-known teacher of English—Joseph Priestley (1733–1804). Priestley began teaching languages and belles lettres at Warrington Academy in 1762, a position later held by the influential elocutionist William Enfield. Priestley was broadly interested in liberal education, which he defined in utilitarian terms as a preparation for a "civil and active life." Priestley was cited as a predecessor by such liberal reformers as Jeremy Bentham and Thomas Huxley in the nineteenth century.

The comparative method and the general utilitarian orientation of the dissenting academies served quite different political functions from the antiquated classicism of the English universities. Dissenters were more evangelical than the established church, and they perpetuated the Puritans' emphasis on popular literacy (see Graff, *Legacies of Literacy*). The more radical tendencies of the Puritans had clear continuities with the natural rights doctrines of dissenters such as Joseph Priestley and Richard Price, but even Priestley and Price were far from Levelers. They were liberal reformers who spoke for the progress of reason toward a utopia of free trade, scientific innovation, and rational religion. While they enlisted literate workers in the cause of parliamentary reform, they felt that the poor would only become more numerous and less industrous if granted relief. As the dissenters gained tolerance and prosperity, academies became less concerned with ministering to the poor than with advancing the interests of the middle classes (see Thompson, *The Making of the English Working Class*). As the dissenting academy tradition lost its organic relationship with the broader public, the academies shifted away from the ideal of a literate laity and a learned clergy to concentrate on providing a liberal education to the middle classes. These developments shaped the introduction of modern science, politics, and culture into higher education and foreshadowed some of the trends that would define the modern research university.

The Dissenters' Departure from Classicism

The first academies were ad hoc schools established in the homes of clergy to preserve dissent against the oppressive measures instituted upon the Restoration. With the establishment of the Anglican Church as part of the national constitution, dissenters were forbidden to teach their children in their own schools, so academies had to be relocated if discovered. Around forty students aged fifteen to seventeen, with some older and many younger, would study for three or four years, and sometimes five or more if they intended on becoming clergy, as many did. The academies were oriented toward producing clergy to perpetuate dissent, political as well as religious. From the outset, the academies formed a well-integrated Calvinist tradition with close Scottish and American ties, and they were guided by a faith that free inquiry would advance knowledge, and with it reasonable reform.

Dissenters soon turned away from Scholasticism to emphasize the continuity between natural religion and natural philosophy in the belief that the book of nature taught the same lessons as the Bible. This line of reasoning is evident in the writings of several of those who were expelled from the English universities by the imposition of the Test Acts, including Edward Reyner, (1600–1668), Thomas Cole (1627–1697), and Philip Henry (1631–1696). According to Reyner's *Treatise of the Necessity of Humane Learning for a Gospel-Preacher* (1663), the study of moral philosophy shows the "*Doctrines . . . Nature* teacheth," and as to natural philosophy, "the knowledge of the Nature of the Creatures is but the *knowledge of God in the Creatures*" (109, 92). To make such knowledge accessible to broad audiences, Cole opposed using

"Scholastick Terms in Divinity" because "the Mysteries of Faith . . . are best understood in their own native simplicity." Henry further argued that "the true learning of a Gospel Minister consists not in being able to speak Latin fluently, and to dispute in Philosophy, but in being able to speak a Word in Season to weary Souls" (qtd. Smith, *Birth* 31, 22). A former student of Cole's, John Locke, would become an important source for the reforms in later academies. The academy of Thomas Rowe (1666–1706) was one of the first to include the works of Locke and Descartes (Smith, *Birth* 43–45), and a student of Rowe's, Isaac Watts, became the best-known advocate of Locke's logical theories. Locke's works were also taught at John Jennings's short-lived academy (1715–1723), where Watts's colleague Philip Doddridge received a broader education than anything formally offered by the English universities. In addition to Locke's logic, and traditional subjects such as mathematics and classical languages, the four-year curriculum included modern languages, geography, experimental science, and political history and philosophy, including the writings of Shaftesbury, Bacon, and Continental natural law theorists such as Grotius and Pufendorf (Doddridge, *Correspondence* 2: 462–75; see also Murray, "Doddridge").

In some of these early academies, English composition and oratory were beginning to be taught. At Jennings's academy, Doddridge outlined and imitated the writings of Sprat and Tillotson, and students practiced English elocution by holding daily debates and critiquing sermons, poems, and essays by Bacon and other advocates of enlightenment. Jennings also discussed modern drama, literature, and the criticism of the *Spectator* and *Tatler*. Before turning to divinity studies in their last few terms, students were directed to confine their own essays to "such subjects as are discoverable by the light of nature" and to support their points with secular sources—"poets and philosophers" rather than "scripture" (Doddridge, *Correspondence* 1: 113). Orations and compositions were mostly in English, and they were not cast in the syllogistic form perpetuated by the dominant tradition (see Jennings; Smith, *Birth*, 114–15; Gibbons 21–59). The traditional emphasis on classical languages was also beginning to be repudiated, as for example at the academy of Joshua Oldfield (1656–1729). Oldfield's *Essay Towards the Improvement of Reason* (1707) stresses the limitations of school logics and the superior importance of "our Mother-Tongue, . . . as it hath been formerly us'd, and as now it stands alter'd, enlarg'd, and improv'd" (130). Rather than treating logic and rhetoric as self-contained subjects of study, Oldfield drew on contemporary theories of human understanding to emphasize the teaching of English and thereby made an "important" contribution to the development of English teaching according to Michael (148).

One of the largest and most significant of the early academies was run by Charles Morton outside London from 1673 to 1686. Morton taught entirely in English and emphasized English composition as well as the other subjects that were becoming the staples of dissenting academies: civil and ecclesiastical history, modern political philosophy, constitutional law, geography, modern languages, and science. As a contributor to the Royal Society, Morton wrote a science text that was "at least fifty years ahead" of institutionalized educational approaches (Girdler 589). Details on what and how Morton taught are provided by pamphlets of two of his students, Daniel Defoe and Samuel Wesley, the father of the founder of Methodism. After studying with Morton, Wesley conformed to Anglicanism, and like other Anglicans he depicted the academies as centers of "republicanism," though he could not help but praise some aspects of Morton's academy. Wesley described the academy's "laboratory" and its experimental equipment and noted that Morton ran the school in a democratic way, "any one having power to propose a Law, and all Laws carryed by the Balat" (Wesley 7, 8). Such customs were quite different from those that the English universities used to distinguish "gentlemen" from "servitors." Morton's academy catered to the needs of more diverse students. Instruction may have been specialized to suit students' career interests (as in the later academies), for Wesley notes that there was "a Distinction of the Faculties, and Employments of every One, whether Law, Divinity, Phisick, or what Else" (7–8).

Wesley's condemnation of the radicalism of the academies was answered by Defoe's *More Short Ways with the Dissenters* (1704). Defoe entered Morton's academy at age fourteen in 1676 and stayed to 1680 or 1681. In *The Present State of Parties* (1712), Defoe praised his former teacher in order to criticize those who did not teach English. The best description of Morton's approach to English appears in Defoe's *The Compleat English Gentleman* (written 1728; see also Leinster-Mackay).[2] According to Defoe, "Morton's class for eloquence" included weekly orations and two weekly compositions, with students role-playing as politicians or ambassadors:

> Thus he taught his pupils to write a masculine and manly stile, to write the most polite English, and at the same time to kno' how to suit their manner as well to the subject they were to write upon as to the persons or degrees of persons they were to write to; and all equally free and plain, without foolish flourishes and ridiculous flights of jingling bombast in stile, or dull meanness or expression below the dignity of the subject or the character of the writer. In a word his pupils came out of his hands finish'd orators, fitted to speak in the highest presence, to the greatest assemblies, and even in Parliaments, Courts of Justice, or any where. (219)

According to Defoe, Morton thus developed effective strategies to teach students to adjust their styles to varied audiences and rhetorical situations, including issues of practical political importance.

Morton's innovations did not go unnoticed. He was arrested for violating the laws against dissenters' teaching, and in 1686 he emigrated to America to escape prosecution. Before departing, he defended himself in a "Vindication drawn up when charged with breaking the 'Stamford Oath.'" Ever since the Catholic Church had suppressed Stamford University in 1334, graduating students at Oxford and Cambridge had sworn the Stamford Oath that they would not threaten the universities' monopoly on learning by lecturing in public on learned topics. According to Morton, Protestant educators did not really want to restrict access to learning and would rather see "Knowledge increas'd and not only confin'd to the Clergy or Learned Professions, but extended or diffus'd as much as might be, to the People in general" (Morton 1: 192). Morton was obviously speaking for the dissenters and their Puritan predecessors and not for the established church and universities, which had adopted a quite restrictive approach to learning. Morton himself had been expelled from Oxford, and the restrictions imposed by the dominant tradition eventually forced him to emigrate to the American colonies. Though his notoriety as an exiled dissenter prevented him from becoming president of Harvard, in 1697 he was appointed vice president, a position created specifically for him. He wrote a series of textbooks in English on moral philosophy and logic for his provincial students, and he challenged the reigning Scholasticism by introducing experimental studies of natural philosophy (see Fiering 238; Morrison 1: 251).

Isaac Watts, Philip Doddridge, and the Teaching of Critical Literacy

To reward the dissenters for supporting the succession of William, restrictions on academies were eased in 1689. The second generation of dissenting educators could thus openly collaborate with each other and with Scottish reformers. The best-known dissenting educator of this period was Philip Doddridge, who ran an influential academy from 1729 to 1751. Doddridge was close with Isaac Watts, whose poor health prevented him from opening his own academy (see Orton 49–54). Watts instead wrote effective textbooks as well as popular devotional literature—poems, songs, and catechisms that went through over six hundred editions and were translated into every language from Armenian to Zulu (see Davis, *Watts* 74–90). Watts's *Logic or the Right Use of Reason* (1724) went through over thirty British editions and seven

American editions by the 1820s. Howell has stated that "it is probably fair to say that in the English-speaking world more eighteenth-century students and serious general readers learned their lessons about logic from Isaac Watts than from any other source," and Watts's *Logic* remained influential through the middle of the next century in America according to Crowley (Howell 342; *Methodical Memory* 177). Watts's practical approach to logic was further popularized by his *Improvement of the Mind: or a Supplement to the Art of Logic* (1741), which was "one of the best known textbooks of the late eighteenth and early nineteenth centuries" (Davis, *Watts* 88). *The Improvement of the Mind, the Second Part with A Discourse on Education* (1751) includes material for teachers on such issues as leading class discussions and teaching the writing process. Through the works of Watts and Doddridge, the "new learning" redefined teaching to foster a critical attitude to received knowledge. Doddridge was very influential within the dissenting tradition itself, while Watts's widely used textbooks made broader contributions to the "democratization of literacy and to practical, public education in reading" (Bartine 64).

Following the epistemological orientation of Locke, Watts based his *Logick* on the "principal operations of the mind" (*Works* 5: 3). Because Watts was broadly interested in improving "the reasoning powers of every rank and order of men," he devoted less space to speculating about the faculties of the mind than to offering advice on how to observe, judge, and discuss experience (*Works* 5: 186). Watts's *Logick* and *The Improvement of the Mind* both emphasize practical strategies for critical inquiry. The first part of the latter work is devoted to methods of improving knowledge, while the second part deals with communicating knowledge. To learn from experience, Watts advised keeping a journal, "enquiring into causes and effects," and generalizing inductively to related phenomena (5: 206). Watts also offered practical advice on how to develop an overview of a book, outline arguments, and critique styles. He stressed the need to be open-minded when confronted with radical beliefs, even those that contradict established doctrines. The second part of the work includes chapters on encouraging free enquiry in the classroom, convincing audiences, using authority without abusing it, preaching, and writing and reading "controversies." Watts also discussed the composing process with recommendations on writing multiple drafts, having them critiqued by others, and revising with an eye to engaging one's intended readers in open dialogue (5: 353–54).

Watts's *Improvement of the Mind* is one of the most pedagogically effective textbooks in the early history of the teaching of English. Watts programmatically initiated readers into the culture of literacy by teaching them how to read, reason, and talk about books and experience in a critical and self-reflexive fashion. Watts helped make the literate culture accessible to broader classes of students. According to Bartine's *Early English Reading Theory* (1992), the "pragmatic" tradition identified with Watts represented an important historical alternative to the "romantic" tradition of Hugh Blair and others who mystified reading and writing with doctrines of natural genius and taste. Watts valued print as a democratizing influence that spread knowledge "through our nation at so cheap a rate" (5: 372). With accessible discussions of how to criticize experience and books, he introduced readers to the values of critical literacy, including a close attention to the grounds of proof, an opposition to traditional prejudices, a skepticism about received authorities, and a guiding faith in individual judgment. This approach was based on the Calvinist assumption that "God has given every man reason to judge for himself" (5: 336). As a dissenter, he was not afraid to argue that tradition held no a priori claim to authority: "all human authority though it be never so ancient, though it hath had universal sovereignty, and swayed all the learned and vulgar world for some thousands of years, yet has no certain and undoubted claim to truth" (5: 334). Out of a faith in critical inquiry, Watts concluded that divine Providence can be discovered "by the light of nature." He thus advised his readers to observe and investigate "natural things," including "human nature" as well as "civil law, or the law of nature and nations" (see *Works* 5: 307–8).

Connections were made among human nature, natural religion, natural law, and the methods of natural philosophy in the study of "pneumatology." Pneumatology's central place in the curriculum is evident in Doddridge's *Course of Lectures on the Principal Subjects in Pneumatology, Ethics, and Divinity* (published posthumously in 1763). While Doddridge defined pneumatology in a traditional way as "the doctrine of *spirits* or the branch of science which relates to them," he began with the faculties of the human mind and the nature of ideas, and subsequent lectures presented a straightforwardly Lockean epistemology. Like studies of pneumatology or "pneumatics" in Scotland, Doddridge devoted less attention to traditional questions about the nature of angels than to the nature of human consciousness and the principles of experimental, or rather experiential reasoning.[3] For support, Doddridge cited Descartes and leading British advocates of enlightenment, including the Scots who transformed moral philosophy according to the epistemological orientation of the new learning: Bacon, Sidney, Shaftesbury, Locke, Boyle, Watts, Berkeley, Hartley, Hutcheson, Beattie, Monboddo, Kames, Duncan, and Reid. These writers' works would transform the core of the humanities—the three language arts of logic, grammar, and rhetoric according to what Hume would call the "science of man" as I will discuss in chapter 7. Doddridge's *Course of Lectures* is clearly a transitional text in this broader transformation.

Doddridge's whole course of instruction was explicitly oriented to serving the needs of the middle classes. According to his student and biographer, Job Orton, only 60 percent of the graduates of Doddridge's academy became ministers, and students with other professional interests pursued different programs of study, a practice that was becoming common in other dissenting academies (Orton 120). Although Doddridge was not the first to teach entirely in English, his broad influence established English as the language of instruction in later academies. Doddridge's curriculum was even more comprehensive than the one he had experienced at Jennings's academy, including logic, rhetoric, geography, metaphysics, geometry, algebra, trigonometry, Newtonian physics, theology, ethics and political philosophy, "natural and experimental *Philosophy,*" and natural and civil history, with particular emphasis given to the history of religious controversies. Pneumatology was strategically important to this curriculum because it maintained the assumption that "Love for the great Architect of this amazing Frame" was instilled by studying nature, whether it be human nature, natural law, or the natural world (*Lectures* 91–92).

Like Watts, Doddridge had a faith in natural reason that led him to take a critical attitude to received beliefs. From the assumption that "there are no *innate ideas* in the human mind," Doddridge concluded that those who relied on tradition to defend accepted beliefs were merely seeking "to impose their own sentiments upon their disciples, as sacred truths stampt on their minds by the author of nature" (*Works* 4: 310). When Doddridge's *Lectures* were taught to Priestley, he found them to be "exceedingly favourable to free inquiry" (Priestley, *Works* 1.1: 23–24). Like Priestley, Doddridge fostered critical inquiry and open debate in the classroom. According to Orton, Doddridge always encouraged students "*to judge for themselves*" and "never concealed the Difficulties which affected any Question, but referred them to Writers on both sides, without hiding any from their Inspection" (101, 100). To ensure that his students did not passively copy down his lectures word for word, as was commonly done in university lecture halls, Doddridge customarily circulated his lectures to be copied later so that students could respond to what he was saying, a custom endorsed by later dissenters such as Priestley. The comparative method of instruction was a conscious attempt to create a classroom dialogue oriented to preparing students to speak to controversial issues. This emphasis on critical literacy redefined the relationship between teachers and students in ways that helped foster the spirit of free inquiry that would characterize the later academies. Such educational practices and purposes provide a powerful historical alternative to the didacticism that characterized the centers of English education.

Doddridge was a major influence on such students as David Fordyce, who had a formative impact on the study of moral philosophy at Aberdeen. Doddridge's academy served as the model for Fordyce's *Dialogues Concerning Education* (1745) (see Jones, "Polite Academy"). Fordyce described an academy in which students freely debated public issues to develop "the Notion of a *Public,* or free Constitution" and become aware of "the Rights and Interests they share" (1: 29). The master of the academy used the comparative method of instruction to teach students to defend their positions and defer only to "Reason" (1: 31). While he praised the ancients for teaching civic virtue, his respondent identified the virtues of modern education with civility and the culture of the heart, and another respondent noted that the ancients had been able to accomplish so much because they studied the language of public life and not "dead Languages" (2: 40–60). Fordyce sent drafts of his works to his former teacher and recommended his colleague George Turnbull for having treated "moral philosophy in the same manner in which natural philosophy has been treated" (Doddridge, *Correspondence* 3: 442, 416). Scots and dissenters shared a commitment to applying the methods of science to the study of moral philosophy. Fordyce's contributions to this project were the point of departure for his own student Alexander Gerard's efforts to reform the Aberdeen curriculum to move inductively from a survey of the arts and sciences to conclude with a course in moral philosophy founded on the "science of human nature," as discussed in chapter 5. Fordyce and Gerard also influenced educational reforms in America, most notably at the college that Benjamin Franklin helped establish as an alternative to Yale and Harvard (see my introduction to Witherspoon's *Selected Writings*).

Such reforms were guided by a faith in natural reason, which could be enlisted to challenge beliefs and practices that limited individuals' natural development. Dissenters helped broaden public education, not just by expanding the curriculum but also by broadening access, including supporting the access of women to education. Watts recommended that women should be able to study logic, "to judge by the reason and nature of things; to banish the prejudices of infancy, custom and humour; to argue closely and justly on any subject; and to cast their thoughts and affairs into a proper and easy method" (5: 378). Watts also felt that women should be able to enjoy the enlightening benefits of studying natural philosophy (5: 380). In taking such positions, dissenters were following through on the belief that human nature was a tabula rasa, with differences in accomplishment due to nurture not nature. Like Defoe, Priestley, and other leading dissenters, Watts was willing to follow such lines of reasoning through to the conclusion that women would be able to advance knowledge if they were taught how. The dissenting tradition helped to create a context in which at least some women could act on such conclusions.

Watts was clearly responding to the interest of women in science, not merely advocating such an interest: "in our age several of the ladies pursue science with success; and others of them are desirous of improving their reason even in common affairs of life, as well as the men" (5: 184).[4] Though dissenting teachers generally tutored female students only privately, academies were more dependent on public support and thus more responsive to social change than well-endowed universities that could afford to cater to a narrow elite.

Doddridge and Watts popularized the values of critical literacy because they believed it fostered rational religion. Doddridge said that he always taught his theological students to be "*experimental Preachers*" with "an Acquaintance with Cases, and an Observation of Facts," including the "*Exercises of the Soul*" and "the Workings of their own Hearts" (qtd. Orton 103). While his terminology sounds incongruous today, Doddridge believed in the continuities among "experimental" reasoning, reasonable religion, and the natural order of human experience. Through the generation of Doddridge, such beliefs were grounded in an evangelical faith that anyone could be taught to recognize those continuities. Doddridge taught his students to respect the "*common People*" and to recognize "their hidden worth, and . . . those noble traces of natural genius" evident even in those "of a very low education" (Orton 104; *Works* 4: 223). In all his writings, he strived for "the greatest plainness of speech" so that even "the lowest" readers could "understand every word," and he had Watts edit his writings to simplify the style still further (*Works* 1: 215). To help the common reader develop critical literacy and an "experimental" sense of his or her personal religious experience, Doddridge wrote works like *The Rise and Progress of Religion in the Soul* (1745, with sixty-five editions through the nineteenth century) and *The Family Expositor* (1739), a five-volume edition of the New Testament with historical commentary on customs and languages to enable families to study the Bible in its historical contexts. Such works followed in the Puritan tradition of fostering public literacy, and they contributed to the expansion of critical literacy in the eighteenth century.

Most English professors would not accept, let alone value, populist evangelism as part of their history. However, one cannot really understand the dissenters and Scots who introduced English into higher education if one ignores their faith in literacy. Almost without exception, the first professors to teach English came from Calvinist backgrounds that valued a literate devotion to the Word. The generation of Watts and Doddridge may be more acceptable because dissenters were becoming less Calvinistic and evangelical as they became more prosperous and worldly. According to Johnson's *Lives of the Poets*, Watts "was one of the first authors that taught the dissenters to court attention by the graces of language. Whatever they had among them before, whether of learning or acuteness, was commonly obscured and blunted by coarseness and inelegance of style. He showed them that zeal and purity might be expressed and enforced by polished diction" (297). Belletristic studies would gain status in later academies, but as Johnson suggests, even with the generation of Watts and Doddridge, religious literature was becoming more literary. Watts's *Horae Lyricae* (1706) and *Divine Songs* (1715) were extremely popular, with the latter going through over a hundred editions by 1850. Watts helped to create the genre of "good godly books" that initiated children into the Word, not by scaring them with damnation, but by entertaining them with stories told in accessible language (see Davis, *Watts* 81). Such works are important to those interested in the teaching of English because, as Michael has discussed, religious literature was "the most potent indirect influence on the literary development of young people" through this period (138). Watts's efforts to make religious literature more engaging to the common reader were combined with an evangelical commitment to broadening the reading public. Such efforts shaped how English was first taught at the college level.

The study of literature continued to be subordinated to the teaching of composition because Calvinists' aversion to worldly refinements had strong continuities with the utilitarian interests of the middle classes. The utilitarianism of the dissenting academies set them in sharp opposition to classicism. Watts assumed that a primary purpose of education was to prepare students for "some proper business or employment" (*Works* 5: 373). Doddridge taught that it would be "imprudence to yourself, and an Injury to the World, to spend so much Time in your Closet, as to neglect your Warehouse; and to be so much taken up with the Volumes of Philosophy or History, Poetry or even Divinity, as to forget to look into your Books of Accounts" (Orton 109–10 n). Doddridge did not view literature or philosophy as ends in themselves: "'tis one Thing to *taste* of these poignant and luscious Fruits, and another to *feed* and *live* upon them" (Orton 91–93). On the other hand, Doddridge advised students to strive to become "masters of our own language" from primary school through college (*Works* 4: 223). Doddridge's own academy stressed composition in all four years of study (see "Rules of Doddridge's Academy"; rpt. Parker, *Dissenting Academies* 147). While dissenters could not understand the value of literature as an end in itself, dissenting academies were more committed than the universities to teaching students how to critique received beliefs and speak to public controversies. The political implications of such lessons began to change as evangelism waned and educated dissenters began to identify more with the educated classes than with those who shared their religion.

Joseph Priestley and the Teaching of English
at Warrington Academy

While George II's reign from 1727 to 1760 was noted for broad public com-
placency and the well-managed party politics of Walpole, the era of the
American and French Revolutions was marked by expanding political activism, though its expression at the polls remained limited.[5] Joseph Priestley
and other liberal dissenters helped foment popular interest in reform, and
their interest in education was an integral part of such efforts. The link between Priestley and the generation of Doddridge and Watts is made by Caleb
Ashworth (1722–1775), who studied with Doddridge and taught Priestley
from 1752 to 1755. According to his *Autobiography,* Priestley wanted to attend
Doddridge's academy, but it had closed upon his death in 1751. Ashworth
adopted Watts's *Logick* and Doddridge's general course of study, and his
academy had moved so far beyond the classical curriculum that Latin was not
even taught. The comparative method was beginning to lead to the Unitari-
anism that characterized many later academies. In addition to being a leading
Unitarian, scientist, and historian, Priestley was one of the most radical practicing rhetoricians in the dissenting tradition (see Crook). As teacher of languages and belles lettres at Warrington Academy from 1762 to 1767, he was
also the most broadly significant teacher of English in the dissenting academy
tradition. Priestley has made recognized contributions to the history of ideas
about rhetoric and grammar, but his theories become far more interesting
when examined as part of the early modern effort to formalize specialized
discursive practices for the studies of science, history, and political economy
(see Bazerman and Russell). Priestley is also important for being one of the
first to provide a utilitarian justification for centering higher education on
such studies.

Warrington Academy opened in 1757 and during its thirty-year existence
became the most famous of the dissenting academies. Advancing the innovations of earlier academies, Warrington offered varied programs of study to
suit students' career goals. Warrington's students had quite different interests
and backgrounds from those at Oxford and Cambridge, according to William
Turner's "An Historical Account of Students Educated in the Warrington
Academy."[6] Only 22 percent became clergy, with 40 percent pursuing careers
in commerce, and roughly 10 percent each in law and medicine. The increasing numbers of students interested in commerce reinforced the utilitarian
tendencies of the academies, particularly the emphasis on applied scientific
studies. Such emphases were supported by the patrons of the academies, with
Warrington supported by such enterprising industrialists as Thomas Bentley,

Wedgewood's partner. To appeal to such audiences, the trustees stressed the school's efforts to advance "Natural Knowledge upon the Foundation of Experiment," particularly "that Part of it which has Connection with our Manufactures and Commerce" (qtd. Gibbs 17–18).

In 1758 an instructor of languages and belles lettres joined the teachers of divinity and natural philosophy. While Priestley applied for the position, it was originally given to John Aikin (1713–1780). Aikin has been called "the first systematic lecturer in English Literature" by George Saintsbury, who held the chair in English literature that was created from Hugh Blair's professorship at Edinburgh (107). Aikin established a program of English studies that was fuller than anything formally offered by the English universities until the end of the next century. With assistants who had studied in Holland and Scotland, Aikin taught grammar, oratory, and criticism as well as British history, logic, French, and classical languages and literature (Turner 16). As in previous academies, English composition and oratory were taught from the first year to graduation, but more attention was also being given to literature. Students read Milton, Pope, Thomson, Young, and Akenside and wrote critical essays on literature as well as philosophy (Turner 20).

Aikin and his colleagues had close contacts with the professors who shaped the departure from classicism in the Scottish universities. In addition to studying and teaching with Doddridge, Aikin had studied at Aberdeen with one of the first university professors to lecture in English, George Turnbull, who was professor of moral philosophy at Marischal College from 1721 to 1727 (see chapter 7). According to one of his students, Aikin "highly" valued the works of his former teacher and was also acquainted with Fordyce, William Duncan, and Turnbull's student Thomas Reid (Turner 13). As noted above, Fordyce had himself studied with Doddridge before going on to write such works as the moral philosophy text in Dodsley's *Preceptor* (1748), which was widely popular in Britain and America. Duncan was a leading proponent of the "new logic" (see Howell 348–61), and Reid's commonsense philosophy shaped American higher education through the middle of the next century. The other faculty at Warrington also had Scottish connections. John Seddon, who helped found Warrington and taught natural philosophy there, had graduated from Glasgow after studies with Francis Hutcheson. As professor of moral philosophy from 1730 to 1777, Hutcheson was one of the first university professors in Britain to lecture completely in English. Like Aikin, Watts, Doddridge, and other dissenters, Priestley was awarded a Scottish doctorate and had close ties with Scottish moral philosophers, though he was a sharp critic of the commonsense doctrines of Reid. Such contacts demonstrate that the institutionalization of English by the Scots and dissenters was a well-articulated educational movement with common sources, though almost none of them have been included within the history of the teaching of college English.

Aikin reluctantly took over divinity in 1761 upon the death of John Taylor, and Priestley began teaching the following year, the same year Blair became Regius Professor of Rhetoric and Belles Lettres at Edinburgh.[7] As discussed in the first chapter, Priestley's most original contribution to English studies was in the area of grammar. He concluded that the fears of Addison, Pope, Swift, and others "that the language of their time would at length become obsolete in this nation are absolutely groundless." He believed that efforts to fix and preserve English could not "produce any effect," that the spread of literacy had in fact stabilized English in Swift's time, and that even if English were changing, free people are free to change their language (*Works* 23: 489). By founding standard usage on the usage of educated people, Priestley took the most progressive position on grammatical correctness in the era (*Works* 23: 198; see Baugh and Cable 182–84). Priestley also helped redefine rhetoric according to contemporary theories of human psychology, particularly the associationalism of David Hartley, who was in fact one of the first to use the term *psychology* for the study of human nature (see *OED*).

Priestley was more interested in teaching and liberal education generally than in theories of rhetoric or grammar. While he revised and published expanded editions of his *Lectures on History* up until the last years of his life, he could not be bothered to make more than superficial revisions in his *Lectures on Oratory and Criticism* when he allowed them to be published in 1777. He advised a teacher interested in his grammar textbook to concentrate instead on assigning and commenting on compositions. He elsewhere recommended that such assignments should be based on works like the *Spectator* and *Robinson Crusoe* (*Works* 1: 298–99, 64, 67). At Warrington Priestley established a library of such texts for this purpose, and he instituted regular "public exercises," including English and Latin compositions, "speeches, and the exhibition of scenes in plays" (1.1: 67, 53–54). Rather than having students serve as copyists, he advised lecturing in a "regular but familiar" way to draw students into the "conversation," with half the time devoted to questions and discussion (24: 20–21). According to his students, Priestley fostered debates of radical ideas in the classroom, and according to his own accounts, he used the comparative method of instruction to teach critical literacy (Turner 26). After debating conflicts in class, students were assigned to research their positions and defend them in "orations, theses, or dissertations" (*Works* 24: 21).

Priestley was a practicing rhetorician who was heavily involved in the pamphlet wars and public debates of the time, but his philosophical interest in rhetoric was subordinate to his broader interest in human psychology. One of his main reasons for publishing his *Lectures on Oratory* was to demonstrate the value of Hartley's associationalism, which he felt solved "almost all the difficulties attending this curious subject, and gives us solid maxims, instead of arbitrary fancy" (*Examination* xii; *Works* 24: 6). Priestley also drew on other associationalists such as Henry Home, Lord Kames, as well as Ward's restatement of classical rhetoric (see *Lectures on Oratory* iii–iv). While he did not reinterpret rhetoric in terms of the "science of human nature" to the extent that George Campbell did, Priestley was a leading proponent of the "new" rhetoric (see Howell 632–47 and Moran). He rejected topical strategies of invention, criticized the elaborate style and form of Ciceronianism, and emphasized a plain style and inductive reasonings from the facts at issue. Priestley's approach to rhetoric was also influenced by his broader effort to understand the specialization of human experience and the formation of disciplinary knowledge (see Bazerman, "How Natural Philosophers Can Cooperate").

Basic aspects of Priestley's theory can be related to his interest in history and science and to his practical engagement with political and religious controversies. He reduced "all kinds of composition" to narration and argumentation: "For either we propose simply to relate *facts*, with a view to communicate information, as in *History*, natural or civil, *Travels*, & c, or we lay down some *proposition*, and endeavour to prove or explain it" (*Lectures on Oratory* 6). Priestley distinguished "true" histories from "novels, romances, and feigned tragedies" (81). While he did not include literature as a distinct category of discourse, he cited works by Shakespeare and Milton as well as contemporary novelists to explore the psychological effects of discourse. Like his Calvinist predecessors, he was willing to accept the Addisonian doctrine that works of fiction could exercise those "*finer feelings* which constitute the pleasures of the imagination," but he also maintained that "some bounds . . . must be set to the licentiousness of the human imagination, particularly that of poets" (*Lectures on Oratory* 73, 67). Echoing Doddridge, Priestley advised that a devotion to "historical romances, familiar essays and poetry" "may be exquisite for a time" but will end up creating "disgust, and a secret dissatisfaction with ourselves" (144).

Priestley's effort to set "some bounds" for the aesthetic experience was consistent with his utilitarian critiques of the literary refinements of classicism. According to Priestley, in ancient times grammar and rhetoric had been the principal studies because philosophy was "then in its infancy." While times had changed, education had not. Classically oriented clerics did not appreciate the "true sources of wealth, power, and happiness" because "commerce was little understood, or even attended to" (*Works* 24: 3). Priestley's

Essay on a Course of Liberal Education for Civil and Active Life (1765) argued that liberal education should be based on the study of history because a critical examination of historical developments leads to a liberal understanding of political economy, religious controversies, and science. For Priestley, philology and literature are "no more than the amusements of childhood" when compared with the science of the human mind and the other "branches of knowledge" advanced by Bacon, Newton, and Boyle (*Works* 15: 23–24). Priestley was an early advocate of reorienting education to include what Thomas Huxley would call the "culture of science." In fact, an essay praising Priestley as a predecessor opens the collection of essays by Huxley in which he opposed Matthew Arnold and argued for emphasizing science more than literature in modern education (see chapter 9). Huxley valued education as a means to advance utilitarian reform, and like Bentham, he cited Priestley as an important example of the educational reformer as liberal political activist. As discussed in the concluding chapter, Bentham and other Utilitarians were instrumental in the founding of London University, which included the first recognized professor of English literature. Almost as soon as literature became a specialized field of study, it was set in opposition to the utilitarianism of commercial society and the provincialism of the popular culture.

Priestley's Utilitarian Philosophy of Liberal Education and Liberal Political Economy

History was fundamental to Priestley's philosophy of liberal education and to his contributions to rhetoric, which he broadened beyond public discourse concerned with political controversies to include an attention to scientific writing. To prepare students for a "civil and active life," Priestley taught several modern history courses at Warrington (*Works* 1: 51). Like Adam Smith, Priestley viewed education as a preparation for "the business of life" and gave priority to science, composition, and other studies with practical utilitarian value. He promoted his history courses by stressing that "COMMERCE has by no means been overlooked" and that merchants will be less likely to look for a quick profit when they have heard "the great maxims of commerce discussed in a scientifical and connected manner" (*Works* 24: 12–13). In order to be able to assess "the true state of the riches of nations," Priestley taught students how to compute wages, standards of living, and national wealth from "data" like commodities prices (24: 111). Such methods gave rise to the science of political economy, but even before *The Wealth of Nations* appeared, Priestley was using historical evidence to argue for a liberal economic philosophy founded on a laissez-faire conception of the free market. He subsequently revised his *Lectures on History* to incorporate the theories of Smith and the other Scottish political economists who contributed to nineteenth-century liberalism.[8] Like Smith, Priestley assumed that education should be judged by the same laws of supply and demand that governed other modes of production.

Priestley helped to systematize the production of scientific knowledge by calling for specialized research carried out through international organizations and supported by the interests of commerce, which were just the sort of trends that would create the modern research university (see *Works* 25: 350). Both Priestley and Smith helped to foster the corporate enterprise of scientific research by working with journals and organizations dedicated to sharing useful knowledge, a trend begun by the Royal Society that was expanding throughout the provinces in the latter half of the eighteenth century. In such works as *The History and Present State of Electricity* (1767), Priestley formalized the conventions of scientific writing, including a carefully referenced review of the literature leading up to an assessment of the current state of research, a systematic description of experimental procedures so that they could be replicated, and a concluding call for further research in the assumption that scientific inquiry was an ongoing collaborative process. According to Bazerman, these innovations document a remarkably modern conception of scientific research as a collaborative enterprise concerned with technological improvements and the advancement of useful knowledge (see "How Natural Philosophers Can Cooperate"). As a follower of Bacon, Priestley assumed that the advance of scientific knowledge depended on two things: "the first is, an historical account of their rise, progress, and present state; and the second an easy channel of communication for all discoveries" (*Works* 25: 362). Like Smith, Priestley worked to advance useful knowledge by writing histories of the progress of experimental research within diverse fields and lectured on rhetoric because he assumed that the advance of knowledge was a corporate enterprise that depended on effective communication. Priestley and Smith were part of the generation who began to establish disciplinary standards for research in the sciences. These standards became the business of universities when disciplinary knowledge became professionalized and universities became integrated into the economy in the ways that Smith and Priestley had argued they should be.

Unlike Smith's, Priestley's theories of education and rhetoric were integrally related to an active involvement in popular politics. Smith assumed the stance of the "impartial spectator" because he was situated at a distance from the centers of political conflict, but Priestley and other dissenting educators joined in public debates over religious freedoms, political rights, and slavery.[9] Priestley was in fact one of the most notorious practicing rhetoricians of his era. In his popular writings on politics and religion, he used the comparative method to critique the historical development of received beliefs, concluding that Unitarian, Arian, and Socinian "heresies" were actually the accepted doctrines of the early church (see *Works* 1: 16). In the "Importance and Extent of Free Inquiry," Priestley went so far as to argue that "should free inquiry lead to the destruction of Christianity itself, it should not . . . be discontinued; for we can only wish for the prevalence of Christianity on the supposition of its being true" (*Works* 15: 78). His "Reflections on the Present State of Free Inquiry" included his notorious statement that Unitarians were "laying gunpowder grain by grain, under the old building of error and superstition, which a single spark may hereafter inflame so as to produce an instantaneous explosion" (18: 544). And when Anglicanism was exploded, "a small change in the political state of things . . . may suffice to overturn the best-compacted establishments *at once*" (18: 544). These lines were quoted by pamphlets and parliamentary speeches calling for continued restrictions on dissenters such as "Gunpowder Priestley." Though he was more controversial than most dissenters, Priestley was within the tradition of reform that they had publicly advocated and privately taught from the first academies. By calling for the right of free enquiry in all spheres of experience, Priestley was carrying the dissenters' faith in critical reason to its logical conclusion, though he left many dissenters behind when he invited them to complete the Reformation by eradicating the worship of Christ (15: 73). Such works helped to politicize the reading public and spread the natural rights doctrines that led to the establishment of the Liberal Party in the next century (see Gibbs 186).

Like his predecessors, Priestley provides clear support for Habermas's claim that the reading public provided a domain for social critique that empowered political reform. Priestley's historically oriented criticisms of religious, political, and economic beliefs were consistent with his commitment to Bacon's doctrine that "Knowledge is power" (see *Works* 24: 32). Priestley believed that scientific experiments threatened unreasonable authorities in the same way that liberal reforms did, concluding that "the English hierarchy (if there be anything unsound in its constitution) has equal reason to tremble even at an air pump or an electrical machine" (25: 375). Whether Priestley was studying chemistry, Christianity, commerce, or the constitution, his goal was a knowledge of the principles that governed the historical development of the phenomenon. A good example of the political power of such knowledge is provided by the work of Priestley's closest associate, Richard Price. Like Priestley, Price is best known as a radical pamphleteer, but he also developed some of the first actuarial models to be used by mutual insurance groups to predict insurance costs from past death rates. Because of his reputation as a political economist, the new government in America invited him to emigrate and become the nation's chief economic advisor, but he declined because of ill health. Price did consult with Parliament on how to reduce the national debt. He advocated a self-supporting insurance program that would require the poor to pay for their own relief. Price believed that the nation and all its citizens should save for the future, which was good practical advice for dissenting merchants but a rather inadequate response to the class of indigent poor that was being created by industrialization (see Thomas).

Priestley and Price treated historical developments as trends that could be studied in a rigorously empirical fashion to reform public policies according to the laws of political economy. Priestley provides an important historical connection between the rise of the science of political economy in the eighteenth century and the utilitarian reforms of nineteenth-century liberalism. Bentham in fact claimed to have discovered the fundamental Utilitarian precept of the greatest good for the greatest number in Priestley's arguments that the "good of the whole is the great rule by which every thing relating to society ought to be regulated" (Priestley, *Works* 24: 221; see also 24: 255; 1: 52 n). Priestley argued for a limited government like that being created in America in the assumption that governments should not overreach their basic purposes of providing security, adjudicating private conflicts, and building public works. Reasoning from the historical experience of prosperous but disenfranchised dissenters, Priestley took a libertarian view that the individual should be left alone "to employ all his faculties for his own advantage; and this he will better understand, and provide for, than the state could do for him" (24: 255; see also 24: 277). From its inception, laissez-faire liberalism was more concerned with encroachments on personal rights than with the problems of the poor, whom Priestley and others of his perspective tended to view as responsible for their own condition (see 24: 227). As discussed in more detail in the chapter on Adam Smith, theorists such as Smith and Priestley mark the departure from classicism in higher education not only because they helped introduce the study of modern cultural and social affairs but also because they developed a modern philosophy of public education.

Like his utilitarianism, Priestley's libertarian political views were a logical extension of the Baconian assumption that knowledge is power. Priestley believed that "ingenuous and speculative individuals will always be the first to make discoveries," and that society would lose the benefits of such discoveries unless "perfect liberty was given to all persons to speculate, and to act as they should judge proper" (*Works* 24: 222). Priestley advanced the ideological and social trends that marked the beginning of the end for classicism, and his works set out the problematics that would come to define liberal individualism, particularly as it was to be institutionalized in the research university. Classicism continued to dominate the English universities through the next century, but in Priestley, one can see the trends that were eroding its authority: a progressive individualism that challenged traditional authorities, a materialism that devalued the aesthetic experience and classicism generally, and a utilitarianism that valued practical applications over abstract speculations. Priestley is an early advocate of the bourgeois utilitarianism that Matthew Arnold termed "provincialism," just the sort of descendent of the Puritans whom Arnold had in mind when he condemned the middle class for its "defective" religion, "narrow range of intellect," and "stunted sense of beauty" (*Works* 10: 10). While Priestley's Utilitarian successors were instrumental in establishing the first professorships of English literature, Arnold helped set literary studies in opposition to the utilitarianism and underlying scientism that Priestley had helped institute at the origins of college English studies.

Not surprisingly, this philosophy of liberal education first emerged in institutions that catered to the middle classes, institutions that for two generations had been removed from the universities at the center of the classical tradition. The dissenters were the first to redefine higher education in response to the economic and political experience of the middle classes, and the tradition they established was filled with a confidence in modern commerce. In his "Proper Objects of Education" (1791), Priestley's faith in progress converged with a millenarian vision of the coming of the modern age:

> The prevailing good sense and humanity of the present age, the rising spirit of commerce and economy together with the sense which all nations now have of the dreadful weight of public debts and increasing taxes, enable us to prognosticate with certainty the approach of those happy times in which the sure prophecies of scripture inform us, that *wars shall cease,* and universal peace and harmony take place. (*Works* 15: 436)

One does not usually look to Scripture for prophecies of commercial utopias, but low taxes justified by scriptural authorities appealed to those who believed in the Protestant work ethic. Priestley addressed himself to the "middle classes of life" because he assumed that the poor were too stupid and the rich too lazy to listen (*Works* 15: 438). Priestley defined the age of modern commerce in the same international terms that he had used to set out the agenda for the advance of science, a context in which narrow national interests become overshadowed by the "true interests" of the free market (24: 8).

While he was one of the most radical advocates of liberal education in the eighteenth century, Priestley's laissez-faire liberalism showed little concern for ministering to the needs of the poor, which had been important to previous generations of dissenting educators. Priestley spoke for the entrepreneurs, scientists, and utilitarian reformers who were beginning to use scientific methods to advance economic modernization, technological innovation, and political reform. Priestley himself helped advance these trends by teaching and writing on economics, science, and politics. Priestley used liberal education to promote liberal reform in ways that furthered the interests of the middle classes. Reformers such as Priestley drew organic intellectuals from the working classes and provinces into debates over how to reform the government, but liberals tended to be less interested in the problems of the poor than in parliamentary representation for the middle classes. Dissenters were active in corresponding societies that spread literate political activism among working people, but in other respects the dissenting tradition was losing its practical engagement with the lower classes. With the generation of Priestley and Price, the mainstay of dissent, Presbyterianism, lost membership to more evangelical sects like Methodism that spoke more directly to the working-class experience, though in less political terms than those used by reformers such as Priestley. As dissenting academies became less involved with addressing broader public needs, English studies became less engaged with fostering social critique and assumed a more belletristic emphasis that was oriented to personal refinement rather than public controversies. As in Scotland, the belletristic interest in self-improvement advanced in tandem with efforts to use the scientific method to explain the individual psyche and the body politic.

Scientism, Belletrism, and the Teaching of English in Late Eighteenth-Century Academies

The career of Warrington's first student, Thomas Percival (1740–1804), documents the changes in class relations and political ideologies that shaped the teaching of English in later dissenting academies. After leaving Warrington, Percival went on to study at Edinburgh, where he became friends with such literati as Robertson and Hume. He completed his medical studies at Leyden in 1765 and then began the scientific research that gained him admission to the Royal Society. Percival corresponded with Voltaire, Diderot, and Condorcet, and he promoted enlightenment through the famous Manchester Literary and Philosophical Society, which he helped establish in 1781. While he was part of the international class of cosmopolitan reformers that included the leading advocates of enlightenment in Scotland, Percival also worked on practical social reforms. He was a close associate of Robert Owen, who introduced more efficient modes of instruction such as peer tutors or monitors to adapt elementary education to the factory system. Percival also worked to liberalize the factory system in which children as young as seven or eight worked from dawn to dusk. Percival's enlightened interest in education is evident in his popular *A Father's Instructions* (1775–1800) and *A Father's Advice to his Daughters* (1777), which helped to teach generations of children how to be middle class. When Warrington Academy was forced to close in 1786 by financial problems and the unmanageability of its increasingly radical students, Percival opened Manchester Academy to continue to provide a liberal education to those intending on careers in commerce and manufacture.

Percival's writings document the faith in science that shaped the teaching of English at Warrington and later academies. Percival's *Moral and Literary Dissertations* (1789) reiterated the close relationship between literary and scientific studies that he had experienced at Warrington. One essay, "On the Alliance of Natural History and Philosophy with Poetry," begins by citing Bacon's dictum that "Knowledge is power" and argues that it is "no less applicable to poesy, than to philosophy" (209). For support of his position, Percival drew on an essay by his teacher John Aikin titled "Essay on the Application of Natural History to Poetry" (212). In a related essay, Percival stated that "the fine arts" gratify "the same faculty which perceives and relishes the charms of nature. And by analogy we may infer, that the exercise, which they give to the taste is favourable to the virtuous affections of the heart." However, anyone with an excessive interest in the "magic delusions of the fine arts, is in danger of having his judgment impaired, his heart corrupted, and his capacity destroyed for the ordinary duties and enjoyments of life" (204).

While Percival placed limits on literary studies that were consistent with the Calvinist background and utilitarian emphases of previous academies, the teaching of English was changing. Priestley's successor at Warrington was John Seddon, who had been tutor of natural philosophy when Priestley taught belles lettres. Notes from Seddon's "Lectures on Philosophy of Language and Grammar" and "Lectures on Oratory" are preserved at Oxford. The two-year program of study was quite eclectic and included "a Course of Lectures upon Oratory . . . conducted upon a Scientific Plan"; lectures "upon Poetry its Several Species, with a Critique upon the principal Poets both antient & modern"; "little dissertations on the other polite arts, as music, painting, sculpture & architecture, which may serve as an acquaintance with them in future life"; and concluding lectures "on the Use & Study of History," particularly English history ("Lectures on Philosophy of Grammar" 2: 308–9). Seddon stressed oratory in political forums as well as the bar and pulpit.

Though he shared his predecessors' concern for the science of human nature and devoted almost one hundred pages to the passions, Seddon's "scientific" approach to rhetoric is actually more classical than Priestley's. However, the most important departure from earlier dissenters is the pervasive attention to literature and other polite arts.

Belletristic concerns became even more prominent in the course taught after Seddon's death in 1770 by William Enfield (1741–1797), who is best known for his elocutionary anthology *The Speaker* (1774), which went through over sixty editions through the nineteenth century. Like Priestley and other earlier teachers at Warrington, Enfield taught "Commerce," and he taught science experimentally. However, unlike Priestley and Seddon, Enfield did not apparently emphasize an active involvement in public controversies. The move toward a more belletristic approach is clearly evident in Enfield's *Mental and Moral Philosophy* (1809), which drew on Scottish moral philosophers to stress the virtues of sentiment. Enfield was responsive to the tendency to conflate ethics and aesthetics that I discuss in later chapters on Scottish belletrists and moral philosophers such as Adam Smith. Like the belletrists, Enfield's works do not address the rhetoric of civic life that had been stressed by dissenters from Morton to Priestley. Echoing Scottish literati such as Kames, Enfield's *Essay on the Cultivation of Taste* (delivered in 1793) stated as a "general maxim —That to *cultivate the Taste,* and *form the Heart* is at least of *equal* importance as to *exercise the understanding and judgment*" (4). Such claims mark a sharp departure from the more utilitarian orientation and Calvinist traditions of Enfield's predecessors.

The academies that succeeded Warrington were free of the external restrictions that limited earlier academies, but internal conflicts made several of the most notable even more unstable than their predecessors. The Unitarian colleges at Hoxton and Hackney in the last decades of the century were both closed when they became too radical for church elders and patrons. The specialization of the curriculum that had been evident at Warrington was deepening as dissenting academies attempted to compete with the increasing number of "English schools" (secular academies offering a full course of practical studies aimed at those intending on a career in business or manufacture). As they became more secular and less sectarian, some dissenting academies became almost indistinguishable from such private schools. With the addition of subjects like surveying and bookkeeping, some academies became technical schools, but notable academies like those at Hackney and Hoxton carried on the broader liberal education of their predecessors. At Hackney, Price taught the rationalist approach to moral philosophy that he published in *Review of the Principal Questions of Morals* (1757). He also lectured on Newton and the mathematical theories that contributed to his work with actuarial models and political economy, and Priestley occasionally lectured on science as well as political philosophy and history. He encouraged students to imitate Franklin and "those which are now conducting the glorious revolution in France," and to the horror of the general public, he and Price even honored Paine with a dinner at Hackney (*Works* 15: 422).

The most important English teacher in these academies was Andrew Kippis, who taught at Hoxton from 1763 to 1784 and at Hackney from 1786 to 1796. Kippis was a student and editor of Doddridge's writings. Like Priestley, Kippis stressed political theory and history, and like Enfield, Kippis also taught English literature, as is evident in the student notes titled "An Essay on the Variety and Harmony of the English Heroic Verse" (1769) and "Introductory Lectures to the Belles Lettres" (1767). According to his student William Hazlitt, Kippis was an effective teacher who spent nine hours a week on English composition alone (see J. W. Smith 174). He lectured extensively on Ward's neoclassical approach to rhetoric, and among the moderns, he drew on such sources as Locke, Fenelon, Rollin, Lawson, Hutcheson, Fordyce, and Sheridan. Kippis took a belletristic approach that assumed that rhetoric was integrally identified with "*Criticism*," but he advised his students to be careful of indulging in "literary luxuries." Despite his reservations about literary studies, Kippis is cited by Altick as one of the first to teach the belles lettres as a "means of kindling genuine interest in the aesthetic values of literature and in reading as a pastime adaptable even to the life of a middle-class tradesman" (44). Equally important in my assessment, Kippis apparently gave as little emphasis to speaking to political controversies as Enfield did.

The belletristic orientation of English studies in the later academies can also be seen in the essays of taste and manners that were included in a student literary journal called the "Academical Repository." The journal was circulated at Daventry Academy from 1785 to 1796, probably by a student literary society there. The hand-copied journal came out in monthly installments and was composed of student essays that had been submitted to a box in the school. The students modeled their compositions on the essays of belletristic journals like the *Spectator*. Light essays sprinkled with French phrases addressed such topics as novel reading and the nature of the sublime. Each issue listed the orations that had been delivered that month, and many of these did deal with practical political issues like capital punishment and legislative reform. However, the distinction between the realms of political oratory and the essay of taste and manners was consistently maintained in the journal itself, which was defined by the refined style and disinterested sensibility of the belletristic essay.

In the end, the dissenters' approach to English apparently became more like the belletristic rhetoric that the Scots institutionalized, which is not surprising given the fact that the dissenters had close contacts with Scotland from the earliest academies.[10] The emphasis on political rhetoric seems to have declined, not just because of the rising interest in belletristic criticism but also as a result of the fragmentation of the dissenting academies' social base. The addition of technical studies and the increased specialization of later academies compounded the identity problem that was created when they lost their unifying religious values and became more like their secular competitors, which at the end of the century were increasingly drawing off the support of potential patrons and students (see McLachlan 5). The dissenting academies were in the end swept away by the movement toward a more utilitarian approach to education that they had themselves instituted. According to Smith's *Birth of Modern Education,* "the industrial revolution finished the process of rendering a curriculum which had been in origin vocational and merely cultural in the most barren sense" (163). Just as classicism had declined into antiquarianism and become irrelevant to contemporary needs, the academies' traditional concern for the natural order of divine Providence lost its popular appeal as the Protestant ethic evolved into the modern age of imperial commerce that Priestley had prophecized. The dissenting academy tradition more or less came to an end with the opening of London University without religious tests in 1828, exactly one hundred years after Defoe had called for such a university in *Augusta Triumphans.*

Conclusion: The Rhetoric of Dissent
and the Rhetoric of Belles Lettres

While the centers of English education preserved the authority of the ancients by maintaining an antiquarian indifference to public life and the contemporary culture, the dissenting academies responded to the broadening of the reading public by redefining liberal education in utilitarian terms that were consistent with the assumptions and priorities of liberal political economy. Like other institutions such as the Scottish universities that served comparatively diverse student groups, the dissenting academies are important sites for assessing how broader social changes contributed to the departure from classicism in higher education. Studies of experimental science, political economy, and English composition suited the disenfranchised but increasingly prosperous students whom the academies depended upon for their survival. Like the other provincials who first introduced college English studies, the dissenters had limited access to the educational and political centers of the dominant culture. While the Scots looked to English studies as a means to cultural assimilation, dissenters were set apart not by cultural differences but by practical political restrictions. Out of a liberal faith that free inquiry would create political change, they developed comparative methods of instruction and a broad curriculum concerned with instilling critical literacy in order to prepare students to speak against the restrictions they faced. The dissenting academies put forward a politically engaged philosophy of liberal education that was far more broadly based than classicism because they served a broader public with a utilitarian interest in public issues and practical knowledge.

In both the dissenting academies and the Scottish universities, pneumatology was a pivotal area for the "experimental" project that began with natural religion, drew on the methods of natural philosophy, and developed into "the science of man." Priestley advanced the effort to formalize the laws of human nature, and he redefined rhetoric in terms of the psychological theories of David Hartley. Like Campbell and Kames, Priestley defined the principles of discourse by the workings of the mind. In the dissenting academies, as in Scotland, the formation of English as an object of study was integrally involved with the constitution of the authorial subject in terms of an "experimental," or rather experiential logic. As I discuss further in the four chapters on the formation of college English in Scotland, the trends in moral philosophy that led to the "science of man" were paralleled by a belletristic tendency to treat style as an index to sensibility. Early eighteenth-century moral philosophers like George Turnbull claimed to be following Bacon and Newton in using an "experimental" approach that demonstrated that human nature and the political world followed natural laws just as the physical world did, and later moral philosophers such as Adam Smith and David Hume took the project one step farther to establish the natural laws of political economy and the "science of man." These intellectual and curricular trends shaped the discursive domain in which English became constituted as an object of formal study, and according to Sharon Crowley, they have shaped the teaching of English into the present day (see *Methodical Memory*).

The history of college English teaching begins not a century ago, as is often assumed, but two centuries earlier at the end of the seventeenth century, when English was first taught to college-level students. The dissenting tradition in the teaching of English best exemplifies Habermas's view that the eighteenth-century expansion of the reading public transformed the public sphere by creating a domain where the middle classes developed a critical understanding of their shared history and political needs, and the dissenting academies present the clearest case of how the transformation of the public sphere shaped the introduction of the modern culture into higher education. Dissenters assumed a critical stance on political and religious beliefs, but literary criticism was given less emphasis than composition. Dissenters had a productive engagement with the expansion of the public sphere, and they effectively prepared students to speak to political and religious controversies and spread useful knowledge. The comparative method fostered critical attitudes to received traditions and established authorities, while the emphasis on composition also served the commercial interests of the dissenters' middle-class students. With Aikin and Priestley, more attention was given to fiction and poetry, though continuing insensitivities to the aesthetic experience prevented literary discourse from becoming established as an object of study in and of itself. While more research is needed, at Warrington after Priestley and in other academies like Hoxton, Hackney, and Daventry, a more belletristic perspective on English studies seems to have appeared. However, neither rhetoric nor literature were to regain the central place that they had within the classical tradition. The liberal individualism that emerged when the humanities were first translated into the modern cultural idiom had utilitarian, materialistic, and technological tendencies that established science as the modern paradigm for how to put knowledge into action, and these tendencies treated literature as little more than an object of study for a leisure hour.

The tendencies toward belletrism and scientism in the later academies had parallels with the introduction of the modern culture into the Scottish universities, which is not surprising given the close ties between the two educational traditions. However, the dissenting academies had important ideological and institutional differences from the Scottish universities. While dissenters shared Scottish moral philosophers' interest in applying the methods of natural science to the study of human nature and political economy, dissenters such as Priestley and Price opposed Scottish attempts to use the concept of a moral sense or common sense as a hedge against skepticism. Priestley's *Examination* of Reid, Beattie, and Oswald shows that he rejected their attempt to place received beliefs beyond question as innate propensities of human nature, and Watts and Doddridge also criticized related trends in Scottish moral philosophy (Watts, *Works* 5: 550–51; Doddridge, *Works* 4: 438–39). Dissenters were Utilitarians who did not value the civic humanist philosophy that formed the communitarian point of departure for Scottish rhetoricians and moral philosophers' examinations of the diversification of civil society because dissenters had been dislocated from the classical curriculum ever since the imposition of religious tests in the English universities in 1662.

The most important difference between the Scots and dissenters may well be not in what was taught but in how it was taught. Dissenters such as Doddridge and Priestley used a comparative method of instruction to foster free inquiry and critical literacy, while Scottish professors generally dictated their lectures for their students to copy down word for word as the received knowledge of their masters. While Scottish belletrists such as Hugh Blair apparently confined student compositions to imitating the style and rhetorical stance of essays of taste and manners of the *Spectator,* dissenters from Morton to Priestley fostered critical debate in the classroom and taught their students to write and speak to public controversies. However, there were important exceptions to this distinction. Popular Scottish professors such as Hutcheson have been noted for having spoken to their students' experience in a more conversational and less didactic manner, and George Jardine was the most effective teacher of composition that I know of in the eighteenth century (see chapter 9). Such pedagogical practices need much more attention than they have traditionally received from historians of ideas about rhetoric because an idea has a very different status and impact if it is presented as a dictate to be memorized or as a position to be debated against conflicting points of view. Such differences may not be evident in the texts that transmit ideas because the difference often lies not simply in what is written but in how it was read and taught, as is evident in the fact that historians of ideas have tended to depict Priestley and Blair as like-minded rhetoricians even though their rhetorical practices could not have been more opposed.

Priestley and Blair were both rhetoricians, in the practical sense of that term. Priestley was a "controversialist," while Blair was a preacher of polite virtues and a leader of the Moderate Party of clergy who helped integrate the Presbyterian Church into the British patronage system, as discussed in later chapters. When situated in its rhetorical context, Blair's cosmopolitan cultural ideology can be seen to have served the same purposes as the sermons that established his public reputation and the political maneuverings that led to his being rewarded with a lucrative professorship. The same sort of connections can be made between Priestley's utilitarian faith in free inquiry and his practical efforts to reform politics and religion and advance useful knowledge through experimental research. Blair was a cultural liberal and political conservative who taught provincials to assume a cosmopolitan perspective on politics at the same time that he was gaining political power as a leader of the Moderate Party of clergy who organized to defend the influence of patrons in the selection of clergy, while Priestley criticized religious and political authorities and advocated liberal education and political economy because he assumed that free inquiry within the marketplace of ideas would overturn unreasonable authorities, empower knowledgeable individuals, and enable them to contribute to public commerce.

While the dissenting academies institutionalized a more politically engaged approach to the teaching of English, the academies lost their practical engagement with the lower classes as dissenters became more prosperous and secular, and less concerned with ministering to the poor. In reactions to continued governmental restrictions, dissenters increasingly insisted that they were no different from the rest of society and should not be publicly persecuted for their private beliefs. Such arguments secularized dissenters' relations with the rest of society in ways that made income or education rather than religion the distinguishing characteristic of social class (see Lincoln 18). Dissenters continued to spread support for reform among the literate working classes in the ways noted in the conclusion to chapter 1. Dissenters were well represented in such radical groups as the Revolution Society, the Society for Constitutional Information, and other corresponding societies that circulated political tracts through the networks of debating societies and working men's clubs that spread political activism in the last decades of the eighteenth century. Conservatives continued to attack dissenters for teaching and publishing radical ideas, but while dissenters advocated political reforms and personal freedoms, they were not the Levelers that they were often portrayed to be.[11] Even radical spokesmen like Priestley and Price considered the lower classes to be unworthy of equal representation and given to an indolence that would only be encouraged by relief from their grinding poverty.

Historians have noted that the radicalism of Priestley and Price had lost touch with the experience of many dissenters and with the lower classes generally. E. P. Thompson has noted that the rational theology of radical dissenters appealed to shopkeepers and trades workers, but the poor found the message too cold and the style too refined to suit their experience (28–35; see also Lincoln 92). With the marked decline of traditional dissenting groups like the Presbyterians and Independents and the rise of more evangelical sects, the more radical possibilities of the Calvinist tradition became dispersed into a vague distrust of the state and a libertarian belief in the authority of the individual experience. As they began to speak for the virtues of enlightened individualism, dissenting intellectuals lost their organic involvement with ministering to the broader public. While the tradition of dissent contributed to the political activism of the working class, more evangelical sects like the Methodists helped reorient working-class aspirations toward the realm of personal salvation. Radical dissenters like Priestley had broadened traditional dissenting demands for religious tolerance and political access into a call for the rights of man, but in the final analysis, the dissenting academies were part of a reformist tradition that is best characterized by the efforts of Percival to improve public sanitation and adapt elementary education to the factory system of exploiting children. The contribution of the dissenting academy tradition to the foundation of London University in the next century is but one example of how eighteenth-century dissent contributed to the liberal reforms of the nineteenth century.

The King's English and the

Classical Tradition in Ireland

The elocutionist movement, in short, shows in striking ways how the oral management of knowledge, threatened ever since the invention of writing, was by now thoroughly debilitated. . . . By the close of the eighteenth century orality as a way of life was in effect ended, and with it the old-time world of oratory, or, to give oratory its Greek name, rhetoric.

—Ong, Review of Howell, *British Logic and Rhetoric*

To lose your native language, and learn that of an alien, is the worst badge of conquest—it is the chain on the soul. To have lost entirely the national language is death; the fetter has worn through.

—Young Irelander Thomas Davis

IN THE DISSENTING academies English studies served the utilitarian needs of the middle classes, but in Ireland the teaching of English was part of the colonial project of suppressing the indigenous language, culture, and religion. Irish Catholics had paid the price for defending an English king at the Battle of Boyne in 1690. For supporting James II, many of the Catholic gentry who had survived Cromwell's subjugation of Ireland were dispossessed. In 1695 Catholic schools were outlawed, and restrictions were imposed on Catholics' abilities to buy or inherit land, with any son able to convert and claim all of a family's property. With the impoverishment of their traditional patrons, the wandering bards who recited poetry in Gaelic in exchange for room and board began to disappear, and the suppression of the indigenous elite and native schools led to the decline of the national language—Gaelic or Irish. Those who became rich from the dispossession of Catholics sought to redress "the want of protestants" by establishing "English schools" (qtd.

Simms 23). The most noted efforts were made by Erasmus Smith (1611–1691), a London turkey merchant and Cromwellian profiteer who amassed over forty-five thousand acres of expropriated Irish lands by 1684. He began by founding schools on his estates to ensure that his dependents learned the King's English and religion, and he then set up a trust to support such efforts throughout Ireland. In 1724 the trust funded two professorships at Trinity College, one in natural and experimental philosophy and one in oratory and history. A holder of the latter chair, John Lawson, became the first university professor to publish lectures on rhetoric and poetry delivered in English.

Lawson's *Lectures Concerning Oratory* (1758) have been read by W. S. Howell as a contribution to the "new" rhetoric inspired by Locke (Howell 616–31), but most of Lawson's ideas are little more than the commonplaces of the classical tradition. Lawson's classicism becomes more significant when situated within the politics of English studies in Ireland. While Trinity actually offered a more rigorous classical education than the English universities, it was located in the provinces and was thus under pressure to meet Irish gentlemen's need to know the language and literature of England. Such needs found their fullest expression outside the lecture halls in Trinity's student societies. In 1747 Edmund Burke established the Academy of Belles Lettres or simply "The Club," which according to several historians was the first student debating society in Britain (see Post 20; Dagg 9–10; Maxwell 141). The records of Burke's Club and the College Historical Society that followed from it in 1770 document students' attitudes to English in the period when it was first beginning to be formally taught. In the next chapter, I examine similar societies and the compositions that remain from the first English classes in Scotland. Such records document the ways students connected their studies with their lives outside the classroom. Students at Trinity and elsewhere tended to be more interested in public controversies than their professors would have liked. In reaction to the revolutions in America and France, university administrators in both Ireland and Scotland attempted to limit topics debated in student societies, and Trinity's student society was actually forced out of the college for debating political topics and allowing the admission of "public" members (those members who were not students but wished to study elocution). One member of that external Historical Society was Thomas Davis, whose sentiments on the loss of Ireland's national language are quoted above (see 'O Cuív 382).

Davis was part of the nationalist attempt to revive Gaelic in the nineteenth century, but in the eighteenth century the Anglo-Irish generally wanted to lose their native speech as quickly as possible. Provincials' efforts to learn to speak like the English are the point of contact between the expansion of the reading public and the movement to standardize educated taste and usage that led to the introduction of English studies into higher education. One of the most popular teachers of English elocution was Thomas Sheridan, who studied rhetoric with John Lawson. Like other leading elocutionists, Sheridan was a provincial who had had to formalize English so that he could teach it to himself. Ironically, Sheridan set "the living voice" in opposition to the "dead letter," with the former "the gift of God" and the latter merely "the invention of man" (*Course . . . on Elocution* ix). Sheridan claimed to be advancing the effort to "fix" English begun by his godfather, Jonathan Swift. While Sheridan and other elocutionists valorized speech as the natural language of the passions, they programmatically set out to "methodize the whole of the English language" by establishing written rules to govern oral expression (*Plan of Education* xviii). The effort to formalize speech into a rule-governed system was a direct response to the expansion of the British reading public that blurred the boundaries between the literate culture and the common language and created a need for works to teach provincials how to speak like the English. Elocutionists' valorization of the natural eloquence of speech takes on particular poignancy when one considers how systematically English teachers worked to eliminate the idioms and oral traditions of the cultural provinces.

English Politics and English Studies in Ireland

While Scotland was a cultural province of England, Ireland was its first colony. For centuries, Ireland had been ruled by a viceroy and settled by immigrants imported to establish plantations on the land of the natives, who were massacred or forced to migrate west. Cromwell's armies killed the most, contributing to an overall population decline of about 20 percent from 1641 to 1672 (Mitchison 7–8). Even more were dispossessed. According to Lecky, between 70 and 90 percent of Ireland was owned by Catholics before Cromwell, while between 20 and 30 percent were left to them by the time he had finished, with Catholics making up about 80 percent of the population at the time (Lecky 35; McCracken 37). By the end of the eighteenth century, the Catholic majority would end up owning less than ten percent of Ireland (see also Kearney 139 and Simms 12–13). Catholics were forced to lease land at two-thirds of the income it yielded. If a Catholic produced a larger crop, the rent increased proportionately. If leaseholders were discovered hiding increased profits, their Protestant discoverer could claim their lease or property. No pretense was made of offering Catholics equal rights before the law. According to the English rulers of Ireland, "the law does not suppose any such person to exist as an Irish Roman Catholic" (qtd. Somerset Fry 167). Protestants referred to Catholics as the "common enemy" and identified themselves as the "Protestant Nation," though broad restrictions were also imposed on Protestant dissenters, mostly Scots, who roughly equaled the Anglicans and surpassed them in Belfast.

According to Cullen and Smout's *Comparative Aspects of Scottish and Irish Economic and Social History* (1977), Ireland may actually have had a more sophisticated economy than Scotland at the beginning of the eighteenth century, but English hegemony had quite different effects in Scotland and Ireland (see also Devine and Dickson). While Scotland benefitted economically from the Union of Parliaments in 1707, the Union of the British and Irish Parliaments in 1799 was but another step in the subjugation of Ireland. The English Parliament treated Ireland as a colonial dependency whose economic interests were subservient to the needs of English commerce. All imports from the colonies into Ireland had to pass through Britain so that customs and handling fees could be charged. The Irish were forbidden to export their leading product, wool, to any country but England, and prohibitive tariffs were imposed on its import there (see Lecky 57; Simms 14). Except in the Highlands, the Union left the Scottish class system destablized but intact, but Ireland was left completely divided against itself by English colonization. Its indigenous elite was replaced by a new ruling class, including absentee landlords like Erasmus Smith who drained the national wealth and used it to fund efforts to suppress the native religion and culture.

In response to the Union, Scottish schools and universities enlisted in the cause of improvement and fostered assimilation by teaching the language and literature of England, but in Ireland there was a vast gap between the intellectual elite and the disenfranchised and oppressed public, creating considerable popular resistance to the efforts of "improvers." While both Scottish and Irish serfs were forced off the land by efforts to improve agriculture in the latter half of the century, only in Ireland did such efforts lead to violent resistance movements opposed to agricultural improvement. Of course Irish Catholics were one of the most subjugated peoples in Europe. As is well known, potato famines in the nineteenth century cut the population in half as a result of starvation and emigration, but the eighteenth century also saw periods of mass starvation. A series of famines inspired Swift's famous *Modest Proposal* in 1729, but the worst starvation came in 1741—"*bliadhain an áir,* the year of the slaughter"—with the death of between two and four hundred thousand people (McCracken 34).

The differing effects of English hegemony in Scotland and Ireland help to explain why the Scottish universities began studying the modern culture,

while Trinity College brought English into the classroom but did not challenge the religious and educational authorities that demarcated the educated
elite from the native population. While Scottish schools and universities were
comparatively accessible, in 1611 Irish Catholics were denied the right to educate their children, creating the lowest levels of literacy in Britain (see Graff,
Legacies). Native institutions like the bardic schools had sustained the oral
traditions of Irish poetry, and when they were outlawed, richer Catholics
took to educating their children at home and then sending them abroad (il-
legally) to an Irish college in a continental university. Poorer Catholics relied
on "hedge schools," generally pitiful groups who gathered in hutches with few
qualified teachers and even fewer books.[1] From the sixteenth century every
Anglican diocese was supposed to found *"a school for to learn English,"* but
the clergy themselves were to provide much of the funding. Out of thirty-
four dioceses, fewer than twenty had founded schools by 1788, with only thirteen open in 1809 (qtd. Atkinson 18, 29; Auchmuty 59). The schools that were
funded were programmatically anti-Catholic and thus set themselves in direct opposition to the vast majority of the public. Royally funded grammar
schools were even less effective. Most were treated as sinecures, and the rest
tended to cater to upper-class Protestants. In 1733, the Society for Promoting
English Protestant Schools in Ireland was incorporated to teach the language
and religion of England. Funds were mismanaged, and only thirty-three
schools were founded by 1750, as compared to almost eight thousand hedge
schools registered in 1824 when laws against Catholic schools were eased
(McCracken 50; Atkinson 53).

As a result of Anglicizing influences and the lack of educational support,
Gaelic or Irish did not really become a popular print language. As discussed
in the first chapter, cheap books and periodicals expanded the English reading public in the latter half of the eighteenth century. In just this period one
sees the beginnings of the modern decline in Irish. While several important
translations of Gaelic poetry appeared in the last decades of the century, few
books were printed in Irish in the eighteenth century other than a handful of
dictionaries, grammars, and works of a religious nature, with Gaelic poetry
continuing to circulate largely in manuscript copies (see 'O Cuív and Bliss).
English had long been used in some formal written discourse, but through
the sixteenth century, even the "Old English" population often spoke Irish.
According to accepted accounts, about two-thirds of the Irish population
spoke Irish as their first language in 1731. By the end of the century, Irish was
spoken by only half the population and by the middle of the next century by
just one-quarter, including a mere 13.6 percent of those under nine years of
age ('O Cuív 383, 423). Efforts to convert Catholics had sometimes used Irish,

but the official view was that Irish was "destructive of the English interest" (qtd. 'O Cuív 375). Gaelic and Catholicism were the mainstays of the Irish identity, but the Catholic Church used English as its official language, and its schools did not give much emphasis to Irish. As a result, in 1806 of over a million and a half who identified their home language as Irish, only twenty thousand stated that they could read it ('O Cuív 381). The fact that Ireland's native language was largely confined to oral traditions gives considerable irony to the idealization of orality by teachers of English such as the elocutionist Thomas Sheridan.

As in England, dissenters in Ireland were generally from the middle class, and they faced broad restrictions on their access to education and politics, restrictions that the Anglican establishment was able to keep in place in Ireland for a time after they were removed in England. Many studied in dissenting academies, and some went on to the Scottish universities, including one of the founders of the Scottish Enlightenment, Francis Hutcheson, who is discussed in chapter 6 as a principal influence on his student Adam Smith. Hutcheson is the most prominent example of the continuities between the educational traditions of the dissenters and Scots, including Scottish dissenters in Ireland. Hutcheson studied in the dissenting academy of James McAlpine before leaving Ireland in 1710 to complete his education at Glasgow, where he studied natural philosophy and the "new" logic (see Leechman, "Account"; Scott). According to Hutcheson and Smith's successor at Glasgow, Thomas Reid, up to one-third of Glasgow students were from Ireland, "stupid Irish teagues" as Reid described them, who came to "attend classes for two or three years to qualify them for teaching schools" (qtd. Haakonssen, Introduction 27).

Hutcheson himself headed a dissenting academy in Dublin before returning to Glasgow to become professor of moral philosophy in 1730. Attempts were made to prosecute him for running this illegal academy, but Hutcheson had powerful friends, most notably Lord Molesworth, who encouraged reformers in Scotland as well as Ireland to broaden higher education beyond scholasticism and sectarianism to prepare students for civic life (see Moore). Molesworth encouraged Hutcheson to publish his first works, six belletristic essays that appeared between 1725 and 1727 in the *Dublin Weekly Journal,* one of the many provincial imitators of the *Spectator.* Three of the essays were responses to essays in the *Spectator,* and none showed any interest in the political controversies then raging around Swift's *Drapier Letters.*

Educational reformers were more successful in Scotland than in Ireland's Anglican college, which was founded in 1592 with funds from Irish lands held by the English queen. According to its historians, Trinity served to "consolidate in the religious and cultural spheres the fruits of victory in the field" (McDowell and Webb 3). Trinity was founded on the model of Trinity College, Cambridge, but more emphasis was given to requiring that professors actually teach. Upon the Restoration, dissenters were exiled from Trinity, and Catholics were not allowed to take degrees until 1793. Despite such restrictions, the student population was more diverse than that of Oxford and Cambridge. During his visit in the eighteenth century, Arthur Young observed that the college "swarms with lads who ought to be educated to the loom and the counting house" (207–8). Unlike at Oxford and Cambridge, enrollment did not decline in the eighteenth century, and the percentage of poorer students did not decrease dramatically. Student enrollment in fact doubled from between four and five hundred to around nine hundred, with poorer students (pensioners and sizars) making up 90 percent of the population from 1724 to 1733 and 79 percent in the last decade of the century (McCracken 51; Stubbs 316–18; McDowell and Webb 86).

Trinity may well have been "the only successful English institution in Ireland" (Auchmuty 129). Teaching did not decline as much as in the English universities, though from 1722 to 1753 no fellow published anything while holding a fellowship (McDowell and Webb 39). From the middle of the century, the college's fortunes rose along with those of the Protestant Ascendancy. The program of studies was more systematic than in the English universities, with quarterly examinations, regular disputations and declamations, and open competitions for some scholarships and professorships.[2] While Locke, Newton, and some experimental science were studied, the curriculum was a pervasively Aristotelian program of studies in metaphysics, ethics, natural philosophy, and logic, with the latter handled "Syllogistically, not with the Flourishes of Rhetoric" according to the "Statutes and Charter" of 1749 (rpt. Bolton 69–70; see also McDowell and Webb 69–73; Maxwell 148–49). The syllogism remained the paradigm for declamations and disputations well into the next century, when a rearguard defense of Aristotle's logic was launched by the archbishop of St. Patrick's Cathedral, Richard Whately. The parallels with the English universities were recognized by one of Trinity's more prominent alumni, Oliver Goldsmith, whose *Present State of Polite Learning* (1759) contrasted universities like Edinburgh that had broadened the curriculum beyond a moribund scholasticism with more traditional universities like those of England and Ireland. According to Clarke's *Classical Education in Britain*, the classical education offered at Trinity was actually "a good deal more thorough than that provided in any other British university," with Trinity taking a less philological and more "literary point of view" (160, 161; see also Clarke, "Classical" 523).

The classical sensibility and religious politics of Trinity had similarities with the centers of English higher education, but Trinity's students were Irish, not English. If they could afford to, Irish gentlemen preferred to go to Oxford or Cambridge, with many staying on to join the English gentry as absentee landlords. Efforts were made to tax the rents leaving Ireland, and in 1734 pamphleteers called for Trinity to keep the rising generation in Ireland by serving as a "publick Nursery" (*Letter to the Young Gentlemen of the University* 5). Another pamphleteer in 1734 complained that the only alternative was to send one's son to England "at a much greater Expence . . . to engage in foreign Friendships, and grow up in such Pursuits as may tempt him to forget his Native Country" (*Letter to G—— W——* 1). The same year another pamphlet defended the faculty by stressing that they were required to teach much more than professors in England. The author agreed that Trinity should help remedy the "afflicted State of this Country" by educating gentlemen in Ireland and reducing the "Numbers, who spend their Lives and Fortunes out of it" (*Second Letter* 36). As Irish Protestants began to think of Ireland as their nation and not just an English colony, they became even more interested in their national university. In the last quarter of the century during the comparatively independent era of "Grattan's Parliament," Provost Hely-Hutchinson revised the curriculum to attract gentlemen by adding instruction in elocution and modern languages.

Lawson, Leland, and the Professorship of Oratory and History at Trinity

In 1724 a professorship of oratory and history and one of natural and experimental philosophy were funded by the Erasmus Smith Trust, with the professorships filled by competitive examinations (Stubbs 208). Thus, as elsewhere, the transition to the vernacular was paralleled by an increased emphasis on scientific studies. Continued increases in the trust led to additional professorships and fellowships. In 1761 the professorship of oratory and history was divided, with Thomas Leland taking the chair in oratory. Both professorships became sinecures by the end of the century, but in the latter half of the next century, the chair in rhetoric provided the basis for the professorship of English literature, as similar chairs did in Scotland.[3] There are basic consistencies between the classical but not moribund curriculum and the literary emphases of the most important professors of rhetoric, John Lawson from 1750 to 1759 and Thomas Leland from 1761 to 1781. None of Lawson's predecessors in the chair published their lectures, and Leland was his only successor to do so, as *A Dissertation on the Principles of Human Eloquence* (1764). Lawson and Leland were both Anglican clergymen and graduates of Trinity, and both largely confined their courses to religious literature, though Leland published more widely than Lawson, including a translation of Demosthenes's *Orations* (1756) and a history of Ireland (1773).[4] While Lawson's *Lectures Concerning Oratory* appeared in editions in 1758, 1759, and 1760, neither his nor Leland's rhetorical theories were widely influential. Historians have in fact treated their lectures as works of "classical scholarship" because they paid less attention to contemporary rhetorical practices than to classical theories (McDowell and Webb 61; see also Maxwell 120).

In his opening dedication to the governors of the Smith Trust, Lawson defended the ancients against advocates of "A Knowledge of modern Languages and of the World" (*Lectures* iv–v). Lawson's defense of the classics is interesting because the trust had emphasized the study of English from its foundation and may have pressed the professors it paid to teach English. Lawson argued that eloquence is best learned from classical models, with studies of modern languages only compounding the "Vice and Folly" of the "unlettered" mind (v). It is unclear whether Lawson actually assigned English compositions (see Stubbs 207; Keesey 55; and Claussen and Wallace x–xi). Because of rising salaries, Trinity professors were becoming less reliant on student fees, and teaching duties were falling more heavily on junior fellows. In contrast, Scottish professors depended on the fees of their students and were thus rewarded for responding to their changing needs, while professors in England were paid even if they did not teach. According to his own account, Lawson's students learned "Criticism" and composition by reviewing classical treatises, and in more practically oriented weekly meetings, students read aloud from a historian or orator to learn "just, distinct Pronunciation" (*Lectures* xi–xii, 23). Lawson assumed that the classics provided the best models and principles of eloquence, but he also recognized that classical theories had to be applied to "our own Tongue" to speak in the pulpit, "Senate," or bar (21). Lawson discussed pulpit oratory in some detail, and he made some effort to teach English, unlike the other leading neoclassical rhetorician of the time, John Ward.

Lawson's *Lectures* are more literary than Ward's summary of the classical precepts of rhetoric (see Keesey). The second lecture outlines the topics to be covered, including "the Rise and Progress of Eloquence among the Antients," "the most celebrated Treatises . . . from Antiquity," and rhetoric's "History in modern Times." Lawson also discussed "Imitation," appeals to the faculties ("Reason," "Passions," and the "Senses"), "Stile or Elocution, as it comprehendeth Ornament, Composition, Figures," and pulpit oratory. The *Lectures* conclude with a final lecture on composing Latin verses that was apparently added because his comments on "dead languages" had irritated classicists (25; see also 433–37). In deference to his fellow classicists, Lawson concluded that learned topics should be addressed in learned languages, and he closed with a Latin poem to show that he could deliver the sort of commonplace verses that students composed to demonstrate their mastery of ancient languages (442–57).

Lawson's course thus began with classical rhetoric, then turned to a neo-classical concern for imitation and stylistic ornamentation, and concluded with epideictic oratory and literary discourse. Throughout his lectures, Lawson sought to "clear the Road marked out by the Antients, to smooth and open it; perhaps in some Places to strike out new and shorter Paths" (*Lectures* 3). Lawson drew extensively on Aristotle, and he idealized the orator who spoke against the domination of his country by a foreign power, Demosthenes, the "Prince, I had almost said God of Eloquence," whose works were translated and published by Leland (34). Lawson generally adhered to classical conceptions of the arts of rhetoric, but he treated invention as a process of managing rather than discovering ideas. According to Howell, invention declined in importance as more emphasis was given to research on the facts at issue. However, Lawson's deemphasis of invention was classicist rather than empiricist, for he treated invention as the process of rearranging commonplaces, rather than as an art for managing the information discovered by empirical investigations.

On other points as well, most notably the relationship of rhetoric and poetry, Lawson touched on ideas at issue in the "new" rhetoric, while often rejecting the trends that had made the ideas an issue. Lawson discussed such germinal concepts as taste and sentiment, but he rejected the turn toward the "science of human nature" that would define the former according to introspective examinations of the latter. Lawson did not accept the view that taste was a mental faculty, and he was particularly opposed to treating an "inward Sense" or "moral *Taste*" as "the Source of Duty and Obligation" (*Lectures* 19). Hutcheson was the leading advocate of the moral sense doctrines to which Lawson referred. As is suggested by the term "moral *Taste*," Hutcheson conflated ethics and aesthetics as closely related matters of sentiment, a line of reasoning that justified studying polite literature as a means to instill polite proprieties. Lawson justified polite refinement in a more traditional way. In discussing a topic like taste, Lawson tended to ask "in what Sense was this Word used in *Greece* and *Rome*, the two great Fountains of that Elegance, which Moderns express by Taste?" (15). Maintaining an adherence to classicism, though not always to classical sources, Lawson blurred the boundaries between rhetoric and taste. Among classicists, Cicero's original interest in teaching citizens to speak to public issues had long become overshadowed by the Ciceronian emphasis on stylistic ornamentation and epideictic discourse. Like Ciceronians and belletrists such as Blair, Lawson emphasized stylistic criticism more than the composition of discourse, and he stressed the composition of epideictic oratory more than political or forensic rhetoric.

Lawson devoted far more attention to ancient theories than to modern public discourse, but he did discuss pulpit oratory. Lawson's popular sermons presented his students with well-known models of how they were expected to put such theories into practice, much as Blair's, Campbell's, and Priestley's writings served as well-known exemplars for their students. Lawson concluded that the eloquence of modern pulpit oratory was due to British religious freedoms. This conclusion was quite ironic, given the fact that Catholics and dissenters had been excluded from his classes at Trinity, and the majority of the Irish population had been dispossessed for their religious beliefs (*Lectures* 96). He advised his clerical students to maintain sharp distinctions between Catholics and Anglicans but to soothe differences with dissenters (369–70). In practice as in theory, Lawson spoke for the Anglican establishment. Lawson was famous for preaching on behalf of private charities, which were all the more needed because Ireland had no poor law. Charity sermons like "The Inequality of Condition advantageous to Society" (1756) comforted the Anglo-Irish by advising them that "Providence" had created poverty for "the regulation of life, the peace of individuals, and [the] flourishing state of the community" (*Sermons* 83–98).[5] Such sermons provided students with models for how to speak of the Irish public.

Lawson did not teach rhetoric as the art of public discourse but as part of the undifferentiated literary category of *eloquence*. For example, after summarizing the works of Aristotle, Cicero, and other classical rhetoricians in lectures three and four, Lawson slipped in a seventh-century poem that presents a vision of the temples of rhetoric and other polite arts, and then he shifted abruptly to discuss modern literary writers such as Milton. Lawson thus moved from classical rhetoric, through neoclassic panegyrics, to modern literature in a manner that is difficult to follow unless one understands *eloquence* in the neoclassical sense of all learned discourse. In lecture eighteen, Lawson explicated Plato's *Phaedrus* and then suddenly shifted to an epideictic poem dedicated to the Earl of Chesterfield and a long poem, "The Judgment of Plato," that imitates the dialogical form of *Phaedrus* (*Lectures* 337–38; 339–51). The continuity here is provided by the assumption that one reads literature in order to write it. Lectures sixteen and seventeen are cast in the form of a dialogue between two orators on the usefulness of reading poetry to learn how to move the passions, and the lectures conclude with two poems, "Venus and Cupid" and "Emiliar an Historical Poem" (314–24). Citing classical commonplaces about the poet's ability to teach the orator how to appeal to the imagination, Lawson attempted to refute the sort of utilitarian views that limited the study of literature within the dissenting academies (272). Though he conceived of literature in classical terms, almost half of Lawson's references are to English writers (Michael 166). Lawson also briefly noted the development of modern literature from Dante through English writers such as Chaucer, Spenser, and Swift, who is judged to be "nearer to uncorrupt Antiquity and Nature" than even Addison (*Lectures* 79). While a full account of the institutionalization of English studies must include Lawson and other classicists like the poetry professors at Oxford, what is perhaps most significant about Lawson's place in the history of the teaching of rhetoric and literature is how easily he can shift from classical rhetoric to modern literature under a classicist's conception of *eloquence*.

Whenever the educated have had limited access to political expression, the study of rhetoric has tended to shift its focus from political oratory to epideictic discourse and then to the study of literature according to George Kennedy (5). This paradigm neatly fits Lawson, the Scottish belletrists, and the general evolution of English studies if one views the development not as a simple matter of rhetoric's reacting to democracy or autocracy but as itself functioning to promote or limit access to political expression in the public sphere. As noted in previous chapters, classicism had come to concentrate on the antiquarian purpose of maintaining learned languages as the boundaries of the learned culture, with the stylistic elaborations of Ciceronian rhetoric serving to distinguish those who had mastered the niceties of classical literature from those who had merely learned Latin. The stylistic emphases of belletristic rhetoric functioned in similar ways to distinguish between the politely educated and the merely literate as the expansion of the reading public increased access to literacy. Like Blair, Smith, and most other rhetoricians, Lawson assumed that "Liberty" is "the Parent of Eloquence" (*Lectures* 93). Such assumptions required rhetoricians to explain why fabled British liberties had not given rise to a new golden age of rhetoric, for none of the leading rhetorical theorists wanted to venture into the domain of contemporary politics to assess the leading orators of the day. Crossing the boundaries between political and civil society would have undermined their rhetorical stance as disinterested critics. This stance and the valorization of a lost age of classical eloquence functioned in an ideological fashion to limit access to political expression, as discussed in later chapters.

While Scots had given up their own national assembly in the hope of economic advancement, Lawson delivered his lectures in a hall right down the street from the Irish House of Commons. Lawson's students were interested in the political debates of the day even if his literary frame of reference had no room for them. Trinity students had their own special gallery to listen to debates in the Commons until 1795, when the gallery was cleared because the students were hissing speakers for being too servile to English interests. While Lawson viewed oratory and poetry from a classicist perspective, his students were more interested in debating contemporary issues than in studying ancient eloquence as a subject unto itself, as becomes clear when I turn to Trinity's student debating societies in the next section.

Lawson addressed English taste and usage indirectly through the classical precepts that served as points of departure for popular commentators. While he used the term *elocution* for delivery on two occasions in his *Lectures,* Lawson generally followed the usage of classical sources and treated delivery as the art of "pronunciation," with the term *elocution* used to discuss style (419, 425). Lawson's student Thomas Sheridan blurred classical categories by using the term *elocution* to discuss delivery. Despite such differences in terminology, Sheridan accepted the conception of delivery taught by Lawson, who criticized "mechanical" approaches and argued that gestures and intonations express the "Sentiments of our Minds" in a "natural" and "universal" language (Lawson, *Lectures* 423, 415). After leaving Lawson's class, Sheridan became known as a leading advocate of what historians of speech have called the "natural" school of elocution to distinguish it from the even more "mechanical" proscriptions of John Walker.

Lawson's only significant successor maintained his basic orientation, most importantly the assumption that "ELOQUENCE in its antient and most extensive sense" includes "not only prosaic but poetical composition" (Leland, *Dissertation* 34). Leland began each term with public lectures on "the progress of English composition," and then he delivered a series of lectures on religious eloquence that he published as *A Dissertation on the Principles of Human Eloquence* in 1764 (xxxix). Leland's lectures responded to Bishop Warburton's attempt to resolve the historical conflict between the highly figured style of Ciceronianism and the recognition that the most sacred of all texts was marked by an unadorned style. Warburton had ingeniously reasoned that the Bible's artlessness showed that it was an impassioned inspiration that stood aloof from changing tastes. Leland's view that figures are the natural "Language of Passion" followed from Ciceronian doctrines, but it created difficulties in accounting for the simple style of the Bible (252). Drawing on the classical source most commonly cited by belletrists, Longinus, Leland argued that the elevated sentiments of the sublime are not inconsistent with simplicity and that the "judicious critic" will not allow stylistic proprieties to detract from the sublime truths of the Bible (102; see also 63–65). According to Leland, conceptions of style are not an arbitrary matter of changing fashions but are instead based on the universals of human nature. To support his case, Leland surveyed classical theories and used moderns such as Shakespeare and Pope as models of the sublime (124).

Leland did not teach rhetoric as the art of public discourse but instead took a literary approach that was quite similar to Lawson's. Like Lawson, Leland touched on many of the issues that were important in the literary criticism of his time. The first half of the *Dissertation* treats figures and tropes as natural expressions of the passions (rather than as a "vicious . . . deviation from the Principles of Metaphysics and Logic"), and in the latter half of the treatise Leland responded directly to Warburton's tendency to treat the figurative nature of discourse as mere arbitrary embellishment (25). Leland's argument for the sublimity of the Bible defended the literary orientation taken not just by Lawson but the Trinity curriculum generally. While Warburton was his specific opponent, Leland also criticized the "new" and the "old" logics, including both "Locke, that enemy of figurative speech," and the Scholastics, who assumed that figures violated the "the logic of definition and division" (19, 29). In this respect, Leland defended a literary conception of style against more narrow philological and logical points of view, including Scholasticism as well as empiricism. While he sought to establish "general principles of RATIONAL CRITICISM" founded on the universals of human nature, Leland, like Lawson, relied heavily on classical authorities for those universals and criticized works like Kames's *Elements of Criticism* that founded critical precepts on modern theories of human nature (74, 67).

In Ireland as elsewhere, the introduction of the modern culture into higher education was marked by an intensifying awareness of historical change and cultural differences, with Leland himself an important historian of the political development of modern Ireland. While Leland's histories were not as influential as Robertson's or Hume's, his *History of Ireland* (1773) reportedly marks "the transition from chronicle to history" in accounts of Ireland's past (Beckett lxiii). Leland treated the history of Ireland up to the defeat of the Catholic defenders of James II in terms of "the progress of the English power in IRELAND" (*History of Ireland* 1: i). Leland did not apologize for the dispossession of Catholics, and he harshly criticized the dissenters' Puritan predecessors. However, he also criticized English policies that denied political freedoms to loyal Irish citizens (1: 10, 3: 392, 1: 342). On this and other points, Leland's history justified the authority of the Anglo-Irish, who were beginning to think of the "Protestant Nation" in more nationalistic terms.

Such terms had revolutionary potential for a subjugated country like Ireland. The leaders of the United Irishmen rebellion of 1798 first learned the art of political oratory in Trinity's student debating societies, which were much more engaged with public issues than the classes of Lawson and Leland. While they translated classical rhetoric into English, Lawson and Leland limited its application to religious literature and did not reinterpret classical concepts to examine public rhetorical practices to the extent that the dissenters or Scots did, for the Anglo-Irish still had a very limited sense of who the Irish public was.

English Studies in Student Societies

As in Scotland and among the dissenters, more emphasis was given to teaching English at Trinity in the latter half of the eighteenth century (see Post). Leland was defeated for the provostship in 1774 by John Hely-Hutchinson, an inveterate place hunter with limited academic credentials. With less concern for academic tradition than for his own popularity, Hely-Hutchinson revised the curriculum to persuade "young Gentlemen of Fortune to finish their Education at home" (5). A contemporary observer viewed the reforms as an attempt to appeal to "men of rank as well as men of science" and noted that the changes were resisted as "not monastic enough" (Barrington 1: 60 n). To attract gentlemen, Hely-Hutchinson established a riding school and professorships in modern languages, and he also improved the college's scientific equipment. Hely-Hutchinson's "Account" (1775) of his reforms opens by noting that the "first Object . . . was to encourage an Attention to Composition and Elocution" (1). To accomplish this purpose, he began requiring compositions of entering students, and he had the Erasmus Smith Trust fund a theater for orations and prizes for compositions, which the "Professor of Oratory and his Assistants" were supposed to submit (2–3). The emphasis on elocution may have been influenced by Sheridan's attempt to establish an elocutionary academy, which is discussed in the next section (see McDowell and Webb 57). Leland had supported these efforts and administered the short-lived academy founded in 1758. Hely-Hutchinson may also have been acting from his own experience in the Irish House of Commons, where he became one of the first British politicians to advocate the theories of Adam Smith (Lecky 135).

Hely-Hutchinson also supported the recently established Historical Society where students debated the issues that were being decided down the street in "Grattan's Parliament." The Historical Society had several predecessors, including the Historical Club founded in 1753 and the Academy of Belles Lettres founded in 1747 by Edmund Burke. The records of debates, compositions, and orations that remain from these societies offer rare documentary evidence of the other side of the educational dialogue—the responses of students to what they were being taught. These societies concentrated on the same two studies as Lawson's professorship, oratory and history, but student societies were apparently more interested in political debates than in the study of history or rhetoric as an end in itself. The Historical Society had seven hundred members by 1780, with as many as a hundred and fifty meeting to hear orations and debate public issues. The Historical Society was in fact more like a popular debating society than a private literary society. Such distinctions are important because, as I discuss in the next chapter, the Scottish literati's attitudes to rhetoric were shaped by their experience discussing English taste and usage in small literary societies that positioned themselves as impartial spectators of political and religious controversies. While the Irish debating societies gave students experience speaking before large audiences on public issues, literary societies were intended to provide a retreat from divisive controversies where gentlemen could gather to correct each other's English.

Burke's club combined elements of a literary society with rules intended to simulate the atmosphere of a public forum. The Academy of Belles Lettres only had between four and eight members, according to the remaining minute book from the spring of 1747, which is reprinted in Samuels's biography of Burke. Burke and his classmates founded the group to learn "speaking, reading, writing and arguing in morality, History, Criticism, Politics, and all the useful branches of Philosophy" (Samuels 228). Twice a week members gathered to deliver orations, critique compositions, read published speeches, and debate the issues of the day. The minutes suggest that some meetings were much like those of a literary society. At one, for example, an essay was read from the *Spectator,* the journal of the Spectator Club that provided the model for provincial literary societies. Burke then read a composition on painting that may have become the second part of *A Philosophical Enquiry into the Origin of our Ideas of the Sublime and Beautiful* (1757), which he began to write as a student (Samuels 248). However, at other meetings members delivered orations as if they were speaking to Parliament on such issues as the taxation of absentee landlords. After a debate over whether the Irish should resist English trade restrictions by buying only Irish manufactures, a rule was passed forbidding "questions relating to the Government of our country wch may possibly affect our loyalty" (Samuels 237). Literary societies often instituted such proscriptions to avoid issues that threatened the group's detached spectatorial perspective. Despite the rule, the club continued to address public controversies such as whether to show clemency to Jacobite rebels or to repeal the death penalty for stealing sheep, with Burke opposing both proposals, the latter on the grounds of "Natural Law" and his characteristic deference to established traditions (Samuels 244, 289; see also Post 23).

Like its predecessors, the "The College Historical Society for the cultivation of historical knowledge and the practice of the members in oratory and composition" was founded in 1770 to provide opportunities for students to learn public speaking and writing. The first extant speech from the chair on June 19, 1771, recounts how the group was established because students were not satisfied with the limits of the classical curriculum, and subsequent speakers also complained about the lack of attention to composition in the classroom (Historical Society, Journals 1: 102; 3: 101; 3: 544). Meetings began with discussion sessions devoted to historical works, and then members delivered orations and debated issues, political as well as philosophical. In addition to the debates and orations, compositions were read by the chair and left for peer critique in the hall, with the author's name subsequently revealed and award-winning compositions copied into the society's essay book, one of the two largest collections of eighteenth-century student compositions that I have been able to find (with the other at Yale). The essays, orations, and minutes of debates make the Historical Society a rich archive for examining how students put rhetorical theories into practice to address public controversies in ways that their professors were failing to do.

The orations recorded in the minute book regularly stress the practical needs served by the society, but the sense of what studies were needed was changing. The group seems to have become increasingly interested in debating public issues and less concerned with studying history. Speakers complained that members were not attending the portion of meetings dedicated to discussing the works of Hume, Gibbon, Robertson, Leland, and other historians. In 1778 the chair echoed earlier complaints that history was being eclipsed by oratory, which is "not the most important end of our institution" (Historical Society Journals 3: 253; see also 3: 442–50). Increasingly, the minutes failed to include abstracts of the historical works that were supposed to be discussed, and the group apparently became more of a debating society, or as one complainant described it, "a Club of Coffee-house Politicians" (3: 251). The conception of whose history should be studied was also changing. A speaker in 1772 stated that the society had been founded to study modern history, or rather "the History of our own Country (for such I will call England) that we might know the Constitution under which we live, and defend it" (1: 201). In 1782, when Grattan's Parliament was granted a semblance of independence from Britain, the society's rule equating "our" history with the history of England was repealed. As a speaker noted, "at this era of Liberty, when Ireland has extorted her Rights, it is the business and indispensable duty of every Irishman to be acquainted with the Laws and Constitution of his Native Country" (qtd. Dagg 46). As they developed a more nationalistic sense of their past, students became more engaged with the controversies of their own society. Debates were held on such issues as the education and political representation of women, religious tolerance, the right to rebel against the government, the freedom of the press, the problem of absentee landlords, and the union of Ireland and Britain.

When votes were taken on such issues, the majority consistently supported conservative positions, but in the turbulent era at the end of the eighteenth century, even questioning the status quo came to be seen as a dangerous pastime for students. Ireland had gained the right to organize Protestant militias for its own defense when troops were withdrawn to the American colonies and kept abroad to fight France. These Irish Volunteers marched on Dublin to intimidate the establishment into supporting Grattan's effort to secure an independent Irish Parliament in 1782. The United Irishmen movement that began in 1791 threatened not just English hegemony but the Anglican ascendancy itself by supporting "republican" ideas like universal male suffrage. Burke's *Reflections on the Revolution in France* (1790), which went through ten editions in a year, helped to create "a stupendous change in the public mind," reversing the trends that were moving toward easing restrictions on Catholics (Plowden 2: 317). Unionists' worst fears were realized when the United Irishmen rebelled with the support of a French invasion in 1798, though the rebellion failed miserably and over fifty thousand people were massacred (Somerset Fry 206). A series of mishaps had prevented the orchestration of local risings with the arrival of the French forces led by Wolfe Tone, who like Thomas Emmet and several other leaders of the United Irishmen learned how to speak to public issues in the College Historical Society at Trinity. In reaction to the rebellion (and with massive amounts of bribery), the Irish Commons voted itself out of existence and was unified with the British Parliament in 1800.

As in Scotland, college administrators responded to the spread of radical ideas by attempting to limit topics of debate in student societies. The continuities between developments in Scotland and Ireland were quite direct. In 1783 the College Historical Society established a mutual membership agreement with one of the leading Scottish societies, the Speculative Society of Edinburgh, which expelled Thomas Emmet for his republican sympathies while he was studying medicine there (Dagg 50). The tensions at Trinity came to the surface on April 10, 1793. The Historical Society was beginning to debate whether the legislature was too corrupt to reform the Constitution when a representative of the administration rose to object to the discussion of modern politics. The society apologized and agreed to forego such topics, but within the next couple of months, the group debated the impressment of servicemen, the benefits to Scotland of its Union with England, and the merits of universal suffrage, with the majority beginning to take more liberal positions. The administration also objected to the presence of "public" members who were not enrolled in the university. In 1794 an expelled student was included among those members, and the society was consequently exiled from the college.

After acceding to all the administration's demands, including prior approval of topics for debates, another College Historical Society was set up within the year, and students were barred from attending the external Historical Society, which eventually closed.[6] The Historical Society within the College largely devoted itself to classical studies and avoided contemporary controversies, if its minutes are actually an accurate record of its debates. The conservative reaction continued, with a governmental visitation in 1798 expelling nineteen students after uncovering four cells of United Irishmen within the college (Dagg 93–96; Maxwell 147). Problems continued into the next century, with the Historical Society closed briefly in 1806, again forced out of the college in 1815, and not readmitted until 1844. The public Historical Society held in the intervening years contributed to the Young Ireland movement that included Thomas Davis, whose statement on Ireland's national language is quoted in the epigraph at the beginning of this chapter.

The minutiae of students' societies will seem unimportant if we continue to define our past as the history of major theorists working in elite institutions, but students' voices need to be heard if we are to understand the dialectical processes by which educational institutions reproduce educated society and sometimes help transform it. Students created occasions to speak and write about public issues because the curriculum was providing few such opportunities. The Journal of the first external Historical Society, which is collected among the volumes of the College Historical Society, includes several speeches criticizing Trinity for allowing the professorships of oratory and history to become mere sinecures. According to Charles Bushe's speech of July 2, 1794, *"The Belles Lettres never can be studied Academically. . . .* Witness . . . your themes never read by your Examiners, Witness your declamations and your disputations never heard by any body and ridicul'd by every body." More attention needs to be paid to how people actually learned to address public audiences on political issues if rhetoric and composition are to be taught in ways that prepare people to write about issues of popular political significance. Ireland's best-known political rhetoricians—Henry Grattan, Henry Flood, and Edmund Burke—all participated in debating societies dedicated to the study of rhetoric (see Bowers 9, 48–50; Somerset Fry 183).[7] The elocutionary movement is the clearest point of contact between such popular extracurricular activities and the institutionalization of college English studies, and leading elocutionists such as Thomas Sheridan were among the first to call for establishing the teaching of English as "a distinct branch of education" (*Lectures* vi).

English Studies Outside the University: Sheridan and the Elocutionists

Sheridan gained popular notoriety by proclaiming that a national orality crisis had arisen because ministers and politicians had not been taught to speak persuasively for public virtue. Sheridan's works show how advocates of English studies were able to appeal to the sort of popular anxieties about cultural and linguistic change that have recently made works on cultural literacy into popular best-sellers. Such works follow in the tradition of Sheridan's sensationalist *British Education: Or the Source of the Disorders of Great Britain; Being an Essay towards Proving, that the Immorality, Ignorance, and False Taste, which so Generally Prevail are the Natural and Necessary Consequence of the Present Defective System of Education* (1756). Sheridan made a living criticizing public education and teaching the public taste with works such as *Course of Lectures on Elocution* (1762), *Lectures on Reading* (1775), *A Complete Dictionary* (1780), *A Rhetorical Grammar* (1781), and *Elements of English* (1786). Sheridan repeatedly argued that instruction in public speaking was needed to check the spread of "irreligion, immorality, and corruption" (*British Education* 1). If the public failed to fund his proposals, the English empire itself would disintegrate as uncontrolled linguistic changes made its greatest orators and poets unintelligible to succeeding generations. To uphold oratory as the bastion of public virtue, Sheridan drew broadly (though not deeply) on the civic ideals of classical rhetoric.[8] While the ancients provided an authoritative model for an oratorical education, Sheridan used classical rhetoric to argue against classicists' emphasis on "acquiring a smattering in two dead languages" (*Lectures* vi). Sheridan reduced rhetoric to a single art, "pronunciation," and redefined it as elocution to appeal to those who wanted to be taught to speak like the English. Sheridan was perhaps the most popular eighteenth-century advocate of establishing English as a formal discipline, and his writings provide insights into how rhetoric was popularized by the formation of such studies.

Sheridan proposed both to "*revive the long lost art of oratory, and to correct, ascertain, and fix the English* language" (*British Education* v). While Swift had proposed a courtly academy as a means of "Correcting, Improving and Ascertaining" English, the effort to "fix" English had become a broader educational project by Sheridan's time, as I discussed in the first chapter. Sheridan often claimed to be a successor to Swift and Johnson. Swift was in fact his godfather, and Sheridan could recount how he refined his elocution under Swift's Augustan tutelage. Sheridan several times reported that Swift asked him about his studies at Trinity: "when I told him the Course of Reading I was put into, he asked me, Do they teach you English? No. Do they teach you how to speak? No. Then said he they teach you *Nothing*" (*Oration* 19–20). Sheridan proclaimed that he would follow his godfather and "methodize the whole of the English language," beginning with the codification of the laws of pronunciation, "the first and noblest part of grammar" (*Dissertation* 4). When "rhetorical grammar" had been formalized, English could be taught in colleges and schools "upon a practicable plan, and in a systematic way" (*Discourse* 52). Like Swift and the later grammarians, lexicographers, and rhetoricians who standardized the conventions of English, Sheridan associated bad English with "Immorality, Ignorance, and false Taste" in order to justify his claim that elocutionary studies would save not only the English language but the English way of life (*Plan of Education* xviii).

Sheridan began his career as an elocutionist by lecturing those who considered themselves English but spoke like the Irish.[9] After publishing *British Education* in 1756, Sheridan lectured in Dublin on the need for an elocutionary academy. In *An Oration pronounced before a numerous body of the Nobility and Gentry,* on December 6, 1757, Sheridan argued that because of the limited attention to English in Irish schools, the gentry were forced to study in England, where they stayed on to become absentees (6). Such arguments obviously had patriotic appeal, for within a month almost one thousand pounds was raised by "the Hibernian Society for the Improvement of Education," with two hundred subscribers, including forty-eight members of Parliament (see Sheldon 237; Benzie 17; Wallace Bacon 16). The group opened an elocutionary academy in 1759 under the direction of Thomas Leland after a series of pamphlets such as *An Enquiry into the Plan and Pretensions of Mr. Sheridan* (1758) convinced Sheridan to give up his original plan to get parliamentary support for his theater, to which the academy was to be attached. Sheridan quickly moved on to lecture on elocution elsewhere in the British provinces, including three series of lectures at Edinburgh in 1761 that helped build popular support for the sort of studies that Blair was introducing into the university at the time. When located in the context of the cultural provinces, Sheridan's claims that elocution would save English society by teaching the British to speak properly seem a bit less absurd. It is not difficult to understand how such claims appealed to Scots and Irish who wanted to attach broader significance to their personal anxieties and ambitions.

The painful irony of the elocutionary movement is that it appealed most to those whose language it set out to eradicate. One of Sheridan's first works was a farce, *The Brave Irishman* (1754), that pandered to the popular taste for stage Irishmen speaking a comical dialect. His elocutionary writings appealed to audiences who were afraid that they too might be laughed at for their own "provincial or vicious pronunciation" (*Course . . . on Elocution* 47). To those not "born and bred" in polite society, Sheridan offered a pronouncing dictionary and manuals on how to speak like the English as well as self-improvement lectures promising to help anyone eradicate the "corrupt" dialect that "custom has established in the place of his birth or education" (*Dissertation* 11). Sheridan claimed that standardizing English throughout the "British dominions" would establish "an entire union" upon "the universality of one common language" (*British Education* 357, 160). Ironically, the leading elocutionists were themselves outsiders who had consciously studied and formalized the idioms of the dominant culture: Sheridan and Gilbert Austin were both Irish, while James Burgh was a dissenter born in Scotland, and John Walker was an uneducated actor who began playing the role of elocutionist in 1768, a decade after Sheridan had made the same change in stage roles. Elocutionists were resented by some for blurring class distinctions, with one "gentleman" suggesting that such "*ornamental*" learning was better left to "*Persons of high Rank and exalted Station*" to avoid making people of "middling" status feel "superior to all Kinds of Industry" (*Letter to a School Master* 12–13).

While some resented their efforts to teach outsiders to speak as ladies and gentlemen, elocutionists appealed to broader audiences by criticizing the educational emphasis on learned languages that had excluded them from the educated culture. According to Sheridan, the fault lay with an education dedicated not just to dead languages but to the "dead letter" of bookish learning. In reaction to the valorization of enlightened reason, Sheridan identified writing as the language of ideas and criticized Locke for failing to recognize that "the passions and the fancy have a language of their own" (*Elocution* viii). This "language of nature, the living speech" was "the gift of God," and it expressed feelings through universally understood gestures and tones, unlike the written word, an artificial "invention of man" that could not readily express sublime sentiments or natural passions (*Elocution* xii, xi; see also 111–56). This natural language of tones and gestures would enable people to say what they felt and be understood with sympathy. Sheridan set the unmediated nature of oral discourse in opposition to the refinements of the literate culture at the same time that he was teaching provincials how to refine their speech to express the appropriate feelings through the correct natural gesture. Such oppositions appealed to provincials who wanted to learn how to speak naturally without feeling anxieties about their accents so that they could speak and feel like a person of literate refinement. To achieve such refinement, provincials alienated themselves from the language and experience of their own society, leaving them able to speak like the English but unable to speak with their own people without grimacing in distaste at their corrupt language and barbarous manners.

The opposition of primitivism and propriety is central to the centrifugal and centripetal forces that shaped the formation of college English as it worked to eradicate provincial traditions and instill a cosmopolitan sensibility. Like elocutionists, belletristic rhetoricians such as Hugh Blair had the sort of hypersensitivity to stylistic proprieties that is common among those at the boundaries of the social class that is distinguished by those proprieties. Blair was also the leading defender of the primitive genius of Ossian, the ancient Highland bard whom Macpherson fabricated from fragments of Gaelic, or rather Irish poetry. Like most of the literati of the Scottish Lowlands, Blair did not know Gaelic or its history. Gaelic-speaking scholars in Ireland were best prepared to document the Irish sources of Macpherson's "epic" tales of ancient warriors battling to defend their homes against foreign invaders, but Irish scholars were initially less concerned with proving that Ossian was actually Ireland's Oisin than with refuting Macpherson's account of ancient Gaelic culture. As O'Halloran has discussed, Irish scholars were representing the ancient Gaelic world as a highly literate and sophisticated culture, a chivalric image that directly contradicted the romantic theories of primitive genius that Scottish belletrists were using to reconceptualize their past in terms that made sense to the dominant culture. Irish scholars initially focused on Macpherson's historical commentary and dismissed the tales themselves as mere "Romances, and vulgar Stories." Only when Ossian was embraced by the popular imagination did scholars in Ireland and Scotland begin to take an interest in their own "receding indigenous culture" (O'Halloran 77, 83).

As popularizers, elocutionists present some of the most obvious examples of the romantic nostalgia and stifling proprieties that shaped the formation of college English. While elocutionists helped make speech a discipline, they did not really teach speaking so much as reading aloud. Elocutionists taught the art of oral interpretation—the delivery of a reading of a text—and not extemporaneous speaking or oral composition. While Sheridan distinguished oral and written language as "two different kinds of language, which have no sort of affinity between them," elocutionists worked methodically to fill in the gaps left in texts by the absence of written marks to indicate intonations, tones, and accents (*Elocution* 22). Sheridan often used "public reading, or speaking," as synonymous terms, but when public speaking is defined as "reading aloud," writing becomes primary, and speech becomes a matter of the "proper delivery" of a reading (*Elocution* 17, 30; *Lectures on Reading* x). Completely inverting the basic claim that speech is the primary "archetype" of discourse, elocutionists scripted oral performances to reduce speech to a set of written rules (*Dissertation* 4). Sheridan and the elocutionists formalized the public reading of written texts by providing rules for pauses, intonations, and gestures, but they generally ignored the art of speaking in the extemporaneous fashion that is characteristic of unscripted speech.

Sheridan was right to claim to be a successor to Swift and Johnson, for he carried the project of standardizing English into the domain of oral discourse to inscribe rules for "speech." To advance this project, Sheridan felt that "the art of speaking, like that of writing, must be reduced to a system; it must have sure and sufficient rules...; [and] it must have masters to teach it, and to enforce the rules by examples" (*Discourse* 36). Speech did not really become a distinct academic discipline until it moved out of English departments in America over a century later, but the elocutionists were the first to establish speech as a recognized profession, or at least a trade, with its own texts, schools, and theories of discourse. John Walker and the "mechanical" school of elocutionists were more important in disciplining speech than Sheridan because they established elaborate rules and notational systems for inscribing the laws of oral discourse, while Sheridan's "natural" approach to elocution did not formalize the rules of speech fully enough to institutionalize an academic discipline. Walker's *Elements of Elocution* (1781) devoted seventy pages to sixteen rules for pauses and more than a hundred pages to rules for inflections, and in *Chironomia: or a Treatise on Rhetorical Delivery* (1806) Sheridan's countryman Gilbert Austin reduced the human body itself to a formal sign system with an extensive collection of pictures on how to position the parts of the body to convey the correct natural sentiment. Like Walker and his successors, Sheridan wrote a "Rhetorical Grammar" to formalize the rules of public speaking in the image of the laws of written syntax, and Sheridan also called for the creation of a new discipline of professional elocutionists.[10]

At the same time that traveling bards and bardic schools were disappearing from Ireland, staged readings were being popularized by the print economy. It is no accident that the two leading elocutionists of the time (Sheridan and Walker) began their speaking careers as actors and then gained national reputations by appealing to the reading public's anxieties about variations in English pronunciation. Sheridan's idea that a theater should provide the basis for a school becomes more understandable when one considers the traditional emphasis on oral recitations in education. However, despite its continuities with the performatory nature of oral traditions, the theater is one of the clearest examples of what Ong has termed "secondary orality"—orality that depends on writing for its very existence and that is understood in terms of the literate experience. Even by Sheridan's time the theater had come to rely on the print economy to build audiences and make play writing profitable, as I discussed in the first chapter. Sheridan kept up his public reputation as other elocutionists began to crowd the stage by holding "Attic Evenings" that included not just orations on elocution but poetry readings and scenes from plays that appealed to a taste for oratory and drama rooted in oral traditions (see Benzie 55–78). Such staged readings are a clear example of the sort of secondary orality that gained nostalgic appeal as the culture of literacy colonized the oral experiences and traditions of the provinces. As part of this project, elocutionists formalized speech into a written system of rules, treating public speaking as reading aloud and inscribing the rules of oral discourse in "rhetorical grammars" for the reading public.

Conclusion: English Studies as Contact Zones

The politics of college English studies are most obvious in Ireland because of the stark realities of the English presence there. For centuries English schools had been used to eliminate the native religion, culture, and language. Ireland's Anglican college aided with this project by providing the Anglo-Irish with opportunities to learn how to speak like the English and master the culture that distinguished them from the Irish public. Similar political dynamics are examined in the next chapter on English studies in Scotland and in the conclusion when we turn to the professorships of English literature established in colleges for women and the working classes in the nineteenth century. Some of the writers who would be canonized as part of "English" literature were Irish, and their dialectical awareness of the limitations and possibilities of the language became part of the discipline.[11] While Ireland was a colony and Scotland a province, a century before the Union of Scottish and English Parliaments intensified pressures for linguistic and cultural unity, King James founded schools in the Highlands to eradicate Catholicism and the "Irishe language" (qtd. *Account of Society in Scotland for Propagating Christian Knowledge* 2–3). A Scottish king sitting on the English throne working to eradicate the language of his native land is a striking example of the complex politics that have shaped the teaching of English. From its formation in the British cultural provinces, college English has been what Mary Louise Pratt has called a "contact zone," a domain where the educated culture has interacted with the traditions and experiences that students from diverse backgrounds bring into the classroom. According to Pratt, such contacts are dialectical because the dominant culture is also changed by its experience of the other, which provides a point of opposition that can create an awareness of the diversity of cultural conventions.

Provincials were the first to introduce modern history, literature, politics, and ethics into higher education because provincials had had to formalize prevailing conventions to teach themselves a culture that was not their own. Those who live comfortably within the dominant culture tend to have a univocal sense of their cultural identity. The English generally define themselves as English first and last, with British assumed to be but a more general synonym, but provincials have a dual identity as Scots or Irish and Britons. English was first studied by those who had to teach themselves the dominant culture, a culture that was not theirs by birth because they were born dissenters, Scots, or Irish. Provincials founded college English studies because they lived in "contact zones" as outsiders who had to teach themselves the proprieties of English taste and usage. They formalized the conventions of English into a rigid set of rules, occasionally colored by a romantic nostalgia for their own receding traditions and pervasively concerned with the modern problem of atomized individualism because of their own alienation from their traditional society. While they were among the first university professors to lecture on rhetoric and poetry in English, Irish professors made only limited contributions to the departure from classicism because they were too alienated from the Irish public experience and too attached to the political and educational status quo to institutionalize a dialectical sense of the dominant culture. However, in their own debating societies Irish students taught themselves how to speak to public issues and debate political and cultural conventions. Outside the universities, Sheridan and the elocutionary movement spoke to provincials' anxieties and their nostalgia for oral traditions in a manner that has parallels with the belletristic rhetoricians who institutionalized college English studies in Scotland. The elocutionary movement is but the most graphic example of how the culture of literacy colonized the oral traditions that were eliminated by expansion of the English reading public.

As I discuss in the next chapters, the expansion of the reading public and the introduction of the public idiom into higher education completely transformed rhetoric because it was the art of discourse traditionally concerned with addressing the public. Shifts in the public sphere have shaped the historical evolution of rhetoric. According to Kennedy, whenever the educated have lost access to public forums, rhetoric has tended to become reoriented from political to epideictic discourse and the study of literature. This view of the development of rhetoric needs to be complicated by an awareness of how rhetoric itself functions to promote or limit access to public discourse. Rhetoric served the needs of the educated as an openly political art when the political world was only accessible to educated male property holders. As educated people lost opportunities to exercise power publicly as citizens, they often continued to do so as priests, educators, or "men of letters." The literary refinements of Ciceronian rhetoric served to maintain the authority of "men of letters" by limiting the learned culture to those who had mastered the stylistic proprieties of ancient languages. In this way, rhetoric has concentrated on those modes of discourse that upheld the authority of the learned culture, at some times in a broader public sphere and at others within a more narrowly demarcated republic of letters. Some elements of the "new" rhetoric were defined by the expansion of democratic political activism in the eighteenth century, particularly the emphasis on critical literacy among the dissenters. Other elements of the "new" rhetoric served to maintain the borders of the learned culture, with Scottish rhetoricians among the leading contributors to the effort to remap the boundaries of polite taste and usage in a time of change. The Irish experience most graphically delineates who was left outside those boundaries because the teaching of English in Ireland was a clear part of the colonial effort to eradicate the indigenous language, culture, and religion.

English Studies Enter the

University Curriculum in Scotland

Education may well be . . . the instrument whereby every individual, in a society like our own, can gain access to any kind of discourse. But we all know that in its distribution, in what it permits and prevents, it follows the well-trodden battle lines of social conflict. Every educational system is a political means of maintaining or modifying the appropriation of discourse, with the knowledge and powers it carries with it.

—Foucault, *Archeology*

WHILE THE DISSENTERS were the first to teach English to college students, the Scots were the first to introduce formal studies of English literature, composition, and rhetoric into the university curriculum. The first university professors to teach English were often rhetoricians, and the translation of rhetoric into English transformed its traditional relations with the ethical and political concerns of moral philosophy. At the same time that rhetoricians began to teach English, moral philosophers started to lecture on modern economics, social relations, and cultural mores. The introduction of the modern culture marks the juncture where moral philosophy began to evolve toward the social sciences and rhetoric became subordinated to belletristic criticism, with both transitions turning on the formation of what Hume called "the science of man" (*Treatise* 43). Histories of the discipline have begun to recognize that English literature was first institutionalized in Scotland, but these histories have not examined how English studies became reduced to literary studies as rhetoric became positioned at the borders of the field and moral philosophy moved beyond them.[1] Those borders were first marked out by the belletristic and scientist trends that are examined in later chapters. In this chapter I situate those trends in their social and institutional contexts. The educational emphasis on personal sentiments and laissez-faire political economy paralleled the "battle lines of social conflict" within related public institutions, most importantly the Scottish Church. Perhaps the clearest parallel is that while Hugh Blair and his colleagues were professing an aversion to factional rhetoric in the classroom, they were establishing themselves as the dominant faction in the Presbyterian Church.

When the formation of college English is situated in the political context of Scotland's union with England, one can begin to understand why rhetoric did not assume the central role in the modern humanities that it had in the classical tradition, despite the fact that rhetoricians were instrumental in translating the humanities into English. Professors of rhetoric and belles lettres such as Hugh Blair relied on their rhetorical skills to gain control of the most broadly influential and publicly accessible institution in their society, the Scottish Church, and many of their students hoped to use such skills to advance in similar ways. Such aspirations were not unreasonable because the church and universities were both relatively broadly based. The Presbyterian Church had a comparatively democratic structure, especially when compared to the Church of England. Access from below was increased by Calvinists' support for public education. Because of its democratic structure, the church was an important site for conflicts between popular traditions and the assimilation of Scottish class interests into the British patronage system. In the 1750s the Moderate Party led by Hugh Blair and William Robertson gained control of the General Assembly of the church by helping to suppress popular resistance to patrons' selection of clergymen. For their efforts, the Moderates were rewarded with some of the most lucrative academic and clerical appointments in Scotland, including Blair's appointment in 1762 as Regius Professor of Rhetoric and Belles Lettres, the first university professorship dedicated to the teaching of English. Blair and his colleagues used such positions to preach and teach moderate enlightenment as a means to counteract the self-interest and divisive factions fostered by the rhetoric of party politics.[2]

The introduction of English into the universities was actively supported by the literary societies where academics gathered with others interested in improvement. Scots created such societies to study English for the same reason that the English studied Latin and the Latins studied Greek: it was the language with prestige and power. Scots interested in polite self-improvement established clubs to read the *Spectator* and imitate its taste and style, in the process internalizing the perspective of the spectator who stands aloof from local controversies and traditional factions. This cosmopolitan sensibility was written into the history of college English studies through the works of Smith, Blair, Campbell, and other Scottish men of letters who defined eloquence and taste in terms that were consistent with their experiences in literary societies. Portions of Campbell's *Philosophy of Rhetoric* were first delivered before such a society, and the public lectures that led to Smith's and Blair's academic appointments may have been sponsored by an Edinburgh society. These societies were instrumental in defining English studies in belletristic and scientistic terms. In literary societies, as in the first classes on English, cultural provincials internalized a cosmopolitan sensibility that may have enabled them to advance in British society but certainly dislocated them from the idioms and traditions of their own society. This process would be repeated throughout the provinces and colonies as English became a world language and English professors took up the task of teaching students how to write from a disinterested perspective for educated audiences and read the classics of "English" literature as the most valued part of their cultural heritage.

After examining the politics of the Moderates and the cosmopolitanism of provincial literary societies, I review the institutional changes that shaped the introduction of the modern culture into higher education. Scottish reformers repudiated antiquarian classicism and broadened the curriculum to study economic modernization, scientific innovation, literary refinement, and cultural assimilation. The most systematic program of reforms came at Marischal College, Aberdeen. There the curriculum was reorganized to move inductively from inquiries into the sciences to examine the logic of natural reason and conclude with "moral science." The professors who lectured on English included moral philosophers, such as Smith, Reid, and Beattie, as well as rhetoricians such as Blair and Campbell who were influenced by them. At Marischal and elsewhere, the transition from ancients to moderns turned on moral philosophy because the studies of "pneumatology" or "pneumatics" was where the "science of man" entered the curriculum. As English became both an object of study and the means of instruction, ancient languages declined to become an introductory course, with traditionalists complaining that students no longer had basic proficiencies in Latin. To a traditional academic, the failure to maintain learned languages would have represented a literacy crisis that ensued because provincial institutions were failing to maintain standards of academic discourse and instill a respect for the classical authorities that defined the learned culture.

Such "literacy crises" mark historical disruptions in the transmission of the educated culture. Such disruptions occur when support for education is inadequate to meet the demands placed on it, as often occurs when the educated culture is expanding to include groups who were not raised within it. The modern literacy crisis that resulted in the delatinization of higher education began with the eighteenth-century expansion of the educated public that was discussed in the first chapter. The introduction of the language of public life into higher education is a formative example of how the humanities were transformed to meet the need for public education in a commercial society. As higher education expanded to include students who traditionally had limited access to the learned culture, and still had limited access to political power, more attention was paid to instilling a common culture, and less emphasis was given to practical political arts such as rhetoric. The clearest example of how the humanities became reoriented to the modern mission of public education is the subordination of rhetoric to belletristic criticism concerned with instilling a taste for the proprieties of civil society. As a rhetorician, I assume that a good way to assess such changes is to situate them in the institutional and social contexts that shaped their guiding assumptions about how one gains the authority to write or speak, whom one is to address, what one can presume to know, and what purposes can be served by communicating it. It is by teaching students how to answer such rhetorical questions that education functions as "a political means of maintaining or modifying the appropriation of discourse."

The Moderate Enlightenment in "North Britain"

Because of its Calvinist heritage, Scotland was actually more broadly literate than the country whose language it studiously imitated. The accessibility of the church and university from below was due in part to the Scots' traditional commitment to public education. Knox had worked to create a literate laity and learned clergy by founding schools and colleges. Even before the Union, such efforts served to unify the country and "civilize" the Highland clans. When the Scottish Privy Council in 1616 called for establishing schools in every parish, it did so to spread "true religion" and the "the vulgar Ingleshe toung" in place of the "Irishe language, which is one of the chieff and principall causes of the continuance of barbaritie, incivilitie."[3] English had obviously not yet been standardized, but literacy was rising from just over 30 percent in the last quarter of the seventeenth century to around 75 percent in 1750 and then to almost 90 percent by the end of the century, levels of literacy that were attained in this period only by areas such as New England and Sweden that were staunchly Calvinist and intensely committed to literate piety (Graff, *Legacies* 169; see also Altick 9–10; Smout 470–71).

While conservatives in England blamed popular literacy for the public unrest of the Puritan era, Scots did not generally accept the view that social stability depended on keeping the poor ignorant. Pamphleteers argued that popular education taught the children of farmers and tradespeople to think for themselves, promote knowledge, and advance through the universities: "Why should not such a youth by the aid of learning, step out of his original rank to enjoy his peculiar happiness to display the faculties of his nature, and to be useful to his country?" (Christison 7–8).[4] Scots may have founded the first circulating library in Britain, and they published some of the cheap reprint series that made polite literature a popular commodity in the last decades of the century. By then, more books were being printed in Edinburgh than in all other British cities combined, London excepted (Ferguson, *Scotland* 219).

With the Union, the center of Scottish politics moved to London, and traditional class relations were complicated by the influence of English interests. Although it had almost one-quarter of England's population, Scotland was given but sixteen seats in the House of Lords (with a total membership of two hundred and six) and six representatives in the Commons (with sixty-eight members). These "representatives" of over a million Scots were elected by several thousand voters, with a single lord often controlling a hundred of those. As Adam Smith noted in the lectures he delivered as professor of moral philosophy, "it is in Britain alone that any consent of the people is required, and God knows it is but a very figurative metaphoricall consent which is given here. And in Scotland still more than in England, as but few have a vote for a member of Parliament who give this metaphoricall consent" (*Lectures on Jurisprudence* 323). The only way Scottish members of Parliament could have much influence in the well-managed party system was to vote in a block, and they were notorious for doing so. Reflecting back on a long career in Parliament, one Scottish MP concluded, "I have heard many arguments which convinced my judgment, but never one which influenced my vote," a comment that highlights the political reality underlying George Campbell's distinction between being convinced and being persuaded to act (qtd. Johnston 215). Managers persuaded representatives to maintain party discipline by promising patronage positions, and the patronage system fostered assimilation by ensuring that the middle classes shared the benefits of Scotland's client status (see Shaw). The most accessible path to preferment was the church, because political and military offices were the domain of the upper classes, and legal studies required higher fees. Most importantly, the educational system was not too enmeshed in classicism or too stratified to prevent those with ability from advancing to positions in the church. Because of their accessibility, the church and universities were important to the ambitions of men of middling fortune, and to the efforts of the upper classes to use the most ambitious to serve the dominant interest.

The committee that oversaw the negotiations for the Union was co-chaired by William Carstares and William Wishart, who were and would be principals of Edinburgh University and moderators of the General Assembly of the Presbyterian Church. Carstares and Wishart helped keep the clergy and other traditional intellectuals from opposing the Union, which many saw as a direct threat to their own authority. Under the terms of the Union, Scotland was to retain its independent religious and educational institutions. However, the Presbyterian Church was divided against itself by British political patronage, which exacerbated traditionalists' resistance to change, and the Scottish universities lost their independence with the centralization of British education in the nineteenth century. The eighteenth-century reforms that made the Scottish universities among the most progressive in Europe were instituted by the generation who founded the Moderate Party in the church. Under the leadership of William Robertson and Hugh Blair, the Moderates integrated the Scottish Church into the British patronage system by suppressing popular resistance to the authority of patrons to select clergy. According to Roger Emerson, "there can be no clearer indication of the conservative and aristocratic temper of the moderates than this willingness to put down the one democratic tendency in their society" ("Social Composition" 30).

Popular opinion and the ability to speak for or against it were important because of the comparatively democratic structure of the Scottish Church. Unlike the top-down organization of the Church of England, the Presbyterian Church had a system of representation that began with male property owners, included regional presbyteries, and culminated in the General Assembly, which debated and voted upon policies and doctrines. Despite the fact that it excluded Catholics, Anglicans, Jews, and atheists, the Scottish Church may have been the most broadly representative institution in eighteenth-century Britain (see Sher, "Moderates"). The democratic structure of the church made it an important forum for the sort of public oratory that can give rise to popular opposition movements, but the Moderates contained such developments by resisting traditionalists in the Popular or Orthodox party, who unlike the Moderates tended to sympathize with the revolutions in America and France. John Witherspoon was a leading opponent of the Moderates until he emigrated in 1768 to become president of Princeton, where he introduced Scottish rhetoric and moral philosophy to students such as James Madison (see Miller, Introduction). On the other hand, the Moderates included cosmopolitan intellectuals among their members (Blair, Robertson, Reid, John Home, Ferguson, Gerard, and Campbell) and associates (Hume, Smith, Henry Home, and Lord Kames). While often denigrated as merely the "mouthpiece of the lairds," the Moderates helped to transform a sectarian country into a British province committed to economic progress and polite improvement (Smout 330).[5] The introduction of English into the universities was part of this transformation.

The Moderates' rise to power documents the rhetorical practices that underlay the theories of such rhetoricians as Hugh Blair, who helped organize the group. According to Sher's analysis, Moderates were never a majority of the clergy, so they had to maneuver to ensure that they were disproportionately represented, and they had to persuade nonaligned clergy and the increasing numbers of lay representatives (*Church* 121–25; see also Clark). The Moderates first organized to defend the authority of upper-class patrons. A compromise had been worked out between the authority of patrons and congregations in 1690, but in violation of the Union, the Tory administration of Queen Anne had reinstituted patronage in 1712. According to Dugald Stewart, Robertson's biographer and contemporary, patronage was "so extremely unpopular" until after 1730 that patrons were hesitant to assert their authority ("Robertson" 1: xxxix). In 1751, a presbytery twice refused to accept a clergyman who was so unpopular that only about five out of a thousand heads of households voted for him (see Sher, *Church;* also Morren 1: 197–99). The minister was installed anyhow, but Robertson and Blair wanted to make an example of the presbytery. After their proposal was soundly defeated by a vote of two hundred to eleven, Robertson and his colleagues published a pamphlet arguing that the decisions of central authorities "must necessarily be absolute and final" or "anarchy and confusion" will follow (Robertson et al. 1: 231). This political rhetoric was powerfully persuasive in a country that had been divided by two armed rebellions. The assembly reversed itself and censured the presbytery. Though Stewart was a leading proponent of the "commonsense" school of moral philosophy, he showed little respect for the public's good sense in this conflict over democratic rights. He approvingly noted that Robertson did not believe "that the people are competent judges" and concluded that Robertson taught them a "useful lesson of that subordination which the peace of society requires" (Stewart, "Robertson" 1: lxv). Until his retirement from the assembly in 1780, Robertson taught his opponents many such lessons in political subordination. Sher has concluded that the Moderates were able to control the assembly well into the next century precisely because they propagated a well-defined ideology that depicted themselves as the party of order and enlightenment (*Church* 89), a conclusion that is quite ironic given their belief that factional ideologies were the greatest threat to disinterested enlightenment.

William Robertson was a major figure in the institutional politics that underlay the cosmopolitan perspective of the literati. In addition to being principal of Edinburgh University and moderator of the General Assembly,

Robertson gained an international reputation as a historian of British politics. According to Stewart, Robertson's "studies were all directed to the great scenes of political exertion; and it was only because he wanted an opportunity to sustain a part in them himself, that he submitted to be an Historian of the actions of others" ("Robertson" 1: xxix). Like the rest of the literati, Robertson did not have access to the forums at the center of British politics, and he regularly expressed his disdain for politics, often in letters currying favors from political managers. To maintain his pretense of impartiality, he relied upon lieutenants to smear opponents, promise preferments, and do the other dirty work of party politics (see Sher, "Moderates"). Robertson was such an effective political manager that during his long tenure as principal of Edinburgh University the faculty senate simply acceded to his decisions and did not vote on a single resolution. Robertson was clearly a very influential politician in the only forums open to him, but his influence as a rhetorician depended on his ability to claim to be a disinterested spokesman for the common good while he worked to suppress democratic resistance to upper-class authorities.

At the same time that they were establishing themselves as the party of Moderate enlightenment in the church and universities, Robertson, Blair, and their colleagues were publishing works that spread more cosmopolitan tastes among the Scottish reading public.[6] While Scotland was more literate than England, the same sectarian traditions that broadened literacy also narrowed its scope of reference. A refined alternative to Scotland's sectarian past was provided by English essayists. The *Tatler* and *Spectator* were imitated and reprinted almost as soon as they appeared, including the *North Tatler* (1710) and the *Tatler of the North* (1711), with the first Edinburgh edition of the *Tatler* in January of 1711, just eleven days after it had ceased publication in London (see Couper 1: 141, 254–56). Scotland's most popular magazine, *The Scots Magazine,* often reprinted essays from English periodicals like the *Rambler* along with Scottish imitations, fostering not just English tastes but a general taste for consumption. Only ten to twenty advertisements were included in each of Edinburgh's two small newspapers in 1763, but the six newspapers existing in 1792 had grown considerably in size and contained from sixty to one hundred advertisements, a growth in advertising that was also evident in other Scottish cities (Couper 1: 154–56). Such trends exercised a strong cosmopolitan influence. For example, when John Home's tragedy *Douglas* was performed in Edinburgh in 1756, he and other Moderates were attacked in pamphlets and speeches in the general assembly for violating Calvinist restrictions on public entertainments. Just twenty years later, assembly meetings were routinely scheduled so that members did not have to miss the theater while in Edinburgh (Sher, *Church* 86).

The Cosmopolitan Perspective of Literary Societies

According to a contemporary observer, after the Union a "taste for polite literature" spread as young lawyers and preachers gathered in literary societies to imitate the taste and style of the *Spectator* (Tytler, *Memoirs* 1: 164). In an effort to remain aloof from the traditional oppositions that erupted in two armed rebellions, these societies often proscribed discussions of politics and religion (see Fyfe 164–65; McElroy). One early society, the Easie Club, was founded by Allan Ramsay in open imitation of the Spectator Club in 1712. An unpublished letter sent that year by a member of the Easie Club to the *Spectator* requested it to publish rules for "civil" societies proscribing heated debates in order to preserve a sense of polite decorum (Buchanon). According to the letter, the Easie Club devoted its meetings to criticizing the style of the *Spectator* in the fashion that Blair's *Lectures* would institutionalize as part of college English studies. According to another account, the club forbade political debates to keep discussions "free of party" and enable members to "live easie and grow Rich in Wit and humour by a free Commerce of minds" (qtd. Rogers, *Social Life* 363). As Ramsay wrote in a poem on his group, "All faction in the Church or State, With greater wisdom still you hate And leave learn'd fools these to Debate" (*Works* 3: 149). By following the example of the Spectator Club and divorcing themselves from the political domain of civic life, such "civil" societies provided an opportunity for educated Scots to step back from the conflicts of their own society, imitate the style and stance of the *Spectator,* and thus internalize a cosmopolitan sensibility.

Such societies ranged in emphasis and membership from small groups of intellectuals interested in enlightenment to more diverse groups with broader social commitments. Perhaps the best known example of the latter was the Select Society, which existed from 1754 to 1764. Many members were classmates or relatives, and most were well connected to the patronage system, including such powerful political managers as Henry Dundas and such literati as Hume, Smith, Robertson, Blair, Boswell, Henry Home, and Ferguson. According to Roger Emerson, the group was "the most important circle of intellectuals in Scotland," and it served to sanction "the norms to which enlightened Scots should conform" ("Social Composition" 291). "The intention of these gentlemen," as pronounced in an article in *Scots Magazine*, "was, by practice to improve themselves in reasoning and eloquence, and by freedom of debate, to discover the most effectual methods of promoting the good of the country" ([1755] 17: 126–27). To ensure that the "freedom of debate" was kept within proper limits, rules were instituted to "prevent improper questions from being handled." According to the "Rules and Orders" of the society, members were forbidden to discuss topics that related to "Revealed Religion, or which may give occasion to vent any Principles of Jacobitism" ("Rules and Minutes" 2). From the list of questions debated by the society, one can see that social problems were discussed, but less often than moralistic questions, with more questions being asked about belles lettres than specific political issues.[7] The only political controversy that the society became practically involved with was the question of whether Scotland should be allowed a militia, which was favored to promote civic virtue in an age of commerce. The English still had too many fears of armed Scots, and the government's rejection of the proposal only redoubled Scots' desire to have a militia. The Select Society established the Poker Club in 1762 to stir up public interest, but according to its "Minutes," the group did little or nothing and soon became inactive.[8]

The Select Society was active in promoting the teaching of English just as such studies were being introduced into the University of Edinburgh. The group sponsored public lectures by Thomas Sheridan on English elocution in 1761, the year before Blair formally became Regius Professor of Rhetoric and Belles Lettres with the support of members of the society. As in Ireland and elsewhere in the provinces, the popular desire to learn to speak like the English is the point of contact between the expansion of the British reading public and the institutionalization of college English studies. Literary societies are where that contact was made. According to an article in *Scots Magazine* in 1761, Sheridan's lectures concentrated on "those points with regard to which Scotsmen are most ignorant, and the dialect of this country most imperfect" (23: 389–90). The two four-week series of lectures were extremely popular, with over three hundred people attending and a two-week course added for women. As a result of the lectures, an observer dryly noted that "a rage for the study of elocution became universal, as if it were the master-excellence in every profession" (Sommerville 56). Sheridan proposed establishing a society to promote "the study of the English toungue, in a regular and proper manner" (*Scots* 390), and *The Scots Magazine* published the "Regulations of the Select Society for promoting the Reading and Speaking of the English Language in Scotland" (23: 440–41). A board of directors headed by Blair, Robertson, Ferguson, and Henry Home made plans to establish schools to teach English, but the Select Society was already in decline, with several unsuccessful attempts to revive it over the next three years ("Rules and Minutes" 161). Nonetheless, members of the society were instrumental in institutionalizing college English studies.

Literary societies were politically important because they provided traditional intellectuals with opportunities to collaborate with country gentry, political managers, and enterprising individuals from business and manufacturing who shared their interest in "improvement." Such groups were often interconnected to create networks that fostered a shared commitment to cosmopolitan tastes among those with ambitions, and those with the power needed to fulfill them. For example, twenty Select Society members were included among the fifty-eight members of the Philosophical Society, which had itself evolved out of the Medical Society established in 1731 and was later absorbed into the Scottish Royal Society that Robertson helped establish in 1782. Like other societies committed to Moderate enlightenment, the Philosophical Society forbade "Religious or Political disputes" to avoid "any Warmth that may be offensive or improper for Philosophical Enquiries" (Tytler, "History of the Society" 25). The group gained an international reputation with the publication of its transactions in 1754 as *Essays and Observations, Physical and Literary*. The preface, reprinted in *Scots Magazine*, laid out an agenda centered on scientific studies that excluded "theology, morals, and politics" because of "the great delicacy of the subject, the imperfections of human understanding, [and] the various attachments and inclinations of mankind" ([1754] 16: 185). The group confined itself to "*natural philosophy* and *literature*" in the assumption that both could be improved by disinterested observation, while politics could not yet be reduced to a science. Such assumptions shaped the introduction of the modern culture into higher education, for neither the "new" rhetoric nor the science of political economy gave much attention to politics in either the classical or practical sense of that term.

As discussed in subsequent chapters, Scottish moral philosophy was being redefined by attempts to apply the empirical method to the study of social relations and human nature. This project was centered at Aberdeen, and it is clearly evident in the group that shaped the most influential theories of rhetoric and moral philosophy to emerge there, the Aberdeen Philosophical Society. In the characteristic manner of a "private literary society," Campbell, Reid, Beattie, Gerard, and other members read and criticized drafts of compositions and read works of taste, most notably those of David Hume (Campbell, *Philosophy* lxv).[9] With its original statement of purpose, the group dedicated itself to the inductive study "either of the human Mind or of the material World" (*Minutes of the Aberdeen Philosophical Society* 78). From 1758 to 1773, the group helped develop the "experimental" school of moral philosophy and rhetoric that included Reid's commonsense philosophy and Campbell's *Philosophy of Rhetoric*, which drew on Reid's response to Hume to found a theory of rhetoric upon the "science of human nature" (*Philosophy* lxvii). As Campbell, Beattie, and Reid would do in their published works, the group discussed moral issues in terms of the laws of human nature, often invoking the faculty of common sense against Hume's skepticism. Campbell developed his interest in rhetoric in the group, composing essays on such topics as "The Nature of Eloquence[,] its various Species & and their Respective Ends" and others on "verbal criticism" (*Minutes of the Aberdeen Philosophical Society* 82). These compositions and the perspective of the group would shape Campbell's *Philosophy of Rhetoric,* for as its title suggests, Campbell's influential text treats rhetoric as a subject of philosophy rather than as a political art.

Literary societies devoted much of their time to mastering English, which Scots often viewed as "a foreign tongue" (Carlyle 543). Educated Scots such as James Beattie were driven by fears of uttering Scotticisms—the idioms that distinguished their speech from English. Like other literati, Beattie painstakingly imitated the proprieties of Addison and other English essayists. In a letter in 1778, Beattie aptly expressed the anxieties that shaped how college English was first taught:

> We who live in Scotland are obliged to study English from books, like a dead language. . . . We are slaves to the language we write, and are continually afraid of committing gross blunders; and when an easy, familiar, idiomatical phrase occurs, dare not adopt it, if we recollect no authority for fear of Scotticisms. In a word, *we* handle English, as a person who cannot fence handles a sword; continually afraid of hurting ourselves with it, or letting it fall, or making some awkward motion that shall betray our ignorance. (rpt. Forbes, *Life and Writings of Beattie* 2: 163–64)

Such defensiveness shaped the assumptions about language and culture that defined the formation of college English. In some respects Beattie was Scotland's Johnson. Like Johnson, he compiled an influential dictionary founded on the idea that "our tongue was brought to perfection in the days of Addison and Swift," with such adulterations as "provincial idioms" only tending "to its debasement" (Beattie, *Scotticisms* 5). The difference is that Johnson collected terms approved by literate usage, while Beattie's dictionary, *Scotticisms* (1787), systematically compiled all the common words that readers were forbidden to use.

The literati's attempt to proscribe popular Scottish idioms is the clearest example of how their efforts to imitate the cosmopolitanism of the British reading public dislocated them from the traditions of their own society. The literati's cosmopolitan sensibility defined how English was studied in literary societies and how it was taught in classrooms. Literary societies provided supportive audiences that encouraged Smith, Campbell, and Blair to situate themselves within what Hume called "the conversible World," a civil society where one could discuss all "topics of Conversation fit for the Entertainment of rational Creatures" removed from the political controversies of civic life (*Essays* 534). Such societies were committed to advancing the enlightened ideas of Bacon. According to *The Transactions of the Scottish Royal Society,* "it was the idea of this great philosopher, that the learned world should be united, as it were in one immense republic, which though consisting of many detached states, should hold a strict union and preserve a mutuall intelligence with each other" (Tytler, "History of the Society" 11). The ideal of an international "union" in "one immense republic" appealed to provincial intellectuals. Civil societies provided networks of collaborators who shared the goal of stepping back from traditional political divisions and establishing relations with a broader middle-class reading public committed to self-improvement and economic progress. These cosmopolitan ideals helped create a central place for belletristic criticism and the science of political economy but left rhetoric in a separate political domain removed from provincials' efforts to advance within civil society.

The cosmopolitan perspective of the literati is evident in one of the better-known efforts to imitate English journals of taste, the first *Edinburgh Review* of 1755. Blair, Robertson, Smith, and other Moderate literati intended it as a biannual review of books published in Scotland, but only two issues appeared, at least partially because the journal was popularly identified with the elitist politics of the Moderates. The preface to the first issue set out the position the journal would assume by noting that after a sectarian history marked by the "violence of parties," the Union with England presented new opportunities: "the communication of trade has awakened industry; the equal administration of laws produced good manners; and the watchful care of the government, seconded by the public spirit of some individuals, has excited, promoted and encouraged, a disposition to every species of improvement" (*Edinburgh Review* ii). According to the literati's understanding of their historical situation, the principal impediment to improving Scottish society was "the difficulty of a proper expression in a country where there is either no standard of language, or at least one very remote" (iii).

To provide such a standard, Smith and other commentators in the *Review* took a sharply proscriptive stance. For example, Smith criticized Johnson's *Dictionary* for failing to censure all words "not of approved use" and rewrote several definitions to make them "sufficiently grammatical" (*Edinburgh Review* 62). Though Johnson's *Dictionary* was too permissive and unmethodical, Scots were advised to study it because they had no "standard of correct language in conversation" (73). In a long letter that concluded the second and last issue, Smith advised his readers to look beyond Scotland, which was just beginning to join "the learned world" and "produces as yet so few works of reputation" (*Edinburgh Review* 79). When speaking of "this country," Smith quickly began referring to it as "England," noting that "since the union, we are apt to regard ourselves in some measure as the countrymen" of Bacon, Boyle, and Newton (81).[10] By assuming a cosmopolitan perspective, the Scottish literati could identify themselves as men of English letters in an "immense republic" that included "the conversible world" but such identifications tended to dislocate the literati from a more organic relationship to the traditions and politics of their own country (see Daiches).

The *Edinburgh Review* did not fail because the public lacked a taste for improvement. The success of journals like *The Scots Magazine* shows that there was a broad audience for periodicals that combined essays of taste and manners with the news of the day. By reprinting selections from works on moral philosophy and belles lettres, such periodicals spread polite tastes among the Scottish reading public at the same time that Moderate sermons were also promoting the virtues of enlightenment (see Dwyer). As elsewhere in the British reading public, such public discourse provided the middle classes with a depoliticized image of their social relations and aspirations. At a time when Scotland was being transformed into a modern society, the literati helped to represent that transformation in cosmopolitan terms that defined self-refinement as social improvement. Essays of taste and manners promoted the virtues of moderation and sensibility, and the literati helped popularize such virtues in order to gain the cultural authority to suppress popular religious enthusiasms and political factions and thus position themselves as spokesmen for modernization, self-improvement, and orderly subservience. Access to such positions was available through education. Because they were accessible to broader classes of students and more responsive to those students' needs than the centers of English education, the Scottish universities are important sites for assessing how rhetoric, moral philosophy, and the humanities generally adapted themselves to the mission of public education, in the modern sense of that term if not the sense perpetuated by English "public" schools.

The Introduction of English— ## A Literacy Crisis in the Learned Culture?

Viewed from the educational centers of the classical tradition, the introduction of the vulgar tongue marked the beginning of the delatinization of higher education that ensued when standards declined as inadequately prepared students were admitted to universities. The perpetuation of classicism depended on the mastery of a narrow canon of classical texts from which one was to deduce all that was worth knowing, with students required to memorize and reproduce received knowledge in commonplace verses and syllogistic disputations that demonstrated that one had mastered the logical and rhetorical forms of the learned culture. From the antiquarian perspective of classicists, the only reason to speak English in a university would be if students had not been taught in grammar schools to understand appropriate academic discourse. The standard of classical languages was in fact declining in Scotland at this time, but the departure from classicism was viewed quite differently by the professors who began lecturing in English on modern cultural and social affairs. The language of public life was introduced into the universities by professors of rhetoric and moral philosophy who challenged not just the confines of the curriculum but its basic assumptions about how knowledge is generated and communicated. Those who introduced the "new" rhetoric and logic into higher education assumed that the best method for advancing knowledge was to reason inductively from the individual experience or phenomenon to the laws that governed the natural order. Such assumptions prompted a complete reformation of the curriculum.

At the end of the seventeenth century in Scotland as in England, antiquarianism enshrouded the curriculum, though the Scottish curriculum was less highly refined because few students had been inculcated into the learned culture in a private grammar school. The first year was spent translating canonical texts—the New Testament, Homer, or a few Greek rhetoricians such as Isocrates. The second year might include the study of Ramus but was largely taken up with mastering the forms of Aristotelian logic, and the last two years were also devoted to Aristotle (largely his ethics and physics) as well as some geometry and perhaps astronomy. As in England, students were initiated into the learned culture by a single tutor or "regent" who taught ancient languages, classical authorities, and syllogistic forms of reasoning that moved from indisputable premises to immutable conclusions. From the 1690s the Scottish universities began to respond to "experimental" trends in natural and moral philosophy, and by 1710 the teaching of natural philosophy had become "fundamentally Newtonian" (Wood, *Aberdeen* 7; see also Emerson, "Science and Moral Philosophy"; Shepherd). The Union of Parliaments in 1707 and the Jacobite rebellions of 1715 and 1745 broadened the challenge to traditional assumptions and created a demand for studies that could be used to improve Scotland's place in Britain—studies of scientific innovations, political economy, and English tastes that could be used to modernize the primitive agricultural culture of the Highlands, expand Glasgow's role as a center of world trade, and enable Scots to speak as British gentlemen.

Scottish higher education was responsive to broader social changes because it was not limited to a narrow social class. Scottish students tended to be younger, less classically educated, and poorer than English university students.[11] For example, Witherspoon entered Edinburgh University at thirteen, Reid at twelve, and Hume and Robertson at eleven. While there were a few private grammar schools, Scottish education was less stratified than the "public" schools of England. Blair and other students from middle-class backgrounds attended "high schools" that emphasized classical languages, while those from more rural areas such as Alexander Carlyle and Adam Ferguson began their education in parish schools that taught reading, writing, and arithmetic along with the rudiments of classical languages for scholars who planned on attending college.[12] Parish schools brought students from a range of social classes together in the same classroom, particularly in the many isolated communities where the children of the local laird might study beside those of his dependents. Poorer students often attended college with financial aid from the parish or its patron. Some were admitted with a letter from their pastors certifying their inability to pay fees, which were about one-third of those at Oxford and Cambridge, and many students received financial aid from university-controlled scholarships.[13] Poorer students were encouraged to go on to college by the Calvinist emphasis on literate devotion and by the accessibility of the Scottish church from below.

The Scottish universities had specific institutional features that made them responsive to students from diverse backgrounds. Entrance exams were not established until the end of the nineteenth century, when the Scottish universities were pressured to conform to the centers of British education. Unlike at Oxford and Cambridge, students were not continually reminded of their social class by their academic vestments and their places at dinner and in academic processions. Also, while England's two universities were located outside its major population centers, four Scottish cities and towns had colleges, with two offering a choice of more than one. Because they lacked the rich endowments of the English universities, the Scottish universities had to compete for students to survive, and such competition fostered innovation (see Wood, *Aberdeen* 61–62). Scottish higher education was also more broadly accessible because it did not have the religious tests that limited the English universities to those who swore to uphold the state religion. Many dissenters thus came north to study. Since most were middle class and had studied in a dissenting academy rather than a classical grammar school, they often supported utilitarian reforms. Students could support reform in a very tangible way because they paid fees directly to the professors whose classes they chose. According to such professors as Adam Smith and Thomas Reid, this system of payment created a competitive marketplace that rewarded professors for being active researchers and effective teachers (*Wealth of Nations* 2: 758–60; Reid, *Works* 734).

If such a system of rewarding teachers of high demand courses had continued to exist, introductory courses such as composition might not have ended up becoming the province of the lowest paid and least experienced teachers, and senior faculty would not be concentrating their efforts on specialized seminars. Of course higher education is not now and was not then a free marketplace of ideas. Scottish universities were gaining freedom from ecclesiastical authorities, who intervened less and less often to maintain orthodoxy from the middle of the eighteenth century. However, political patronage was increasing dramatically. In 1690, only four of forty-nine professorships were royally sponsored, but in 1800, twenty-four of seventy-two professors owed their positions directly to the English king. Even those who were not appointed to a royally financed chair like Hugh Blair's Regius Professorship of Rhetoric and Belles Lettres often received their jobs through party patronage. According to Emerson, "academic staffs changed in outlook about as rapidly as did the elites which gave them office but not at a much faster rate" ("Scottish Universities" 457). That rate of change was accelerated by the Union and intensified still further after the defeat of the rebellions of 1715 and 1745.

The reformation of the curriculum followed closely upon the Union of Parliaments in 1707. Principal Carstares of Edinburgh University was the most influential Scottish educator of the time because of his close ties to King William. Like many of his colleagues, Carstares had contacts with dissenters in England and had studied in the Calvinist universities of Holland, which were already teaching modern history and the vernacular. Carstares introduced a series of reforms that would be adopted elsewhere.[14] Regents had traditionally taught all the subjects in the curriculum, but Carstares established professorships in "Logic and Metaphisick," "Ethics and Natural Philosophy," and "Pnewmaticks and Morall Philosophy." Moral philosophy was meant to be the capstone of the curriculum, but the course was free of student fees and overlapped with the one in ethics and natural philosophy (see Grant). The moral philosophy course did not become as significant as those at Glasgow and Aberdeen until Ferguson took the chair in 1764 with the provision that he could charge student fees (see Sher, "Professors of Virtue"). As the study of contemporary ethics and politics gained importance, classical languages began to lose their interdisciplinary presence. Greek would be taught by a single faculty member, rather than being a pervasive part of the whole philosophy course and integrally involved with the study of syllogistic reasoning. Latin also became the province of a single professor of "Humanity" and largely became confined to the first year (see Grant 263–64). These changes mark the beginning of the modern decline of the classics in public education (see Withrington 173–74).

English was introduced into the university between the two Jacobite rebellions when reforms began to yield results after a period of political turmoil and economic stagnation. The defeat of the rebellion of 1715 led to a purging of faculty with allegiances to the old order, particularly at Aberdeen, where virtually all the professors were deposed for Jacobite sentiments in 1717. The rising generation of faculty accepted the Union and sought to improve Scotland's place in it. Most notable was Francis Hutcheson, professor of moral philosophy at Glasgow from 1729 to 1746. Hutcheson has traditionally been viewed as a primary source of the whole Scottish Enlightenment (see Scott). More important here, he was one of the first university professors to teach in English, though Glasgow divinity professors had "dropped into English" at times (H. M. B. Reid, *Divinity* 198). Moral philosophers were often among the first to lecture in English, including John Pringle at Edinburgh from 1734 to 1745 and Thomas Reid's teacher, George Turnbull, at Marischal College from 1721 to 1727. The moral philosophers who began lecturing in English on contemporary political and ethical issues were rejecting classicism, not classical humanism. Hutcheson, Turnbull, and Pringle drew on the civic ideals of Ciceronian humanism, but they recognized that the language of public life was now English and not Latin. The students of Hutcheson and the other moral philosophers of his generation would reorient the humanities to suit the needs of a "commercial society," devaluing divisive civic eloquence in order to maintain the decorum of civil society and avoid disturbing the natural laws of political economy. The transition from civic humanism to civility was consistent with the cosmopolitanism of the literary societies where Scots gathered to imitate the style and sensibility of the *Spectator,* and with the idealization of the "impartial spectator" by Hutcheson's student Adam Smith.

The introduction of the vernacular is one of the most important and least examined developments in the history of higher education. The adoption of English is the pivot point for the transition away from classicism. For the first time in over a millennium, the language of public life was being used and studied in college classrooms. The introduction of English did not end antiquarianism, but the arcane studies and ritualistic disputations that had maintained the boundaries of the learned culture must have come to seem quite confining, if not downright ridiculous, when students began discussing contemporary issues and no longer had to concentrate their attention on learning a technical jargon in a dead language. According to one professor, when English began to be used, "the eyes of men were opened to the unsuitable

nature of the subjects which they treated," and they called for "radical reform" in "public education" (Jardine, *Outlines* 25). Just as it is not surprising
that English was first used by professors of moral philosophy who wanted to
speak to contemporary social and cultural issues, it is no accident that when
English became the language of instruction, professors across the curriculum
began to challenge the authority of the ancients.

The interdisciplinary trends that shaped the transition from the ancients
to the moderns are evident in the description of the Edinburgh curriculum
published in *Scots Magazine* in 1741 by Robert Henderson, a librarian at the
university. As elsewhere, a deepening awareness of cultural differences was
leading to a more self-reflexive approach to the study of history. The professor of history was looking beyond the classical world to examine modern history and the art of composing histories. The practice of lecturing in Latin was
defensively justified as a means to make the language "familiar" to students
(Henderson 373). Trends in natural religion and natural philosophy were
converging to redefine moral philosophy. Pringle's course is described as beginning with a "physical enquiry" into sensory phenomena and concluding
with the study of "Natural Theology; or the existence and attributes of God
demonstrated from the light of nature" (373). Strikingly absent is any reference to Aristotle, who was traditionally the foundation for ethics in particular
and the curriculum in general. Generations of regents had taught Aristotle's
physics along with his metaphysics, but ancient authorities were giving way
to an experimental approach to natural philosophy, with a "set of Experiments" used to teach sciences like optics and hydrostatics that could be examined experimentally. An experimental course was being taught by the
famous Newtonian mathematician Colin Maclaurin, who conducted experiments for a public audience of women as well as for his students (Henderson
372; Maclaurin v). The emphasis on experimental science was establishing
Edinburgh's international preeminence in medicine, with professorships in
anatomy, botany, chemistry, and the theory and practice of "Physick." While
medicine remained an extracurricular study in England, the Scottish universities helped professionalize medicine by institutionalizing it as an area of
academic research and formally certifying its practitioners.

Programmatic educational reforms were also being instituted elsewhere,
most notably at Marischal College, Aberdeen, where the whole curriculum
was reorganized according to the inductive logic of the sciences. Sources of
these reforms can be found in the works of George Turnbull, professor of
moral philosophy at Marischal from 1721 to 1727, who is discussed further
in chapter 7, and Turnbull's successor David Fordyce links the reforms at
Marischal with the innovations in the dissenting academies that Fordyce had

himself experienced as a student of Philip Doddridge. The proposals of Turnbull and Fordyce were implemented by Fordyce's student and successor Alexander Gerard. Gerard published the reforms at Marischal in *Scots Magazine* in 1752 (14: 606) and then in *A Plan of Education in the Marischal College* (1755). According to Wood's history of the curriculum, the most striking innovation is "the increasingly dominant role played by the natural sciences in the arts curriculum" (Wood, *Aberdeen* 163). Gerard worked from the assumption that "the only basis of Philosophy is now acknowledged to be an accurate and extensive history of nature, exhibiting an exact view of the various phenomena for which Philosophy is to account" (Gerard 3–4). Marischal's competitor, King's College, soon publicly committed itself to advancing science. In *An Abstract of Some Statutes and Orders of King's College in Old Aberdeen* (1754), Turnbull's student Thomas Reid repudiated "the logic and Metaphysic of the Schoolmen" and professed the college's emphasis on "Natural and Experimental Philosophy."

With the institutionalization of Lockean assumptions about the primacy of inductive reasoning, higher education was reoriented away from transmitting static bodies of knowledge toward advancing "useful knowledge." While educators had long assumed that deductions from classical authorities were the natural way of reasoning, Gerard and his contemporaries believed that the only reliable method of advancing knowledge was by reasoning inductively from the phenomena studied in the particular area of inquiry. According to Gerard, individuals can reason logically from experience without formal instruction, and in fact, it is only by "observing the natural reasonings of mankind, that just *rules* of reasoning can be discovered" (17). Gerard maintained that the study of philosophy "must be entirely founded" on history, especially natural history, "the immediate foundation of almost all the arts of life, agriculture, gardening, manufactures, medicines, & c." (29, 31). After studying natural and civil history, students turned to "*Natural* and *Experimental* Philosophy," "criticism and the *Belles Lettres*," mathematics, and related subjects, with the final year dedicated to pneumatology, natural religion, natural law, and moral philosophy (28–32). With these changes, classical languages were largely confined to the first year, and the curriculum moved away from classicism toward a program of studies concerned with historical change and inductive reasonings from experience, the same program of studies that was being instituted in the dissenting academies at the time.

The "science of man" became a unifying emphasis of the whole curriculum as it was redefined by the logic of the individual experience. In the revised curriculum, the study of "the constitution of man" connected research on the individual arts and sciences with the concluding studies of ethics and politics: "moral Philosophy is founded as well as Logic on Pneumatics, and must therefore come after it. The constitution of man, and his several active powers must be explained, before his business, his duty, and his happiness can be discovered" (Gerard 23). The study of psychology under the traditional rubric of "pneumatics" or "pneumatology" preserved the continuity between natural religion and natural philosophy by using the experimental method to demonstrate the providential order of human nature. Aberdeen moral philosophers were leading advocates of this project, but pneumatics or pneumatology played the same pivotal role elsewhere in Scotland and in the dissenting academies as the area of moral philosophy that developed from "the science of man," to "the science of human nature," and then to the "science of mind" or "psychology." Pneumatics was where the epistemological trends in logic, rhetoric, and moral philosophy first converged on the modern project of disciplining the individual consciousness according to the logic of enlightened reason. This project served cosmopolitan purposes and identifies the reforms at Aberdeen with the efforts of the Edinburgh literati to promote self-improvement as a means to social advancement through cultural assimilation.[15]

While reformers saw the movement beyond the ancients as essential to advancing modern higher education, traditional intellectuals saw such reforms as a decline and not an advance. The introduction of remedial Latin classes at Glasgow and Edinburgh early in the century suggests that a mastery of learned languages could no longer be assumed as a prerequisite. The faculty of King's College were complaining in 1763 that the basics of Latin had to be taught "in the way of a common Grammar School" (qtd. Wood, *Aberdeen* 58). Prevailing instructional practices suggest that learned languages were declining: the increasing reliance on basic translation exercises, the need to conclude Latin lectures with English summaries, and the frequent reiteration of official requirements that students were supposed to speak Latin. Standards had dropped so low by the end of the century that the descriptions of university curricula in Sinclair's *Statistical Account* readily note that Greek was taught at a rudimentary level and that additional professors of "humanity" were needed to teach the basics of Latin. Teachers of Greek were reportedly forced to popularize their courses to attract fee-paying students. According to Clarke's *Classical Education in Britain,* the professor of Greek at Glasgow from 1774 to 1821 tried to interest students by declaiming on "the liberty, the literature and the glory of ancient Greece, while tears of enthusiasm rolled down his cheek" (144). According to such accounts, professors had to resort to popular declamations to motivate students who needed remedial work to appreciate learned languages.

As I discuss in more detail in the concluding chapter, the institutionalization of the "new" rhetoric in the eighteenth century has basic parallels with the reintroduction of rhetoric into American English departments two centuries later, when open admissions led to the introduction of "basic" writing courses for those who were deemed to be too ill-prepared to study the classics of English literature. In both cases, more broadly based colleges introduced courses that elite institutions considered to be beneath them, and this so-called decline in standards occurred at the same time that previously excluded groups were gaining access to education. Such "literacy crises" mark junctures where the educated culture is having difficulty reproducing itself because it is expanding to include broader classes of students, new forms of knowledge, or cultural traditions that it has not yet assimilated. As they are assimilated, the educated culture becomes more attentive to the diversity of experience, the history of social relations, and the relations of the personal and political. More attention is also paid to how people read, write, and think because the processes no longer seem natural when they have to be taught to those who have not learned them as part of their natural upbringing. From one perspective, the need for such "remedial" instruction marks an era of decline, but from another, it marks a historical opportunity for cultural transformation because education is straining to maintain the hegemony of the dominant culture and the processes involved have been called into question and can be subjected to productive critical analysis.

Whether one defines it as a decline or an opportunity to reform the learned culture, the introduction of the public idiom into higher education transformed its relations with the public. As broader classes of students gained access to the educated culture, intense scrutiny was devoted to how individuals internalize cultural conventions, and efforts were made to formalize such conventions so that the less educated could be taught to respect them. The expansion of the reading public and the standardization of English were discussed in chapter 1 in terms of the centrifugal and centripetal forces in discourse that surface most clearly at the boundaries of the educated culture. These trends had their greatest impact on higher education in those institutions that were most broadly accessible to the public—the Scottish universities and English dissenting academies. The standardization of English within provincial universities themselves is clearly documented in the Minutes of the Edinburgh Faculty Senate (see Morgan and Hannay 212–39). In the seventeenth century, most of the motions were in Latin, but some were also in Scots, with numerous spellings, terms, and phrasings that are unfamiliar to standard English speakers. From 1700 to 1740, Latin became less common, and the vernacular moved steadily toward standardized English, with variations from accepted usage virtually nonexistent after the 1750s —the period when English was beginning to be formally taught in the classroom. At Edinburgh as elsewhere, English was first taught by professors who had had to begin by teaching it to themselves.

English Studies Enter the University Curriculum

The first university professor to lecture on English literature, composition, and rhetoric was apparently John Stevenson, professor of logic and metaphysics at the University of Edinburgh from 1730 to 1777 (see Miller, Introduction). Crawford has called Stevenson "the herald of the new subject" of English literary studies, while Court has deemphasized Stevenson's significance in order to claim Smith as the first professor of English literature (Crawford 27; Court 18). Only fragmentary accounts of Stevenson's course of instruction remain. His "Lectures on Logic" show the influence of Bacon and Locke, though at least one of his students felt that he was overly attentive to syllogistic reasoning (see Sommerville). According to another student, one of the three hours of his course was devoted to Heineccius's *Logic* and a compendium of Locke's *Essay,* and a second hour was spent studying classical philosophy. In the third he lectured on Aristotle's *Poetics,* Longinus's *On the Sublime,* and "a judicious selection from the French and English critics" (Carlyle 47–48). Other accounts of the course also cite the works of Dryden, Addison, Cicero, and Quintilian. Students such as William Robertson, Hugh Blair, and John Witherspoon praised Stevenson for having had the most formative impact on their education. Stevenson's influence on Blair and Witherspoon is especially significant because they became the most influential teachers of English in Britain and America in the eighteenth century.

Stevenson apparently took a belletristic approach that was consistent with the paradigm that Blair institutionalized. From the outset, the paradigm of rhetoric and belles lettres emphasized polite taste and deemphasized rhetoric's traditional concern for civic discourse. Stevenson's belletristic perspective can be surmised from the collection of thirty-seven student essays that remain from his classes. This rare collection documents students' contributions to the classroom conversations that preceded the published works of Blair and the other "new" rhetoricians. Several of these essays adopt the style and sentiments of the essay of taste and manners that was popularized by the *Spectator* and taught by Blair and other early professors of English. For example, David Clerk's essay "Taste" (1740) argues that taste is a natural faculty founded on "plain common Sense" that is in "Sympathy" with the natural order ("Book of Essays" 123). Even before the lectures of Blair and Smith, students such as Clerk had learned that taste is "not confined" to matters of literature or language, but "comprehends the whole Circle of Civility and good manners, and regulates Life and Conduct" (128–29). As in the essays of the *Spectator* and the literary societies modeled on them, this "Circle of Civility" included polite manners but not public politics. According to Clerk, "the Design of Schools, the Use of Universities, the Benefit of Conversation should all center" on taste, "and no one can properly be stiled a Gentleman, who has not made us[e] of every Opportunity to enrich his own Capacity, and settle the Elements of Taste" (128).

Another essay, George Drummond's "Rules of Conversation" (1740), outlines the proprieties that maintained the "Circle of Civility." These rules include the same proscriptions against heated debates that were implemented to preserve the polite decorum of literary societies. Whether "we are Magistrates, Judges, Men of Business, or however station'd in the Scale of Life, we must pay a regard to the particular Decorum, and Elegance of manners, that's suitable to our condition" ("Book of Essays" 105). Drummond stresses that "if we would generally please, and avoid bringing scandall on our professions," we must "divest our selves as much as possible of our public characters" (106). We must be careful "how far we enter into disputes, especially upon delicate subjects where our religious, or even political principles may too far interest our positions in the argument" (107). The art of polite conversation depends on the "moderation of good manners," and mastering that art is "the most natural and certain method of rising in the world and making one's fortune" (101). To assimilate into polite companies, "we must carefully adapt our behaviour and conduct to their designs, study to fall in with their views, accomodate our selves to their temper" (103). Drummond also notes that "the History of our own Country" shows anyone that the "art of making himself agreeable by the charms of a well regulated conversation" is more important than oratorical "Eloquence." These students' essays are motivated by the same anxieties about cultural assimilation that are evident in the works of Smith and Blair discussed in later chapters, and here as there, those anxieties lead the authors to distance themselves from public controversies and the rhetoric associated with them.

Few professors would want to be judged by their students' compositions because even the best tend to lack nuance. It is precisely the nuances of the essay that contain its critical potential, but these students' essays are as lacking in irony and critical self-awareness as the popular anthologies and elocutionary manuals that taught such students to read essays of taste and manners to learn how to speak with the voice of the *Spectator* or *Idler*. Like such sources, these student essayists present refined sentiments in a polished style to demonstrate that they had mastered the proprieties of civil society. Stevenson's students' essays suggest that some of the lessons popularized by the *Spectator* and taught by Blair's *Lectures on Rhetoric and Belles Lettres* were being learned by provincials in Blair's own school days. Of course no one ever accused Blair of originality. In many respects, his theories merely rationalized the anxieties of middle-class provincials and formalized the conventions they sought to master. To be admitted within the "Circle of Civility," provincials recognized that they needed to remember their place, avoid speaking up on controversial topics, and studiously imitate the tastes of their betters. Provincial students wanted to learn how to be "stiled a Gentleman," and they were willing "to divest" themselves of their "public character" and remain silent on the sort of disputes that had been the civic locus of classical rhetoric. Such attitudes and anxieties were clearly evident in the literary societies and college classrooms where English studies were first defined in terms of the paradigm of rhetoric and belles lettres.

The political purposes of this depoliticized paradigm become clear when one examines how the first university professorship dedicated to the teaching of English was founded to reward a leader of the Moderate Party for establishing subservience within the church. In the decade after they suppressed popular resistance in the Presbyterian Church, the Moderates were given some of the best clerical and educational posts in Scotland. As the leader of the Moderates, William Robertson received two sinecures and the principalship of Edinburgh University, which together yielded an income of three hundred and sixty pounds, making him perhaps the best-paid clergyman in Scotland. The Moderates were at the peak of their political influence because of their close contacts with the ministry of their countryman Lord Bute, young King George's principal advisor. Bute's personal secretary was the Moderate clergyman and dramatist John Home. As early as 1756, Home was maneuvering to establish a professorship in rhetoric, but it was originally intended not for Blair but for another Moderate, Adam Ferguson, who had been unsuccessfully touted for the professorship in moral philosophy in 1754. In a letter to Lord Milton in 1756, Home stressed that the need for a professor to teach "eloquence in the Art of speaking" was greater for a "Scotchman than any body else as he lies under some disadvantages which Art must remove." In 1757 a Moderate ally wrote to Gilbert Elliot (Bute's political agent in Scotland) praising the literati's efforts, including Ferguson's work on "a very ingenious System of Eloquence or Composition in general" (qtd. Sher, *Church* 108, 88). Ferguson would instead be given a professorship in natural philosophy and then moved to the chair of moral philosophy in 1764 when its occupant was bought off with a sinecure of two hundred pounds. If Ferguson had become professor of rhetoric, he might not have taken the belletristic approach that Blair institutionalized because Ferguson was devoted to the civic humanist tradition that maintained rhetoric and moral philosophy's shared concern for politics into the eighteenth century.[16]

Blair's professorship was established after a very successful series of public lectures delivered by Adam Smith at Edinburgh from 1748 to 1751, perhaps under the sponsorship of the Philosophical Society or another literary society.[17] Smith was reportedly selected because "his pronunciation and his style were much superior" to Scots who had not had the benefit of studying in England (qtd. Bryce 7). At Edinburgh and then as professor at Glasgow, Smith lectured on the "science" of political economy at the same time that he was lecturing on rhetoric and belles lettres. As discussed in the next chapter, Smith is the most important example of how the trend toward belletrism in rhetoric was paralleled by the movement of moral philosophy toward the social sciences. The "science of man" was the point of origin for both of these trends, as is evident in the course in logic that Smith taught at Glasgow in 1751 before moving to the chair in moral philosophy, which he held from 1752 to 1764. According to one account, Smith dismissed deductive reasoning with a few introductory comments and then lectured on rhetoric and belles lettres. Smith justified his approach by noting that "the best method of explaining and illustrating the various powers of the human mind" was through "an examination of the several ways of communicating our thoughts by speech, and from an attention to the principles of those literary compositions which contribute to persuasion and entertainment" (Stewart, *Collected Works* 10: 11).

After Smith's departure for Glasgow, public lectures on rhetoric and belles lettres were continued at Edinburgh by Robert Watson until 1756, when he became professor of logic and rhetoric at St. Andrews (see Bator, "Formation of the Regius Chair" and "Lectures of Robert Watson"). Blair gave public lectures from December 1759 until 1760, when he was made professor without pay. In 1762 he formally became Regius Professor of Rhetoric and Belles Lettres. In a letter in March 1762 to Gilbert Elliot thanking him for taking up the affair with Bute, Blair had requested that "belles lettres" be added to the title of the chair to give it a more "modern air" (NLS Mss 11009: 111). Blair's correspondence shows that he was very concerned that he be allowed to charge students fees, rather than just be paid a flat salary for delivering public lectures. From its first year Blair's course attracted many students, and he sold the copyright to his lectures for the huge sum of fifteen hundred pounds in 1783. The incomes of most professors were rising at the time, from an average salary of thirty pounds in the first half of the century to around one hundred and ten pounds by the end of the century (Emerson, "Scottish Universities," 460). With salaries equal to many doctors and lawyers, professors were becoming comfortably middle class, and perhaps none was more comfortable with the middle-class reading public than Hugh Blair.

Blair was the first university professor I know of who was formally appointed to teach English, but English composition, rhetoric, and criticism were also being taught by professors of logic and moral philosophy. In addition to Smith at Glasgow and Watson at St. Andrews, James Beattie taught rhetoric at Marischal as professor of moral philosophy from 1760. Beattie's *Elements of Moral Science* (1790–1793) discuss "the Popular Essay, the Sermon, and the Oration" (2: 569–84). Beattie draws on classical rhetoric but upholds Addison's *Spectator* as more preferable to political discourse "dictated by party-spirit" (2: 573). Rather than teaching rhetoric as a political art, Beattie concentrated on polite taste and usage. He advised students to avoid the idioms of their own nation because such "barbarous language debases the taste" and "taints the mind." If Scottish words are allowed into English, "our speech must in a few years be barbarous. But this, every person of taste, who loves his country, understands its language, and wishes well to its literature, will do every thing in his power to counteract" (2: 524–25).[18] As Beattie became an increasingly strident opponent of republicanism and skepticism, he placed even more emphasis on teaching polite taste as a means to instill a deference to the proprieties of the dominant culture. He went so far as to conclude that "I am one of those who wish to see the English spirit and English manners prevail over the whole island" (qtd. Wood, *Aberdeen* 124). Professors like Beattie taught students to view their native culture as "barbarous," identify themselves with the language and literature of England, and studiously imitate refined taste to improve not just their minds but "their" country as well.

Even at the origins of college English, professors apparently found it easier to lecture on criticism than to teach composition, for less evidence exists of the writing done in the first courses on English than in student societies. As discussed in the chapter on English studies in Ireland, such societies provided occasions for students to work on their English at a time when the curriculum provided few such opportunities. Compositions were assigned by such notable professors as Pringle, Stevenson, and Ferguson, but one cannot be sure how much composition was emphasized even in courses on rhetoric. In the 1760s the rhetoric class at Glasgow was criticized for failing to recognize that "to excel in composition, constant and almost daily practice is necessary: the rules did not teach composition; composition produced the rules" (Thom 316). Students also complained about the lack of attention to composition. Alexander Carlyle criticized his composition course at Glasgow with William

Leechman for including only one writing assignment each term and concluded that he had learned much more from his writing and reading in a student society (95, 85; see also Leechman). Along the same lines, while praising Stevenson's teaching, Sommerville felt that groups like the Belles Lettres Society had contributed more to his progress "in literature, in composition, and in solid intellectual improvement" (39–40).

Professors tended to be ambivalent about student societies, praising them for encouraging study, but also worried that they were not under faculty control. Like other universities, Glasgow several times attempted to suppress its student societies. While Robertson supported them at Edinburgh, Blair advised students to limit their discussions to what was "useful and manly," particularly topics directly related to their studies or which have a "relation to morals and taste" (*Lectures* 1: 241). One such group was the Belles Lettres Society cited by Sommerville. According to its "Proceedings," it was "instituted that proper opportunities might not be wanting where gentlemen of Taste might communicate their Opinions to one another and receive mutual improvement" (53–54; see also Bator). On this and other points, the "Proceedings" acceded to the Addisonian doctrines that Blair taught in the classroom, but some of the questions discussed were more explicitly political than those that professors taught and discussed in their own literary societies, including questions about the freedom of the press and the merits of the Union. Within several weeks of Principal Robertson, Blair, and other faculty members' becoming honorary members in April and May of 1760, a committee was formed to examine the minutes because the society had considered many "very Improper subjects of debate" ("Proceedings" 71). After that time, there is a noticeable decline in the number of political topics discussed.

The history of another Edinburgh student society, the Speculative Society founded in 1764, shows that political topics were becoming increasingly problematic as public unrest intensified in the last quarter of the century. The Speculative Society has already been cited in chapter 3 for having had contacts with Irish student societies. The society was founded by half a dozen students for the purpose of "improvement in Literary Composition and Public Speaking" (*History of the Speculative Society* 2). As in other societies, students met weekly to debate issues and practice their English elocution by reading essays, including their own compositions. The society also included Robertson, Stewart, and other faculty as honorary members. The rules founding the society were intended to maintain polite decorum, but like the Belles Lettres Society, the Speculative Society did not confine itself to traditional moralistic topics. The group questioned accepted positions on controversial issues, including the enslavement of Africans, the persecution of Jews, and the restrictions on Catholics. The group also discussed political rights and representation. The group got into trouble in the last two decades of the century when the revolutions in England and France made such topics more than merely academic. A conservative faction attempted to expel those with republican sympathies. Hume and other former members returned to push for expulsion and resigned in protest when a contingent of liberals led by Francis Jeffrey and Henry Brougham defeated them (*History* 31–34; see Dagg 51). Jeffrey and Brougham spoke for a rising generation of liberal reformers. As discussed in chapter 9, they went on to found a second *Edinburgh Review* and helped establish a secular university with a utilitarian orientation, the University of London. The University of London included the first professorship dedicated to the study of English literature, a study that almost immediately was set in opposition to Utilitarianism and provincialism.

Debates between liberal reformers and more conservative Scottish literati disturbed the disinterested civility of the literary societies that had supported the introduction of English studies. According to one observer, the war with the American colonies "became a principal object of conversation in every company and often excited angry debates, which impaired the pleasures of social life" (Sommerville 198–99). As political debates divided civil society, liberal ideas became suspect, and protégés like John Millar lost favor with mentors like Henry Home for expressing distrust of established authorities.[19] Radical Whigs splintered the ruling political interest, and when revolution abroad led to reaction at home, the literati's associate Henry Dundas suppressed dissent and imposed state controls on the press, making it difficult for his intellectual colleagues to claim to be cosmopolitans speaking from an impartial position in civil society. Urbanization, commercialization, and increasing social mobility further undermined the shared commitment to improvement that had brought traditional intellectuals together with political managers, men of business, and the gentry.[20] In the last decades of the century the middle classes were becoming dissatisfied with being cast in the role of disinterested spectators of politics. As they lost their traditional deference for the absentee aristocracy, the bourgeoisie became increasingly jealous of the gentry's ability to manipulate elections and began to organize for the purpose of political reform and not just polite self-improvement.

Literary societies had brought ministers, lawyers, country gentlemen, and merchants together around a shared interest in improvement, but when the interests of such groups diverged, literary societies began to close. The Select Society had already ended in 1764, the Philosophical Society of Aberdeen disbanded in 1773, the Literary Society of Glasgow closed in 1778, and the Philosophical Society of Edinburgh was absorbed into the Royal Society in 1783. As political divisions fractured civil society, literary societies gave way to popular debating societies and specialized organizations that limited their membership by professional affiliation or social class. According to McElroy, from 1770 to 1800 "there was an unmistakable division upwards: aristocrats, intellectuals and scholars separated themselves and gathered together in societies which were no longer open to those in the middle ranks of society" (87). Unlike literary societies, debating societies such as the Pantheon and Forum defined themselves as public forums for people to speak to popular audiences on political issues.[21] Public debating societies were often centers of political agitation that had contacts with dissenters and the corresponding societies that spread critical literacy and political activism among the working classes. Such societies were an anathema to literati like Blair, who criticized "public and promiscuous Societies, in which multitudes are brought together who are often of low stations and occupations, who are joined by no common bond of union, except an absurd rage for Public Speaking" (*Lectures* 2: 240). Blair taught his students to identify themselves with a more refined and less "promiscuous" public, a civil society unified by cosmopolitan tastes and an aversion to the passions of popular politics.

Conclusion: Belletrism, Scientism, and the Rhetorical Stance of the Spectator

In this chapter I tried to show how the departure from classicism in the Scottish universities was influenced by political developments in related institutions, particularly the integration of the Scottish Church into the British patronage system and the spread of cosmopolitanism through literary societies modeled on the perspective of the *Spectator*. Literary societies provided a place where provincials committed to self-improvement could assume an impartial perspective on traditional political conflicts and concentrate on mastering the proprieties of "conversible society." In the church, the perspective of the disinterested observer proved to be an effective rhetorical stance for the Moderate clergy who established themselves as the dominant political faction by defending the authority of patrons against the democratic traditions of their own society. The Moderates are an important historical example of how traditional intellectuals serve the dominant interest while claiming to speak from a disinterested position free from the prejudice of any particular class. The leaders of the Moderates were rewarded for their efforts with influential clerical and academic posts. From these positions, professors such as Hugh Blair and William Robertson began to teach the modern culture from a depoliticized perspective that upheld assimilated Scots' authority as disinterested spokesmen for self-improvement and social progress. When this perspective is situated in its practical rhetorical context, one can understand why the rhetoricians who founded college English established trends that would eliminate rhetoric from the humanities, eventually exiling political discourse to the social sciences and confining the study of English to the study of literature.

The literary societies in which Scots composed their theories of rhetoric and culture shaped the conceptions of audience and purpose assumed by those theories. In these societies, provincials could envision themselves as part of a cosmopolitan reading public where "the commerce of Letters is alike open to all" (Fordyce, *Dialogues* 1: 19). From their experiences in literary societies, Smith, Blair, and Campbell came to define modern rhetoric by the free exchange of sentiments between responsive auditors in "conversible society." Faced with such audiences, those who introduced English into the university assumed the rhetorical stance of the impartial spectator who speaks from a disengaged and hence disinterested perspective. To master this stance, provincials imitated the *Spectator* and studiously eliminated all idioms and attitudes that challenged the decorum of civil society. In this chapter, I used these literary societies to begin to sketch out *cosmopolitanism* as an ideological formation and process, including the proprieties that demarcated civil society and the process through which individuals internalized those proprieties. Literary societies are important sites for studying cosmopolitanism as both a cultural ideology and a process of enculturation because they encouraged educated Scots to identify themselves with the educated public at a formative stage in British history.

For centuries in Scotland and elsewhere, an education in classical literature, ancient languages, and scholastic reasoning had effectively preserved the boundaries of the learned culture. From the educational centers of that culture, the introduction of English would have looked like a literacy crisis that began when provincial universities failed to maintain learned languages and began teaching the "vulgar," in the sense of both the common people and their language. As this literacy crisis deepened, learned languages would become confined to small departments at the periphery of the curriculum, and English departments would take up the work of maintaining standards of academic literacy and instilling a respect for the literary classics of the educated culture. Scottish educators were the first to repudiate classicism and proclaim that Aristotle had finally "resigned his empire to Bacon and Newton" ("Statistical Account of Marischal" 21: 114). The emphasis on ancient languages was condemned for having been "exclusively adapted to the education of churchmen" and "indifferent . . . to the progressive improvement of the times" (Reid, *Works* 734; Jardine, *Outlines* 14). According to such reformers, ancient languages had preserved the antiquated orthodoxies of outmoded elites by providing "a mysterious semblance of learning" and concealing "from common observation, and even from the masters themselves, the intrinsic defects of the system which they continued to pursue" (Jardine, *Outlines* 14). The rejection of classicism had become so established by 1760 that when the professor of ancient languages at Aberdeen complained of few students, Principal Chalmers rebuked him severely: "now that Education is put upon a more rational and useful footing, there are many Students who know nothing either of Latin and Greek. Their plans & schemes for Life" depend on more "useful knowledge" (Aberdeen Mss: K.44). No Oxford or Cambridge don would have made such a statement in the eighteenth century, nor perhaps in the nineteenth for that matter.

The Scots who taught the language and literature of England were intensely aware that what they studied was not part of their heritage by birth but had to be consciously acquired by mastering the conventions of the dominant culture. Their anxieties about their mastery of English were institutionalized in a conflicted conception of culture that combined a nostalgia for the primitive genius of receding traditions with a programmatic attempt to eradicate the language of those traditions. Such "dialogical" oppositions had a formative impact on college English studies. As universities expanded beyond the traditional elite and became reoriented to the modern mission of educating the public, the production of discourse became subordinated to the reception of discourse. The paradigm of rhetoric and belles lettres was consistent with the nature of the reading public as a consumer society, but it disengaged the humanities from political action in the public sphere. Rhetoric had had a central role within the classical tradition as the art of persuading the public to follow the leadership of the educated, but the humanities in the modern period have tended to assume a more disinterested perspective on the public sphere. Grammar schools and universities had long served the needs of the elite by perpetuating the learned languages and classical authorities that maintained the boundaries of the educated culture, but from the eighteenth-century onward, the boundaries of the educated culture have been less easily defined and more contested, leaving educational institutions unsure of whether they are educating political agents or observers.

The expansion of the educated public and the standardization of educated usage involved dialectical forces that were reproduced within higher education, not just in the subordination of rhetoric to belletristic criticism, but also in the evolution of moral philosophy toward the social sciences. The "science of man" emerged out of the traditional study of "pneumatology," which among the Scots and the dissenters was shifting its focus from natural religion to human nature. For Smith and other leading moral philosophers, the "Newtonian method" provided a means to generalize from the study of man to the study of "human society" as "an immense machine" (*Theory of Moral Sentiments* 316). Moral philosophers became aware of the diversity of cultural conventions with the expansion of the "civilized" world, and they used the methods of science to account for the customs of foreign cultures and the economic changes that were transforming their own society. In the century before Marx, Smith and other moral philosophers such as John Millar developed a "science" of political economy that formalized the relations among land, labor, and capital.[22] In response to an intensifying awareness of cultural diversity and social change, moral philosophers established the "science of man" to demonstrate that "man is every where the same; and we must necessarily conclude that the untutored Indian and the civilized European have acted upon the same principles." "The general laws of our constitution" would explain alien cultures by scientific certainties that maintained traditional proprieties (Millar iii). In these ways, the "science of man" provided a stable reference point and reliable methodology for defining the laws that governed politics, morés, and morals as well as the conventions of educated discourse.

In subsequent chapters, the theories of rhetoric that contributed to the formation of college English studies are examined against the redefinition of moral philosophy by the "science of man." Into the eighteenth century, rhetoric and moral philosophy were indebted to a common tradition with the same two sources, the civic humanism of Cicero and Aristotle. As moral philosophers began to speak as scientists, they became less concerned with civic eloquence and more interested in mastering the laws governing psychology and political economy. Civic humanism is used as a point of departure for assessing the movement toward the social sciences that shaped the assumptions upon which college English studies were founded. Professors of moral philosophy such as Francis Hutcheson and George Turnbull are transitional figures who were influenced both by civic humanism and by the effort to apply the methods of natural philosophy to moral philosophy. With Hutcheson's student, Adam Smith, moral philosophers came to assume the perspective of the "impartial spectator." While Smith and his colleagues were among the first university professors to teach rhetoric in English, the departure from classicism would end up removing rhetoric from its traditional place at the center of the humanities. Belletrists like Smith and Blair focused on taste, while Campbell founded his project on the "science of human nature," but both perspectives treated discourse as essentially an internal phenomenon concerned with mental faculties rather than with putting shared knowledge into political action.

Civic humanism had suited a *polis,* and even a republic of letters, but the traditional opposition of the public good and private corruption did not make sense in a commercial society defined in laissez-faire terms that devalued the political sphere, made economics more than a private matter, and further blurred the opposition of the private and the public by constituting the social as a domain that was public but not political—a distinction inconceivable within civic humanism. The first major British theorist of modern society was Adam Smith, and his works popularized the virtues of sociability, the power of consumption as the driving force in "commercial society," and the model of a laissez-faire political economy that devalued not just politics but the public sphere generally as a domain where people use rhetoric to adjudicate conflicts, celebrate shared values, and deliberate over the best courses of action. Smith's works mapped out the discursive domain within which English was first constituted as an object of university study. That domain was the carefully demarcated sphere of civil society where individuals conduct the business of daily life and express their feelings freely, as long as they remain free of the passions and party interests of popular politics. This domain was idealized in print and realized in practice in the literary societies where educated Scots stepped back from the divisive controversies of the time and imitated the perspective of the *Spectator* as a model of the decorum of the polite reading public. While such a perspective proved to be conducive to the development of literary criticism and the social sciences, it cast the individual in the stance of critical observer and not political agent, in practice a highly rhetorical stance but in theory one with little need for rhetoric.

Adam Smith and the Rhetoric

of a Commercial Society

Philosophic theories of knowledge made the same appeal to the self, or ego, in the form of personal consciousness identified with mind itself, that political theory made to the natural individual, as the court of ultimate resort.... From philosophy the idea crept into psychology, which became an introspective and introverted account of isolated and ultimate private consciousness. Henceforth moral and political individualism could appeal to "scientific" warrant for its tenets and employ a vocabulary made current by psychology:—although in fact the psychology appealed to as its scientific foundation was its own offspring.

—Dewey, *The Public and Its Problems*

MORAL PHILOSOPHY WAS the field of study where "philosophic theories of knowledge" appealed to the logic of the individual experience to formalize the "sciences" of psychology and political economy, with both assuming the vantage point of the autonomous individual that they had themselves established as their "scientific foundation." In the age of science, rhetoric was left with little to do but manage the flow of information between isolated individuals and help them refine their private tastes. Before they began speaking as social scientists, moral philosophers often played the role of popular moralists, preaching and teaching the values of the educated culture to popular audiences, while rhetoricians taught the educated how to draw on popular beliefs to speak to public controversies. In periods when the educated culture has been called upon to explain itself in new ways to broader classes of students, rhetoric and moral philosophy have often been infused with the energy that is generated when social change ruptures traditional systems of belief, undermines established positions of authority, and prompts reexaminations

of moral and discursive conventions. In response to the expansion of the educated culture in the eighteenth century, the political concerns of rhetoric
and moral philosophy became contained within "an introspective and introverted account of isolated and ultimate private consciousness." Few figures
are more broadly important in this development than Adam Smith, who introduced the "new" rhetoric into the university curriculum at the same time
that he was delivering the lectures on moral philosophy that gave rise to his
Theory of Moral Sentiments and *Wealth of Nations,* which are foundational
works for the emergence of modern "moral and political individualism."

The Scottish Enlightenment, according to Pocock, was the historical point
where "the locus of virtue shifted decisively from the civic to the civil," from
civic virtue in political action to that more diffuse "blend of the economic,
cultural and moral which we call the social for short" ("Cambridge" 240).
Following from that shift, moral philosophy expanded to include political
economy, psychology, and cultural anthropology, and English studies subordinated the composition of public discourse to stylistic criticism concerned
with instilling a respect for the proprieties of civil society. Pocock has established the civic humanist tradition as the point of departure for the Addisonian concern for civility, while other historians such as Knud Haakonssen have
examined the continuities between the natural law tradition and the Scots'
efforts to reason inductively from the individual experience to the laws governing the general species, domain, or "economy." According to Fordyce's
widely popular *Elements of Moral Philosophy,* this "science" "builds its Reasonings on plain uncontroverted Experiments, or upon the fullest Induction
of Particulars." It begins with "human nature, its moral powers and connections, and from these deduces the laws of action; and is defined more strictly
the 'Science of Manners or Duty.'" ("Elements" 2: 243; see Bryson, *Man and
Society* 249). The natural law and civic humanist traditions provide a broader
historical context for the examination of the scientistic and belletristic trends
in moral philosophy and rhetoric that I develop in the first section of this
chapter.

In the second section, I examine how Smith drew on the Addisonian
attention to social interactions and sympathetic reactions to develop a model
of the social construction and psychological internalization of shared values.
The model of the "impartial spectator" served to instill self-control in a society that was losing its faith in traditional values, but the turn inward to
concentrate on psychological motivations reoriented rhetoric away from
questions about how to accomplish practical purposes. Rhetoric's traditional
focus on purposeful action located it at a central discontinuity in the whole
enlightenment project. The Baconian tautology that knowledge is power

contained a conflicted conception of human nature that failed to resolve how knowledge has the power to act. Proponents of enlightenment generally assumed that action was motivated not by reason but by the passions or will. Rhetoric had been grudgingly accepted as necessary to move the will to persuade people to act, but to mediate between action and reflection, Smith and other Scottish moral philosophers focused not on the will to act but on the sympathetic imagination because it was less disruptive and more responsive to refinement. To promote social harmony and instill self-control, Smith focused not on the perspective of the agent, who may act from self-interested passions, but on the observer who sympathizes with others who act from disinterested motives. To feel such moral sentiments, the individual must step back from a conflict and assume the perspective of the disinterested spectator. While such a perspective may be appropriate for a critic or scientist, it is one step removed from the viewpoint of the political agent. Within this disciplinary paradigm, appropriate motivations and refined responses gained priority over political agency. Rhetoric and moral philosophy lost their productive engagement with public action and became a critical enterprise concerned with instilling appropriate moral sentiments and aesthetic responses.

After reviewing how Smith's theory of personal sentiments contributed to the belletristic tendencies of the "new" rhetoric, I turn in the third section to assess how Smith's conception of commercial society failed to resolve anxieties about atomized individualism because it did not envision a productive function for civic discourse. Within laissez-faire political economy, public discourse became almost completely confined to persuading others to do business with us. In the "practical system of morality," that Smith added to his last revisions of *The Theory of Moral Sentiments,* "prudence" became the virtue of self-restraint divorced from the civic conception of practical wisdom, *phronesis* or *prudentia*—the ability to reason from shared values to resolve public conflicts. Smith's "prudent man" of business was but another personification of the "impartial spectator," who made his only appearance in *The Wealth of Nations* as an image of provincials who have a disinterested perspective because they are too far removed from the centers of political conflict to be involved in them. Smith's works on rhetoric and moral philosophy document the problems and priorities that shaped the introduction of the modern culture into higher education, most notably the alienation of the individual from the public in laissez-faire liberalism, but also the broader reorientation of the liberal arts away from the perspective of the political agent to that of the critic or scientist.

The belletristic sensibility became central to ethics in Smith's *Theory of Moral Sentiments;* the science of political economy was set out in *The Wealth of Nations;* and these trends converged on the formation of English studies in Smith's *Lectures on Rhetoric and Belles Lettres.* While little attention has been paid to the relations between Smith's theories of rhetoric and moral philosophy, the importance of his *Lectures on Rhetoric and Belles Lettres* has been well recognized. Howell has presented Smith as a champion of the "new" rhetoric, while Court has argued that Smith was the first professor of English literature.[1] According to Howell, Smith broadened rhetoric's domain beyond persuasive orations about political issues to include literary and scientific discourse, while at the same time rejecting rhetoric's "ritualistic form" and topical strategies of invention in favor of a plain style and an inductive form of proof (536–75; see also Bazerman, "Money Talks"). Rather than centering my analysis on his lectures on rhetoric, which were not published until rediscovered in the twentieth century, I examine how Smith's influential theories of moral sentiments and political economy mark out the trends in moral philosophy that bordered the discursive domain in which English literature, rhetoric, and composition became constituted as objects of formal academic study. Following Smith, Hugh Blair treated style as an index to sensibility and deemphasized rhetoric's traditional engagement with political and legal controversies, while Campbell's *Philosophy of Rhetoric* formalized the "new" rhetoric according to the laws of "the science of human nature." As the trends toward belletrism and scientism advanced, an increasingly narrow conception of literature would eclipse rhetoric, and college English studies would lose the concern for practical political action that had been shared by rhetoric and moral philosophy in the civic humanist tradition.

The formation of college English foreshadows broader developments in the modern relations of the humanities and the public sphere. The domain of popular politics that had been studied by rhetoric and moral philosophy became the province of the social sciences. The modern reduction of politics to a science reflects the development of a public sphere where "technological rationality has become political rationality" (Marcuse xvi). According to Hans Georg Gadamer, the modern definition of practical understanding according to the instrumental logic of science stands in sharp contrast with the conception of practical rationality at the center of Aristotle's civic humanism. This conception identified rhetoric and moral philosophy as closely related political arts concerned with drawing on shared beliefs to address public problems. Civic humanism served elitist and sexist political purposes by valorizing the normative authority of public discourse in a society where the public was limited to freeborn males, but I believe that a critical reassessment of civic discourse can help establish a historical counterpoint to the possessive individualism of laissez-faire liberalism, which is the acknowledged descendent of the natural law tradition. Our pressing need to reconstitute a sense of the civic has been discussed by a range of figures, including Henry Giroux and others who could hardly be accused of nostalgia for classical republicanism. In the modern period the teaching of rhetoric and composition have not generally been identified with this project because the very concept of a modern rhetoric is an oxymoron in British universities, and composition instruction has generally been reduced to basic skills by the instrumental rationality that has acted as a powerful counterforce to trends in the humanities, most notably English departments' devotion to nonutilitarian nonfactual forms of discourse.

From Civic Humanism and Natural Law to Civility and Political Economy

The natural law tradition contributed to the formation of liberal individualism and the modern effort to use the "experimental" method to discover the natural laws that govern human nature and political economy, while the civic humanist tradition connects Scottish moral philosophy with the broader history of philosophies of politics as a practical domain of purposeful action.[2] The terminology of *natural laws* enabled moral philosophers to claim to be adopting the methods of the natural sciences while maintaining a faith in the Providential order of the world. To establish a natural authority for individual rights, natural law doctrines tended to remove individuals from their civic duties and situate them in a higher rational order or a set of contractual relations founded on a pre-social "natural" world. Scottish moral philosophers expunged the rationalist tendencies of Continental sources such as Heineccius, Grotius, and Pufendorf and defined natural laws in more empirical terms to assess the material development of society from primitive agriculture to modern commerce. Civic humanism provided a countervailing sense of how commerce corrupted public virtue by fostering private luxuries and factional interests. In order to understand how modernization was transforming their traditional society, Scottish moral philosophers reinterpreted the civic ideal of the citizen orator in Addisonian terms of civility to maintain the virtue of "sociability" in an increasingly diversified commercial society. Natural law doctrines provide the historical context for assessing the modern relations of scientism and liberalism, while civic humanism provides a context for considering how rhetoric became displaced from its central role in the humanities as higher education took up the mission of teaching the public to internalize the values of educated society—a mission that had not been important when universities educated a narrow elite whose public authority was uncontested.

The close ties between civic humanism and rhetoric can be traced back to the origins of the humanities, most notably to Aristotle and Isocrates, the leading students of Platonic idealism and sophistic relativism.[3] Sophists introduced the study of rhetoric to Athens from provincial city states such as Syracuse (see Enos). As in the eighteenth century, the study of rhetoric was formalized by provincials who had grown up outside the dominant culture and had consciously taught themselves its systems of values and modes of argument. As they traveled among the Greek city states teaching the art of rhetoric, Sophists encountered diverse systems of belief and came to conclude that politics and morals were a matter of convention and not nature. When Gorgias, Protagoras, and other Sophists introduced the study of rhetoric to the center of Greek culture, they justified it in humanistic terms by arguing that absolutes cannot be known, that there are two sides to every issue, and that "man" is the measure of all things (Freeman 125–30; see also Havelock; Jarratt). Plato opposed the relativistic moral philosophy and opportunistic rhetoric of the Sophists, but his student categorized the uncertainties of civic discourse as part of his broader effort to develop a political philosophy concerned with the realization of moral potential through practical action. Aristotle developed a philosophy of practical wisdom or *phronesis* that assumed that one can rarely act with certainty but one should act toward what appears best in the particular situation (see Selfe). In a parallel departure from the positions of his teacher Gorgias, Isocrates developed a humanistic philosophy of education that broadly surveyed literature, history, and politics to prepare citizens to speak with practical wisdom from the historical experience and values of the dominant culture (see Jaeger; Marrou; and T. Poulakos). From Isocrates through Cicero, civic humanism justified the humanities as a broad preparation for public life, and rhetoric as the means for putting a liberal education into political action.

The civic ideal of "the good man speaking well" valorizes public action over abstract speculation or private virtue (see, for example, Cicero, *De Officiis* 1.43.153). This ideal was situated in the social morés and moral conventions that shaped the duties of a citizen. As Pocock has discussed, civic humanism assumes that "the development of the individual towards self-fulfillment is possible only when the individual acts as a citizen, that is as a conscious and autonomous participant in an autonomous decision-making political community, the polis or republic" (*Politics* 85). The notion of a *private citizen* was an oxymoron for civic humanists. One who is incapable of participating in the *polis* is by definition an *idiotes*, with *idios* meaning "private" or "opposite to public" as well as "peculiar" or "strange" (Liddell and Scott). A good citizen must have practical wisdom, the ability to deliberate effectively to achieve the best possible ends (Aristotle 1141b10, 1140a25–30). Practical wisdom or prudence is necessary because social action turns on a relativistic judgment of the possibilities and constraints of a particular situation. Practical wisdom was fundamental to Aristotle's whole understanding of rhetoric and ethics as concerned with doing the right thing at the right time to solve a public problem (1094b, 1140b1–30). "The great merit of Aristotle," according to Gadamer, "was that he anticipated the impasse of our scientific culture by his description of the structure of practical reason as distinct from theoretical knowledge and technical skill" ("Hermeneutics and Social Science" 312; see also *Truth and Method*).[4]

Practical wisdom or *phronesis* was put into civic action through the art of rhetoric. For civic humanists such as Aristotle, Isocrates, and Cicero, rhetoric is the situational art of discovering the available means of persuasion in a particular conflict. To use those means to achieve the best possible ends, the rhetorician must have practical wisdom. The art of rhetoric, like practical wisdom, engages the whole person, including *pathos* and *ethos* as well as *logos,* because what is best cannot be known with certainty but can be felt and valued by those with practical experience and a broad humanistic education in the traditions of the culture. Debating public controversies provides opportunities for citizens to develop the highest moral excellences by working through political conflicts to achieve the best ends possible at this moment in this situation. Rhetoric and ethics thus share a common domain—the indeterminate and conflicted sphere of public politics where the good cannot be known but must be acted upon. Rhetoric and ethics also share a common teleology, for both are concerned with deliberating over how to achieve the best possible political ends, a matter not of absolutes but of *kairos*—that which is appropriate in this situation on this occasion. Such a judgment is rhetorical and ethical, and finally political. The ideal of "the good man speaking well" made the wealthy citizen who is undistracted by private needs the voice of the public good and denied wisdom, and even humanity, to women, slaves, and others who were denied the virtues of citizenship. Precisely because the civic ideal of practical wisdom in political action is so concerned with how one gains the power to speak from "shared" values, civic humanism provides a context for examining how rhetoric and moral philosophy were transformed by the modern expansion of the educated public to include groups who had to be taught to internalize its values.

Civic humanism remained influential into the eighteenth century, but it evolved to suit changing political relations. Civic humanism had its broadest political impact in the early modern period through its influence on the "Commonwealthman" tradition of Sydney and Harrington, who turned to the civic virtues of a mixed constitution in order to mediate between the "vices" of popular democracy and unrestrained autocracy (see Robbins; Pocock *Politics* 105–6). In Scotland, civic ideals were also invoked by Andrew Fletcher of Saltoun, who spoke against the Union by arguing that a distant capital would provide few opportunities for the Scottish gentry to fulfill their civic duties. Civic humanism had an enduring appeal to the elite because it maintained that only the landed gentry could speak disinterestedly for the public good. With the expansion of commercial society, anxiety about the corruption of civic virtue "was eased apart from its political frame and relocated in a framework of social relationships that were defined in social, economic and cultural terms" (Phillipson, "Adam Smith" 200). Smith's teacher Francis Hutcheson contributed to the Addisonian tendency to associate civic virtues with polite refinement rather than political debates and helped to bring commerce and personal rights into the domain of moral philosophy, as discussed further below. Hume rejected the civic concentration on the public good as irrelevant to most individuals' experience and reasserted the sophistic view that justice was based on mere "artifice and human conventions" (*Treatise* 532, 548; see also *Essays* 52–53). For Smith, commerce was not simply a source of private vice but of public wealth, and in his works the public sphere becomes divided between a restricted political domain and a broader civil society where individuals should be left free to do business, governed not by political authorities but by natural laws. Smith's philosophy lies in the space between Hutcheson and Hume, at "the limits of the civic tradition" (Robertson, "Scottish" 141). It was in this space that English studies became constituted as an object of university study.

While Pocock has sharply opposed theories of natural rights and civic duties, Scottish moral philosophers were practical moralists who drew eclectically on both traditions. Scots learned of the "laws of nations" in the Calvinist colleges of Holland, and early Scottish moral philosophers like Hutcheson and his teacher Gershom Carmichael taught Continental and Lockean conceptions of natural law along with the virtues of civic humanism, with Cicero the classical source for both (see Moore and Silverthorne). Cicero popularized the Stoic doctrine that human beings are rational creatures who possess rights by nature of their participation in the rational order of the cosmos (*On the Commonwealth* 215). By abstracting from existing political relations, the Stoics helped to create a context in which the individual could be conceived apart from his, or even her, public duties. The Stoical tendency to treat the individual as a microcosm for the rational order of the cosmos was also popularized by more modern sources such as Shaftesbury, who argued that the "economy of the passions" within the individual reproduced "the economy of the species or kind" in which "the private interest and good of every-one . . . work towards the general good" (Shaftesbury 1: 289, 336, 338). Shaftesbury was also an important source for the Addisonian tendency to reinterpret civic virtues as sociability in the assumption that benevolence "can never find exercise for itself in so remote a sphere as that of the body politick." Thus, people can "better taste society, and enjoy the common good and interest in a more contracted publick" such as conversible society (qtd. Scott 164–65).

Shaftesbury's most important successor, Francis Hutcheson, is a transitional figure whose works show how civic duties and natural rights were first adapted to commercial society by provincials who were committed to economic modernization and cultural assimilation but lacked political power.[5] Like civic humanists, Hutcheson defined the body politic as "a society of free men united under one government for their common interest," and he rejected the Hobbesian view that political society necessarily infringed upon personal freedoms (see Hutcheson, *Works* 4: 302, 283). Hutcheson viewed his own works as but an introduction to the ancients, particularly Aristotle and Cicero (4: iv, i). However, Hutcheson's understanding of civic ideals is often shaped by his readings of Shaftesbury. From Shaftesbury Hutcheson learned to internalize the civic opposition of private interests and the public good in terms of egoistical and altruistic feelings mediated by a moral sense, which he identified as a source of aesthetic as well as ethical sentiments (see Raphael). Following Hutcheson, and more directly Hume, what became known as the "science of human nature" internalized the conflict between self-interest and the common good in the domain of personal sentiment. At the same time, the science of political economy would redefine political relations in terms of economic transactions, with conflicts between self-interest and the public good resolved by the "invisible hand" of the natural law of supply and demand without individuals ever having to become practically involved in publicly debating political purposes or the means to achieve them.

These trends are clear in how Hutcheson redefined the domain of moral philosophy. Hutcheson divided moral philosophy into ethics and the "law of nature," with the latter subdivided into "*private rights*," "*Oeconomicks*," and "*Politicks*" (*Works* 4: i). Economics thus becomes part of moral philosophy along with "private rights" via natural law doctrines that depict the private sphere as a realm of "natural liberty" that predates the social contract.[6] "Oeconomicks" was still evolving toward the modern conception of the term, as is evident in the fact that financial duties and business transactions are actually included in a division titled "Elements of the Law of Nature." The con-

cluding part of the work, "Oeconomicks and Politicks," follows civic humanists by displacing economics from the public to the domestic sphere of *oikos
nomos*, household laws, or as Hutcheson terms it, "the laws and rights of the
several members of a family" (4: i). The classical conception of domestic
economy had excluded commerce from the public domain of civic virtue (see
Aristotle 1258a20), but Hutcheson is able to bring economics into the purview
of moral philosophy by locating self-interest and the common good in a moral
economy in which the citizen as "sober, frugal oeconomist" works industri-
ously to satisfy his personal needs in a manner that benefits society (4: 322).
Hutcheson's emphasis on "private rights" and economics advanced the movement of the natural law tradition toward the possessive individualism that
would replace the ideal of an active public life with the libertarian view that
the individual has a right to be left alone to pursue personal advancement.

The trends toward scientism and belletrism were beginning to redefine
how moral philosophers thought of the relationship between the political
and the personal. Hutcheson advocated applying the empirical methods of
the natural sciences to the "economy" of the individual experience and the
political system. According to his student, William Leechman, Hutcheson
proceeded from the assumption that "in the same way that we enquire into
the structure of an animal body, of a plant, or of the solar system a more exact
theory of morals may be formed" (Hutcheson, *Works* 5: xiv–xv). To make a
science of ethics and politics, Hutcheson drew on Shaftesbury and the natural
jurisprudence tradition to formulate "the general *Rights* of HUMAN SOCIETY,
or Mankind as a System" (6: 104). Personal morality and political economy
are brought into harmony by assuming that the "moral faculty" serves the
"more extensive interest of the system" (5: 222). Like Smith, Hutcheson tends
to associate moral sentiments with polite refinement. According to Hutcheson, the moral sense is closely identified with "the senses of beauty and harmony, or, with Mr. Addison, the *imagination*" as well as with a "*sympathetick*
... fellow-feeling" for others (*Works* 5: 15). In response to Addison's *Spectator*
essays on the "Pleasures of the Imagination," Hutcheson's first work, *An Inquiry into the Original of our Ideas of Beauty and Virtue* (1725), took a psychological approach that was similar to that which belletrists would adopt to
teach style as an index to the personal character of an author. "Both Hume
and Smith learned from Hutcheson to keep aesthetics in mind when thinking
about ethics," according to the editors of Smith's *Theory of Moral Sentiments*
(Raphael and Macfie 14).

Like his two major successors, Hutcheson relied on the concept of a spectator to mediate the discontinuity between the general political economy and
the moral economy of benevolent and self-interested passions.[7] According to

Hutcheson, as we observe and reflect on our moral and aesthetic responses, we refine our sensibility and strengthen the "*sympathetick*" sense that prompts us to greater "fellow feeling" for others (*Works* 5: 19, 21). The spectator thus provided a mechanism for reason to refine the imagination through reflection on experience. The fact that the spectator is merely an observer and thus disinterested was basic to the whole effort to resolve the contradictions between self-interest and benevolence because "the agent himself perhaps may be moved by a view of advantages . . . ; but such advantages won't engage the approbation of others" (4: 18). Instilling the perspective of the disinterested spectator became central to moral philosophy with Smith because the balance of egoism and altruism ceased to seem so natural in a commercial society. More attention had to be paid to how people actually internalize prevailing values to prevent social diversification from eroding traditional hierarchies and thus undermining the subservience necessary to an orderly society.[8] In theory, the spectator moderates the self-interested feelings that motivate acts, but the practical dislocation from the perspective of the agent remains problematic, particularly in considering political agency.

While he was more concerned with political rights than his student, Hutcheson was no more interested in political advocacy than Smith. Smith's philosophy of "natural liberty" assumed little more than the individual's right to be "left perfectly free to pursue his own interest," with politics ideally concerned with little more than the libertarian essentials of abjudicating private conflicts, maintaining public works, and defending national security (*Wealth Of Nations* 687). While Hutcheson's theories were used by advocates of natural rights, his lectures did not value or encourage a practical involvement in political causes.[9] Even when Hutcheson was forced to admit that legitimate conflicts can occur, his only practical advice was to reiterate that "such as sincerely aim at acting the virtuous part, will always easily discern what equity and humanity require unless they are too much influenced by selfishness" (*Works* 4: 155). From such a perspective, rhetoric can never be more than a threat precisely because the rhetorician never speaks from a disinterested perspective. Hutcheson concluded that in a pure democracy the ignorant public will inevitably be ruled by demagogues: when "all the free men meet in the assembly, there is no hope of wisdom, no avoiding seditions, no stability of councils. Suspicion and envy can be raised, by artful selfish demagogues, against all virtue and eminence" (*Works* 6: 265). Following this same line of argument, civic humanists had taught rhetoric to prepare citizens to speak with practical wisdom against demagogues, but Hutcheson apparently found the art of debating political conflicts to be too distasteful to be worth discussing.

While the disinterested observer is a rather aloof vantage point for the citizen who needs to know how to speak to political conflicts, it does aptly suit the perspective of a social scientist or literary critic. Smith took a detached perspective in order to define politics, ethics, and aesthetics according to the natural laws of political economy and human psychology. Civic humanists had maintained that public debates put shared values into political action, thus fulfilling the moral potential of citizens, but faced with a heterogeneous public where traditional values were being undermined by social diversification, Smith and his contemporaries turned away from scenes of political conflict in an effort to establish more reliable methods and stable points of reference. The "science of man" required the formation of a new rhetoric, a rhetoric defined by the personal sensitivities of the belletristic critic and the inductive method of the social scientist, not the practical wisdom of the political orator. If one reads Smith's *Lectures on Rhetoric and Belles Lettres* in the context of his moral philosophy, one can see how his sentimental ethics and laissez-faire political economy led to an emphasis on stylistic criticism and a devaluation of public debate. In basic respects, the perspective established by the tradition of Hutcheson, Hume, and Smith led directly to the belletrism of Hugh Blair and the scientism of George Campbell, whose works foreshadow the trends that would erase rhetoric from the two cultures of the modern arts and sciences. Nowhere are these continuities more evident than in the general turn inward to study how discourse revealed the sentiments of the individual authorial subject.

Moral Sentiments and the Subordination
of Rhetoric to Belles Lettres

Pocock has argued that the transition from the civic to the civil in Scottish moral philosophy was shaped by the Addisonian tendency to redefine political duties as a matter of sociability. By distancing itself from the party politics of the periodical press, the essays of taste and manners of the *Spectator* could disinterestedly survey popular morés and interpersonal relations to examine how individuals revealed their personal character and social position through their taste in dress and deportment. According to the editors of *The Theory of Moral Sentiments* (1759), Smith may have taken his most characteristic term from the dedication to the first volume of the *Spectator,* where Addison positioned himself as "an impartial spectator" and defined his audience as concerned with gaining "acknowledged merit" through polite refinement (*Moral Sentiments* 15 n). Smith taught such readers that ethics was not a matter of acting purposefully to advance civic virtues, but of reacting sympathetically to individuals and learning to appreciate the harmony of the larger moral and political economy (see 326). The virtues of personal refinement appealed to readers who wanted to believe that their efforts to assimilate into polite society had moral value and social significance. Smith's concept of "the impartial spectator, the man within the breast," especially appealed to those at the periphery of civil society who were anxious about violating its proprieties and wanted to internalize a spokesman to tell them how to respond appropriately. In this and other ways, Smith's ethics were consistent with the experience of the middle-class reading public—a civil society that defined its members as tasteful consumers and not political participants.

Like his teacher, Smith associated moral feelings with a sympathetic imagination in a manner that identified ethics with aesthetics. Smith modeled the spectatorial perspective on the way we view a picture or poem, and he identified morality with a "delicate" taste that is "precisely suited to its object" (21, 20). From the opening pages of *A Theory of Moral Sentiments*, virtue is associated with "the most exquisite sensibility," and readers are invited to join "us" in feeling "pity and compassion" as we imagine the "torments" and "agonies" of individuals being hung and tortured (9). As we develop a sociable "fellow-feeling" for suffering individuals, we also come to realize that we share such refined feelings with others. As we adjust our reactions to achieve "harmony and concord" with those we look up to, we become socialized and internalize a "spectator" who helps us to calm our passions to what is considered appropriate (22). For examples that evoke refined sentiments, Smith drew widely on the expanding domain of print literacy, citing classical moralists as well as modern histories, contemporary accounts of "savage" cultures, and "the poets and romance writers, who best paint the refinements and delicacies of love and friendship, and of all other private and domestic affections" (143). While only those with the "most acute and delicate sensibility" can achieve an "exact propriety," even "the rude vulgar of mankind" are capable of "mere propriety" because they possess "the great demigod within the breast, the great judge and arbiter of conduct," who will compel them to follow the minimum "rules of conduct" (25, 247, 163).

Smith's moral philosophy is grounded in a concern for how shared values are socially constructed and internalized, or as Dwyer has termed it, "the complex interpersonal negotiation that takes place in the achievement of group norms" (54). According to Smith, people cannot develop an internal spectator without someone to mirror their feelings and thus enable them to refine their sentiments to internalize accepted conventions (*Moral Sentiments* 110). Smith was aware that this view of how morés become morals tended to suggest that moral standards are merely social norms, and he made important revisions in the second and sixth editions (1761 and 1790) to abstract the impartial observer from existing social conventions.[10] Faced with revolutions abroad and instability at home, Smith became more concerned about the diversity and unreliability of prevailing values (see Mizuta). In the sixth edition, Smith rewrote the section following his discussion of how the impartial observer is formed from reflections on social interactions. He gave new stress to the "natural and proper" foundations of its judgments, using the term four times in as many sentences to abstract from social conventions to universal categories. According to Smith, "praise and blame express what actually are; praiseworthiness and blame-worthiness, what naturally ought to be the sentiments of other people" (*Moral Sentiments* 126). These revisions show Smith trying to bridge the gap that Hume had pointed out between descriptions of what is and prescriptions for what ought to be. These questions about how to generate an *ought* from an *is* would also be central to the debate between Hume and the commonsense moral philosophers over how moral authority can be founded on empirical observations, as I discuss further in chapter 7. Such questions may seem peripheral to rhetoric, but insofar as it is concerned with arguing about what ought to be done, questions about moral authority are fundamental to rhetorical practice even if they are unexamined in rhetorical theory.

Smith's attention to the social interactions that instill prevailing values could have formed the basis for a civic conception of modern rhetoric, but his theory is less concerned with the public purposes of discourse than with the personal motivations that inspire it. Civic rhetoricians and moral philosophers valued practical wisdom because they wanted to teach people how to achieve the best possible ends, but purposeful action is never disinterested. To establish his claim that the spectator is truly disinterested, Smith dismissed utilitarian judgments of acts according to their effects and focused instead on "the sentiment or affection of the heart, from which any action proceeds, and upon which its whole virtue or vice depends" (*Moral Sentiments* 67). As already noted, this shift from practical effects to personal motivations is evident in the moral philosophy of Hutcheson, and Hume also concluded "that when we praise any actions, we regard only the motives that produced them, and consider the actions as signs or indications of certain principles in the mind or temper" (*Treatise* 529). This concentration on questions about how to judge motives, rather than on how to achieve practical goals, is consistent with the general idealization of the disinterested sensibility and with the introspective turn of the "new" rhetoric. This turn reoriented rhetoric away from its productive engagement with achieving political purposes and enlisted it in the essentially critical project of assessing individuals' motives and responses.

Smith's belletristic approach to rhetoric followed from this introspective turn. Smith's stylistic criticism focused on the sentiments that motivate discourse rather than on the political effects it achieves. As in the belletristic rhetoric of Blair, the composition of purposeful public discourse was given less emphasis than stylistic criticism concerned with instilling polite proprieties, proprieties that provincials had to be formally taught because "we in this country are most of us very sensible that the perfection of language is very different from that we commonly speak in. The idea we form of a good style is almost contrary to that which we generally hear" (Smith, *Rhetoric and Belles Lettres* 38). Smith gave particular emphasis to "perspecuity" because a clear style best conveys the sentiment that motivates the discourse, and thus best evokes "*sympathy*" (22). Smith assumed, according to Bevilacqua, that sympathy "accounts for the rhetorical efficacy of vivid expression" (563). However, Smith gave less attention to producing rhetorical effects than to critiquing how such effects reveal the psychological workings of sympathetic sentiments, and he treated language not as a set of purposefully used conventions but as a transparent medium for presenting natural sentiments (see *Rhetoric and Belles Lettres* 51–52).

To instill such sentiments, Smith taught his students to analyze how the styles of authors such as Pope and Addison reveal their individual characters, with an examination of Addison's style providing an occasion for extolling the virtues of the "modest man, who naturally delivers himself in sentences of a moderate length and with a uniform tone" (*Rhetoric and Belles Lettres* 49). To reinforce the moral of his stylistic criticism, Smith included a long digression on the ideal of the "plain" and "simple" styles as indices to dispassionate sensibility (32–35). As with Blair and other belletrists, Smith's stylistic criticisms of the personal sentiments that motivated essayists such as Addison reduced the essay to a univocal instrument for instilling sensibility and divorced it from the heteroglossia of the periodical press discussed in the first chapter. In this way, the essay was taught as a means for instilling polite proprieties rather than as a self-reflective genre that had the potential for social critique. This pedagogy was consistent with Smith's concern for the internalization of prevailing norms and with his lack of concern for the political purposes of rhetoric. This perspective was institutionalized as the paradigm of rhetoric and belles lettres, and it foreshadowed the conflicted movement in modern composition courses from essays of personal experience to the conventions of academic discourse, a movement oriented to internalizing a disinterested stance and a clear style that effaces the purposes served by its modes of representing experience (see Trimbur).

Like Blair and the others who subordinated composition to criticism, Smith spent little time discussing strategies for composing discourse to achieve an intended purpose. "New" rhetoricians generally rejected classical invention strategies aimed at tapping the productive capacities of discourse. Because he was so committed to stylistic criticism, Smith concluded that rhetoricians such as Cicero also dismissed invention and arrangement "as very slight matters" and concentrated on "the ornaments of language" (*Rhetoric and Belles Lettres* 142). This conclusion may be consistent with Ciceronianism but not with Cicero's own writings. Classical rhetoricians studied the art of drawing on shared beliefs to speak to public conflicts and emphasized invention strategies such as stasis theory as useful in determining whether a conflict turned on a matter of fact, definition, evaluation, or procedure. Smith and the other "new" rhetoricians were uniformly uninterested in stasis theory because they were not concerned with teaching students to speak to public conflicts. The rejection of invention is the decisive step in the subordination of composition to criticism, and it is a key element of the "new" rhetoric according to Howell, who praised Smith as a modern for discovering that in the age of science one must merely report the facts of the case. More critical historians such as Sharon Crowley have agreed that the dismissal of invention was a definitive element of early modern rhetoric but have condemned it for denigrating shared beliefs as a form of knowledge and molding the individual consciousness in the image of disinterested rationality.[11] Whenever rhetoric loses its practical engagement with the productive capacities of shared knowledge and deliberative discourse, composition will be taught through criticism, and the critical stance of the disinterested observer will tend to replace the rhetorical stance of the political agent as the vantage point that students are taught to assume as educated individuals.

While Smith's *Lectures on Rhetoric and Belles Lettres* ignored the political debates of his own time, he used the politics of ancient rhetoric as a cautionary tale to teach his students about the corrupting influences of popular politics. Smith's comments on classical oratory are important because they show an attention to the political contexts of rhetoric that is notably absent from his discussions of modern rhetoric (see, for example, 148). Smith noted that like the rest of the "Old Eloquence," classical forensic oratory was highly emotional and poorly reasoned because it was addressed to popular audiences, including juries who were no better "than the mob in the pit of an ill-regulated play-house" (173). On the other hand, Smith praised rhetoricians like Demosthenes because they led coalitions of "gentlemen" (patricians and rich plebians) against the lower classes, "the rabble and mob, and the most wretched and miserable set of men imaginable" (150). Similarly, the rhetorical excesses of Roman oratory were a symptom of the political corruptions that resulted from the absence of a strong middle class to restrain the "extravagances" of the upper and lower classes (151). Such comments provide clear insights into Smith's practical attitude to the public and help to explain why he avoided discussing the political rhetoric of his own time. Smith, like Blair, assumed that it was in poor taste to speak to the vulgar public on political matters. While "eloquence" was to be respected as a classical ideal, its contemporary relevance was limited by a tasteful aversion to practical politics.

Like Blair and other provincial rhetoricians, Smith could see the civic purposes of ancient rhetoric, but when he turned to contemporary discourse, he concentrated on belletristic genres and avoided political rhetoric. Smith assumed that an age of science had little need for public debate. Because a lawyer addresses trained judges rather than an ignorant jury, he "can do no more than tell over what facts he is to prove" (*Rhetoric and Belles Lettres* 190). Modern political orators must speak in a similarly dispassionate and disinterested fashion because they no longer speak to broad public audiences. As Smith lectured on the ancient art of rhetoric, political orators were remapping the world on the floor of Parliament (see Oliver), but Smith pointedly ignored the oratory of the House of Commons, not to mention popular political debates and pamphlets. Instead, he confined himself to the proprieties of civil society:

> The order and decorum of behaviour which is now in fashion will not admit of any the least extravaganzes. The behaviour which is reckoned polite in England is a calm, composed, unpassionate serenity, noways ruffled by passion. . . . Politeness, again in England, consists in composure, calm and unruffled behaviour. The most polite persons are those only who go to the opera, and any emotions would there be reckoned altogether indecent. And we see that, when the same persons go out . . . to a bear-garden or such like ungentlemanly entertainment, they preserve the same composure as before at the Opera, while the rabble about express all the various passions by their gesture and behaviour. (*Rhetoric and Belles Lettres* 191–92)

A provincial like Smith imagined that an English gentleman maintained the self-restraint of a spectator at the opera even while at a bear-baiting. He had to reiterate that he was speaking of "Politeness" as it existed "again in England" because he knew that the proprieties of civil society were divorced from his audience's practical experience—a critical distance that was fundamental to the disinterested authority of such cosmopolitan ideals.

Smith and his successors disassociated rhetoric from its classical concern for legal controversies and political conflicts and turned for models to more cosmopolitan forms of discourse, particularly the essays of taste and manners that maintained the proprieties of the polite reading public. The essays of Addison and the other commentators on polite taste provided models of the sympathetic imagination, and students were taught to concentrate on internalizing its stylistic proprieties and ignore the essay's potential as a means to critique social conventions. The focus on the psychological dimensions of discourse was maintained by both of Smith's major successors. While it was Campbell who reinterpreted classical rhetoric to found it upon a "science of human nature," it was Blair's more eclectic belletrism that came to define early college English studies, particularly in America.

At the same time that rhetoric was expanding to include belletristic and even scientific forms of discourse, rhetoric was narrowing its depth of focus from the purposeful use of discourse to stylistic proprieties, and it was being reoriented from public discourse to matters of personal sentiment.[12] The emphasis on stylistic distinctions served the need of the middle classes to distinguish themselves from the less educated, and it helped establish English studies as a means to make such distinctions. However, the emphasis on stylistic criticism as a means to instill polite sentiments contained a basic "paradox." As Daiches has discussed, the "rhetorical analysis of literature" produced a basic "paradox of Scottish culture, the co-existence of a cooly rational tone and method with a belief in the moral value of feeling" (82). By using stylistic proprieties to regulate the production and the reception of discourse, Smith and later belletrists worked to contain the political purposes of rhetoric as well as the aesthetic effects of literature.[13]

The belletrism of the "new" rhetoric was supported by the conflation of ethics and aesthetics as matters of refined sentiments, while the deemphasis of civic discourse was consistent with the emerging science of political economy. As I discuss in the next section, Smith's laissez-faire political economy devalued the public domain as a sphere of purposeful political action. For Smith, the rise of commerce and liberty do not depend on political leadership but on the "natural laws" of political economy and human psychology that govern the historical evolution of society from primitive agricultural communities through feudalism to "commercial society." Cultural and political changes are the unintended outcomes of developments in the modes of production that do not depend on purposeful action or collective decision making. For example, as a primitive lord sought more elegant goods, his wealth was naturally diverted from his retainers to independent tradespeople. This natural desire for cultural refinement distracted the country lord from his civic duties, expanded commerce and thus civil society, and "introduced order and good government, and with them, the liberty and security of individuals" (*Wealth Of Nations* 412–13).[14] Possessive individualism, free commerce, and civil society advance naturally, with laissez-faire liberalism opposing itself to the rhetoric of party politics in order to speak from a disinterested perspective on the laws of nature. From this perspective, rhetoric is at best irrelevant and at worst the principal hindrance to the "free" exercise of the natural laws that promote progress.

The Political Economy of Rhetoric in a "Commercial Society"

The emphasis on political discourse in the civic humanist tradition provides an historical point of reference for critiquing Smith's theories of moral sentiments and belletristic criticism, but even starker contrasts emerge when one compares his vision of "commercial society" to the classical conception of the public sphere. While civic humanists treated economics as a private matter of personal business and domestic economy, Smith's political economy subordinates politics to economics, not only by treating politics as a threat to economic improvement, but also by defining the political sphere as a subordinate part of a larger rule-governed system or economy. According to Smith's laissez-faire political economy, "perfect liberty" is achieved not by political debate or collective action but by allowing the "natural" laws "gravitating" within the economy to operate unhindered by governmental intervention (*Wealth of Nations* 75). To reduce politics to a science, Smith reasons in a Newtonian fashion to determine the universal law that operates like gravity to govern the whole system or economy. Left unhindered by political intervention, the "invisible hand" follows the law of supply and demand and disperses wealth in a way that best serves the "publick interest" (456). With the public good taken care of by natural laws, practical wisdom becomes confined to the modern sense of *prudence*—the stoical self-control needed to delay gratification and work hard to attain one's private interests.[15] As I discuss in this section, when the public sphere is devalued and prudence becomes mere self-restraint, rhetoric loses its public significance and becomes confined to persuasive transactions between individual economic agents, which is about the only legitimate function left to persuasive public discourse in Smith's vision of civil society.

Civic humanists understood that the art of politics is less than a science but more than a craft, but Smith associated politics with the machinations of factional interests that could only disrupt the "natural laws" of political economy. For Smith, political economy was part of "the science of a legislator," a science opposed to "the skill of that insidious and crafty animal, vulgarly called a statesman or politician" (*Wealth Of Nations* 468; see also 428). The devaluation of practical politics and the valorization of science mark sharp departures from the civic view that citizens achieve their greatest potential by developing their practical wisdom through political action. The ideal of the citizen orator had made the established elite the spokesmen for the public interest, but Smith claimed authority in more modern terms by opposing factional interests to the disinterested expertise of the sciences. As the educated claimed authority not as citizen orators but as uninvolved observers, critical reflection became disengaged from practical action. Smith recognized that impartiality is rarely more than a pretense in party politics: "the real, revered, and impartial spectator, therefore is upon no occasion at a greater distance than amidst the violence and rage of contending parties" (*Theory of Moral Sentiments* 155–56). Only when we step outside a conflict and allow our passions to cool can we "identify ourselves, as it were, with the ideal man within the breast," but since the moment to act has passed, disinterested reason "can frequently produce nothing but vain regret and unavailing repentance" (158).

Just as Smith's ethics center not on actions but on reactions and motivations, his political economy makes political agency at best irrelevant to the public good. In the larger economy, moral sentiments work in concert with the ways of the world to reward the industrious and isolate the unjust, and thus "to promote the same great end, the order of the world, and the perfection and happiness of human nature" (*Theory of Moral Sentiments* 168). The "same great end" of human nature and political economy is unproblematic because "the Author of nature" has created "the oeconomy of nature." Our instincts for "self-preservation, and the propagation of the species" prompt us to work toward the ends that are best for us individually and the economy generally (78). However, when one shifts down from the larger economy to practical questions about how people can draw on shared values to resolve conflicts, one finds the same discontinuity between theory and action that is evident throughout Smith's science of political economy. Given the "depraved state of mankind," we cannot know the effects of our acts, and "fortune, which governs the world," makes the broader social consequences of our acts even more unknowable (78, 104). Since the results of human action "depend, not upon the agent, but upon fortune," the effects of an act are less morally significant than the sentiments that motivate it (93). While Smith's theories of human nature and political economy enabled moral philosophers to speak as social scientists, practical reason is devalued because the political outcomes of human action are unknowable and morally less significant than the sentiments that motivate an act.

In his last revisions of *The Theory of Moral Sentiments* before his death, Smith worked to remedy such practical limitations by adding a section, "Of the Character of Virtue," which he intended as "a practical system of Morality" (*Correspondence* 320). In these revisions, Smith tried to resolve the contradictions between sympathetic sentiments and an economy driven by self-interest. In his most elaborate discussion of the business ethic, Smith idealized the "prudent man" who learns the virtues of long-term investments from the impartial spectator:

> In the steadiness of his industry and frugality, in his steadily sacrificing the ease and enjoyment of the present moment for the probable expectation of the still greater ease and enjoyment of a more distant but more lasting period of time, the prudent man is always both supported and rewarded by the entire approbation of the impartial spectator, and of the representative of the impartial spectator, the man within the breast. (*Theory of Moral Sentiments* 215)

According to the editors of *The Theory of Moral Sentiments*, this passage shows that the economic man is a moral agent, thus obviating "*das* Adam Smith problem"—the problem of reconciling Smith's apparently contradictory emphases on self-interest in economics and sympathy in ethics (Raphael and Macfie 9). However, rather than associating prudence with practical reasoning toward shared ideals, Smith treats prudence as a means to self-interest. As a model of situated practical reasoning, prudence was integral to the civic ideal of the orator who speaks with practical wisdom for public virtue, but Smith's "prudent man" is a private man of business who confines himself as much as possible "to his own affairs" (215). Though duty may require "service to his country," he "would be much better pleased that the public business were well managed by some other person" (216). Prudence thus becomes confined to the self-interested reasonings of private business, particularly those concerning "the care of the health, of the fortune, of the rank and reputation of the individual" (213).

While civic humanists valued prudence as a means to achieve shared political goals by overcoming *fortuna*, fortune or fate, Smith identified prudence with the self-restraint needed to achieve personal fortune. Practical reasoning is devalued by being divorced from the domain where shared values are negotiated against practical problems. Smith's emphasis on personal sentiments and his lack of concern for practical reason in political action are consistent with his laissez-faire liberalism, and that philosophy was consistent with the experience of the middle-class reading public. While discussing how the rich depend on the middle classes for managers, Smith cautioned his readers not to let their personal ambitions become political:

> Are you in earnest resolved never to barter your liberty for the lordly servitude of a court, but to live free, fearless, and independent? There seems to be

one way to continue in that virtuous resolution; and perhaps but one. Never enter the place from whence so few have been able to return; never come within the circle of ambition; nor ever bring yourself into comparison with those masters of the earth who have already engrossed the attention of half mankind before you. (*Theory of Moral Sentiments* 57)

Though he may at times be duty bound to accept public offices, the self-restrained man of business avoids becoming involved in politics in order to maintain his freedom as an economic agent in civil society.

Smith's final revisions of *The Theory of Moral Sentiments* document his concern that commercialism was undermining the self-restraint necessary to maintain subservience within society. Along with adding a section on "practical morality," Smith revised the conclusion of the first part of the work. He deleted a concluding chapter that had used Stoicism to valorize self-control and added a chapter boldly titled, "Of the corruption of our moral sentiments which is occasioned by this disposition to admire the rich and the great, and to despise or neglect persons of poor and mean condition." Smith had originally concluded by discussing how a respect for one's betters instills social subservience. He had recommended that each individual stoically accept an assigned position in the social order, considering "himself as an atom, a particle, of an immense and infinite system, which must, and ought to be disposed of, according to the conveniency of the whole" (59). Stoicism had thus been used to valorize the self-control needed to prevent atomized individualism from fragmenting the social order, but as the changes he prophesied deepened, Smith clearly lost faith in classical doctrines of self-control (see Dwyer 169–70). In the new conclusion, he condemned the desire to imitate the tastes of the leisure class as "the great and most universal cause of the corruption of our moral sentiments" (61). He noted that "wealth and greatness are often regarded with the respect and admiration which are due only to wisdom and virtue" (61–62). While Smith felt that human nature was becoming corrupted by "fashion," he concluded that those in the "middling and inferior stations of life" have to maintain basic proprieties so that people will do business with them (63). As his anxieties about social diversification deepened, Smith could only retreat into a cynical reliance on middle-class proprieties because he did not conceive of civil society as a public sphere where political changes can be debated against shared values (see Dwyer 183).

Smith did allot one practical function to persuasive discourse in the public sphere, a function that like prudence is associated with the exercise of self-interest in civil society. In perhaps the best-known passage of *The Wealth of Nations*, Smith noted that "it is not from the benevolence of the butcher, the brewer, or the baker, that we expect our dinner, but from their regard to their own interest. We address ourselves, not to their humanity but to their self-love, and never talk to them of our own necessities but of their advantage" (27). Smith here upholds what Phillipson has described as "the moral value of the process of higgling and bargaining which took place in the market places of a free commercial society" ("Smith" 191). This commerce of discourse is defined in explicitly rhetorical terms in the parallel passage in the lectures on moral philosophy that Smith delivered at the same time that he was teaching a "private" class on rhetoric and belles lettres. Smith had used the same examples to make the same point about the natural "disposition to barter, which is the cause of the division of labour" (*Jurisprudence* 493). The division into classes is not due to the natural abilities of those with wealth: "the real foundation of it is that principle to perswade which so much prevails in human nature" (493). Thus, persuading people to do business is the basic dynamic that holds civil society together: "We ought then to cultivate the power of perswasion, and indeed we do so without intending it" because our "whole life is spent in the exercise of it" (494). While Smith thus recognized that rhetoric permeates public life, he dispersed it from political forums to the commerce of discourse in civil society, which works "freely" within an abstract economy governed by natural laws that operate beyond practical reason or collaborative decision making.

Another of the last revisions of *The Theory of Moral Sentiments* shows how Smith increasingly relied on the impartial spectator to maintain self-control in a commercial society where the only shared value is the virtue of self-interest.

> The man of real constancy and firmness, the wise and just man who has been thoroughly bred in the great school of self-command, in the bustle and business of the world. . . . He has never dared to forget for one moment the judgment which the impartial spectator would pass upon his sentiments and conduct. He has never dared to suffer the man within the breast to be absent one moment from his attention. With the eyes of this great inmate he has always been accustomed to regard whatever relates to himself. . . . He has been in the constant practice, and, indeed, under the constant necessity, of modelling, or of endeavouring to model, not only his outward conduct and behaviour, but, as much as he can even his inward sentiments and feelings, according to those of this awful and respectable judge. (146–47)

This "inmate" will serve as "judge" of every thought and feeling until the laws that govern his imprisonment have been internalized. This "demigod within the breast" personifies the God within man recast in the role of the objective observer (131). Functioning like a religious conscience, the spectator served to instill self-control in a society that was losing its faith in traditional values with the advance of atomized individualism.[16] The impartial spectator internalized the disinterested rationality of the sciences to fill the void left by the absence of shared values in a commercial society.

Smith's impartial spectator presents the most incisive image of the psychological dynamics of hegemony that I know of in the history of moral philosophy.[17] It aptly mirrors the experience of those whose social position leaves them with cultural insecurities that they attempt to resolve by dutifully imitating respected modes of behavior and expression. Smith's ethics valorized the virtues of assimilation, and he concluded his foundational contribution to the science of political economy by noting that provincials are best situated to judge politics because they are removed from the centers of conflict:

> In all great countries which are united under one uniform government, the spirit of party commonly prevails less in the remote provinces than in the centre of the empire. The distance of those provinces from the capital, from the principal seat of the great scramble of faction and ambition, makes them enter less into the views of any of the contending parties, and renders them more indifferent and impartial spectators of the conduct of all. The spirit of party prevails less in Scotland than in England. (945)

Here in the conclusion, the impartial spectator makes perhaps its only appearance in *The Wealth of Nations* as an image of the disinterested perspective of provincials who stand as mute observers at the periphery of the political sphere. Because Smith assumed that the "natural laws" of political economy will serve the public interest if left free from politics, he was not bothered by his own recognition that provincial spectators might be too removed from the centers of political debate to speak for their rights (see 619–22).

From its origins, laissez-faire liberalism has been more interested in protecting individual rights than in developing groups' abilities to express themselves politically. Smith assumed that "natural liberty" meant freedom from governmental controls, not the freedom to participate in political governance (*Wealth Of Nations* 687). The shift to laissez-faire liberalism from civic humanism marks a major transition in the practical politics of public discourse as well as in the political purposes of the humanities. That transition turned on a reorientation from the rhetorical stance of the civic orator to the critical stance of the disinterested observer. This stance was assumed by Smith and the other belletristic critics and scientistic moral philosophers who introduced modern cultural and political studies, and it was central to the broader effort to adapt education to a commercial society that did not have a clearly defined elite with the cultural authority to speak for the public. From the "new" rhetoric of the eighteenth century to the new rhetoric of the twentieth, rhetorical studies have tended to be justified primarily by the need for citizens to be effective critics of public discourse, not by their need to speak and write on public issues. American composition classes tend to be organized around the genesis from personal to academic essays, thus beginning with an autonomous individual and concluding with the conventions that demarcate the academy, especially its emphasis on disinterested argumentation. This emphasis on essayistic literacy was instituted by the first professors of English, as discussed in chapter 8, and that emphasis has remained a constant in rhetoric and composition because the modern humanities are oriented to educating the public, a public far more diverse than that of the polis but also farther removed from the centers of political power.

Conclusion: Rhetoric's Displacement by the Transition from Civic Humanism to Laissez-Faire Liberalism

Civic humanism provides a point of departure for assessing how the relationship of rhetoric and moral philosophy was reformulated when the humanities were first translated into English. Within the civic humanist tradition, rhetoric and moral philosophy shared a well-integrated theory of practical wisdom in political action personified by the ideal of the citizen orator who could speak to public conflicts with practical wisdom. The ideal of the "good man speaking well" clearly served to perpetuate the patriarchal authority of the upper classes, but the idealization of practical wisdom in civic action does provide a historical point of reference for examining how practical reasoning and purposeful action became redefined within higher education as it adapted to the diversification of educated society by taking on the mission of instilling sociability in educated individuals. Science expanded its claims to authority over a public sphere that ceased to be valued as a domain of purposeful action, and literature and art began to be considered as matters of personal genius rather than expressions of shared values. The formation of the science of political economy and the conflation of aesthetics and ethics in terms of personal refinement were important steps in the modern movement of the humanities toward the two cultures of the arts and sciences. Smith attempted to ameliorate the underlying trend toward atomized individualism by emphasizing sympathetic fellow-feelings and the internalization of shared values through the "impartial spectator." Such emphases were meant to maintain a personal sense of social responsibility, while depersonalizing political agency. The depoliticization of rhetoric was consistent with the transition from civic to liberal humanism, the devaluation of the public sphere, and the pressures on modern education to assimilate broader classes of students into the dominant culture.

Civic humanism had valorized the public sphere as a domain for resolving legal conflicts, deliberating over political policies, and celebrating civic values, while the natural law tradition tended to displace individuals from their political duties in order to claim a higher authority for individual rights. Civic humanists such as Adam Ferguson criticized commercial society for making the individual "a detached and solitary being" set "in competition with his fellow-creatures," whom "he deals with" as he "does with his cattle and his soil, for the sake of the profits they bring" (Ferguson, *Essay* 19). Smith also recognized that the specialization of labor alienated individuals from shared values, but he could offer nothing more than stoical self-control to remedy atomized individualism because he did not view the public sphere as a domain for resolving conflicts by renegotiating shared beliefs. While the "impartial spectator" originates in social interactions, its movement toward abstract ideals and disinterested objectivity rationalizes Scottish intellectuals' own disengagement from the cultural traditions and political conflicts of their society. The "great inmate" internalized this alienation from a devalued public sphere in the form of a second self who monitors every reaction, but is too disengaged to guide practical action. As ethics became personal and politics became economic, prudential public discourse became limited to the expression of self-interest. Civil society came to provide an alternative to a public that had become too impersonal to have value to individuals. As a result, civic virtue became sociability, and rhetoric became subordinated to stylistic criticism intended to instill the sensibility of the dispassionate observer.

While civic humanists educated a stable elite with a shared sense of tradition, the professors who translated the humanities into English faced broader classes of students. Rhetoric had been central to a classical conception of the humanities because the art of addressing the public was important to maintaining the leadership of the educated classes. Though rhetoricians were instrumental in introducing the modern culture into the university, rhetoric and composition were subordinated to criticism in the assumption that few students would have the occasion to speak as civic orators but all could advance in civil society if they mastered the tastes of the dominant culture. Smith used stylistic criticism to teach students the virtues of the plain and simple man of business with a stoical self-restraint personified by the impartial spectator. Students were taught to step back from political controversies, refine their sensibility, and leave the public good to the natural laws of political economy. The reconceptualization of civic virtue in terms of civility left politics in a separate domain that was irrelevant to the economic ambitions and cultural insecurities of the middle classes. Scottish moral philosophers were too removed from public life to develop a politically engaged humanism, and they taught their students that progress depended on cultural

assimilation and commercial expansion and not on political action. As a result, Scottish moral philosophers became practical moralists without a practical political voice, a problem that deepened when moral philosophers began
speaking as social scientists in the nineteenth century (see Bryson, "The
Emergence of the Social Sciences from Moral Philosophy"; Sloan, "The Teaching of Ethics in the American Undergraduate Curriculum, 1876–1976").

The first university professors to lecture on modern culture and politics
were interested in the social construction and psychological internalization
of changing values because their sectarian society was being culturally assimilated into a world empire. While the workings of cultural hegemony were
formalized and taught by Scottish professors of rhetoric and moral philosophy, the dissenters took a more explicitly political approach that was oriented
to teaching critical literacy because they were less concerned with cultural assimilation than with reforming the political restrictions they faced. Unlike
Smith and his colleagues, dissenters such as Priestley maintained that "in a
free country, where even private persons have much at stake, every man is
nearly interested in the conduct of his superiors, and cannot be an uncon-
cerned spectator of what is transacted by them" (*Works* 24: 24). It was not the
critically literate activist but the impartial spectator that became the characteristic stance of the modern humanities because it was more consistent with
the logic of laissez-faire liberalism. Smith's writings document the belletristic
and scientistic trends that began to shape the humanities when they were first
translated into English to meet the needs of educating broader classes of students than those who had been included in the educated culture when it was
bordered by learned languages. Following trends that are set out in Smith's
moral philosophy, Campbell's *Philosophy of Rhetoric* systematically redefined
the trivium of logic, grammar, and rhetoric according to the "science of
human nature," and Blair's popular *Lectures on Rhetoric and Belles Lettres*
taught the reading public to internalize the proprieties that distinguished
civil society from the popular culture and party politics.

7

Campbell's *Philosophy of Rhetoric*

and the "Science of Man"

> Here then is the only expedient, from which we can hope for success
> in our philosophical researches, to leave the tedious lingering
> method, which we have hitherto followed, and instead of taking now
> and then a castle or a village on the frontier, to march up directly to
> the capital or center of these sciences, to human nature itself; which
> being once masters of, we may every where else hope for an easy vic-
> tory. . . . There is no question of importance, whose decision is not
> compriz'd in the science of man; and there is none, which can be de-
> cided with any certainty, before we become acquainted with that sci-
> ence. In pretending therefore to explain the principles of human
> nature, we in effect propose a compleat system of the sciences built on
> a foundation almost entirely new, and the only one upon which they
> can stand with any security.
>
> —Hume, *Treatise of Human Nature*

THE INTRODUCTION TO Hume's *Treatise of Human Nature: Being an Attempt to introduce the experimental Method of Reasoning into Moral Subjects*
(1739–1740) set out his project to conquer "human nature itself" and use it as
a base for new systems of "*Logic, Morals, Criticism and Politics*" (43). In the introduction to *An Inquiry Concerning Human Understanding* (1751), Hume explicitly distinguished his approach to "moral philosophy or the science of
human nature" from those that treat "man chiefly as born for action" and en-
list the arts of "poetry and eloquence" in moving audiences with scenes
drawn from "common life" (15–16). Hume thus distanced his project from the
traditional concern for purposeful action that had associated moral philosophy with rhetoric and the affairs of common life, and even his worst critics
accepted his invitation to apply a "microscope" to their mind to examine
their psychological reactions to experience (*Inquiry* 74). To preserve the logic

of experience against Hume's criticisms of cause and effect reasoning, Thomas Reid and his colleagues established a mental faculty they called "common sense." Commonsense philosophers such as Reid, Henry Home, and George Campbell were instrumental in defining the "new" logic according to the experimental reasoning of the sciences (see Howell). Campbell's *Philosophy of Rhetoric* (1776) not only made a prominent contribution to the "new" logic, it systematically redefined rhetoric according to the "science of human nature," and it also included the first concerted attempt to formalize correct usage by inductively generalizing from existing conventions. Thus, while it was Hume who most aptly set out the modern project of using "the scientific conquest of nature for the scientific conquest of man" (Marcuse xiv), it was his critics who programmatically reconceived the three language arts according to that project.

In terms that echo Hume, Campbell set out to use "the science of human nature to ascertain with greater precision, the radical principles of that art, whose object it is, by the use of language, to operate on the soul of the hearer, in the way of informing, convincing, pleasing, moving, or persuading" (*Philosophy of Rhetoric* lxvii). Campbell's *Philosophy of Rhetoric* has been "widely acknowledged" as a "turning point in the history of rhetorical theory" (Bevilacqua, "Philosophical Origins" 1; see also Ehninger; Bitzer). While Campbell was the most systematic advocate of the "new" rhetoric and the most "liberal" proponent of defining correct usage according to literate usage, he was also an important advocate of the commonsense philosophy that has been widely criticized for propagating a close-minded empiricism that upheld established beliefs as the dictates of nature (see, for example, Martin, May, and Berlin, "Writing Instruction"). Debates over whether morality was a matter of nature or convention have shaped the shared development of rhetoric and moral philosophy ever since Plato condemned the sophists as relativists. Hume and the commonsense philosophers were having much the same sort of debate, and for the same sort of reasons: established beliefs had ceased to seem natural because society was changing and becoming more aware of the diversity of cultural conventions. Campbell's reconceptualization of the trivium was part of the broader effort to establish "natural" foundations not just for the conventions of discourse but also for the ethical and political values that had been called into question by the formation of commercial society, the expansion of print literacy, and the emergence of science as an authoritative system of knowledge.

From ancient times, rhetoric had been criticized by philosophers for concerning itself with the realm of *doxa,* in the dual sense of mere opinion and appearance. The term at issue in the debate between Hume and the commonsense philosophers contains a similar dichotomy of related but distinct concepts. The word *sense* is often used to refer to a natural sense or faculty, but it also means the sense or meaning that is created from an experience or text. Both senses of the word are included within the historical development of the term *common sense*. The term has been used to refer both to a natural faculty that makes sense of the input from the five senses and to the beliefs held in common by a group or society. Commonsense philosophers often equivocated between these senses, sometimes appealing to the good sense of the common person, and at others asserting that a natural sense demonstrated the non-sense of skepticism. The former appeal invites people to question ideas against their experiences. Though it may be merely a rhetorical question, intended to instill and not really to challenge the idea, such an appeal can also be rhetorical in a broader sense, for it makes shared beliefs a site for intellectual reflection, popular debate, and possibly even critical transformation. On the other hand, when common sense is defined as a natural faculty, received beliefs and customs are placed beyond debate, and intellection and intellectuals claim a natural authority that places them above the realm of the common experience, enabling them to speak as scientists but leaving them unable to speak to the public in a dialectical fashion from received beliefs in social action.

The realm of common sense—the often tacit domain of conventional values and popular beliefs—became a site for debate because the authority of traditional beliefs and traditional intellectuals was being challenged by changes in systems of knowledge and class relations. "It was natural that 'common sense' should have been exalted," according to Gramsci, "when there was a reaction against the principle of authority represented by Aristotle and the Bible. It was discovered indeed that in 'common sense' there was a certain measure of 'experimentalism' and direct observation of reality, though empirical and limited" (*Prison Notebooks* 348). Commonsense philosophers tried to answer the question of how moral authority can be generated from empirical observation, a question that arose almost as soon as the scientific method was applied to moral philosophy. Such questions had to be answered if the educated were to maintain their power to speak for traditional values and thus determine whose traditions would be valued. As Gramsci observed, "the relation between common sense and the upper level of philosophy is assured by 'politics,' the political relations of the 'intellectuals' and the 'simple'" (331). By defining common sense not as the simple good sense of the common person but as a natural sense, the "science of human nature" enabled traditional intellectuals to preserve their authority as natural and hence unquestionable, even as the basis of that authority was shifting from the domain of natural religion to the natural sciences.

Clerics could speak for science against skepticism because they had faith in the providential order of human psychology and political economy. From his first significant publication, Campbell aligned himself with those who turned to common sense to claim a natural authority for traditional beliefs. Campbell's *Dissertation on Miracles* (1762) was an attempt to defend the veracity of historical testimonies to miracles against Hume's critique of the empirical evidence for them in *Philosophical Essays Concerning Human Understanding* (1748). As principal and professor of divinity at Marischal College, Campbell participated in the Aberdeen Philosophical Society with two of the leading proponents of commonsense philosophy, Thomas Reid and James Beattie.[1] The group was obsessed with Hume's writings, and its concerns shaped the inception and composition of Campbell's *Philosophy of Rhetoric*, portions of which were first written for delivery to the group. Like the other defenders of common sense, Campbell drew on Hume's introspective examinations of human nature while attempting to curtail the general evolution of empiricism toward skepticism. Aberdeen commonsense philosophers such as Reid and Campbell were among the leading proponents of the "new" logic, and the effort to reform the curriculum according to the logic of the sciences received its greatest institutional expression at Aberdeen, as I discussed in chapter 5. A brief review of how the natural law tradition contributed to the development of "scientism" at Aberdeen will thus complement my preceding analysis of the transmission of the civic and natural law traditions through Hutcheson to Smith.

As an introduction to the debate over common sense, I begin with a brief review of the emergence of the "science of man" at Aberdeen, particularly in the works of Reid's teacher George Turnbull. Turnbull first laid out some elements of commonsense philosophy, particularly its attempt to define human nature by the empirical method of natural philosophy. Like Hutcheson, Turnbull is a transitional figure whose works document how the "science of man" emerged out of the study of pneumatology as moral philosophers adapted doctrines of natural laws and civic virtues to the effort to advance the enlightenment project of Bacon and Newton. The faith in the providential order of human nature enabled moral philosophers to synthesize natural law doctrines with the methods of natural philosophy. As Hume's kinsman Henry Home noted in the first response to Hume in defense of common sense, "all morality" is founded on "the laws of our nature, . . . of which every person partakes who is not a monster" (*Essays* 38). For Home and his successors, the workings of common sense could be studied in a Newtonian fashion because human nature is a "complex machine, composed of various principles of motion, which may be conceived as so many springs and weights, counteracting and balancing one another" (140–41). The belief that psychological faculties were governed by natural laws provided the basic justification for formalizing logical, grammatical, and rhetorical conventions according to the "science of man." The turn toward the psychology of the autonomous individual is the definitive step in the transition from classicism to modernism, and it was instrumental in orienting modern composition and literary studies to the disciplinary project of molding personal character through the teaching of discourse.

The "Science of Man" at Aberdeen

Hume's *Treatise of Human Nature: Being an Attempt to introduce the experimental Method of Reasoning into Moral Subjects* was not alone in arguing that the "science of man" should be the foundation for "all the sciences" (42). In the same year that the third book of the *Treatise* appeared, George Turnbull's *Principles of Moral Philosophy* (1740) appeared with a title page emblazoned with a motto from Bacon heralding the benefits of applying the empirical method of natural philosophy to moral philosophy.[2] In his dedication, Turnbull stated that he attempted "to account for MORAL, as the great *Newton* has taught us to explain NATURAL Appearances" (1: i). The logic of science would first be applied to reforming the curriculum at Aberdeen, as discussed in chapter 5, and those reforms were consistent with Turnbull's *Observations Upon Liberal Education* (1742), which had argued that all the liberal arts should be founded upon an "experimental knowledge of human nature." Upon such a foundation,

> every conclusion is deduced from internal principles and dispositions of the human mind, and their operations, which are well known to all who have carefully studied mankind; and is therefore confirmed by experience, in the same manner that natural philosophers establish their physical doctrines, upon observations evincing certain properties of bodies and laws of motion. (1)

As a regent at Marischal from 1721 to 1727, Turnbull's "Newtonianism" had a formative impact on his students and his successors, including Thomas Reid, David Fordyce, Alexander Gerard, and James Beattie.[3] These moral philosophers made Aberdeen a center for the study of the "science of man," with Reid a leading advocate of "the ideology of scientism" (Wood, "Science and Virtue" 146).

Turnbull advanced those trends that would lead to moral philosophy being called *moral science* by his successors at Aberdeen, but Turnbull was also a practical moralist who drew on the civic humanist tradition to argue for an active engagement in public politics. Like Hutcheson, Turnbull's political philosophy drew on classical civic humanists and Commonwealthmen such as Harrington and Sydney. From such sources, Turnbull argued for the existence of a "natural aristocracy"—men of "superior wisdom" whose right to lead (but not to command) is exemplified by their ability to speak eloquently to the public (Heineccius 2: 21). Turnbull's civic orientation is most evident in his claims that an active public life fulfills the highest potential of human nature, and thus political freedom must include the rights to speak and act, rather than just the right to be left alone to pursue one's private interest. Such positions were influential in America, with Turnbull cited by Witherspoon and Franklin to support educational reforms at Princeton and Philadelphia. Like other Scottish moral philosophers, Turnbull broadened civic assumptions about public life to include "well employed industry," or what John Witherspoon termed "virtuous industry" (Turnbull, *Observations* 191; see Miller, Introduction, *Witherspoon*).

Though he was less reductivist and more practical than many Newtonian moral philosophers, Turnbull was committed to the Newtonian project of reducing diverse phenomena to a single governing principle. Turnbull felt that "perhaps the moon and planets are not more regular in their motions, to the eyes of an astronomer, than human affairs are to those" with a knowledge of history and human nature (*Observations* 76). While he hoped that moral philosophers would one day be able to establish laws that would have the explanatory power of gravity, Turnbull was attentive to the diversity of practical reasoning in varied fields of study and experience: "the nature and degrees of moral, probable, or historical evidence, tho' left out of what is commonly called logic," are perhaps "the most essential part of a science that merits to be called the art of reasoning. . . . And it can never be more successfully taught than in reading history" (*Observations* 383–84). While induction provided the paradigm for "experimental" reasoning, Turnbull at points acknowledged that diverse phenomena may have a logic of their own. Turnbull's successors at Aberdeen followed through on this line of reasoning to argue for replacing instruction in syllogistic reasoning with studies of the inferential modes of reasoning used in various disciplines. The "science of man" unified the curriculum and the systems of thought it formalized by founding logical and sociological processes upon the psychological laws of human nature. At King's College, Aberdeen, in 1753, Turnbull's student Thomas Reid helped establish a curriculum that culminated with a year devoted to "the Philosophy of the Human mind and the Sciences that Depend upon it," with the latter including "Logic, Rhetorick, The Laws of Nature and Nations, Politicks, Oeconomicks, the fine Arts and Natural Religion" (qtd. Wood, *Aberdeen* 67). According to Wood's account, these reforms followed from the doctrines of Turnbull.

Turnbull's edition of Heineccius's *Methodical System of Universal Law; or the Law of Nature and Nations* (1742) shows how Newtonian moral philosophers drew on natural law doctrines to maintain a faith in the providential order of the world. Turnbull discussed Heineccius's positions in long notes and supplementary essays that form a rich dialogue between the empiricism of Scottish moral philosophy and the rationalism of Continental jurisprudence. While praising Harrington and others for reasoning "from natural causes . . . as natural philosophers do," Turnbull criticized Heineccius for not founding the "*moral state*" on the "*physical state*": "For whence can a man's duties or obligations . . . be inferred but from his physical state, from his frame, condition, rank and circumstances" (Heineccius 2: 119, 18). More explicitly than Hutcheson, and perhaps even Smith, Turnbull reconceived political doctrines of natural law according to the logic of the natural sciences: "Natural Philosophy is . . . the science of the laws, according to which nature operates in producing its effects, and to which human art must conform in order to produce certain effects. And the settled methods, according to which nature works, and human arts must work, in order to produce certain effects are called *laws of nature*" (Heineccius 2: 247). The natural laws of politics would be determined by an inductive investigation of history and "experimental" inquiries into psychology. The Newtonian impetus to reduce diverse beliefs and behaviors to a single governing law such as gravity or supply and demand marks the historic juncture where moral philosophy began to move toward the social sciences, and Turnbull helped institute that transition in higher education.

Like most Scottish moral philosophers, Turnbull began his course on moral philosophy with pneumatology in the assumption that human nature provided the natural laws that governed historical changes and cultural differences. Like Hutcheson, Smith, and the commonsense philosophers, Turnbull assumed that a natural sense common to all worked in concert with the general political economy to promote the good of humanity. Whether termed sympathy or a moral or common sense, this assumption had a complex history that was related to the concept of a *sensus communis*. From the classical period, *sensus communis* was used in varied ways to refer to innate reason, shared beliefs, the sense that synthesizes sensory input, or civic virtue. This last sense is present in Cicero's works, which associated *sensus communis* with *humanitas* or *communis humanitas* and cited it in the context of "common practice, custom and speech" in *De Oratore* (1.3.12; see Bugter). The link between Cicero and the moral-sense doctrines that influenced Smith is

Shaftesbury's "*Sensus Communis:* An Essay on the Freedom of Wit and Humour," which treated the common sense as the source of the sympathetic feelings for others that promote the common good (see Van Holthoon). Civic humanists from Cicero through Vico tended to identify common sense more with the common beliefs that were imbedded in social institutions and shared traditions, while the natural law tradition founded its claim to authority not on civic duties but on the faculty of natural reason that worked in concert with the rational order of the cosmos. However one plots the complex history of common sense, it is an historical point of contact between evolving conceptions of the individual psyche and the body politic, sometimes serving as a site for debates of shared conventions, and at others as a strategy for placing such matters above discussion as a matter of natural law.[4]

Turnbull's emphasis on common sense was his most important contribution to the Aberdeen school of moral philosophy, according to Norton (see *Hume* 163–70). A commonsensical faith in the providential order of experience continued to link natural philosophy, natural religion, and moral philosophy in the works of the moral philosophers who succeeded Turnbull, most notably David Fordyce from 1742 to 1751, and James Beattie from 1760 to 1797. However, the defense of common sense became more strident after Hume demonstrated that assumptions about final causes were inconsistent with the logic of human experience because cause and effect relations were merely mental associations and not certain evidence of a natural order created by a governing intelligence. The concept of a common sense as an innate mental faculty served to reassert the natural authority of established beliefs, while the debate over the nature of common sense helped reorient the study of rhetoric away from popular conflicts over shared values to the laws governing human nature.

Insofar as *common sense* is defined as the knowledge held in common by a society—the often tacit assumptions people commonly draw on to make moral decisions and act on social issues—then common sense must be a concern of rhetoric and moral philosophy if they are to be dialectically engaged with the popular experience. Ironically, this conception of common sense is closer to Hume's position than it is to the common-sense philosophers, who defined common sense as a natural faculty rather than as a body of shared conventions and beliefs. The reaction to Hume led to a narrowing focus on epistemology that limited the sciences of man to the "science of human nature." Like Hume, Turnbull published on political history and theory, but in the works published by the two leading commonsense philosophers, Thomas Reid and Dugald Stewart, moral philosophy became confined almost entirely to the "science of mind."[5] Following this introspective turn away from the broader historical and political concerns of Turnbull, rhetoric came to concentrate on the effects of discourse on the individual auditor and became disengaged from public debates of political controversies and changing values.

Making a Sense of the Common

The "new" rhetoric and logic were both heavily influenced by the commonsense school of moral philosophy that included Henry Home, Beattie, Reid, Stewart, and Campbell, as well as the most important rhetorician in early America, John Witherspoon, whose interest in epistemology was subordinate to his practical engagement with politics (see Miller, Introduction). Like other defenders of common sense, Campbell accepted Hume's epistemological line of inquiry but attempted to check its skeptical conclusions by positing innate propensities to believe in the self and the world, concluding that those who deny such beliefs are beyond reason. Following Hume, Campbell assumed that impressions are associated within the mind according to three relations (resemblance, contiguity, and cause and effect); such impressions are to be categorized in terms of their vivacity; vivid impressions encourage belief; passion is the source of action; and sympathy with others moves us with the passions that they feel (see Bitzer). Against Hume's critique of cause and effect and the reliability of the senses, Campbell defended common sense as essential "to all deductions concerning life and existence," particularly "moral reasoning" (*Philosophy of Rhetoric* 42). Before examining how Campbell and his colleagues redefined all three of the language arts to adapt them to the "science of human nature," I want to review what was at issue in the debate over common sense itself.

Campbell and the commonsense philosophers strenuously opposed Hume's skepticism because it directly challenged their effort to apply the scientific method to the study of human nature to demonstrate the natural order of Providence.[6] Hume's critique of the empirical method is well known. After positing that only the principle of cause and effect could possibly provide a "just inference from one object to another," he demonstrated that "*reasonings concerning causes and effects are deriv'd from nothing but custom*" (*Treatise* 145, 234). We can thus "never really advance a step beyond ourselves," and our self is shown to be but "a bundle or collection of different perceptions, which succeed each other with inconceivable rapidity, and are in perpetual flux" (116, 300). If we cannot rely on cause and effect relations in our own fluctuating experiences, we certainly cannot assume that "*whatever begins to exist, must have a cause of existence*," which was precisely the assumption that Turnbull and others had used to justify studying nature as God's handiwork (*Treatise* 126; Turnbull, *Observations* 353). Hume also pushed doctrines of moral sentiments toward subjectivism by noting that "when you pronounce any action or character to be vicious, you mean nothing, but from the constitution of your nature you have a feeling or sentiment of blame from the contemplation of it" (*Treatise* 520). Hume's *Treatise* treated vice and virtue as merely "perceptions in the mind," and his *Enquiry Concerning the Principles of Morals* defined virtue as "*whatever mental action or quality gives to a spectator the pleasing sentiment of approbation*" (520–21; *Philosophy* 265). From this perspective, justice was nothing more than an "artificial virtue" that "arises artificially, tho' necessarily from education, and human conventions," as was also true "of allegiance, of the laws of nations, of modesty, and of good-manners" (*Treatise* 628). With Hume, empiricism thus seemed to lead only to atomized individualism, and moral sentiments threatened to become nothing more than mere subjectivism.

Reid and his colleagues reacted to the passage from Hume's *Treatise* quoted at the beginning of this chapter by condemning him for "promising with a grave face, no less than a complete system of the sciences, upon a foundation entirely new—to with, that of human nature—when the intention of the whole work is to shew, that there is neither human nature nor science in the world" (*Works* 101). As Reid understood it, the problem was not just Hume's skepticism about the reliability of the senses but the empiricist definition of human nature as a *tabula rasa,* with the atomistic tendencies of such a definition evident even in Locke (Reid, *Works* 103; see also Campbell, *Rhetoric* 262). The doctrine of the moral sense had been sufficient to refute the egoism of Hobbes and Mandeville and defend benevolence as an innate part of human nature. To refute Hume's skepticism, the moral sense was broadened into a "common sense," an innate set of propensities to believe in the stability of the interpretive subject and the objective world. Commonsense philosophers repeatedly stressed that the world is as we see it, that common language and common opinion testify to the veracity of our sense of the world, and that the denial of common sense was simply nonsense (*Rhetoric* 42). Commonsense philosophers sought to claim a middle ground between empiricism and rationalism, taking from the former the method of induction, and relying on the latter for the view that certain propensities of human nature are prior to experience and cannot be reduced to sensory phenomena. From this position, commonsense philosophers could claim to be advancing the "science of human nature" without calling into question the truths of natural religion.

The reactionary tendencies of commonsense philosophy were first criticized by Joseph Priestley's *Examination of Dr. Reid's "Inquiry in the Human Mind on the Principles of Common Sense," Dr. Beattie's "Essay on the Nature and Immutability of Truth," and Dr. Oswald's "Appeal to Common Sense in Behalf of Religion"* (1774) (see Bevilacqua, "Campbell, Priestley, and the Controversy Concerning Common Sense"). According to Priestley, "a panic fear of scepticism" had led to the "triumph of sense over reason," an unnecessary triumph because Hume's critique of empiricism was but a "pitiful sophism" that did not hinder the advance of knowledge (*Examination* 205, 7). As a materialist, Priestley had no doubts about the logic of cause and effect, and he viewed common sense as nothing more than conventional associations. As a dissenter, Priestley objected on political as well as intellectual grounds to any attempt to claim a natural authority for social conventions because he did not feel there was any natural obligation to obey established authorities (230).[7] According to many accounts, commonsense philosophy's tacit support for the status quo helped establish it as the dominant educational philosophy in Restoration France and post-Revolutionary America, where it "offered an enlightened and extremely effective means of controlling the imagination to a society which believed in the need for such control" (Martin viii; see also May). Drawing on such accounts, historians of rhetoric such as James Berlin have attributed the close-minded conservativism of modern composition teaching to the ongoing influence of commonsense realism.

Commonsense moral philosophy served conservative purposes insofar as it treated received beliefs as the dictates of nature, but the appeal to common sense also had democratic potential. Reid did place certain "truths" above rational proof, arguing that those who had attempted to prove them logically had done more harm than good (*Works* 713). Commonsense philosophers sought to explain how and why people behave morally in everyday life, and they recognized that speculative reasoning played a small role in common life. Reid often claimed to speak for the shared beliefs of the "common man" (*Works* 100). Reid sometimes treated "the *common sense of mankind*" in terms of the sort of shared knowledge that directs "the common affairs of life," and he accepted that "*good sense* . . . is often found in those who are not acute in reasoning" (*Works* 118). Reid's tendency to equivocate between common sense as a natural faculty and the good sense of the common person was criticized by Benjamin Rush, who suggested to Thomas Paine that he use the title *Common Sense* for his critique of conventional political assumptions; and Scottish commonsense philosophers also influenced other advocates of the American Revolution, most notably Thomas Jefferson, who avidly studied the works of Reid, Home, and Hume throughout his life. According to Garry Wills, such influences led Jefferson to conclude that the Declaration of Independence had simply served "to place before mankind the common sense of the subject" (qtd. *Inventing America* 190).[8] However, to find a philosophy of "common sense" that is grounded in an examination of the social construction of shared knowledge, one must look not to the commonsense philosophers so much as to Smith and especially Hume, who was a "common-sense moralist and skeptical metaphysician," according to Norton.

Unfortunately, it was as a natural sense and not as common opinion that "common sense" was invoked to redefine rhetoric and moral philosophy according to the "science of man." The commonsense philosophers contributed to a broad reassessment of the three language arts: logic was defined not as the dialectical art of reasoning from shared beliefs but as inductive generalizations from the individual experience; rhetoric was systematically reconceived according to the mental faculties of the autonomous auditor; and grammatical conventions were standardized to distinguish correct English from common usage. All of these efforts were guided by commonsense philosophers' attempts to define the human experience by the logic of the sciences. In fact all four of the "new" logicians whom Howell concluded his account with were commonsense philosophers—Reid, Home, Campbell, and Stewart (Howell 372–437). Commonsense philosophy also shaped Campbell's effort to define the purposes of rhetoric according to the mental faculties addressed rather than by the social ends achieved. While one might expect a proponent of inductive reasoning to begin with examples of how rhetoric effects change in common life, Campbell's analysis is oriented not to scenes of political debate and moral conflict but to introspective examinations of how language affects the mental faculties. In rhetoric, as in moral philosophy, commonsense philosophy helped shift the focus from the sociological to the psychological, and rhetoric became more concerned with the workings of the individual consciousness than with the practical art of drawing on common beliefs to speak to public issues.

The Redefinition of Logic, Rhetoric, and Grammar by the "Science of Man"

Few theorists have reformulated all three of the language arts as systematically or as influentially as George Campbell. Campbell's criticism of the syllogism, according to Howell, is "the most famous chapter on logic in any rhetorical treatise ever written" (401). Campbell's canons of "grammatical criticism" were used to standardize usage in English classrooms and textbooks into the twentieth century, and his introspective approach to rhetoric "shaped the philosophical context in which rhetoric would be defined throughout the nineteenth century" (Johnson, *Nineteenth-Century Rhetoric* 20). Campbell was more systematic than other epistemologically oriented rhetoricians such as Priestley, but in concentrating more systematically on the workings of the faculties, Campbell paid less attention to actual rhetorical practices than Priestley had. Campbell was less interested in the practical art of rhetoric than in formalizing discourse as a rule-governed system founded on the laws of the "science of man." Campbell's theory of discourse is the clearest example of how language studies were transformed by the transition from classicism to modernism, with rhetoric moving decisively away from its dialectical engagement with popular opinion to become a vehicle for constituting the autonomous individual according to the logic of science. Crowley's *Methodical Memory* has examined this disciplinary project in considerable detail, and so I only briefly review how it systematically redefined the core of the humanities, the three language arts of logic, rhetoric, and grammar.

Commonsense philosophers shared an allegiance to the logic of reasoning inductively from the individual experience.[9] Reid's influential "Account of Aristotle's Logic" first appeared in a work on cultural anthropology, *The History of Man* (1774), by the first advocate of common sense, Henry Home. According to Laudan, Reid "was the first major British philosopher to take Newton's opinions on induction, causality, and hypothesis seriously" (106). As advocates of Newtonianism, Reid and commonsense philosophers had a formative impact on the style, epistemology, and methodology of British science (see Olson's *Scottish Philosophy and British Physics, 1750–1880*).[10] Reid opposed the logic of scientific inquiry to traditional modes of reasoning and concluded that while the logic of Locke and Newton had established "laboratories and observatories" to advance knowledge, the syllogism had only produced "numberless disputes, and numberless sects" (Reid, *Works* 712). Echoing such views, Campbell argued that because a syllogism merely reformulates conclusions contained in its premises, it cannot generate new knowledge. Thus a syllogism is but "*logomachy,* or in plain English, the art of fighting with words and about words" (Campbell, *Rhetoric* 69). Campbell, Reid, Kames, and Stewart were instrumental in establishing induction as the paradigm for educated inquiry according to Howell, who treated the transition from deduction to induction as an historical advance within the history of ideas rather than as a paradigm shift related to broader changes in the sociology of knowledge.

With the commonsense school of moral philosophy, the paradigm for the generation of knowledge shifted decisively from deductions from received traditions to inductive generalizations from the individual experience. This transition shaped the curricular reforms at Aberdeen discussed in chapter 5. The educated culture was expanding its claims to knowledge beyond the well-demarcated sphere of the learned tradition and asserting its authority over broader social, technological, and economic trends. Deduction could not expand the power of knowledge, for according to its critics, a syllogism contained its conclusions in its premises and depended on established beliefs for those premises. Most importantly, the syllogism assumed an audience who shared its traditions and was thus able to value its ability to "invent" new insights from received beliefs. Deductive reasoning, rhetorical common-places, and classical arts of invention lost their validity as the educated cul-ture expanded to include groups who did not share a clearly defined set of beliefs from which one could readily generate answers to questions about common experience. The classical ideal of the citizen orator who speaks with practical wisdom from shared beliefs was discussed in the last chapter, but the classical art of reasoning from popular opinions was dialectic. As discussed in Aristotle's *Topics* and by later civic humanists, dialectic was the model of practical reasoning to be used in popular argumentation because it worked from assumptions held by "all, most, or by the most notable" and refined that common sense into the best sense possible in the indeterminant situations where more rigorous demonstrations are impossible (*Works* 104a 9–10). Commonsense philosophers helped to popularize the logic of science by claiming that it is nothing more than common sense, but commonsense phi-losophy was not dialectical in either the classical or contemporary senses of that term because it did not work from received beliefs but from natural laws.

Following through on the premises of the "new" logic, Campbell's *Philos-ophy of Rhetoric* redefined rhetoric according to the "science of human na-ture" (lxvii). Campbell broadened "eloquence" beyond the classical art of persuasive oratory to define it in more modern terms as "that art or talent by which the discourse is adapted to its end." He then reoriented the study of rhetoric from the political to the psychological domain and categorized the ends of discourse by the mental faculties that are engaged by each genre: "all the ends of speaking are reducible to four; every speech being intended to en-lighten the understanding, to please the imagination, to move the passions, or to influence the will" (1). The aims addressed by each are information or conviction, admiration (including "the sublime"), animation, and persua-sion. Campbell then discussed the means of addressing the individual facul-ties and the characteristics of each type of discourse (2–4).

As in Hume, Smith, and the Hutchesonian tradition generally, *sentiment* and *sympathy* were key terms for explaining the workings of "eloquence."

According to Campbell, "it is the intention of eloquence to convey our sentiments into the minds of others," with sympathy the "main engine by which oratory operates on the passions" (139, 96). Sympathy was central to Smith's theory of moral sentiments, and Campbell drew on such sources when he concluded that "what is addressed solely to the moral powers of the mind, is not so properly denominated the pathetic, as the *sentimental*" (*Rhetoric* 131). Like Smith, Campbell defined rhetoric in terms that were consistent with the sentiments of conversible society but which were carefully distanced from the contestatory nature of political debate. Following Hume, Campbell treated moving the passions as a matter of "enlivening and invigorating the ideas of imagination" so that they "resemble the impressions of sense and the traces of memory" (94). While he could not accept Hume's view that a belief is nothing more than a "lively idea," Campbell agreed that "lively ideas have a stronger influence than faint ideas to induce belief," and he devoted most of the third part of *The Philosophy of Rhetoric* to stylistic criticisms of how "vivacity" is created (73; see Hume, *Treatise* 134). Campbell focused on how mental impressions are represented in discourse because he understood language in Baconian terms as a window on the mind—a transparent medium for conveying vivid impressions that will engage the imagination to move the will to act. Such conceptions focused attention not on the craft of composing and using language purposefully but on the disciplinary project of instilling a respect for the laws that governed the natural workings of the mental faculties.

Following the epistemological turn of moral philosophy, Campbell reoriented rhetoric away from practical action toward the psychological reactions of sensitive auditors. Like other "new" rhetoricians, Campbell assumed that the art of rhetoric could offer little aid with the invention of discourse and that it was largely a matter of managing the communication of mental impression through discourse. As Crowley has discussed, "eighteenth-century discourse theory displaced inventive potential out of communal discourse and relocated it within individual minds" (68). Even when discussing "moral reasoning," Campbell focused on empirical evidence and the mental processes of the isolated individual and ignored the dialectical art of drawing on shared values to resolve public conflicts (Campbell, *Rhetoric* 43–58; see S. Crowley 21–22).[11] Campbell's theory of rhetoric centered on the isolated auditor who exists in an idealized domain that is as untroubled by party interests and traditional prejudices as the bourgeois reading public and liberal political economy were understood to be. According to Crowley, Campbell's conception of the sphere of rhetoric is "curiously serene and univocal: communication takes place in an ideal discursive world where rhetors always know exactly what they intend, and where, with the proper care, their thoughts and intentions always and inevitably make their way into the receptive minds of capable listeners and readers" (S. Crowley 30). Within this discursive domain, one need only establish the presence of a belief and it will be accepted, for a disinterested appraisal will demonstrate whether it is common sense or non-sense.

While Campbell rejected the basic assumptions of classical rhetoric, he relied on it for the more practical elements of his theory, particularly its traditional emphasis on the elements of the rhetorical situation. For each of the three domains of public discourse ("the bar, the pulpit, and the senate"), he discussed "the speaker, the hearers or persons addressed, the subject, the occasion, and the end in view, or the effect intended to be produced by the discourse" (*Rhetoric* 99). Despite the practical potential of this conception of rhetoric as situated purposeful action, Campbell did not actually examine existing rhetorical practices. When he did refer to contemporary public discourse, he used terms like "fanaticism," and "party-spirit" to dismiss the divisive rhetoric of party politics (109, 97). Campbell's philosophy of rhetoric, like that of Smith, rested on the ideal of "sympathy," an ideal that was consistent with their idealization of polite sentiment but that was incompatible with the sort of conflicts that are an undeniable part of politics. Amid such conflicts, "party-men" lose "all sympathy" for their opponents (97). Like other Moderate clergy such as Blair, Campbell showed little faith in the good sense of the common people: "from a consciousness, it would seem, of their own incapacity to guide themselves, they are ever prone blindly to submit to the guidance of some popular orator" (97–98). Campbell's chapter on the oratory of the bar, the pulpit, and the senate is the most practical one in his work, but it is also one of the shortest. It is confined to a "cursory view of the differences" among the types of discourse intended to "exemplify and illustrate" his general "philosophy of rhetoric," which is centered on the psychology of the individual auditor, not public discourse (99).

While the influence of Campbell's theories of logic and rhetoric has been well established, less attention has been paid to his efforts to apply the scientific method to grammatical studies, despite the fact that fully two-thirds of *The Philosophy of Rhetoric* is devoted to grammatical analyses of the stylistic characteristics that are introduced in the first chapter (most notably, perspicuity, vivacity, elegance, and vehemence) (see Ulman). While his rhetorical theory defined and modeled mental responses to discourse, his extensive attention to "verbal criticism" was meant to bring order to discourse itself. The two longest chapters in the book are on perspicuity and vivacity and include elaborate categorizations of faults in word choice and sentence style. The ideal is a clear style that unproblematically reproduces "lively ideas" (221). This ideal and Campbell's standards for judging usage would be used to correct students' essays long after Campbell's *Philosophy of Rhetoric* was superseded by composition texts such as those of Alexander Bain. Like other moral philosophers and logicians at Aberdeen, Bain was committed to the project of applying the logic of the natural sciences to the study of human nature in order to determine the laws that governed human expression and human experience generally.[12]

While he assumed that "language is purely a species of fashion," Campbell set out to establish a scientific authority for grammar as "a collection of general observations methodically digested" (*Rhetoric* 139, 140). A grammarian was to observe patterns of "general usage" and select those usages that are *reputable* (not simply "common"), *national* (as opposed to "provincial" or "foreign"), and *present* (not "obsolete" but not merely "fashionable" either). Where usage is "divided," the grammarian sought perspicuity and simplicity by applying nine principles of "verbal criticism" to make the language "univocal" (151–69). Grammarians were to be disinterested observers and codifiers. Their mastery of the laws of grammar would give them the authority to censure idioms that "prevail among the populace," even if their usage is "uniform and extensive" as long as they "are considered as corrupt, and like counterfeit money, though common, not valued" (142). Campbell's rigorous method thus gave the critic the authority to condemn common idioms in the name of common sense. The critic upheld the idioms of "men of rank and eminence" and "reputable" writers, including those in the provinces who have mastered the dominant idiom, but excluding "the far greater part of mankind, perhaps ninety-nine of a hundred, [who] are, by reason of poverty and other circumstances, deprived of the advantages of education, and condemned to toil for bread, almost incessantly, in some narrow occupation" (144, 142). Working people's narrow range of experience leaves their language as stunted as their intellect. Campbell thus established the disinterested authority of a scientific approach to grammar and then used that authority to demarcate literate usage from the language of common people.

As discussed in the first chapter, Campbell contributed to the formation of English as an object of formal study, and that formation was shaped by the dialectical forces at work in discourse, including centrifugal forces that moved outward to include broader domains and audiences within the dominant discourse and centripetal forces that worked to establish a univocal set of standards within that expanded domain. All the trends discussed in this chapter were part of these dialectical trends: a grammatical theory that claimed the authority of common usage but proscribed the idioms of the common person, an inductive logic that modeled the experiential reasoning of daily life in the image of the disinterested logic of the sciences, a rhetoric

that used forms of public discourse to teach the sentiments of conversible society, and a moral philosophy that upheld "common sense" as the dictate of
nature and not the product of common experience. On the one hand, these
trends helped to break down the antiquarianism of higher education by challenging its concentration on dead languages, ritualistic displays of syllogistic
reasoning, and the stylistic refinements of Ciceronianism. On the other hand,
these trends served to formalize the contemporary culture, and human nature itself, as a rule-governed system of discourse, thus bringing order, reason, and hence authority to the conventions of educated discourse at a time
when the boundaries of the educated culture had been blurred by the expansion of print literacy.

Conclusion: The "New" Rhetoric and the "Science of Man"— As Natural as Common Sense

In the passage quoted at the beginning of this chapter, Hume set out to conquer the "capital" of the sciences, "human nature itself." Epistemologically
oriented rhetoricians like Priestley and Campbell also felt that they were con-
quering "*a new world,*" or at least "a new country, of which, though there have
been some successful incursions occasionally made upon its frontiers, we are
not yet in full possession" (Priestley, *Examination* xix; Campbell, *Rhetoric*
lxxv). The conquest of human nature would bring order to rhetoric and
moral philosophy in the same way that pneumatology had served to maintain the continuities between natural philosophy and natural religion by up-
holding the providential order of nature. Turnbull had been able to apply the
method of the natural sciences to human nature with confidence that "the
transition from facts and final causes of the one kind, to those of the other,
is exceeding natural and easy" (*Observations* 349). After Hume asked a few
simple questions about how one can generate a moral obligation from an
empirical observation, the step from "facts" to "final causes" no longer seemed
quite so "natural":

> In every system of morality, which I have hitherto met with, I have always re-
> mark'd, that the author proceeds for some time in the ordinary way of rea-
> soning, and establishes the being of a God, or makes observations concerning
> human affairs; when of a sudden I am surpriz'd to find, that instead of the
> usual copulations of propositions, *is,* and *is not,* I meet with no proposition
> that is not connected with an *ought,* or an *ought not.* (*Treatise* 521)

After Hume, the continuity from what *is* to what *ought to be* had to be
reestablished if empirical observations were to have moral authority. Hume's

critics attempted to bridge the gap between the two by claiming that the step from the one to the other was as natural as common sense.

For over a century, commonsense philosophy was able to preserve the continuity between science and religion by providing acceptable answers to questions about how one can derive moral imperatives from statements of fact. The providential order of human nature had to be maintained to prevent the expanding awareness of cultural differences and historical changes from leading to the obvious conclusion that morals and mores were indeed a matter of mere convention and not nature. Questions about how to derive an *ought* from an *is* also raised broader questions about the nature of motives, the purposes of action, and civic duties and natural rights. Such concerns inevitably had an impact on rhetoric as well as moral philosophy because rhetoric is the art of persuading people about what they *ought* to do. The theory that Campbell derived from commonsense philosophy shifted the scene of rhetorical action away from public debates over common beliefs and interiorized it in the workings of the mental faculties, creating perhaps the most intellectually interesting and certainly the most systematic theory of discourse written in English in the eighteenth century. His major nineteenth-century successor, Alexander Bain, and others concerned with "mental science" followed Campbell in assuming that theories of rhetoric should center upon the mental responses of auditors. Campbell's *Philosophy of Rhetoric* is perhaps the first "scientific" theory of rhetoric, and it became an important part of the effort to appropriate the rising authority of the sciences without undermining traditional beliefs. This effort succeeded as long as it had to—until traditional intellectuals had secularized their relations with the public and were able to claim authority as professional scientists and critics.

Every theory of discourse contains an epistemology, an ethics, and a politics, for every theory models what can be known, how people should respond, and what purposes are to be served. What is most striking about Campbell's theory is how programmatically it constituted the authorial subject and then used the "science of human nature" to formalize logical, rhetorical, and grammatical conventions. Campbell formulated an integrated theory that includes a psychological rhetoric, an experiential logic, and a scientific grammar. This theory was used to teach students the conventions of educated discourse into the twentieth century. According to Sharon Crowley, "the influence of Campbell's *Philosophy of Rhetoric* on subsequent rhetorical theory was enormous. It was cited or quoted in textbook after textbook throughout the nineteenth century up to as late as 1920" (175 n; see also Johnson, *Nineteenth-Century Rhetoric* 20). Crowley has established Campbell as a key figure in the teaching of college English. His theories were used to model students' compositions in the image of enlightened reason and exclude those who could not reproduce appropriate sentiments in approved ways. A century after Campbell's *Philosophy of Rhetoric*, textbooks were still teaching that invention is "not a thing to be taught. It is a part of one's native endowment, and of his general intellectual accumulations. . . . No amount of ingenuity or pumping will draw water from a well that is dry" (qtd. S. Crowley 76). After all, if language is merely the representation of mental experiences, then individuals who cannot express themselves correctly must be mentally defective.

The "new" rhetoric and the "science of man" were as natural as common sense because they followed the same natural laws that it did. Turnbull and his contemporaries appropriated doctrines of natural law from the political tradition that reached back through Continental sources to the Stoics and redefined them according to the logic of the sciences in order to create sciences of human psychology and political economy. Both centered on the perspective of autonomous individuals who are free to say, think, and do what they will as long as they follow the laws that are a natural part of the system, a system that balanced the common good and self-interest within human nature as well as the general political economy. Within this liberal political economy, rhetoric could never be more than the art of conveying mental impressions among autonomous individuals and would generally be seen as a threat because its identification with self-interest and party factions threatened the logic of the whole system. As Dewey has discussed, the "economic 'laws'" governing "the free play of competitive exchange, designated the law of supply and demand, were 'natural' laws," and as such they "were set in opposition to political laws as artificial, man-made affairs" (90).

The opposition of nature to mere convention was central to the arguments between Hume and the commonsense philosophers over the "science of human nature," a science that alienated intellection and intellectuals from common life in the same way that Smith's laissez-faire liberalism and the resultant atomized individualism did (see Dewey 86–90). However, philosophies of common sense can be oriented to drawing on conventional beliefs to transform and not just maintain established beliefs and practices. Like Dewey, Gramsci was very concerned with how shared beliefs create a sense of commonality that can generate collective action to transform society. Gramsci's emphasis on common sense as the grounds of intellectual reflection oriented to political action provides a powerful counterpoint to the philosophy of common sense that first defined the discipline of college English. From the outset, students were disciplined to internalize a disinterested perspective on public controversies and a disengaged conception of culture that divorced literary classics from the popular experience. From the outset, the autonomous individual and a depoliticized belletristic conception of culture have been natural counterparts to liberal political economy in public education. This paradigm was able to claim a natural authority because it aptly represented the experience of the bourgeois reading public, particularly the experience of provincial intellectuals who had divorced themselves from the popular culture, historical experience, and shared values of their own societies in order to identify themselves with the cosmopolitan stance of the impartial spectator.

Common sense need not be a reactionary assertion of nature against change. It has been and can be more dialectical. According to Gramsci,

> Every social stratum has its own "common sense" and its own "good sense", which are basically the most widespread conception of life and of man. Every philosophical current leaves behind a sedimentation of "common sense": this is the document of its historical effectiveness. Common sense is not something rigid and immobile, but is continually transforming itself, enriching itself with scientific ideas and with philosophical opinions which have entered ordinary life. (*Prison Notebooks* 326 n)

Scottish commonsense philosophy was quite historically effective (far more than most of its critics) at establishing itself as a philosophy of public education and popular morality. The educated culture was expanding to include groups that had not been born within it, and higher education was beginning to take on the modern responsibility of initiating broader classes of individuals into the dominant culture—the "common sense" of educated people. To serve this purpose, moral philosophy and rhetoric turned inward to concentrate on the processes of instilling and communicating "natural" sentiments, and the dialectical possibilities of critiques of common sense were contained within the belletristic and scientistic trends that contributed to the formation of the two cultures of the arts and sciences. Today common sense tends to be as little valued within the academy as political rhetoric or popular values, but its civic potentials need to be reconsidered as rhetoric expands its frame of reference beyond academic discourse and becomes more involved with community literacies, cultural studies, and political controversies—the contemporary trend that I return to in the conclusion.

Campbell's *Philosophy of Rhetoric* helped establish the disciplinary project of teaching composition through criticism. The only textbook to have more influence on the formation of college English was Hugh Blair's *Lectures on Rhetoric and Belles Lettres* (see Johnson, *Nineteenth-Century Rhetoric* 65–66). With Blair, rhetoric became more concerned with instilling taste than correcting usage but no less concerned with disciplining the authorial subject. Blair gave more attention to belles lettres than to rhetoric because he assumed that few readers would have opportunities to speak to public controversies but all would need taste to be accepted into civil society. Belletrism was repudiated in the next century when English studies developed more rigorous disciplinary knowledge, but from the origins of college English studies, they have been most concerned with the criticism and not the composition of discourse, which is of course ironic given the fact that Campbell, Blair, and the others who established college English studies professed to be rhetoricians. Rhetoric, both as a type of discourse and as a theory of composition, would be pushed to the margins of English studies, and then exiled from the humanities as English departments became literature departments. Rhetoric has never fit very well into either of the two cultures of the modern arts and sciences. Its concern for the situated and self-interested nature of purposeful discourse challenges the disinterested logic of the sciences and the refined sensibility of the arts. These oppositions became evident in Smith and Campbell, and they became widely institutionalized when Blair's *Lectures* became the standard textbook in college English courses.

Hugh Blair and the Rhetoric

of Belles Lettres

The purity of bourgeois art, which hypostasized itself as a world of freedom in contrast to what was happening in the material world, was from the beginning bought with the exclusion of the lower classes—with whose cause, the real universality, art keeps faith precisely by its freedom from the ends of the false universality. Serious art has been withheld from those for whom the hardship and oppression of life make a mockery of seriousness.

—Max Horkheimer and Theodor Adorno,
Dialectic of Enlightenment

SCIENTISM HAD THE MOST influence on the formation of college English through Campbell's effort to define the "new" rhetoric according to the "science of human nature," but it was Blair who instituted the emphasis on belletristic criticism that would characterize college English studies. Campbell's *Philosophy of Rhetoric* (1776) went through twenty-one editions through the next century, while Blair's *Lectures on Rhetoric and Belles Lettres* (1783) went through over five times that many (Golden and Corbett 140). Like Turnbull, Reid, and other advocates of the "science of man" at Aberdeen, Campbell wrote a systematic treatise that did not adopt the appealing style of the essay of taste and manners that Hume had turned to when his own *Treatise* was ignored by the reading public and fell "deadborn" from the press.[1] By contrast, Blair's *Lectures* provided an accessible survey of the proprieties of taste and usage (see Golden and Ehninger; Ehninger and Golden). Even before their publication, Blair's *Lectures* had circulated so widely through students' notes that a reviewer quoted from a set to criticize Blair for timidly cutting his criticisms of Johnson's Latinate style (*English Review* [1783] 2: 24–25). Blair's *Lectures* became the standard text for the first college English classes, and when read against the remaining archival evidence, they provide useful insights into how English was first taught within the university. While Blair's influence on "current-traditional rhetoric" has been well established, historians of literary studies have been understandably disinclined to claim a belletristic cleric as the founder of their discipline, even though the first professors of English literature acknowledged him as their predecessor and occupied chairs that had often been first established as professorships of rhetoric.[2]

Because Blair's *Lectures* became "a staple of instruction for half the educated English speaking world," they document how rhetorical and literary studies were popularized when they were translated into English and taught to the sort of readers and students who had been excluded from the learned culture when it was contained within learned languages (Schmitz 3). Blair's provincial students and readers had to be formally taught the taste and style of the educated culture because they were not born and raised within it. Blair's *Lectures* helped them alleviate their anxieties about the conventions of style and taste and appealed to their nostalgia for unrefined passions and untutored genius. The opposition of convention and nature gave explanatory power—the power to explain experience—to Blair's discussions of correct taste and natural passion, stylistic proprieties and primitive genius, and the progress of politeness and ancient eloquence. Such oppositions made sense to provincials because they understood the conventional nature of culture from their own experience of having had to teach themselves its modes of expression and response. By emphasizing stylistic niceties and romanticizing natural genius, Blair alienated provincial students from their own traditions, and from the dialectical potential of their experience as outsiders. A similar alienation from the popular cultures and political experiences of the provinces is evident in how Campbell made common sense into a natural faculty and how Smith characterized the dialectical consciousness of outsiders in the form of the second self who judges every response and gesture from the perspective of the impartial spectator.

The anxieties of provincials may seem only marginally relevant to college English, but they were imbedded in the priorities and forms that have defined the discipline. The paradigm of rhetoric and belles lettres served the needs of the reading public by subordinating the production of public discourse to stylistic criticism that instilled a taste for the proprieties of civil society. The emphasis on taste was but the clearest example of how the teaching of English was adapted to the needs of the reading public as a consumer society. Standards for taste had been set by the belletristic essays of the *Spectator*, and Blair devoted more detailed attention to those essays than to any other models, even though he said almost nothing about the genre itself. In his four lectures on Addison's essays on "The Pleasures of the Imagination," Blair confined his comments almost entirely to syntax. Blair did not fail to formalize the essay simply because it was an emerging genre at the time, for little critical commentary would be published on the essay even after it became a basic part of the discipline, in part because the essay resists categorization, but also in part because its conventions are seen to be so personal and idiosyncratic that they cannot be formalized (see for example Good). As in later English courses that uncritically stressed the essay, Blair treated style as a matter of personal voice that should be as natural and unlabored as conversation. The essay has the potential to be a dialectical form of cultural critique, as I discussed in the first chapter (see also Spellmeyer). However, when it is taught as an arhetorical form that enables individuals to speak freely from their experience, it merely reproduces the laissez-faire polity of civil society by assuming that individuals are free to do what they will as long as they obey the laws that are a natural part of the system. Blair helped institutionalize this arhetorical perspective by removing the essay from the social contexts of its creation and reception, ignoring its structure and purposes, and concentrating on style as an expression of personal character.

Perhaps the greatest irony of the history of college English is that it began with a Scotsman who praised the natural genius of a fabrication of his own culture that was calculatedly created to appeal to the tastes of the dominant culture. Blair's critical reputation was first established by his commentary on Ossian, the blind bard that Blair's protégé James Macpherson created from scraps of old Gaelic verses. Blair was also well known as a preacher of moderate sentiments. The five volumes of Blair's *Sermons* (1777–1800) went through over seventy-five editions in as many years (Harding xxviii). Dwyer has even claimed that the *Sermons* are "next to the *Spectator* . . . the best-selling work in the English language written in the eighteenth century" (19). As a preacher and teacher of polite proprieties and romantic primitivism, Blair helped formalize the centripetal and centrifugal forces that first defined college English. As creativity was romanticized and instruction came to concentrate on instilling stylistic proprieties, invention became unteachable and correctness became an end in itself. While belletristic commonplaces would be repudiated by the critics who succeeded Blair, college English perpetuated cosmopolitan values and provincial insecurities as it expanded beyond the British provinces to emerging universities within England itself and then throughout the colonies of the English-speaking world. The Ossianic affair is but the most notorious example of how indigenous traditions were colonized by this expansion, and Blair's rhetorical practice as a preacher of moderate sentiments documents the political purposes served by the spread of cosmopolitan values.

A Rhetoric for a Reading Public

As Bourdieu discussed in *Distinction: A Social Critique of the Judgement of Taste* (1984), social groups "distinguish themselves by the distinctions they make" (5). More than anything else, Blair's course taught provincials how to distinguish themselves by making tasteful distinctions. Blair began his course by lecturing on the faculty of taste and related critical precepts such as sublimity and genius, and then he concentrated on stylistic criticism for the rest of the first volume of his *Lectures*. Blair devoted the second part of his course to ten lectures on oratory (with a sermon the only modern example cited) and thirteen lectures on expository writing and literary genres ranging from tragedy to lyric poetry. While a wide range of discourse was still included in the area of study, Blair's course centered on stylistic criticism concerned with the "Pleasures of Taste . . . which we receive from poetry, eloquence or fine writing" (1: 92–93). As English studies began to concentrate on reception, reading was becoming defined as a leisure activity divorced from the utilitarian and political purposes served by writing in daily life. Such distinctions would become increasingly important as "literature" became more narrowly defined as nonfactual nonutilitarian discourse. Blair was the first professor of English precisely because he was not simply a professor of rhetoric. He was in fact the first British professor of "rhetoric and belles lettres," a title that he had himself requested because he believed the term *belles lettres* would give a "modern air" to the proposed professorship in rhetoric.³ Such a change was appropriate, for Blair instituted a belletristic perspective that would eventually place rhetoric at the periphery of the humanities in courses that were too practical to be considered literary.

Blair's *Lectures* are a formative juncture in this development. Blair introduced his course by paying homage to the classical conception of the liberal arts that identified eloquence with practical wisdom and civic virtue.

> Speech is the great instrument by which man becomes beneficial to man: and it is to the intercourse and transmission of thought, by means of speech, that we are chiefly indebted for the improvement of thought itself. . . . What we call human reason is not the effort or ability of one, so much as it is the result of the reason of many, arising from lights mutually communicated in consequence of discourse and writing. (1: 1)

Such ideas were imbedded in the inclusion of *ratio* in *oratio,* for civic humanists assumed that the ability to reason collaboratively through language was what distinguished human beings from animals and made civilization possible. According to Blair, without the power of speech, "reason would be a solitary, and, in some measure, an unavailing principle" (*Lectures* 1: 1). Because discourse embodies the shared culture, "the study of Rhetoric and Belles Lettres supposes and requires a proper acquaintance with the rest of the liberal arts. It embraces them all within its circle, and recommends them to the highest regard" (1: 4). While Blair thus began with the ideals that placed rhetoric at the center of a liberal education, by the end of the first lecture he shifted to viewing rhetoric "not so much as a practical art as a speculative science," a viewpoint maintained throughout most of his course (1: 8).

Blair shifted from composition to reception in order to adapt rhetoric to the needs of a heterogeneous reading public. While rhetoric was a "practical art" for those few who might speak from positions of public authority, most were destined to be only readers:

> Of those who peruse the following Lectures, some, by the profession to which they addict themselves, or in consequence of their prevailing inclination, may have the view of being employed in composition, or in public speaking. Others, without any prospect of this kind, may wish only to improve their taste with respect to writing and discourse, and to acquire principles which will enable them to judge for themselves in that part of literature called the Belles Lettres. (*Lectures* 1: 5)

While Blair reiterated the traditional view that "in the study of composition, we are cultivating reason itself," he assumed that most of his readers would not "addict themselves" to "either composition or public speaking." He concluded that "the same instructions which assist others in composition, will assist them in judging of, and relishing, the beauties of composition" (*Lectures* 1: 6, 8). Taste is particularly well suited to leisured study in those "vacant spaces, those unemployed intervals" (1: 11). A "cultivated taste" not only increases one's pleasure but also instills a responsiveness "to all the tender and human passions, by giving them frequent exercise." Taste is also a social virtue "in an age when works of genius and literature are so frequently the subjects of discourse . . . in polite society" (1: 12, 9).

To adapt rhetoric to "polite society," Blair concentrated not on how to use discourse purposefully but on how to respond tastefully. Taste is defined as a "natural sensibility" that is "more a-kin to a feeling of sense, than to a process of understanding," but tastes can be improved by "the application of reason and good sense to . . . productions of genius" (*Lectures* 1: 21, 16, 22). This conception of taste drew on the assumption in the Hutchesonian tradition that reason provides the understanding of the means to an end, but actions and reactions are prompted by natural passions or feelings. When we respond to a work of art, "we are pleased, through our natural sense of beauty. Reason shows us why, and upon what grounds, we are pleased" (1: 22). Thus, "all the rules of genuine Criticism" are "founded on feeling" (1: 38). Following Hume's essay "Of the Standard of Taste," Blair reduced the two basic "characters of Taste" to "Delicacy and Correctness," with the former identified with "natural sensibility" and the latter a matter of critical judgment (Blair, *Lectures* 1: 23; see Hume, *Essays* 226–49). The creation and reception of discourse are the dominion of the natural faculties of genius and taste, which cannot be taught but can be corrected. While Bourdieu has argued that the mystification of elite tastes tends to treat "taste in legitimate culture as a gift of nature," taste had to be divided into natural and critical components if critics were to have the authority to correct the gifts of nature and teach them to anyone who lacked a natural responsiveness to them (1).

Critics gain the authority to correct popular tastes by speaking disinterestedly for "those feelings and sentiments that are found, on the most extensive examination, to be the common sentiments and feelings of men" (*Lectures* 2: 250). Neoclassicists could assume that literature was merely an imitation of nature because their audiences shared beliefs about what was natural. Moral philosophers attempted to maintain such beliefs by founding them on an innate sense common to all reasonable people. While such arguments were still convincing with regard to basic moral values, Blair had to account for the diversity of tastes in a heterogeneous reading public in order to establish the critic's authority to correct public taste. Since no "standard of Taste" was universally acknowledged, readers needed to be taught to inspect their own "experience" and learn to recognize that taste is founded "upon sentiments and perceptions which belong to our nature," as long as it is not corrupted (1: 33–34). The "genuine Taste of human nature," like doctrines of common sense, claimed the authority of "common sentiments," not those of the common person but those of "men placed in such circumstances as are favourable to the proper exertions of taste" (1: 35, 32). What is common in human nature had to be distinguished from what is common in society if critics were to have the power to correct what is common but unnatural (1: 27, 31). The "caprice of unenlightened Taste" is corrected by disinterested assessments that become the judgments of history (1: 31). In this way, "the judgment of Criticism, and the voice of the Public, when once become unprejudiced and dispassionate, will ever coincide" (1: 39).

Blair's *Lectures* are marked by a pervasive concern for correcting productions of genius and popular tastes, but his discussions of standards such as clarity are undercut by a nostalgia for the "Sublimity" of unrefined "Genius." In his third lecture Blair addressed "Genius" and "Sublimity," and then he devoted the next two lectures to the "*Progress of Language.*" Provincial literati like Smith and Blair often speculated about natural genius and the sublimity of primitive languages, concluding that language had originally been intensely metaphorical because of the immediacy of unexamined experience and the limited vocabulary available to describe it. After reviewing the "progress" of politeness, Blair devoted a dozen lectures to grammatical and stylistic proprieties and then concluded the first volume with five "Critical Examinations" of the standards of correctness—Addison and Swift. The most interesting aspect of this movement from primitive genius to polite proprieties is how ambivalent Blair was about it. His account of the "progress" of language is marked by a longing for the creative genius of unrefined language, and along the way he admitted that criticism can correct but not create, that the progress of politeness left culture chaste but barren, and that productive genius and sublime responses cannot be understood or explained. This ambivalence about refinement is a characteristic element of the provincialism that defined how English was first taught within the university. Such ambivalences echo throughout the *Lectures,* even in those sections devoted to instilling the virtues of refinement.

For Blair, as for Smith, the virtues of style and character were one and the same because individuals' characters are revealed both in how they express themselves and in how they respond to others. Blair noted that "the General Characters of Style, particularly, the Plain and the Simple, and the characters of those English authors who are classed under them" was "taken" from a "manuscript treatise on rhetoric" written by Smith (*Lectures* 1: 381). As in Smith's *Lectures on Rhetoric and Belles Lettres,* "perspicuity" is treated as a "fundamental quality of style," and the traditional concern for figures and tropes as signs of impassioned sentiments is replaced by the ideal of the unadorned style that more accurately represents experience and more naturally conveys the sensations it evokes (Blair, *Lectures* 1: 185, 1: 363–64). Following Smith, Blair assumed that a style has such a close "reference to an author's manner of thinking" that an author's style documents the natural merits and weaknesses of his or her personal character (1: 183). Blair devoted far more attention to the criticism of style than to the other four arts of rhetoric combined (invention, arrangement, memory, and delivery) because he assumed that the improvement of style is integrally related to the refinement of character. Smith and Blair both presented Addison as the ideal of the polite style and sensibility. Blair devoted four lectures to explicating the style of Addison's essays to provide his students with models for their own essays, as I discuss in the next section.

Just as Blair treated style by the personal sentiments that it conveys, he defined literary discourse by the psychological effects it evokes. The concept of sublimity was pivotal to the transition from the traditional emphasis on the elaborate style to a concentration on the responses of readers. Blair rejected the view that the highly figured style taught by rhetoricians is the language of the sublime because sublimity lies not in refined words but in sentiments of a "solemn and awful kind, and even bordering on the terrible," including especially feelings of "vastness," "obscurity," and particularly scenes of "darkness, solitude, and silence" (*Lectures* 1: 47–51). The sublime style cannot be rationally explained or formally taught, "the utmost we can expect is, that this fire of imagination should sometimes flash upon us like lightning from heaven, and then disappear" (1: 76). Such statements have led to Blair's being categorized as a "pre-romantic" (see Monk; and Abrahms). Of course these ideas were far from original, and Blair was not the only Scottish critic to espouse them.

Home's *Elements of Criticism* (1762), according to Tompkins, is where "literary criticism becomes a science." With the reorientation to the psychology of the isolated reader, "the reception of works of art comes to be treated not as an event in the social world with social consequences for author and audience, but as an object of scholarly and scientific investigation" (Tompkins 215–16). "Criticism" was characterized by Home's biographer as a "severe" and even "ascetic employment of the faculties, which demands a cool and dispassionate frame of mind, and a sobriety of thought remote from all enthusiasm; and where the habit of criticism prevails, the ardour of feeling is proportionally abated and subdued" (Tytler, *Memoirs* 1: 438–39). Despite the concern that criticism "subdued" sentiment, the suppression of "enthusiasm" was seen as a beneficial effect, and not just because "this moderation of our emotions is absolutely essential to the formation of a good taste" (1: 440–41). While the redefinition of literature by its psychological effects on isolated readers paralleled the epistemological turns of the "new" logic and rhetoric, it also served the political need to teach broader classes of readers and students to distance themselves from traditional enthusiasms and internalize the proprieties of civil society.

As they refashioned themselves according to the tastes of the dominant culture, provincials became dislocated from the traditions and idioms of their own society and ended up being silenced by their "natural" inability to express themselves in a language that was not their own. By alienating students from their "common" experience and popular culture, the emphasis on correctness ensured that students would have little to say until they had internalized the style and sensibility of educated discourse. In this way, Blair's *Lectures* helped to strengthen the boundaries of the learned culture that had become blurred by the spread of cheap print literacy. The limitations imposed by Blair's approach become even more relevant when one looks at how he taught composition. While he valorized ancient eloquence, he taught students to imitate contemporary essayists, not orators. The essayists he upheld as models had often used the essay to advance party interests and critique popular morés, but Blair reduced the essay to a univocal medium for instilling refined sentiments and never discussed broader matters of organization and development, let alone the social contexts and political purposes that had made the essay a popular genre.

After discussing how Blair put his conception of rhetoric and composition into pedagogical practice, I turn in succeeding sections to the critical and rhetorical practices that followed from the paradigm of rhetoric and belles lettres. Blair's commentary on Macpherson's fabricated Gaelic epic documents how the emphasis on English tastes dislocated provincials from the broader traditions of their own society. Along the same lines, at the same time that Blair and his colleagues were teaching students that civil society had become too polite to tolerate the heated oratory of ancient political rhetoric, they were using rhetoric to establish themselves as the dominant faction in the Scottish church and suppress popular resistance to their political authority.

Ancient Rhetoric in Modern Practice: *The Proprieties of the Essay*

Blair's *Lectures on Rhetoric and Belles Lettres* is where classical theories of public oratory first met the emphasis in modern composition courses on the essay, but Blair devoted almost half of the second volume to discussing the three genres of public oratory. He discussed "the manner suited to each; the proper distribution and management of all the parts of discourse; and the proper pronunciation or delivery of it" (2: 1). Like Campbell, Blair reiterated rhetoric's practical concern for purpose, audience, and situation, but he dismissed invention as an unteachable matter of natural genius and concentrated instead on the "delivery" of discourse. This managerial view of rhetoric was consistent with the critical stance that is assumed throughout Blair's *Lectures*. While Blair valorized the civic ideals and practical essentials of classical rhetoric, he did not discuss the political oratory of his own era because he was far more concerned with instilling polite sentiments than in teaching students how to speak to public controversies. Blair is the best example of Potkay's argument that "professing politeness" served to "consolidate" the "governing class" by showing the impropriety of "the openly democratic ideal of ancient eloquence" (6–7).[4] While he reiterated the classical ideals that justified the study of rhetoric, Blair contained the contemporary relevance of such ideals by emphasizing that rhetoric has limited influence in a society where politics is governed by patronage, conflicts of interest are resolved by the rule of law, and the reading public has too much taste to become involved in political controversies. What one needed to advance in such a society was not popular oratory but polite taste, and the best way to learn it was by studying the style of essays of taste and manners. By defining style as a matter of personal voice and establishing the correction of stylistic niceties as the business of composition teaching, Blair limited the critical potential of the essay. While the essay was a blurred genre that had been popularized by the party politics of the day, Blair helped institutionalize the essay of taste and manners as a model for educated discourse and a means to initiate students into it.

The first two lectures of the second volume of Blair's *Lectures* examine the development of "eloquence" from Greece through Rome to the modern period. This development is described with the same sort of nostalgia evident in Blair's discussion of the general "progress" of language and literature from a state of "original genius" (2: 257). The eloquence of classical rhetoric was due to the fact that ancient orators were citizens, not professionals or pedants. They "were not Orators by profession; they were not formed by schools, but by a much more powerful education; that of business and debate, where man sharpened man, and civil affairs carried on by public speaking called forth every exertion of the mind" (2: 257, 14). Reasoning from this civic conception of rhetoric as the means and end of public virtue, Blair stressed that "high, manly, and forcible Eloquence" is found only "in the regions of freedom" (2: 9). According to Blair, only when the ancient Greek states achieved freedom did they study rhetoric, and whenever democracy has given way to tyranny, rhetoric has become "confined within a narrower range; it can be exerted only in the pulpit, or at the bar; but it is excluded from those great scenes of public business, where the spirits of men have the freest play" (2: 9).

Blair's idealization of the democratic eloquence of classical rhetoric becomes ironic when one considers that the only modern examples of popular oratory that he cites are in the "narrower range" of pulpit eloquence. In line with his view that language had advanced from primitive genius to reasoned refinement, Blair concluded that eloquence has little influence in modern politics because "a certain strictness of good sense" puts us "on our guard against the flowers of Elocution" (1: 42–43). Even in Parliament, "the noblest field" of political oratory, the power of rhetoric is limited by "ministerial influence" (2: 43). Blair's comments are quite striking when one considers that he had associated rhetoric with democracy and that his own era is generally regarded as the golden age of modern political oratory. At least one of Blair's reviewers criticized him for failing to follow through on his idealization of democratic eloquence and discuss the oratory of such influential rhetoricians as Pitt and Burke (*English Review* [1783] 2: 24–25). Blair was not simply displaying the modern academic's lack of interest in popular politics. His library included an ample number of works on current political debates (see Amory), and he was himself an influential practitioner of the art of rhetoric. As a leader of the Moderate faction in the Scottish Church, Blair was quite deft at the rhetoric of party politics. In public forums as in the classroom, Blair claimed authority as a disinterested spokesman for moderate sentiments against factional enthusiasms and remained aloof from party politics, while at the same time he was using the practical arts of rhetoric to subdue popular resistance to patronage and "ministerial influence."

Blair's conservative political agenda influenced his practical understanding of public discourse in obvious ways, but more subtle limitations become apparent when the classical precepts he recounted are contrasted with the modern perspective on rhetoric that he helped to institutionalize. Blair recognized the merits of the classical emphasis on the purposeful nature of discourse, and he reiterated traditional advice on how to arrange and deliver ideas (*Lectures* 1: 402–7). From classical theories and his own practical experience, Blair had learned that an effective orator speaks to a rhetorical situation in a fashion that is suited to "the subject, the hearers, the place, the occasion" (2: 58). Despite the practical strengths of such assumptions, Blair's whole approach to the teaching of composition is based on his view that all that can be taught is how to correct, organize, and deliver what has been generated by natural genius. Blair is praised by Howell for rejecting classical heuristics and recognizing the primacy of empirical evidence in the age of science, but Howell was less concerned with the teaching of composition than with the history of ideas. The erasure of invention from rhetoric in the eighteenth century has been critiqued in detail by Crowley (see *Methodical Memory*). Classical aids to invention such as the *topoi* have recently been reclaimed as part of composition instruction because they can help writers and speakers to locate the issue at question in a debate and draw on shared beliefs to resolve the conflict. Blair was uninterested in invention, not simply because he was committed to the logic of induction, but also because he viewed creativity as a natural process that is "beyond the power of art" (2: 180).[5] Blair's conception of the creative process led him to conclude that "critical rules are designed chiefly to shew the faults that ought to be avoided. To nature we must be indebted for the production of eminent beauties" (1: 38).

Reasoning from assumptions that are still used to justify composition teachers' devoting most of their time to correcting students' essays, Blair apparently confined his students' writing to copying his lectures and imitating his critical explications of belletristic essays. Unlike most professors, Blair did not even hold an "examination" hour dedicated to discussing students' questions and compositions (Bryce 5). While we have student essays from the classes of Blair's own teacher, John Stevenson, all that apparently remains from Blair's courses are the notes that his students painstakingly copied as he read out his lectures word for word.[6] Remarks in manuscript copies of those lectures suggest that Blair's students wrote the same sort of "critical examinations" that he presented as models in his lectures on the essays of Addison and Swift. In one set of notes, Blair began a lecture on a *Spectator* essay by stating "I am now to examine that paper of the Spectator, which I some time ago gave you, as an exercise to criticise upon, and as an illustration of the Rules concerning Style formerly laid down. I have received a good many papers, and I am pleased" (Edin. Univ. Mss. DC.106, 456). Blair's approach to teaching composition had limitations that are obvious today, but they were also obvious in his own day to teachers who were committed to teaching rhetoric as a practical art. While Blair's students seem to have spent their time copying his polished sentiments and imitating his stylistic commentary, dissenters such as Joseph Priestley were having students explore conflicting views of controversial issues and then research and write compositions arguing their own positions. The dissenters' emphasis on critical debate was integral to their efforts to prepare students to speak for religious and political dissent, while Blair's pedagogy was oriented to teaching people how to read with taste.

While the archival evidence is limited, it suggests that Blair's students wrote essays that imitated his own commentary on the style of Addison and Swift, commentary that includes exactly the sort of mincing criticisms that too many teachers still make on students' essays. Blair's painstaking criticisms of each and every sentence in Addison's essays on "The Pleasures of the Imagination" thus present important insights into how composition was taught by the first university professor appointed to teach English rhetoric, literature, and composition. Blair never bothered to discuss what the essays were about, how they might be situated in broader debates or social contexts, or what purposes they served. In a ruthlessly methodical fashion, he corrected each and every sentence with the sort of tedious attention to formal proprieties that have convinced generations of students that their English teachers are less interested in what they write about than in how they punctuate it. Blair looked for and found frequent erroneous, infelicitous, and inharmonious phrases, and he strained to misread parallelisms and references that would only seem unclear to a reader who is intent on maintaining proprieties, including such popular bugbears as using *this* and *that* to make summary references (Blair, *Lectures* 1: 423). Blair's commentary is confined almost entirely to syntax because his whole approach to composition is concerned with correcting faults and not with exploring generative structures or examining how authors responded to their contexts. While he had noted the importance of audience and purpose in earlier lectures, Blair did not apply these rhetorical concepts to the models that he had his students imitate in their compositions. Blair thus established the arhetorical approach to the teaching of composition that Trimbur has termed "the rhetoric of deproduction" (see "Essayist Literacy and the Rhetoric of Deproduction").

Blair immersed his students in the painstaking mastery of stylistic niceties in a way that was quite similar to the stylistic emphases of Ciceronianism. For example, in response to a sentence from the *Spectator* such as "a man of a polite imagination is let into a great many pleasures, that the vulgar are not capable of receiving," Blair devoted a paragraph to the use of *that* instead of *which*, propounding the sort of elaborate rules that have been repeated in textbooks and violated by writers ever since they were first formulated to reduce the conventions of English to a logical system. What is not examined is the basic idea that this sentence expresses. Such ideas were placed beyond question by the pedagogy itself, which taught students to tacitly internalize the sensibility and stance of the belletristic essay as they concentrated their attention on mastering its stylistic conventions. Such an approach was consistent with Blair's view that criticism was confined to correcting the products of genius. He also defended his concentration on "faults, or rather blemishes and imperfections" by noting that one can only read the "best authors" with "pleasure, when one properly distinguishes their beauties from their faults" (*Lectures* 1: 79). An emphasis on correctness was also needed because of the "peculiarities of dialect" of his Scottish students, whose "ordinary spoken language often differs much from what is used by good English authors" (1: 430). Whether Blair's concentration on correctness increased his students' "pleasure" in reading is doubtful, but the attention to stylistic proprieties probably appealed to the insecurities of those who believed that learning how to speak like the English would enable them to advance in polite society.

While it was Campbell who systematically redefined rhetoric according to the psychology of the individual auditor, Blair was instrumental in institutionalizing stylistic criticism of syntactic proprieties as part of the discipline of college English. Like Campbell and Smith, Blair is a well-recognized founder of what has become known as current-traditional rhetoric. Like his colleagues and successors, Blair taught students to concentrate on mastering the style of educated discourse and distance themselves from discourse that addressed legal conflicts and political controversies. According to Crowley, "what was left to student writing was to demonstrate progressive mastery of the smaller conventions governing discursive decorum" (*Methodical Memory* 152). This emphasis on polite proprieties dislocated rhetoric from the political domain and situated it within the confines of civil society. Students were taught to situate themselves not as purposeful agents in political society but as disinterested observers who had mastered the niceties of correct usage and polite taste. The dislocation of rhetoric from the public experience is clearly evident in belletrists' inability to see a place for political discourse in modern society, but the best example of the Scottish literati's alienation from the traditions of their own society is Blair's valorization of Macpherson's Ossian as a Bardic spokesman for the native genius of Scotland's receding oral traditions.

The Ossianic Bard and Belletrism

Macpherson drew on some fifteen Gaelic sources to compose his "epic" tales of the blind Highland bard Ossian, but Ossian spoke the language of sensibility that was the characteristic idiom of literati such as Hugh Blair, who guided the composition of Macpherson's works and explained them to the reading public. Determining the cultural authenticity of Macpherson's Ossianic epics is perhaps less important than recognizing how richly they inscribe the dynamic heteroglossia of the cultural provinces.[7] To adapt his Gaelic fragments to the tastes of the British reading public, Macpherson drew on Greek and Roman models and the eclectic neoclassical and protoromantic doctrines that Blair synthesized for his Scottish students. Blair himself did not know Gaelic and was indifferent to the Gaelic literary revival that followed the political subjugation of the Highland clans, but he was immediately taken with the fragmentary "translations" that Macpherson had composed at the insistence of John Home in 1759. Blair pressed Macpherson to translate his "epic" and helped support him while he did so. Ossian validated Blair's view that the sublime was to be found "amidst the rude scenes of nature, amidst rocks and torrents and whirlwinds and battles. . . . It is the thunder and the lightning of genius. It is the offspring of nature, not of art" (*Critical Dissertation* 121). Rather than being expressions of natural genius, the poems were an artful imitation of the sort of romantic primitivism that Blair was popularizing. After Macpherson published *Fragments of Ancient Poetry, collected in the Highlands of Scotland* (1760) and then *Finigal, an Ancient Epic Poem* (1762) and *Temora, an Ancient Epic Poem* (1763), Blair composed the *Critical Dissertation on the Poems of Ossian* (1763), which served as the standard introduction in editions of Macpherson's *Works of Ossian* (1765). Blair's reaction to Ossian had a formative impact on the lectures that he was beginning to deliver, and the reputation Blair gained as the defender of Scotland's native bard helped strengthen the popular appeal of those lectures when they were published.

Even before he officially became Regius Professor of Rhetoric and Belles Lettres, Blair was devoting one of his concluding lectures to the fragments that Macpherson had translated.[8] In a letter in 1762, Blair referred to his forthcoming professorial "commission" and described the popular acclaim he received for his lecture on Ossian, which was attended by "many People of Distinction & of Taste" (National Library of Scotland Mss. 3219: 1). Like the rest of the bourgeois reading public, Blair was transported by Ossian's sublime sentiments, and the sensations invoked by Ossian proved he was a genius:

> Has he the spirit, the fire, the inspiration of a poet? Does he utter the voice of nature? Does he elevate by his sentiments? Does he interest by his descriptions? Does he paint to the heart as well as to the fancy? Does he make his readers glow, and tremble, and weep? These are the great characteristics of true poetry. (*Critical Dissertation* 217)

Hume wrote Blair that Ossian had become his "child . . . by adoption," and when Johnson and others challenged Ossian's genealogy, Blair collected testimony and included it in his *Critical Dissertation* to prove that Ossian was a native-born genius of an ancient Scottish lineage (Sher, *Church* 250). A later Scottish commentator dryly noted that Blair's criticism of Ossian was "ingenious and acute, and as good as could possibly be written by a gentleman lecturing on a language he did not know, of a past he had not studied, of a poem on whose origin he was utterly mistaken" (Graham 126).

While Ossian was readily accepted by Lowland Scots like Blair who knew little about the oral traditions of the Highlands, the literati were not merely dupes. As Sher has discussed, "they made it known what they were after and how important it was to them to get it; Macpherson gave them what they wanted." Ossian was important as a source of patriotic pride because Parliament had just denied Scots the right to establish a militia (Sher, *Church* 254, 257–61). Ossian spoke directly to Scots' nostalgia for lost martial virtues: "Raise, ye bards of other times, raise high the praise of heroes; that my soul may settle on their fame . . . and cease to be sad" (Macpherson, *Works of Ossian* 1: 119). With displaced patriotic zeal, Blair and his colleagues defended their "Homer of the Highlands" (*Critical Dissertation* 138). Blair marveled that the works had "all the essential requisites of a true and regular epic," which was not surprising since Macpherson had calculatedly imitated them

(*Critical Dissertation* 41). When Blair asked Johnson with pride if any modern man could possibly have written such a work of genius, Johnson responded that it could have been written by "many men, many women, and many children" (qtd. Monk 120). Even when scholars began to doubt Ossian's authenticity, the poems' sensationalism maintained their popular appeal. Translated into all major European languages, Ossian was passionately studied by such influential figures as Schiller, Jefferson, and Napoleon (see DeGategno). Few literary works have created such a popular sensation, and Blair was there to explain such sensations according to the sentiments of civil society.

While traditionally viewed as a precursor to Romanticism, Ossian was not only a primitive genius but a man of taste who expressed sentiments that were valued by provincial literati such as Blair. Blair advised readers that "no sentiments can be beautiful without being proper," and as to Ossian, "no poet maintains a higher tone of virtuous and noble sentiment, throughout all his works" (*Critical Dissertation* 119, 122). While the heroes of classical epics could be vengeful, prideful, and rather crude, Ossian's warriors could shed a tear for a vanquished enemy and always showed respect for a lady in distress. According to Blair, Ossian himself was "endowed by nature with an exquisite sensibility of heart; prone to that tender melancholy which is so often an attendant on great genius; and susceptible equally of strong and of soft emotions" (27–28). It was important to demonstrate Ossian's polite "sensibility" to show that he was a natural genius from an heroic age and not simply a savage Highlander. An appendix to Sinclair's famous *Statistical Account of Scotland* (1791) included typical expressions of displaced patriotism that romanticized Scotland's past in order to claim "high credit" for Scotland for "having produced one of the greatest poets that has appeared in any period of history" (1: 1).[9] Echoing Blair, Sinclair defined "the two great characteristics of Ossian's poetry" as "tenderness and sublimity." Sinclair also stressed that Scotland's ancient bard had "a heart penetrated with noble sentiments, and with sublime and tender passions; a heart that glows and kindles the fancy; a heart that is full, pours forth the ardent feelings with which it is impressed" (1: 2; Blair, *Critical Dissertation* 37).

While Ossian spoke the language of polite sentiment, his native tongue was supposed to be Gaelic, and his popularity fostered interest in the traditions that were being eradicated as Highlanders were forced off the land. As the Highland clans were being replaced with Highland sheep, Gaelic societies were founded in London and Edinburgh. Expatriate and Lowland Scots tended to be more interested in such cultural accoutrements as the kilt than in the problems of the dispossessed. According to Durkacz's *The Decline of the Celtic Languages,* the politics of Gaelic societies did not extend beyond a "romantic Toryism" that treated Gaelic as "a museum piece for the refined sentiments and heroic endeavours of the misty Celtic past" (192, 197). According to the report of a committee set up to investigate the Ossianic poems, they could not easily be authenticated because oral traditions were disappearing with "the change of manners in the Highlands, where the habits of industry have now superseded the amusement of listening to the legendary narrative or heroic ballad" (qtd. Burke, *Popular Culture* 250). Gaelic was promoted by the Moderates' evangelical opponents, who circulated free Gaelic Bibles and established Gaelic schools throughout the Highlands. According to Durkacz, Moderates generally showed "an instinctual distrust" of the political potentials of such missionary activities (99). Blair himself devoted less time to preaching for aid to the poor than to teaching his readers how to refine their tastes in those leisure hours when they were feeling nostalgic for the "heroic ballads" of receding oral traditions.

Belletristic Rhetorical Theory in Political Practice

As I discuss in chapter 5, Blair was a leader of the Moderate Party that gained control of the Presbyterian Church in the middle of the century by defining themselves as spokesmen for orderly subservience, and the Moderates' support for the authority of patrons in the selection of clergy helped to transform the comparatively democratic Scottish Church into a well-integrated part of British party politics. As a reward for their efforts, Moderate leaders such as Blair and Robertson were given the best educational and clerical positions in Scotland, including Blair's professorship of rhetoric and belles lettres. Like George Campbell, whose sermon against the American Revolution was circulated free of charge by the government, Blair was a politically important public orator, particularly in the last quarter of the century, when the revolutions in America and France led to calls for reforms in Britain. Blair was in fact one of the most popular preachers of the century, and his *Sermons* provide an influential model of the sort of public discourse that followed from his rhetorical theory. Blair popularized the view that polite refinements fostered moral sentiments by teaching individuals to balance self-centered feelings with sympathy for others. As in Smith's works on moral sentiments and liberal political economy, the ideal of the sympathetic imagination served to instill the virtues of self-restraint as a means to maintain subservience and hence order in a changing society. Blair's moderate religion could tolerate a heretic such as Hume, but it could not tolerate popular resistance to political authority. This combination of cultural liberalism and political conservatism carefully maintained the boundaries between civil society and the political sphere that had been demarcated by Smith's laissez-faire liberalism.

Blair's *Sermons* were an unparalleled popular success. The publication of the first volume in 1777 brought him a two-hundred-pound pension from the king, and Blair received six hundred pounds for the third volume alone (Finlayson x). By its appearance in 1790, the former two volumes had already gone through fifteen editions according to a letter by Blair of April 14, 1790 (National Library of Scotland Mss. 588: 1374). Blair's *Sermons* preached the sentiments that he taught in his *Lectures*. Blair's *Lectures* advised against the "warmth" of the evangelicals and the "studied coolness" characteristic of traditional Presbyterians, and his *Sermons* were themselves praised for occupying that "middle place between the dry metaphysical discussion of one class of preachers, and the loose incoherent declamation of another" (*Lectures* 2: 44; Finlayson, *Sermons* 5: 497 n). Blair avoided traditional doctrinal controversies and preached the virtues of polite sentiment. Boswell aptly characterized their popular appeal when he noted that Blair's sermons "lighted things up so finely, and you get from them such comfortable answers" (qtd. Schmitz 1). Because they provided "such comfortable answers," Blair's sermons were imitated, if not simply read, by Anglican as well as Presbyterian clergy throughout Britain (see Golden). According to the *Monthly Review* of 1784, Blair's sermons "have gained so universal a reputation, as to render religious and moral instruction fashionable" (70: 175).

Blair's "fashionable" religion paid more attention to polite refinement than to divisive doctrines or the needs of the poor. Blair often spoke of the "sublimity" of religious sentiments in the same sort of terms that he had used in his *Lectures* and even recommended a spirit of romantic "melancholy" about death (*Sermons* 1: 297). Other sermons preached the virtues of polite sentiment that were being taught by moral philosophers such as Hutcheson and Smith. In his sermon "On Sensibility," Blair advised his readers to moderate between Hobbesian "self-love" and Hutchesonian "social and benevolent instincts" by working hard to advance their own self-interest but also to "weep with them that weep" (2: 293–94). Blair's sermon "On Moderation" advised against impassioned beliefs and counseled that those with moderation will achieve success because they are not distracted from gradual but steady social advancement. In "On Fortitude," "On Idleness," "On Luxury and Licentiousness," and numerous other sermons, he advised that "the sober, the industrious, and the virtuous . . . prosper in the world." According to this comforting praise for the Protestant work ethic, "the opulent are not prohibited from enjoying the good things of this world." What is forbidden are "thoughtless and intemperate enjoyment," wasting one's time, and neglecting one's responsibilities (4: 115–28). Like Smith and other professors of moral philosophy, Blair taught his audiences to accept their station in society with stoical self-restraint: "First, as private men and Christians, let us cultivate those virtues which are essential to the prosperity of our country. The foundation of all public happiness must be laid in the good conduct of individuals; in their industry, sobriety, justice, and regular attention to the duties of their several stations" (5: 143).

Like Campbell and other preachers and teachers of moderatism, Blair promoted the virtues of self-control and the politics of subservience in order to preserve the social order while advancing liberal tolerance. In many of Blair's sermons, as Sher discusses, "it is sometimes difficult to distinguish between submission to Providence and submission to the existing system of social 'ranks' and orders" (*Church* 185; see also Dwyer 45–50). While defending political orthodoxy, the Moderates tolerated intellectuals who espoused unorthodox views, most notably Hume. Blair himself defended Hume against an effort to have him censured by the General Assembly of the church. Blair's *Observations upon . . . the Writings of Sopho, and David Hume* (1755) argued in a scholarly fashion that Hume had been quoted out of context and was actually skeptical about the proofs of reason and not the existence of the world. Blair preserved the boundaries between civility and politics by arguing that "the proper objects of censure and reproof are not freedom of thought, but licentiousness of action; not erroneous speculations, but crimes pernicious to society" (2). The Moderates defended tolerance even when riots spread across Scotland after Parliament considered extending basic civil rights to Catholics. Campbell's *Address to the People of Scotland Upon the Alarms That Have Been Raised in Regard to Popery* (1779) argued against using the traditional authority of the church to compel public orthodoxy. Campbell stressed that human judgment is fallible, that those who know least tend to be most certain of their opinions, and that the Christian method is "persuasion, not compulsion" (9). This stance was consistent with the liberal view that religious opinions are personal matters, but it was strikingly removed from the theocratic authority that Calvinists had wielded when they publicly punished those who failed to maintain the compulsory attendance at church on Sunday.

While they defended personal freedoms, Blair and Campbell spoke against allowing the public order to be disturbed by private opinions expressed in civil society. Blair, Campbell, and other leading Moderates like Gerard preached subservience to authority on fast days set aside by the government for public reflection on developments in America and France. Campbell's *The Nature, Extent, and Importance of the Duty of Allegiance* (1776) was even printed and circulated free by the government to help suppress sympathy for the American revolution, which ran high among the Moderates' evangelical opponents. Campbell cited the biblical precepts traditionally used to preach political quietism: render unto Caesar his due, obey higher powers in the state as in heaven, and accept the world as God made it. Campbell argued that "private interest" was far less important than the "public" need for "tranquility and order" (15, 11). Rejecting the social contract as a meaningless and dangerous fiction, he subordinated personal rights to "*public utility,*" maintaining that "in matters of government and legislation, that which immemorial custom has established, unless opposed by some natural or divine law, is always regarded as obligatory" (21–24, 12, 18). Given the variability of opinion, especially among "the mere populace, the unthinking multitude," one must accept the rule of law (40). Blair's sermon, "On the Love of Our Country" (1793) also attacked the "spirit of discontent" and "visionary projects of reformation" that have "sprung up among us" and advised that "plain good sense" dictates that one should avoid such extremes and work hard for personal advancement, which is available even to those of "ordinary rank and humble birth" (*Sermons* 5: 135–46). Such were the politics of common sense.

While Campbell was somewhat removed from the machinations of church politics at Edinburgh, Blair was a leading political manager of the Moderate Party, second only to Principal Robertson. Blair may have been even more influential behind the scenes than he was in the pulpit. He helped the Moderates establish themselves as the party of order within the church by working to ensure the selection of clergy loyal to the party. Blair regularly corresponded with influential politicians such as his former student Henry Dundas, who dominated Scottish politics during the "reign of terror" that was instituted to suppress dissent after the French Revolution (Sher, *Church* 306). Blair frequently stressed the need to select clergy who are "firmly attached both to the present Ministry & to the Moderate interests" in order to have clergy to speak against "the lower classes of men" who challenged the public authority of patrons (National Library of Scotland Mss. 3464: 20; 588: 1296). These letters show how rhetorically effective Blair was at courting the "ministerial influence" that he referred to in his *Lectures* as one of the main reasons why political rhetoric had become less important in the modern world. Through his role in the selection of candidates and his duties as professor, Blair exercised an influence over younger clergymen that was unequaled by anyone else in the church at the time, according to one of his young contemporaries (Hill 206). Through his personal contacts as well as from the pulpit, Blair helped to liberalize the theology of the Scottish church, while also working to make it an orderly part of the British patronage system.

Blair's efforts were opposed by the popular party in the church. One of the leading opponents of the Moderates was John Witherspoon, who became the most important American advocate of the "new" rhetoric when he emigrated to become president of Princeton in 1768. Witherspoon's *Ecclesiastical Characteristics* (1753) satirized the polite pretensions, political machinations, and liberal theology of the Moderates, particularly their efforts to court the favor of the upper classes. The fourth "Maxim" of the *Ecclesiastical Characteristics* ridiculed the polite sermonizing on social virtues popularized by Blair, and the eighth attacked the Moderates for supporting the authority of upper-class patrons against the interests of the "common people." While he was a former classmate of Blair's and would become a leading American advocate of the civic humanist and Commonwealth ideals popularized by Hutcheson, Witherspoon opposed the tendency in the Hutchesonian tradition to conflate ethics and aesthetics because he saw how the idealization of refined sentiments contributed to the elitist political practices of the Moderates, as I discuss in my introduction to *The Selected Writings of John Witherspoon*. After Witherspoon's emigration, the popular party broadened its activism beyond the issue of church patronage to spread support among the working and mercantile classes for the revolutions in America and France (see Landsman). Religious dissent in Scotland thus developed into broader political activism in the same way that it had among the English dissenters, and like Priestley, Witherspoon taught rhetoric not as a human science or as belletristic criticism but as the art of speaking to public political conflicts.[10]

While they depoliticized rhetoric by disassociating it from its classical emphasis on addressing public controversies, Blair and Campbell were very politically influential as practicing rhetoricians. According to John Hill, Blair's successor in the Moderate leadership, Blair had a major impact on public opinion:

> Many, who could not judge correctly upon political subjects, were ready to be directed by him, whose sentiments upon religious topics they believed to be unerring. He declared from his pulpit, that no man could be a good Christian that was a bad subject. The opinions of those French philosophers, who wished to destroy subordination, and to loosen the restraints of law, he rejected with abhorrence. . . . Sentiments like these from the mouth of such a man, spoken at such a time, could not fail to be productive of the happiest effects on the public mind. (Hill 191–92)

Speaking not as politicians but as disinterested clergymen, Blair and Campbell preached the virtues of self-control, orderly subservience, and liberal tolerance in ways that maintained the political status quo while advancing personal freedoms in civil society. The pulpit was an important public forum in Scotland, and not just because of its theocratic traditions. The comparatively democratic structure of the church and the greater accessibility of the universities meant that articulate members of the working classes could be drawn into positions of leadership as public spokesmen for moderate enlightenment. Such a situation helped to make rhetoric important enough to be studied, but also problematic enough that it needed to be taught with taste.

Conclusion: The Introspective Turn Toward Belletristic Sentiments and the "Science of Man"

Campbell's *Philosophy of Rhetoric* exemplified the strengths of the scientific method as then understood. He moved systematically from a few simple principles founded on the "facts" of "mental science" to develop a comprehensive model that explained the workings of discourse according to the laws of human psychology. Blair's *Lectures* are less committed to science and more concerned with the task of instilling polite sentiments through the stylistic analysis of literature—a task that was consistent with the tendency to treat ethics and aesthetics as matters of personal sentiment. While belletristic criticism and the "science of man" contributed to trends that would eventually divide the humanities into the two cultures of the arts and sciences, both trends began with the assumption that the study of discourse revealed the laws that governed the individual mind, and both constituted discourse as an object of study by introspective inquiries into its psychological effects. After discourse had been founded on the laws of human nature, criticisms of taste and usage could be used to correct "unnatural" enthusiasms and instill self-restraint. Discourse and human nature defined each other for Blair, Campbell, Smith, and for all those who worked to develop human sciences through introspective analyses of the expression of ideas and sentiments. While such concerns were consistent with rhetoric's traditional attention to the effects of discourse on audiences, the shift from public debates to personal responses marks a basic transition in the history of rhetoric, a transition that arose out of the expansion of the reading public and contributed to the formation of college English.

Blair reoriented rhetoric from production to reception to adapt language studies to a reading public who needed to be taught polite taste more than the art of using discourse as a mode of practical action. While only those few who "addict themselves" to public speaking or composition needed to study rhetoric as a productive art, all would benefit from learning to develop a taste for the polite style (*Lectures* 1: 5). While Blair justified the "study of polite literature" by maintaining that "the exercise of taste is, in its native tendency, moral and purifying," he also stressed that such studies could serve as a leisure activity for even the "most busy man, in the most active sphere" (1: 13, 11). Blair's *Lectures* aptly suited the tastes of readers with increased leisure time and rising social aspirations. While Adam Smith was the first great theorist of consumer society, Blair's emphasis on taste also suited a public that was defined by the consumption and not the production of discourse. Blair provided readers with the sentiments that would ennoble them and the taste that would help them to gain acceptance in civil society. Like Smith, Blair treated style as the embodiment of personal character and turned to the *Spectator* as a model of the dispassionate style and rhetorical stance of the disinterested observer. As they internalized the stylistic proprieties of the essays of the *Spectator*, students became alienated from their own traditions and their dialectical experience as outsiders, and the essay became divorced from the political contexts and purposes that shaped its composition and reception.

In a time of increasing social unrest, Blair's *Lectures on Rhetoric and Belles Lettres* helped popularize the values of sensibility, sociability, and the other moderate virtues that maintain the proprieties of civil society. Such values were also being spread by the literary anthologies that were read along with treatises on rhetoric to provide model essays for imitation, anthologies like *The Flowers of Literature, or Treasury of Wit and Genius; Containing the Essence of the Beauties of Johnson, Swift, Fielding, Pope, Goldsmith, Hervey, Sterne, Watts & C* (1783). Other literati were also teaching the public politeness, most notably Blair's colleague Henry Mackenzie, who wrote the popular novel of sentiment *The Man of Feeling* (1771) and the essays of the *Mirror* (1779–1780) and *Lounger* (1785–1787) that imitated the models Blair taught in the classroom. Essays of taste and manners provided a tasteful alternative to the intensifying public debates of the time. Smith's *Theory of Moral Sentiments*, Blair's sermons on the moderate sensibility, and Mackenzie's belletristic essays and sentimental novels were part of an ongoing dialogue about the virtues of sociability in a society that felt threatened by political change and atomized individualism (see Dwyer, *Virtuous Discourse*). These works, like those of Hutcheson and Hume, encouraged readers to look inward, reflect on their responses to experience, and learn self-restraint by refining their tastes and eliminating party prejudices and factional interests. These works situated themselves and their readers within the domain of civil society, a domain where interpersonal relations and freely expressed sentiments fostered personal improvement, as long as one remained above the popular political enthusiasms that Smith had represented as the greatest threat to social progress and economic improvement.

Since an individual's style was an index to his or her character, belletristic criticism was seen as a means to mold sensibility as well as style. Unfortunately, the concentration on stylistic conventions tended to stifle the delicate feelings that it sought to nurture, and the idealization of natural genius, primitive sublimity, and ancient eloquence meant that individuals had limited access to discourses with real political and cultural power. Such ideals dislocated the provincial literati from the traditions and experience of their own popular culture. While provincials nostalgically valorized the sublime genius of their native culture, they internalized stylistic niceties that systematically silenced their shared traditions. As already noted, Home's biographer felt that criticism might suppress the delicate sentiments but that a refined taste was worth the cost because criticism also helped eradicate enthusiasm and instill moderation. Home's own *Elements of Criticism* presented a similar perspective on literary studies: "by uniting different ranks in the same elegant pleasures, they promote benevolence: by cherishing love of order, they inforce submission to government; and by inspiring delicacy of feeling, they make regular government a double blessing" (1: v). Blair helped to define college English by this belletristic philosophy of criticism and the political ideology that it served. With the adoption of Blair's *Lectures* as a standard text, college English came to concentrate on stylistic proprieties; literature and rhetoric moved toward the personal domain; and the productive capacities of discourse became "natural" aptitudes that were beyond the reach of most individuals.

The provincialism of this approach to teaching culture is perhaps most evident in the conflicted relations of the Edinburgh literati with Scotland's genuine native bard, Robert Burns. Burns was welcomed into the heart of the Edinburgh literati as an example of unrefined genius, unlike another Scots vernacular poet, Robert Ferguson, who was too educated to be condescended to, especially after he satirized the "man of feeling" in his poem "The Sow of Feeling," (see Smith, "Eighteenth-Century Ideas of Scotland"; Daiches 89–92). Burns's poetry has the humor and rhythm of common life, the immediacy of physical experience, and a genuine sympathy for the common sense of the folk culture. Unfortunately, he persisted in valuing the idioms that the literati were attempting to eradicate. The literati tried to teach him to write like a gentleman, with Blair advising him that "no man can be a good Poet without being somewhat of a Philosopher" (National Library of Scotland 3408: 3–4; see also Ferguson, "Burns and Hugh Blair"). The literati's response to Burns, according to Daiches, is the best example of their total inability "to deal with a whole area of imaginative literature," particularly that area of literature that was closest to the popular imagination of their own society (77). From the outset, college English studies has worked to preserve the "purity of bourgeois art" by excluding the popular culture. In a parallel manner, the "science of human nature" naturalized "common sense" by defining it as an innate faculty rather than the shared good sense of common people, and the science of laissez-faire political economy sought to exclude politics and the political arts from the public sphere to avoid disturbing the workings of such natural laws as supply and demand (Horkheimer and Adorno 135).

The literati could take pride in the fact that their essays, histories, and philosophies established a respectable place for Scottish writers in the republic of English letters, but the era of the Moderates is notably lacking in the domain of poetry, fiction, and other "works of the imagination" (see Craig, Daiches). According to Smout, even the most important writers spoke to the nostalgia for lost traditions that had led to Ossian's being canonized as the Homer of the Highlands: "Scott deliberatively, and Burns unwittingly, . . . provided the public with the nostalgic stability and sense of nationhood in the past that it sensed it was losing in the present" (499). Such nostalgia was consistent with the dialogical trends that shaped the formation of English as an object of study in the cultural provinces. The first professors of English gave more emphasis to criticism than to composition, and their emphasis on stylistic proprieties tended to alienate students of English from the traditions and idioms of their own culture. The alienation of literary studies from the popular culture would deepen as English professors developed more rigorous disciplinary methods for distinguishing "literature" from the popular culture and the rhetoric of popular politics.

The relations between the formation of college English and the development of the modern public sphere are important because the expansion of the reading public had the potential to establish a popular domain for critical reflection of the sort that Habermas has idealized, and rhetoric and moral philosophy were involved with the public forums and popular values that constituted that domain. Except for the dissenters, who opposed the political restrictions that made them outsiders in their own country, provincials were less interested in critiquing the dominant culture than in assimilating into it. The provincial anxieties and aspirations that first established college English retained their influence into the nineteenth century, when the discipline developed a broader importance and a narrower field of study as higher education expanded to teach the dominant culture to the lower classes and women. By narrowing the domain of study to literary discourse, divorcing itself from the popular culture, and marginalizing rhetoric's practical involvement with the production of public discourse, college English failed to establish a critical stance that was productively engaged with the popular traditions and public controversies that presented opportunities for social critique when the educated culture was expanded and destablized by the spread of cheap print literacy. While college English was never really meant to serve such purposes, except perhaps by the dissenters, the potential was there at the formation of the discipline and remains within it still wherever students have opportunities not just to appreciate or even to criticize the dominant culture but to compose alternatives from the traditions and experiences that they bring to the classroom.

" 'Rhetoric' in Modern Times

Really Means 'Criticism' "

Detachment, disinterestedness, indifference—aesthetic theory has so
often presented these as the only way to recognize the work of art for
what it is, autonomous, *selbständig,* that one ends up forgetting that
they really mean disinvestment, detachment, indifference, in other
words, the refusal to invest oneself.

—Bourdieu, *Distinction: A Social Critique of the Judgement of Taste*

My account of the introduction of college English studies in Britain
concludes where most histories begin, with the establishment of the first professorships of English literature. The first was established with the founding
of the London University in 1828, and then in the 1860s, a century after English first entered the university curriculum, professorships were created in
Scotland and America, and finally even at Oxford and Cambridge in the last
decade of the century. One of those professors at Edinburgh, George Saintsbury, looked back to the founder of his professorship, Hugh Blair, and praised
him for "accepting to the full the important truth that 'Rhetoric' in modern
times really means 'Criticism'" (463). Other early professors of literature such
as those at London also cited Blair as a predecessor, but critics who have been
farther removed from the transition from *rhetoric* to *criticism* have not generally accepted Blair and his contemporaries as the founders of college English, even though professorships of English literature were often refashioned
from chairs of rhetoric (see Palmer, McMurty, and William Riley Parker). In
the assumption that the study of English is more or less synonymous with the
study of literature, in the modern sense of that term, historians of the discipline have concluded that English studies only became a discipline when literary studies moved away from rhetoric and became a specialized area of

scholarly inquiry. Journalism and other utilitarian forms of public discourse moved outside the discipline, and in Britain if not in America, rhetoric became a historical footnote for those interested in teaching "English for academic purposes."[1]

While most histories of college English begin with the nineteenth century, reforms in the eighteenth-century cultural provinces contributed to the establishment of the first professorships of English literature. The dissenting academy tradition contributed to the founding in 1828 of London University, the first English university to be without religious tests. In 1831 King's College was opened by supporters of the established church, and when the two institutions formed an uneasy union as the University of London in 1836, professorships of English literature were part of both King's College and University College (see Bellot). At the same time that Utilitarian reformers like Jeremy Bentham, James Mill, and Henry Brougham were working with a group of dissenters to establish London University, Mill and Brougham were collaborating with other liberal Scottish Whigs on the *Edinburgh Review,* which was assailing Oxbridge for its narrow classicism. The utilitarian assumptions underlying these positions had first been applied to higher education by Scottish professors of moral philosophy such as Adam Smith, and dissenters such as Joseph Priestley had been the first to redefine higher education itself in utilitarian terms to serve the needs of students who were more likely to work in trade and manufacture than to retire to a country parish or estate. In important respects, the Utilitarianism of James Mill and Bentham is the conduit through which developments in Scotland and the dissenting academies contributed to the reforms of the nineteenth century, including the establishment of first professorships of English literature.

Historians have viewed the history of college English differently because they have different perspectives on what college English is. I have reviewed how the teaching of English was first introduced into higher education in order to examine how it was transformed as it expanded beyond the traditional elite and took up the modern mission of educating a more heterogeneous public. To conclude my historical account, I survey the establishment of the first professorships of English literature and then use the debate between Matthew Arnold and Thomas Huxley as a case study for assessing how the conflict between the ancients and moderns became redefined in terms of the opposition of literature and science. Almost as soon as utilitarian reformers founded the first professorship of English literature, literary studies became defined by their opposition to the utilitarianism that would eventually establish the sciences' dominance of the modern research university. Arnold divorced criticism from practical affairs and public politics in order to establish its "disinterestedness," while advocates of the "culture of science" such as

Huxley made ultimately more convincing claims to authority and viewed the profession of "Literature" as simply a part of the "old Rhetoric" (*Essays* 206). Whether one defines it as new or old, rhetoric was nearing the end of its historical importance in the British university curriculum. With such influential promoters of scientific efficiency as Alexander Bain, rhetoric's practical concerns became reduced to mechanical skills, and the profession of English became a critical enterprise that lacked the productive engagement with public politics and popular values that had been shared by moral philosophy and rhetoric before the former moved toward the social sciences and the latter was subordinated to belletristic criticism.

The Expansion of Higher Education in Nineteenth-Century England

In the nineteenth century, English studies continued to gain importance in broad-based institutions as the reading public continued to expand. In addition to the college founded at London in 1828, reformers founded colleges at Manchester in 1850, at Leeds in 1874, at Sheffield in 1879, at Birmingham in 1880, and at Liverpool and Nottingham in 1881. These institutions were often shaped by the Utilitarianism of Bentham and James Mill, with the former claiming Priestley as a predecessor and the latter a student of the Scottish Enlightenment.[2] At the end of the eighteenth century, English literature had become publicly accessible through the cheap reprint series that had appeared when the perpetual copyright was removed, as I discussed in the first chapter. Nineteenth-century anthology series made the classics of English readily available to the reading public. Several series were published in editions of hundreds of thousands, with *Chandos Classics* reportedly selling a phenomenal three and a half million copies between 1868 and 1884 (Altick 243). These series and the critical commentary that accompanied them established English literature as the "poor man's classics" (Palmer 78). The editors and professors who taught the public how to read literature included individuals such as Henry Morley, who was professor of English language and literature at University College in the latter half of the nineteenth century, when such professorships were becoming widely established throughout Britain. Morley edited series of reprints of literary masterworks, multivolume historical accounts of British literature, and complete library sets of the modern canon of the educated culture for those who wanted to buy a shelf of the classics to educate themselves, or at least to serve as a conspicuous sign that they had the taste to buy the right books.[3]

London University was founded as a public stock company to educate "the youth of our middling rich people" (qtd. Silver 40). Bentham, Brougham, and others had worked with a conference of dissenters to establish the college, and the guiding assumptions from the outset were Utilitarian (see Bellot 21–23). The curriculum of London University, later renamed University College, had more in common with the dissenting academies and Scottish universities than with the English universities. The emphasis was on professional studies, primarily law and medicine, but the range of subjects included sciences, modern languages, and political economy as well as classics and mathematics. According to Bellot, "deliberate imitations of Scottish practice" included "the extended range of subjects of university study, the lecture system, the non-residence of the students, their admission to single courses, the absence of religious tests, the dependence of the professors upon fees, and the democratic character of the institution" (8). As in Scotland, English was the language of instruction. According to most histories of college English, the first professorship of English was the professorship of English language and literature at London University that was first held by Thomas Dale. Dale was a dissenting clergymen, a significant point given the fact that University College was so concertedly secular that Matthew Arnold condemned it as that "Godless institution on Gower Street" (qtd. Lawson and Silver 258).

Reverend Dale was professor of English language and literature at University College from 1828 to 1830 and professor of English literature and history at King's College from 1835 to 1840. According to his *Introductory Lecture Delivered in the University of London* (1828), Dale lectured on the history and "philosophy" of English, English literature, elocution, and composition. In a fashion consistent with his evangelical background, Dale's two-year program of English studies was straightforwardly moralistic: "in all my Lectures, more particularly when treating upon that glorious and inexhaustible subject, the LITERATURE of our country—I shall esteem it my duty—and I trust I shall find it my delight—to inculcate lessons of virtue, through the medium of the masters of our language" (30; see Palmer 20). Dale followed in the tradition of Hugh Blair's *Lectures on Rhetoric and Belles Lettres,* which he edited in 1845. Dale's introduction to Blair's *Lectures* opens with detailed criticisms of Blair's own style, with the rest of the introduction devoted to remedying Blair's inadequate attention to the historical development of Anglo-Saxon and English. The professors who followed Dale gradually moved beyond the belletristic emphasis on style to give more stress to the historical study of English and its literature, but polite sentiments continued to be stressed as a means to instill sensibility in the age of science.

Dale was succeeded at King's College in 1840 by F. D. Maurice, who was one of the founders of Queen's College for women in 1848 and the Working

Men's College that evolved out of the public lectures at King's College in 1854. One of several early professors of English literature to have ties with colleges that expanded higher education to address a broader educated public, Maurice became the first principal of the Working Men's College after being dismissed from King's College in 1853 for challenging the doctrines of the established church. Maurice's *Sketches of Contemporary Authors* (1828) and *The Friendship of Books and Other Lectures* (1874) document the values that English literature was meant to teach. While literature was taught to spread a patriotic respect for English history and culture, Maurice particularly valued the personal "friendship" between readers and writers. Our "friend" the poet is not "a more special man than we are; he is more of a common man. The human sympathies have been more awakened in him than in us." Maurice's assumption that "the heart of the critic is in sympathy with the heart of the writer" had clear continuities with the emphasis that earlier professors of English had placed on the sympathetic imagination (*Friendship* 314, 388). Smith valued sympathy because it maintained sociability in an increasingly depersonalized society, and Maurice also viewed the "culture of the heart" as a remedy to a commercial society in which "production, and accumulation, have become the vocation of the world" (*Sketches* 118). With Maurice, the opposition of romantic sentiments to popular utilitarian values was beginning to reduce the study of English to the study of literature, with literature defined as nonutilitarian nonfactual discourse that cultivated the imagination (see Winterowd and Blum).

As it became defined by such oppositions, the teaching of literature was beginning to assume a shape that is readily recognizable to modern professors of literature. From 1865 to 1890 English literature became a distinct area of university study throughout Britain and America. At this time the professorship of English literature at University College was held by Henry Morley, whose career and teaching are described in McMurty's *English Language, English Literature: The Creation of an Academic Discipline*. McMurty has claimed that Morley was "the first to devote an academic career solely to English studies," though one could make the same claim for Hugh Blair's academic career a century earlier if one does not define the study of English as the study of literature (50). Morley published anthologies and critical works on English literature, and he was a popular teacher who lectured in an enthusiastic fact-filled fashion on the historical development of English and its literature. In his years as professor, enrollment in the two-year program of English studies grew from 52 to 159. In addition to graduation examinations for the degree in English instituted in 1882, Morley's students wrote essays and responses to such essay questions as "Describe briefly the argument by which Wordsworth justified the style of his 'Lyrical Ballads'"; "Compare with references to first principles, the styles of any three important living writers"; "Write a short essay on the principles of criticism"; and "Discuss separately the considerations that determine choice and portion of words in an English sentence" (McMurty 53). Such questions, which were consistent with graduation examinations, suggest that literature was becoming a well-demarcated scholarly domain with its own purposes and "arguments," which were studied to demonstrate mastery of the subject area, rather than to learn practical skills that could be used to develop other sorts of arguments.[4]

Morley taught a "Maidens' class" for women, and from 1878, he also lectured on English at Queen's College for women, which had been established in 1848. Women began to gain access to higher education through the extension classes and public lecture series that were being established at the time, partially as a result of groups like the Ladies Educational Association, which originated in the North of England in the 1860s and soon spread throughout Britain and America. According to McMurty, women were well represented in lectures on English literature, and women's colleges were among the first institutions to integrate such studies fully into the college curriculum (11–13). According to the first professor of English at Queen's College, Charles Kingsley, "it is the primary idea of this College to vindicate women's right to an education in all points equal to that of men; the difference between them being determined not by any fancied inferiority of mind, but simply by the distinct offices and character of the sexes" (Kingsley, *Works* 20: 240).

While literature was becoming a well-demarcated area of study in the classroom, early professors of English such as Kingsley still wrote for popular rather than scholarly audiences on a range of topics that situated literary studies in the broader agenda of liberal reform. Kingsley was a novelist as well as a clergyman and published essays for a journal called *Politics for the People* (1848), which sought to dissuade the lower classes from the radical politics of the Chartists (see Kingsley *Letters and Memories*). Like his predecessors, Kingsley taught literature as a means to cultivate polite sentiments and instill a respect for the national culture. He stressed that such studies were well "adapted to the mind of woman" because they called "into fullest exercise her blessed faculty of sympathy" (*Works* 20: 258). His introductory lectures provide insights into how the entrance of women into higher education engendered concepts such as "sympathy." Through her "vocation as priestess of charity," a woman's heart can

> deliver man from bondage to his own tyrannous and all-too-exclusive brain—from our daily sin of looking at men, not as our struggling and suffer-

ing brothers, but as mere symbols of certain formulae, incarnations of sets of opinions, wheels in some iron liberty-grinding or Christianity-spinning machine. (20: 258–59)

Women's ability to "look instinctively at the world" would help to remedy the dehumanizing tendencies of a utilitarian "liberty-grinding" political economy. Such oppositions document how the moralizing sentiments that had shaped English studies from their origins were adapted to the expanding mission of public education as more diverse groups were assimilated into the educated public.

From its origins in the cultural provinces, college English had been oriented to teaching students to internalize the proprieties of English taste and usage, and as the educated public expanded to include the working classes and women, English literature gained importance as a means to teach students to respect the common culture. Such respect could not be learned by rote. It had to be felt. Like earlier professors and critics, the first professors of English literature modeled the psychological responses of enculturated readers, and some emphasized essays as a way to help students express their feelings. Kingsley set up a student-centered pedagogy by asking students in his opening lecture what they wanted to study. Kingsley assumed that "pupils themselves are very often best able to tell their teachers what sort of instruction they require" (*Works* 20: 229, 41). Kingsley's course generally began with analyses of early English ballads to "discover many of the great primary laws of composition, as well as the secrets of sublimity and pathos in their simplest manifestations," and then he discussed Chaucer, Shakespeare, and later writers (20: 238). Literature was used to teach style as well as sentiment, and Kingsley promised to spend half of each class reading and discussing students' essays. He advised students to form their style not by the doctrines of Blair and Kames but by a "critical examination" of the best literature. "As Professor Maurice warned me when I undertook this lectureship, my object in teaching you about 'styles' should be that you may have no style at all" (2: 237). The view that students' essays should have "no style at all" suggests that the conventions of the essay were already so well institutionalized that they were understood to be the natural way for students to express themselves.

Historians have tended to use the introduction of English studies into colleges for women and the working class as evidence of the discipline's marginal status in elite institutions, but if one does not center the history of English studies on more conservative universities, then the position of English studies in those institutions that were working as agents of social change becomes more important than its grudging acceptance by the traditional elite. Centrifugal as well as centripetal forces were at work in the mechanics' institutes and working men's colleges that developed out of them. The London Mechanics' Institute was established in 1823, twenty more opened in 1824, and seventy more in 1825. These institutions offered access to libraries and classes in practical scientific areas as well as subjects intended for personal self-improvement like English literature. According to a survey of forty such institutions in James Hole's *The History and Management of Literary, Scientific, and Mechanics Institutions* (1853), about one-third of the lectures were devoted to scientific studies, while more than half were devoted to English literature and composition (see Palmer 31–33). Such institutions helped to spread learning to the working classes, while also trying to ensure that what they learned was appropriate to their position in society. While conservatives worried about the widespread demand for courses in political economy, mechanics' institutes were also attacked by working-class journals like the *Poor Man's Guardian* because radicals believed that polite proprieties were emphasized to limit more explicitly political discussions (see Silver 41–44; Lawson and Silver 261–62). The conflicts between middle-class reformers and working-class radicals mark out the contested boundaries of the reading public and the institutions that were positioned at those boundaries—institutions that included some of the first professors of English literature.

Rather than only looking within the discipline at the professionalization of literature, we need broader accounts of the changes in literacy that made English literature into the "poor man's Classics" (Palmer vii). Utilitarians worked to expand working-class literacy because they wanted literate workers to join them in supporting reforms, as is evident in Brougham's *Practical Observations upon . . . Education* (1825), a pamphlet he put together from his articles in the *Edinburgh Review*. Like other Utilitarians, Brougham argued that education would make the poor independent and productive, while governmental relief would simply increase their numbers and their indolence. Brougham called for promoting cheap reprints, *"Book Clubs," "Reading Societies,"* workers' institutes, and libraries, citing the Library Company of Philadelphia that Franklin founded in 1731 as a model for such self-supporting and self-governing efforts (25). He stressed that workers should themselves determine what they wanted to read. According to Brougham, the English working classes tended to read more for entertainment, but "habits of reading" were more broadly established in Scotland, where workers often read more serious works such as Bacon's essays (6, 4). Brougham believed that working people had the time and motivation to read if cheap reading material and opportunities for collaborative learning were made available. He specifically opposed limitations on literacy such as a current tax on paper, "which is truly a tax upon knowledge, and falls the heaviest upon those who most want instruction" (3). Like other Utilitarians and their predecessors such as Priestley, Brougham criticized governmental efforts to restrict the circulation of books on political history and political economy because they promote the "good of the working classes, as well as of their superiors" (7). However, Brougham did not limit working-class reading to the merely utilitarian: "a high degree of intellectual refinement and a taste for the pleasures of speculation, without any view to a particular employment, may be united with a life of hard labour, even in its most humble branches, and may both prove its solace and its guide" (27). Such views explain why the Utilitarians were instrumental in founding some of the first professorships of English literature, and they suggest that the purposes served by opposing literature to utilitarianism were more complex than they might appear to those within the discipline.

Institutions such as University College and the workers' colleges contributed to the same Utilitarian agenda that was served by the Society for the Diffusion of Useful Knowledge, which was founded by Mill, Brougham, and other reformers in 1827. In 1820 Brougham had introduced a bill in Parliament in an unsuccessful attempt to broaden English grammar schools along the lines of the generalist curriculum of the Scottish parish schools. Vicesimus Knox, the Oxford don discussed in the second chapter, responded with *Remarks on the Tendency of a Bill now in Parliament to degrade Grammar Schools* (1820), which argued that social relations were being destablized by Utilitarians' efforts to spread practical scientific learning (see Adamson 48–49). While liberals can be defined by their efforts to teach the working classes practical skills and self-improvement, conservatives sought to perpetuate the classical authorities of the grammar schools and English universities. As discussed in the second chapter, the antiquarian devotion to classicism inculcated the culture of a gentleman through years of painstaking study of ancient languages, and those who wore the class ties of prestigious public schools were taught a common cultural ideology founded on an insurmountable faith in their own superiority. In the face of increasing social diversification, classical studies became even more important to preserving the authority of the traditional elite. Groups like the Clarendon Commission of 1864 reiterated the restriction of education to classical languages, and the classics continued to dominate an Oxbridge education into the twentieth century.[5]

The narrow classicism of the centers of English education was repeatedly criticized by Brougham, Francis Jeffrey, and other liberal Scots in the journal that they founded in 1802, the *Edinburgh Review,* which was much more successful than the short-lived *Edinburgh Review* established by Adam Smith,

Hugh Blair, and the moderate literati (see chapter 5). The second *Edinburgh Review* was "one of the great moulders of public opinion in early nineteenth-century Britain, and especially perhaps of middle-class opinion" (Ferguson, *Scotland* 267). The *Review* included calls for reform by James Mill, and contributors from 1807 to the 1830s took every possible opportunity to attack the classicism of the English universities. Authors repeatedly asserted that education should instill "the great principle of utility" as "the managing, the presiding, the governing sentiment in the breast of every member of society" (*Edinburgh Review* 14: 189). However, in the English universities, "the great principle of utility is vilified and disgraced throughout the whole course of study" because "classical learning occupies an immense proportion of the field of education." "Nothing would so much tend to bring classical literature within proper bounds as a steady and invaluable appeal to utility" (15: 188–89, 51). While the attacks on classicism could be seen as a sign of the expanding influence of liberal reform, they were actually a response to the increasing centralization of British education, for it was the Scottish universities that were being forced to conform to the centers of English education and not the other way around.

English Literature and English Politics in the Scottish Universities

Scottish reformers were concerned with the English university system because they were being pressed to become part of it. Scots' attitudes to assimilation changed markedly as a result of such pressures. According to Phillipson, "if the process had been seen in the eighteenth century as controllable from within, in the nineteenth it appeared as a pressure operating from without, as something which was controlling the development of much of Scottish life but which Scotsmen could not themselves control" ("Public Opinion" 144). Beginning in 1826, several royal commissions worked to bring the Scottish universities into a centralized system of education. With each visitation, they were pushed to implement a more specialized curriculum and raise standards to make the universities more scholarly and less accessible, like Oxford and Cambridge. While the English universities concentrated on classical languages and mathematics, the Scots tended to take a less philological approach to the former and a more humanistic approach to the latter.[6]

Though many Scots defended the merits of their system, less flexible programs of study were instituted, and the age of admission was raised. Following the Universities Act of 1858, English studies became a formal part of the standard curriculum, and professorships in English literature were widely instituted, often by renaming chairs of rhetoric and belles lettres or rhetoric and logic. Those chairs of rhetoric had been established by Scots who assumed that assimilation meant progress, but assimilationist pressures were now undermining those institutional features that had made the universities responsive to social change.

Despite such trends, a more generalist approach to the teaching of English was carried on by notable professors such as George Jardine, a student of Adam Smith's who held his former professorship of logic at Glasgow from 1787 to 1826. Jardine's course was divided into four parts:

1) "An analysis of the faculties of the mind, chiefly those of the understanding.—Illustrated by the principles of language and of general grammar";

2) "The art of improving those faculties of the mind, by which a knowledge of the causes, properties, and relations of things is acquired.—Illustrated by the history of logic, and explanation of the principal rules of that art";

3) "The art of improving the powers of taste.—Illustrated by the history of the principal arts of taste and of criticism"; and

4) "The art of improving the faculty of communication.—Illustrated by the history of eloquence and of rhetoric." (*Synopsis* 5–6)

As in the eighteenth century, this program of study was founded on the assumption that the study of human psychology or "pneumatology is the centre and capital of the Sciences and Arts" (*Synopsis* 6–7). In studies of the "science of human nature," the student was "assisted in making experiments on himself, in the application of inductive reasoning in the discovery of the laws of mind" (9). Unlike Blair, however, Jardine was very involved with teaching. After an hour of lectures on "the proper method of improving the faculties of reason, of taste, and of communication by speech and writing," an additional hour or two were spent on "Examinations and Exercises" in the assumption that composition was the best way to improve reason and taste (1, i). Jardine emphasized the need for carefully sequenced compositions on literature, history, and logic. In addition to reading and commenting on essays himself, he also had students collaborate on their peers' essays to help ease the paper load imposed by his two hundred students (ii–v).

According to Davie and Horner, Jardine's *Outlines of Philosophical Education* (1818) is an example of the Scottish tradition at its best, though I believe his pedagogy also has much in common with the practically engaged approach of the dissenters. In his account of the curriculum at Glasgow, Jardine's colleague Thomas Reid praised Jardine's course in "general grammar, rhetoric, and belles lettres" for repudiating deductive reasoning, emphasizing student compositions, and advancing the science of human nature (*Works* 735). As a provincial who was committed to teaching, Jardine attempted to reorient the liberal arts to educating a broader public:

> philosophical education, as it is generally conducted in our universities, is too much confined to the mere communication of knowledge; and . . . too little attention is bestowed on the formation of those intellectual habits of thinking, judging, reasoning, and communication, upon which the farther prosecutions of science, and the business of active life, almost entirely depend. (*Outlines* v)

Jardine contrasted this philosophy of the liberal arts with an "exclusive" emphasis on classical learning and concluded that Scottish universities placed greater value on "science both physical and mental, than . . . the most accurate knowledge of the ancient tongues" (418–19). Jardine's student Francis Jeffrey defended the Scots' generalist approach to the liberal arts before the Royal Commission of 1826 by arguing that it was better suited to public education because it was best able to "liberalise and make intelligent the mass of our population" (qtd. Davie 27).

The Scottish universities were the first to introduce the study of the modern culture because they were the first to take up the modern mission of educating the public. From Hutcheson through Jardine, the public was taught to look inward and study the "science of human nature," a science formalized from introspective examinations of the psychological processes involved in cultural assimilation, with the dominant culture internalized in the form of a second self to monitor every action and reaction. Most markedly with Campbell and the commonsense philosophers, rhetoric and moral philosophy were reoriented away from public debates over shared values to view common sense as a psychological rather than sociological matter. The limitations of commonsense realism are clear in the teaching of Dugald Stewart, the most influential commonsense philosopher and perhaps the most popular moral philosopher in the English-speaking world in the nineteenth century. Stewart's *Outline of Moral Philosophy* presents the substance of the course that he began teaching at Edinburgh in 1793. Stewart divides moral philosophy into three parts: "the intellectual powers of man," "his active and moral powers," and "man, considered as the member of political body," with the last area of study also concentrating on the "essential principles of our constitution" (*Works* 2: 11). Stewart did not publish on politics in his lifetime, though his *Lectures on Political Economy* were published posthumously. Stewart's approach, like his predecessors, advanced the "science of human nature," or as Alexander Bain termed it, "psychology." As moral philosophy gave rise to the sciences of psychology and political economy, it lost the engagement with purposeful practical action that it had shared with rhetoric in the civic humanist tradition.[7]

These trends explain why a nineteenth-century psychologist such as Bain had the same sort of impact on rhetoric that a political economist had had in the prior century. As is clear in the case of Jardine and in the dissenting academy tradition generally, provincials were concerned with the psychology and sociology of learning because they had had to consciously teach themselves the dominant culture. This engagement with pedagogy is important because when professors have to teach a practical skill such as composition, they cannot simply lecture on received systems of knowledge without considering how they are being interpreted by students. Scottish professors' attention to composition limited efforts to institute the more classically oriented approach favored by the centers of English education according to a professor who testified to the Royal Commission of 1826: "with regard to classes of Logic and Moral Philosophy—they are both to be considered in their practical tendency classes for teaching composition" (qtd. Davie 28). Then as now, many professors felt that such teaching took too much time away from the efficient transmission of knowledge. Bain helped to make public education more efficient by reducing teaching and learning to sciences with such works as *English Composition and Rhetoric* (1866), *Mental and Moral Science* (1868), and *Education as a Science* (1879). According to Bain, "the great principle of Division of Labour" dictated that subjects should be broken down into basic skills, with English teachers having "nothing to do with the matter, except in relation to the manner" (*Education* 357). Science and mechanical correctness had had a natural affinity from the beginnings of the "new" rhetoric, but when the need for efficiency in public education became a compelling factor, the combination of science and mechanics became a deadeningly efficient routine of drills to skills that divorced formal conventions from matters of public significance.

Following the belletrism of Blair as well as the scientism of Campbell, Bain founded his theory of rhetoric on mental faculties and treated style as the unifying concern of rhetoric, composition, and literature. According to Bain, "there are three principal ends in speaking,—to inform, to persuade, to please. They correspond to the three departments of the human mind, the Understanding, the Will, and the Feelings" (*Composition* 19). While their models differ as to the number of faculties, Campbell's epistemological approach was clearly Bain's point of departure (see also 214). Like Campbell and Blair, Bain dismissed invention and concentrated on correctness. Like many professors of literature at the time, Bain treated the principles of rhetoric as "the basis of

literary criticism," but he did not make literature into a subject unto itself because he assumed that the principles of style make literature "self-explaining"
(*Education* 355). Literature remained primarily a means to improve composition; thus, moderns were preferred to classics; prose was to be studied more
than poetry; and extracts were seen as better than whole works to avoid students' being distracted by the "matter" of the passages being criticized (*On
Teaching* 15). Bain rejected the traditional emphasis on essay writing in the
courses taught by such "celebrated and successful teachers, as Jardine," because essays were but the "crude devices of the infancy of the education art"
(*On Teaching* 23–24). In the age of science, writing and reading were to be
taught methodically as basic skills through an efficient regimen of exercises
dictated by the mental faculties. Bain's scientific efficiency advanced utilitarian ideals in just the sort of reductivist way that would set them, and the teaching of composition founded upon them, outside the realm of "literature."

Bain's educational philosophy and practice marked out some of the trends
that would divide modern higher education into two opposing cultures, but
he saw no problems in applying the logic of the sciences to the arts and humanities. Concluding that the era when "higher knowledge was . . . made to
flow through two dead languages should now be considered as drawing to a
close," Bain reconceptualized "Liberal Education" to advance the trends toward scientism and belletrism that were established by his predecessors (*Education* vi–vii). According to Bain's six-year program of study, which extends
from the high school to university, "The Renovated Curriculum" would include three divisions: the sciences, the humanities, and English composition
and literature. The humanities are divided between history and "Universal
Literature," with the former including social sciences like political economy
and the latter covering the whole "Literature of the World" (390–92). "Universal Literature" would be based on "the beau-ideal of Rhetoric and Belles
Lettres as conceived by the chief modern authorities in the department, as for
example, Campbell and Blair in the last century" (391). The priorities of the
curriculum are clear in Bain's comment that "I would not call Science alone a
Liberal Education, although a course that implied a fair knowledge of Natural Science, and a wide grasp of Sociology, would be no mean equipment for
the battle of life" (392). Bain's approach had a pervasive impact. According
to William James in 1876, "the two philosophers of indubitably the widest
influence in England and America since Mill's death are Messrs. Bain and
Spencer" (qtd. Potter 117 n). Bain was particularly influential in modernizing
composition teaching according to such historians as Donald Stewart,
Kitzhaber, and Connors. Bain's influence helps to explain the limitations of
modern rhetoric and composition, for his approach included no sense of the

aesthetic experience of literature, the political uses of rhetoric, or the creativity involved in the composing process.

At the same time that composition teaching was being reduced to a science, professorships of rhetoric and belles lettres were being redefined as chairs of literature. After Blair's death in 1800, his professorship remained little more than a sinecure until William Edmonstone Aytoun occupied it in 1845. During his tenure from 1845 to 1865, enrollment rose from thirty to fifty. Edmonstone was an important member of the Edinburgh literati—a poet, compiler of popular ballads, and essayist for the *Edinburgh Review*'s Tory competitor, *Blackwood's Magazine*. According to the university *Calendar* for Aytoun's last year at Edinburgh, his course included lectures on composition and public speaking, "examinations" of the style of English authors, and "a complete review of British literature . . . each epoch being considered referentially to the external history and social development of the country." Instruction in rhetoric was limited to what was "strictly practical and useful," but like most professors of literature, he still had to teach composition, a task that led him to complain about having to grade a weekly pile of essays that was large enough "to roast an ox" (qtd. Meikle 102). In 1827 the course in English was added to graduation requirements, and by 1864 graduation examinations in English had come to include only two questions on rhetoric and two on the English language, but eight on English literature. In 1865, the professorship of rhetoric and belles lettres was redefined as a chair in rhetoric and English literature to reflect the increased attention to literature and the departure from belletrism. Professorships in English literature were also established at Glasgow in 1862, at Dundee in 1882, at Aberdeen in 1893, and at St. Andrews in 1897. Several of these positions were held by scholars who helped establish English literature as a scholarly discipline (see Horner and McMurty).

From Ancients and Moderns to the Opposition of Literature and Science

In this era, according to J. S. Mill, "educational reformers and conservatives" were no longer simply arguing over "ancients and moderns" so much as "whether general education should be classical—let me use a wider expression, and say literary—or scientific" ("Address at St. Andrews" 138). As Mill's comment suggests, the modern opposition of literature to science was in some respects a continuation of the former debate. The conflict between what C. P. Snow has termed the "two cultures" of the arts and sciences came into clear focus in an exchange between an Oxford professor of poetry, Matthew Arnold, and a professor of physiology at the University of London, Thomas Huxley. Arnold began his lectures as professor of poetry at Oxford in 1857 with "On the Modern Element in Literature" and concluded a decade later with "Anarchy and Authority." Unlike his predecessors and nineteenth-century successors at Oxford, Arnold lectured in English, and during his tenure, he produced works such as "The Function of Criticism at the Present Time" that shaped the founding ideals of modern literary studies. Arnold wrote "Literature and Science" (1885) in response to Huxley's argument that a literary education was inadequate in the age of science. While their cultural theories are too complex to be fully characterized here, several of their basic claims about whether science or literature should define modern education are suggestive of later developments. With Arnold, criticism becomes committed to the task of eradicating "provincialism," particularly the Utilitarianism of Benthamites. While Arnold helped establish the critical stance of modern literary studies, Huxley is important because he spoke for the broader ideological and institutional trends that would shape the modern university, trends that had begun to emerge when the humanities were first translated into English in the previous century.

In important respects the debate between Arnold and Huxley is the point where utilitarian justifications for the teaching of English were repudiated as elite institutions began to establish the study of literature as a subject unto itself. As already noted, Utilitarianism provides the point of contact between eighteenth-century reforms and the founding of the first professorships of English literature, but "the culture of the heart" was soon set in opposition to the utilitarian values of the times. When they first brought the modern culture into the classroom, rhetoricians had aligned themselves with the sciences, but nineteenth-century men of science were beginning to argue for the primacy of what Huxley called the "culture of science," a culture that had its own methods for putting knowledge into action. Huxley's collection of essays, *Science and Education,* opens with an essay lauding Priestley as an early spokesman for the progress of reason, and the collection includes a dozen speeches on the virtues of science that were delivered at the founding of institutions intended to advance practical learning—working men's colleges as well as research universities such as Johns Hopkins University. While Huxley spoke for diverse institutions concerned with expanding scientific learning, Arnold spoke from the center of the learned culture and defended its traditional authority. Arnold felt that classical languages should remain central to all education, and he defended the church control of education that had made the English universities bastions of the status quo, rejecting the secularism of University College as a violation of "the great principle that Christianity should be the base of all public education" (qtd. Adamson 69).

With Arnold, the centers of English education took up the project of eradicating "provincialism" as public education became centralized. Arnold regretted that his predecessors had failed to set up a central academy to "purify" English: "the less a literature has felt the influence of a supposed centre of correct information, correct judgment, correct taste, the more we shall find in it this note of provinciality" (*Works* 3: 244–45). Only when culture is "rid of provinciality," can writers create "classical prose, prose of the centre" (3: 246). Arnold's first lecture at Oxford, "On the Modern Element in Literature," began by defending the central role of classics in education and ended by defining Periclean Greece as more "modern" than the reign of Elizabeth because the Greeks possessed the "critical spirit" of modernism, while Elizabethans uncritically mixed factual accounts with outrageous fantasies (1: 23–27). Arnold condemned the public as "Barbarians, Philistines, and Populace" and concluded that "the English middle class presents us at this day, for our actual needs, and for the purposes of national civilisation, with a defective type of religion, a narrow range of intellect and knowledge, a stunted sense of beauty, a low standard of manners" (10: 6, 10). Arnold opposed the classics to all that was "defective," "narrow," "stunted," and "low" in modern society, and his ideal of "classical prose of the centre" followed in the tradition of Swift and Johnson to distinguish between the classically educated and merely literate, even as the basic sense of "Classics" was expanding beyond the ancients.

In his years as professor of poetry, Arnold turned from writing literature to presenting it as "a criticism of life," a criticism that is essentially characterized by its *disinterestedness* (3: 270). Toward the end of his tenure, Arnold published his influential *Essays in Criticism: First Series* (1865). The lead essay, "The Function of Criticism at the Present Time," stressed that "Criticism, real criticism" is "a disinterested endeavor" concerned with "the best that is known and thought in the world, irrespective of practice, politics, and everything of the kind" (3: 283, 271). Arnold stressed that the critic "must keep out of the region of immediate practice in the political, social humanitarian sphere," not only to oppose the utilitarianism that dominates that sphere but also because criticism requires the perspective of a "spectator" who is "disinterested" (3: 275, 283). Noting that the "bane of criticism in this country. . . . is that practical considerations cling to it and stifle it," Arnold sought to demarcate a "pure intellectual sphere" detached from "ulterior, political, practical considerations" (270). Literary criticism was thus fundamentally opposed to Utilitarian values, not simply because they evaluated experiences and ideas by their utility, or even because the definitive value was the greatest good for the greatest number, but also because the whole value system began and ended with practical considerations. Nothing could be more opposed to Utilitarianism than the idea that intellectuals should confine themselves to a pure intellectual sphere divorced from practical affairs. The purity of this sphere was defined in opposition to popular values, and such oppositions demarcated the literary from the practical in ways that proved quite unproductive for the humanities.

The ideal of a disinterested criticism that was divorced from practical utility was consistent with classicism, though not with civic humanism. Arnold believed that his ideal of a disinterested criticism that would correct the provincialism of modern tastes was not a departure from the classicism of the English universities, referring to his own "puny warfare against the Philistine" as but another battle in the war that his "beloved" Oxford had raised "against them for centuries" (3: 288). This positioning of the humanities in opposition to practical affairs and the popular culture was consistent with Oxford's traditional aloofness from the public, but this stance was quite different from the more integrated role that Scots and dissenters had envisioned for public education. Arnold's effort to "purify" criticism is important, I think, because the modern humanities have suffered from their failure to establish practical involvements with the public sphere. Though Arnold himself was a public intellectual of the sort who have been rare in the modern humanities, Arnoldian humanism maintained its purity by divorcing ideas from practical applications in the assumption that "ideas cannot be too much prized in and for themselves." Arnold maintained that "there is the world of ideas and there is the world of practice," with the two domains necessarily kept distinct so that disinterested judgments can be made (3: 265). In Arnoldian humanism, as in earlier conceptions of the "disinterested spectator," critical distance entailed practical disengagement, a disengagement that would leave the realm of social praxis to the instrumental logic of the sciences.

In "Science and Culture" Huxley responded to Arnold's definition of culture as "the best that has been thought and said in the world," particularly "the criticism of life contained in literature" (qtd. 142). According to Huxley, Arnold had made two basic claims: "a criticism of life is the essence of culture," and "literature contains the materials which suffice for the construction of such a criticism" (143). While Huxley accepted the former claim, he asserted that "for the purpose of attaining real culture, an exclusively scientific education is at least as effectual as an exclusively literary education" and concluded that a liberal education should contain them both (140). Huxley had reservations about Arnoldian humanism, but he was unreservedly critical of classicists as "monopolists of liberal education" (137). Huxley directly challenged the authority of tradition and the literature that embodied it. According to Huxley, a "scientific 'criticism of life'" "appeals not to authority, nor to what anybody may have thought or said, but to nature" (150). Praising Priestley as an early defender of the cause of applying reason to education, politics, and religion, Huxley addressed himself to the most current "crises" in "a long series of battles, which have been fought over education in a campaign which began long before Priestley's time, and will probably not be finished just yet." According to his account of the ongoing battle between the moderns and ancients, the conflict had shifted with the arrival of a "third army ranged under the banner of Physical Science" (136).

The conflict, as Huxley understood it, was between two different views of "liberal education," which Huxley defined as a "broad" education suited to a "free" people (238). Such conceptions of liberal or general education were defined by the assumption that those being educated were the general public and not merely a narrow elite.[8] According to Huxley, a liberal education should emphasize science, both as a "subject-matter" and as a "discipline which the learning of science involves" (166). As a "discipline," science trains the mind, and as a subject, science is important in "getting on" in the "practical affairs of life" and in the professions, among which he includes engineering, an inclusion that would transform the whole conception of the learned professions (113, 239). Like earlier educational reformers among the Scots and dissenters, Huxley assumed that science provides the best "educational discipline" because "it supplies in a better form than any other study can supply, exercise in a special form of logic, and a peculiar method of testing the validity of our processes of inquiry" (162). These views had first been introduced into education by the Scots and dissenters who reformed the curriculum according to the logic of science, and Huxley was an influential advocate of making "scientific culture" a major part of public education from elementary through university studies (162).

In "Universities: Actual and Ideal" (1874), Huxley outlined the "ideal" curriculum as including all the fine arts, "Moral and Religious philosophy," and natural science (206–07). Huxley cited Kant as an authority, though with qualifications: "Kant has said that the ultimate object of all knowledge is to give replies to these three questions: What can I do? What ought I to do? What may I hope for?" Huxley argued that his curriculum would provide answers to the first two questions, and as to the third, "Do what you can to do what you ought, and leave hoping and fearing alone" (207). When "hoping and fearing" are set outside education, literature is certain to become secondary to more "practical" studies, as it would in fact become in the research universities that Smith and Priestley envisioned and Huxley ceremoniously inaugurated. According to Huxley, the advance of science inevitably undercut the authority of literary classics because the physical sciences provide an understanding of facts "to which the tradition of a thousand years was as insignificant as the hearsay of yesterday" (210). Dismissing a classical education as "scandalously insufficient and almost worthless," Huxley noted that there are several ways to determine "the value of purely literary education" (207). In any such determination, one should remember that "books are the money of Literature, but only the counters of Science," which bases its knowledge on fact not fiction (213). Such knowledge is accessible to all who learn the "discipline" of science.

Huxley was concerned with educational access and practical usefulness because he was a largely self-educated working person, having received his degree from the University of London by examination after apprenticing with a doctor. Many of the speeches that Huxley made on behalf of the "scientific culture" were delivered in provincial cities such as Birmingham, Liverpool, and Aberdeen, where colleges were established or reformed to advance useful knowledge. As "a plebian who stands by his order," he was proud to inaugurate institutions that would make such knowledge accessible to the public (205). When he spoke at the opening of Johns Hopkins University, he stressed that his ideas "are entirely in accordance with the measures you have adopted," particularly the emphasis on specialized research supported by fellowships and experimental equipment, which were just the sort of emphases that would come to define the modern research university (257). Upon such ceremonial occasions, Huxley provided boosterism for the scientific enterprise, observing that

> this distinctive character of our times lies in the vast and constantly increasing part which is played by natural knowledge. Not only is our daily life shaped by it, not only does the prosperity of millions of men depend upon it, but our whole theory of life has long been influenced, consciously or unconsciously, by the general conceptions of the universe, which have been forced upon us by physical science. (149)

This view of social progress and the education best suited to advancing it had first been introduced into higher education in the eighteenth-century cultural provinces, and in the nineteenth century it was advanced by liberal reformers such as Huxley who maintained the liberal belief that science would make society more productive and harmonious.

Echoing views that dissenters and Scots like Priestley and Smith had advanced when they introduced the sciences of political economy and psychology into the curriculum, Huxley argued that a liberal education should teach people to deal "with political, as they now deal with scientific questions." The study of "sociology" would instill "agreement upon common principles of social action" among "both the capitalist and the operative" (157–58). In fact, science had already gained such authority among educational reformers that Huxley was concerned that its ascendancy would eclipse other forms of knowledge: "there are other forms of culture beside physical science; and I should be profoundly sorry to see the fact forgotten, or even to observe a tendency to starve, or cripple, literary, or aesthetic, culture for the sake of science" (122). Huxley feared that the modern "scientific culture" would do just that, for he made a point of distinguishing himself from "a kind of sect, or horde, of scientific Goths and Vandals, who think it would be proper and desirable to sweep away all other forms of culture and instruction, except those in physical science" (163).

While Huxley tried to distinguish himself from the scientific barbarians who had become influential enough to be viewed as a threat, Arnold clearly saw Huxley's views as part of that threat. He responded to Huxley's "Science and Culture" with "Literature and Science" (1881), a lecture he delivered in America in response to trends he observed in American culture. Arnold later described the lecture as "my doctrine on Studies as well as I can frame it" (10: 462–63). Arnold argued that the classics remained the best education, even for a modern commercial society like America. According to Arnold, Huxley had reduced literature to *belles lettres,* a term of derision Arnold used for "a superficial humanism" concerned with "decorative" arts. Arnold maintained the classical definition of "literature" as "humane letters" and treated science as "specialist" knowledge that failed to connect the intellectual with the moral and aesthetic (66–67). Huxley often did assume a simplistic belletristic dualism of "intellect" and "feeling, or that which, before the name was defiled, was called the aesthetic side of our nature, and which can neither be proved nor disproved, but only felt and known" (175). In Huxley's frame of reference, what cannot be proved should not be hoped or feared, and such a perspective will inevitably position the arts at the margins of serious studies. While literary studies would be influenced by Arnold's view that critics should make a disinterested appraisal of the best that has been thought and said, Huxley is important because he spoke to the ideological and institutional trends that would define the priorities of the modern university, and the place of literary studies within it.

Conclusion: The Function of Criticism in Public Education?

Utilitarianism has exercised an increasing influence on higher education ever since the educated public expanded beyond classically educated upper-class males. Utilitarian values first emerged in the dissenting academies and Scottish universities because they were more responsive to the social aspirations of the middle classes than the centers of English education. Reformers repudiated classicism as mere antiquarianism and introduced the study of English literature and composition, experimental science, and the "sciences of man" to adapt higher education to "commercial society." In the nineteenth century, a coalition of Utilitarians and dissenters established the first English university to challenge Oxford and Cambridge's hegemony, and that university was designed to make "useful" knowledge accessible to the middle classes in order to advance reasonable reforms within society. The University of London openly imitated the reforms of the Scottish universities, including their emphasis on the teaching of English. However, from the establishment of the first professorships of English literature at the University of London, literary studies were set in opposition to the utilitarianism that had contributed to their institution. The idea that literature should stand for "the culture of the heart" against the commercialism of the age was not inconsistent with the sentiments taught by professors of rhetoric and belles lettres, but rhetoric had also included more practical concerns within the teaching of English that were lost when it became merely literary and divorced itself from the popular culture and public debates over political reform.

The teaching of reading and writing are mutually enriching activities, a truism that was as obvious in the classes of George Jardine or Joseph Priestley as it is in any effective English course today. In the eighteenth century, English was taught as a practical art for communicating ideas and as "imaginative" literature that instilled an appreciation for the finer things in life, with rhetoric providing both the strategies of composition and the categories for critical analysis. Belletristic rhetoricians introduced English literature into higher education to teach the reading public refined tastes, and as education expanded to include the working classes and women, the teaching of literature became even more explicitly concerned with instilling a shared respect for the values of English literature. A range of mid-nineteenth-century textbooks from elementary readers to literary anthologies helped establish British literature as a subject with a history to be learned and a canon to be appreciated (see Michael 262–63). The consolidation of literature as a field of study served the practical purpose of instilling a patriotic understanding of the national culture, a purpose that became increasingly important as the educated public expanded. While the teaching of English had initially adapted to such centrifugal and centripetal forces by subordinating rhetoric to belletristic criticism, the domain of critical study was not narrowed to nonutilitarian nonfactual discourse until the nineteenth century. As English studies became synonymous with literary studies, and literature became understood in the modern sense of the term, the old rhetorical connection of reading with writing disappeared, and students were taught to read literature as productions of genius and not as something that they themselves might compose (see Palmer 39).

Matthew Arnold helped establish the mission of literary criticism as the eradication of provincialism. This mission was consistent with the function that English studies had served since they were first introduced into provincial universities, but he divorced criticism from the political sphere even more concertedly than his predecessors had. Arnold had a more humanistic understanding of the function of criticism than the belletrists who had taught English as a means to eradicate the provincial idioms and tastes of their students, but the basic purpose remained correcting the values of the less educated, a purpose that had not been served by the humanities when higher education was confined within learned languages. Arnold uncompromisingly condemned not just popular values but the whole domain of common opinion in ways that provincial professors of rhetoric and moral philosophy never did. Provincial proponents of self-improvement and cultural assimilation did not have the authority of speaking from the center of the culture, and they wanted to improve provincial society, not simply critique its provincial puritan values. They worked to translate those values into utilitarian efforts to modernize the economy, educate the public, and thus promote social stability and individual opportunity. Arnold helped define literary studies in opposition to utilitarianism, and such oppositions inevitably marginalized such practical studies as rhetoric and composition and divorced the teaching of English from the ethical and political concerns of moral philosophy.

Arnold positioned the function of criticism in a cosmopolitan domain beyond the realm of political rhetoric and popular values. According to Arnold, the eras that produced the greatest literature were those that were most disinterested. The Renaissance and Periclean Greece "were, in the main, disinterestedly intellectual and spiritual movements; movements in which the human spirit looked for its satisfaction in itself and in the increased play of its own activity," unlike the French Revolution, which "took a political, practical character" (3: 263–64). The first professors of English had also positioned themselves as disinterested observers, and they also did so for less than disinterested purposes, as I tried to demonstrate when I examined the political practices that followed from the rhetorical theories of traditional intellectuals such as Hugh Blair. While Arnold defended the church's traditional control of education, he was not himself a churchman. While some of the first professors of English literature were churchmen, increasing numbers were not, though that does not mean that professors of literature were not traditional intellectuals.

When a group of intellectuals claims not only that they are disinterested but that their disinterestedness is what gives their position authority, then one can conclude two things: the authority of these intellectuals is being contested against changing social needs, and this group of intellectuals has a less tangible claim to serving the public interest than some other group has. To establish a higher authority for their representations of the shared culture, professors of literature distanced themselves from the utilitarian reformers who were challenging traditional authorities and from the promoters of scientific education who could make far more concrete claims for the benefits of what they taught. Professors of literature dismissed the world of work and the political sphere as domains dominated by utilitarian values and scientific methods that were antithetical to the "culture of the heart." Divorced from such practical domains, literary studies could be situated on a higher cosmopolitan plain and established as an autonomous discipline that disinterestedly served the middle classes' interest in cultural refinement while remaining disdainful of their practical needs and values. As English studies became reduced to literary studies, professors of literature would increasingly struggle against the popular perception that theirs was a profession devoted to leisured reading. This perception could be dismissed as mere utilitarianism until utilitarian values took over public education. The belletristic emphases of English studies have prevented criticism from becoming more productively engaged with literacy, political debates, and popular values ever since rhetoric was first subordinated to belletristic criticism, and these problems only intensified when the study of English was reduced to the study of literature, in the modern sense of that term.

Conclusion

Is the History of Classics a Model for the Future of English Departments?

> The mode of being of the new intellectual can no longer consist in elo-
> quence, which is an exterior and momentary mover of the feelings and
> passions, but in active participation in practical life, as constructor, or-
> ganiser, "permanent persuader" and not just a simple orator (but su-
> perior at the same time to the abstract mathematical spirit); from
> technique-as-work one proceeds to technique-as-science and to the
> humanistic conception of history, without which one remains "spe-
> cialized" and does not become "directive" (specialized and political).
>
> —Gramsci, *Selections from Prison Notebooks*

THE DEPARTURE FROM classicism that shaped the formation of college
English may seem rather quaint today, for ancient languages are now the
business of small departments at the periphery of the curriculum—a stark
contrast with less than a century ago, when classical languages and literature
dominated the centers of higher education. The literacy crisis that culminated in the delatinization of higher education can be dated from the introduction of English in the eighteenth-century British cultural provinces. The
history of classics should be a powerful historical example for those who have
defined English departments as departments of literary classics. In British
universities, rhetoric is no longer studied or taught in any concerted way as
far as I know, and in America the typical English department is less influential than the colleges of communications that study the popular media and
utilitarian forms of discourse that English departments dismiss as nonliter-
ary.[1] The most respected English departments in America have not deigned
to recognize composition and rhetoric as a discipline, and other English departments have recently allowed the teaching of composition to be moved

into separate programs or departments. What a discipline excludes from study defines it in ways that are ignored by histories of the ideas contained within it. Because rhetoric and composition were excluded by the profession of literature, I have tried to look back beyond that profession and examine how professors in the eighteenth-century provinces first began to teach the modern culture, including English literature and composition as well as modern history, political economy, psychology, and science. When we look beyond the limits of current disciplines, we can begin to understand how those boundaries were established and how they have positioned the work of college English. The formation of college English was bounded by the transformation of the reading public by print, and the work of English departments is currently being redefined by a literacy "crisis" that may end up making the classics of English literature into an antiquarian study.

The educational centers of England generally remained aloof from the "new learning," while modern science, history, politics, ethics, literature, and composition were introduced into the curriculum in provincial colleges. The core of the humanities was transformed by the "science of man" to define logic as the art of reasoning from the individual experience, rhetoric as the means of conveying sentiments between isolated auditors, and grammar as the science of distinguishing literate usage from common idioms. I have examined how these reforms changed what was studied as well as how it was taught because I believe that learning and teaching are sites where one can observe the intimate dynamics of cultural reproduction and, at times, transformation. I also examined the rhetorical practices that followed from the "new" rhetoric because I believe that rhetoric can best be understood when it is situated in the domain between the educated culture and the popular experience. Research on this domain can, I think, provide important insights into how intellectual developments are shaped by the changes in class relations and social conditions that determine what is important enough to argue about, who gets taught to make such arguments, and what purposes those arguments serve. As an attempt to value practice, my argument has significant practical limitations. My methods tend to be rather traditional, at points self-consciously so because I value traditions as ongoing arguments about the experiences and goals of the groups who identify with those traditions (see my "Reinventing Rhetorical Traditions"). However, at some points my analyses have probably been naively and perhaps even nostalgically traditional.

The civic humanist tradition is for me a useful point of reference in thinking about the relations of popular values and practical action, but others will find in Aristotle, if not in Isocrates, nothing more than the outmoded values of an oppressive elite.[2] As Habermas has discussed, "the Hellenic public sphere, as handed down to us in the stylized form of Greek self-interpretation has shared with everything else considered 'classical' a peculiarly normative power," a power that has only in this century entered "a process of decomposition" even though "publicity continues to be an organizational principle of our political order" (*Structural Transformation* 4). I have used civic humanism as a point of reference for considering how social diversification expanded rhetoric and moral philosophy to include an attention to modern discourse, ethics, and politics. Rhetoricians broadened their domain of study beyond persuasive public oratory to begin to examine scientific writing and other forms of discourse such as the essay that had been peripheral to their focus on public controversies, and moral philosophers looked beyond religious conceptions of human nature and the civic virtues of the political elite to examine the psychological processes involved in cultural assimilation and the social changes created by modernization. While I have used civic humanism to critique the atomized individualism that emerged with the formation of the sciences of psychology and political economy, such analyses can easily slip into nostalgia if the public sphere is idealized as a normative domain where "shared" values are used to determine the common good. The public and the private became blurred by the expansion of civil society, and it is within this domain that college English studies originated and have remained. That domain was also closely associated with the emergence of modern gender categories, and my failure to use gender as a category of analysis is one of the most serious practical limitations of my historical account.[3]

My analyses have been based on a traditional understanding of rhetoric —one that situates practical action in specific contexts to assess what purposes it serves and how these can best be attained. Rhetoric has traditionally emphasized the situational nature of purposeful action and has treated critical reflection as an aid to action, with the purposes of action defined by the dialectical contingencies of audiences, texts, authors, and speakers on this occasion at this time. Rhetoric has been associated with popular opinions and situational ethics ever since Plato and the Sophists argued over whether rhetoric was merely a set of techniques for making opinions persuasive to the ignorant or the art of exploring the dialectical possibilities of situations. When the boundaries between the educated elite and the broader public were blurred by the decline of learned languages and the spread of print literacy, the art of speaking to public controversies was subordinated to belletristic criticism intended to teach the reading public to maintain the proprieties of civil society. Rhetoricians who were positioned outside the centers of the educated culture introduced the study of English into the university curriculum, and their field of study was bounded by the theories of human psychology and political economy developed by moral philosophers. From the stance of the impartial spectator, politics could be viewed as a science, and ethics and aesthetics became matters of polite sentiment rather than purposeful action. However, for professors of English to be able to speak as disinterested critics, they had to cease to present themselves as rhetoricians.

This argument, I believe, not only helps explain why rhetoric and composition became marginalized in the modern humanities but also values that position by showing that the borders of the educated culture have been its most dynamic area of development. If I am right that the history of college English began not at the centers of the educated culture but in the provinces with professors and students who translated the learned culture into a new language because the classics did not make sense of their experience, then one would expect that the future of the discipline may now be emerging not simply in the latest theoretical trends contained within it but also in those courses that are most broadly involved with the changing experiences of students. From my work as an administrator and teacher of lower-division courses in literature and composition, I have come to believe that the future of college English studies, at least in public universities and colleges in America, is now being determined by what is happening to the general education curriculum. While developments there are obviously influenced by theories of multiculturalism and feminism, such movements have themselves arisen out of the general expansion of higher education to include traditionally excluded groups. Such broader institutional changes are now transforming the basic purposes of the humanities. The research mission of the humanities is being deemphasized because it is not seen to yield knowledge of utilitarian value, and liberal education is being held accountable to the practical needs of the world of work.

While they can be criticized against the values of Arnoldian humanism or other forms of classicism, these developments are part of a basic reevaluation of the public benefits of higher education. Departments of literature are increasingly being judged by the very values that were repudiated by the first professors of English literature. Departments that fail to develop a new accounting of their work may well end up becoming the classics departments of the twenty-first century. English departments have served as the educational bastions of the culture of the book, but the texts and modes of reading that they have valued are losing their broader currency among educated people. Rather than bewailing these trends as a crisis in cultural literacy or the death of "literature," Richard Lanham's *The Electronic Word: Democracy, Technology and the Arts* (1993) has redefined literary studies in more rhetorical terms to present a productive alternative to an antiquarian veneration for literary classics. Rather than challenging the marginalization of rhetoric and composition within English departments, I want to try to exploit that position to broaden the base of the humanities, but before I advance that line of argument, I want to review the arguments that I made in the preceding chapters.

Teaching the British English

The history of college English has too often been read from the inside out and from the top down, centering on developments in elite institutions and ignoring teaching as well as the broader political functions and institutional conditions of education. Such accounts have excised rhetoric as a set of practical strategies for claiming disciplinary authority, if not also as a particular area of study that lacks modern disciplinary status. Once a discipline is established, it ceases being openly rhetorical precisely because its purposes and strategies have become established as a natural part of work in the field rather than as an attempt to resolve the practical problems that were contained within that area of inquiry. To understand the problems that the formation of college English was meant to solve, I began with the eighteenth-century expansion of cheap print literacy that transformed the public sphere, giving rise to efforts to standardize educated taste and usage, and thus reestablish the boundaries around the educated culture that had been blurred by the decline of learned languages. These efforts included the first dictionaries of literate usage, the grammars that formalized that usage into a logical system, and also the attempts of elocutionists to eradicate provincial idioms and script speech itself by filling in gaps in written texts with elaborate notational systems on the correct ways to express "natural" feelings. The dialectical interaction between the expansion and standardization of educated discourse popularized the essay of taste and manners that would be instituted as a means to teach taste, but which also had the potential to critique accepted mores against changing needs. As it came to be taught, the essay reproduced the logic of laissez-faire liberalism by valorizing personal voice and representing its purposes and conventions as natural laws rather than as purposeful responses to particular social situations.

While the centers of English education maintained the boundaries of the learned culture by emphasizing learned languages and highly refined modes of expression and reasoning, the dissenters who were forced out of Cambridge and Oxford began to teach modern science, history, politics, rhetoric, and composition to adapt higher education to the needs of their middle-class students. The antiquarianism of the centers of English education is evident not just in what they taught but also in how they failed to teach much of anything at all. Oxford and Cambridge were both notorious for not taking teaching seriously. Most professors did not even bother to lecture, and tutors tended to teach in an unreflective fashion that immersed students in the mastery of a dead language and the outmoded forms of Ciceronian rhetoric and Aristotelian logic. Like the apprenticeships common in oral and scribal cultures, the informal transmission of highly formalized modes of knowledge preserved the cultural capital of those who possessed it by not calling the received tradition into question against current needs. Also, those who had acquired the educated culture by rote memorization could not easily explain it to those who had not. The dissenting academy tradition introduced not just modern subjects of study but also modern ways of teaching. The comparative method of instruction was adopted to teach students to debate conflicting views of established beliefs. Dissenters assumed that critical literacy advanced reasonable religion, economic progress, personal freedom, and the laissez-faire political economy that would defend reason, progress, and freedom. Provincial colleges and universities began teaching English in an effort to meet the need for public education in commercial society.

The provincial traditions that contributed to the formation of college English provide case studies of the pedagogical and political dimensions of educational change. The dissenting academies show how the introduction of the modern culture was shaped by the practical needs of the middle classes. The teaching of English in Ireland provides the clearest case of how English studies served colonial purposes by alienating students from their national language and culture. While the records of Irish student societies show that students often used their studies for their own political purposes, the alienation from the lived experience is graphically evident in the works of the influential Irish elocutionist Thomas Sheridan, who valorized "the language of nature, the living speech" while systematically eradicating the idioms that provincials naturally spoke (*Lectures on Elocution* xi). Scottish professors translated the humanities into English to teach the virtues of self-restraint and refined taste to students who had not been inculcated into the learned culture through the study of learned languages. The works of Scottish professors of rhetoric and moral philosophy document how the three language arts were transformed as the logic of science became established as the natural mode of reasoning from the individual experience, the grammatical conventions of English became codified, and rhetoric was reoriented from the productive capacities of shared beliefs to the psychological responses of the isolated auditor.

The sciences of psychology and political economy that emerged out of the study of moral philosophy contributed to the belletristic and scientistic trends that subordinated composition to criticism and devalued the public sphere as a domain for debating popular beliefs and political controversies. Moral philosophy began its modern development toward the social sciences with the emergence of the "science of man" out of pneumatology. Pneumatology or pneumatics traditionally studied the human spirit and the nature of the divine but was redefined when the logic of the natural sciences was applied to the study of human nature. The "science of man" provided moral philosophers with a reliable methodology and point of reference to judge social changes and cultural differences against the natural laws that maintained the balance between self-interest and the public good in human psychology and the political economy. The science of political economy that was formalized by Adam Smith documents the laissez-faire liberalism that made rhetoric at best a means to communicate sentiments between autonomous individuals, and at worst the art of arousing the heated passions and factional interests that disturbed the natural order of the human psyche and the body politic. As politics became a science and ethics and aesthetics became a matter of personal sentiment, rhetoric became disassociated from the civic ideology that had placed it at the center of the humanities. Rhetoric was subordinated to belletristic criticism concerned with instilling the cosmopolitan tastes that maintained the decorum of civil society.

The proprieties of "conversible society" were internalized in the form of the impartial spectator who monitors every thought and gesture to ensure that they are not motivated by self-interest or factional loyalties. This divided consciousness aptly characterized the experience of provincials who studiously internalized cosmopolitan tastes and values in a manner that alienated them from the idioms and traditions of their own society. Smith studied how individuals become assimilated as they learn to imitate more refined modes of behavior and expression—the process that expands the existing cultural hegemony by making its proprieties part of the experience of those not born within it. Outsiders who have taught themselves the conventions of the dominant culture can develop a critical awareness of how shared values are socially constructed and psychologically internalized, but Smith effaced the contested nature of this dialectical process by defining it as a "natural" human tendency to identify with those who exercise tasteful self-restraint. The ideal of the impartial spectator taught individuals to make a disinterested assessment of experience by positioning themselves above the self-interested motives that prompt people to act. Such self-restraint was valued as a means to prevent social diversification from undermining established hierarchies and traditional values. Self-restraint was taught to the expanding reading public by treating taste as a means to distinguish between the truly polite and the merely popular, and thus distinguish oneself as a member of civil society.

The rhetorical stance of the impartial spectator was consistent with the positions that social scientists and literary critics were establishing, but it removed individuals from the perspective of the political agent that had been assumed by rhetoricians. From the natural sciences, the social sciences adopted the stance of the objective observer who stands outside experience and reasons inductively to codify the natural laws that govern it. "Disinterestedness" also became established as the characteristic that distinguished "the work of art for what it is, i.e. autonomous" (Bourdieu 4). To position themselves as disinterested critics of provincial tastes, the founders of modern literary studies such as Matthew Arnold carefully marked out a boundary around the domain of literature to set it off from the practical sphere of popular values and political conflicts. This "sacred frontier," as Bourdieu has termed it, inscribed an "ethos of elective distance from the necessities of the natural and social world" (5). This disinterested ethos was basic to the emergence of the two cultures of the modern arts and sciences, and its logic was contained within the discursive forms that were first used to teach the modern culture. The first university English courses presented the essays of the *Spectator* as models of taste and style, with the critical potential of the genre effaced by concentrating on syntactic proprieties and ignoring the social conditions and political purposes that made the essay a blurred genre. Social relations were formalized into a science of political economy that devalued the public sphere as a domain for collective decision making and purposeful action, and the conventions of common sense and popular argumentation became defined by the natural workings of the mechanistic faculties of the "science of human nature."

To establish their disinterested authority, literary critics and social scientists had to divorce themselves from the practical contexts and purposes that had shaped the studies of rhetoric and moral philosophy.[4] By creating a critical distance between intellectual reflection and social action, the intellectuals who introduced modern politics and literature into higher education helped reestablish the boundaries around the educated culture that had been blurred by the expansion of the educated public. Disinterested ideals such as moderation and taste served the practical interests of traditional intellectuals who owed their positions to political patronage but needed to appear to be above politics if they were to teach the public to believe that cultural assimilation meant social progress. Of course nothing is less disinterested than rhetoric in action. Rhetoric could not be made into a science or an art without abstracting it from its practical engagement with popular values, conflicts of interest, and deliberative decision making. The modern effacement of the rhetoric of popular politics from the two cultures of the arts and sciences is not merely of concern to specialists in rhetoric and composition, or even just to humanists who are being pressed to account for the practical values of the liberal arts.[5] It is a problem for students who are taught the modes of reasoning and expression that demarcate the educated culture without being taught that they are rhetorical conventions that were formalized to serve practical political purposes, including the exclusion of less educated people such as themselves.

From a Historical Perspective, What Then Are the Practical Values of Rhetoric and Composition?

As a historian, I am suspicious of the tendency to reduce historical developments to object lessons for current practitioners, but as a rhetorician, I am compelled to relate historical reflection to practical action to avoid making history a mere antiquarian concern. Historians such as Sharon Crowley have established that "Current-traditional rhetoric is a direct descendant of the work of the British new rhetoricians" (Crowley 56; see also Berlin, *Writing Instruction*). I would like to conclude by making a different sort of connection, one that stresses not historical continuities but the parallels between historical situations. The origins of college English have broad institutional and cultural similarities with the current position of rhetoric and composition in American higher education. English literature and composition were first taught by rhetoricians in comparatively broad-based provincial institutions, and rhetoric and composition have reemerged as an area of scholarship in the last two decades in English departments in more broadly accessible institutions in America.[6] In reaction to a moribund classical tradition that was losing its authority within the educated culture, the new rhetoric of the eighteenth century formalized discursive practices that served the needs of provincials who wanted to feel ennobled by refined sentiments and master correct English usage to be accepted into educated society. Similarly, in the twentieth century, the new rhetoric was institutionalized in English departments that were pressed to teach more than the classics of English literature because their students were seen to need instruction in the basics of educated discourse. In both periods, educational reforms were shaped by broader changes in educated discourse, by the expansion of print in the late eighteenth century, and by the transformation of print by new technologies in the late twentieth century (see Lanham). In the eighteenth century as in the twentieth century, these educational changes began not at the centers of the educated culture, but in provincial institutions, which today means institutions that have comparatively "low" admissions standards, including most land grant universities, public colleges, and especially community colleges, where most courses in rhetoric and composition are currently taught.

The dialectical interaction of access and consolidation is part of the centrifugal and centripetal dynamics that shaped the formation of college English and positioned it within broader developments in education and the educated culture. Then as now, expansions of the educated culture yield efforts to formalize and standardize its conventions to reestablish the distinctions between those who know its proprieties and those who don't. Such efforts concentrate on those areas where the dominant culture comes into contact with marginal groups because that is where boundaries are drawn and access is granted or denied. The dynamics of that process are most intense at the borders of the dominant culture because proprieties do not seem so natural when they have to be taught, and groups who have not been inculcated into the dominant culture have a potentially dialectical awareness of the contested nature of its conventions. Teachers who have a critical awareness of such dynamics recognize the possibilities and limitations that they impose on teaching entering students how to write and read in ways that will enable them not just to gain access to higher education but also to develop a critical awareness of its conventions and priorities. Such teachers have developed a rich philosophy of "problem-posing" pedagogy that assumes that literacy is more than decoding because it involves a dialectical process of critical reflection and practical action that enables one to criticize texts against one's own experience and use them to accomplish one's own purposes (see Shor, Freire, and Giroux). Such critical awareness situates a problem in practical contexts that can be used to question whose purposes will be served by "solving" it.

I have attempted to apply this perspective to the history of college English by looking beyond its accepted borders to examine the purposes that defined them and the dialectical potential contained within them. Within the field, philosophies of critical literacy can be domesticated into student-centered reforms that emphasize essays of personal experience that are not all that different from the belletristic essays and introspective orientation that were established in the first university English courses. However, a problem-posing perspective can also challenge us to reexamine what problems composition courses have been meant to solve. Such bridge courses are supposed to provide access to students who need extra work on the basics of academic discourse, but the bridge has generally gone one way—moving students from personal essays to the conventions of academic writing. The modern reduction of rhetoric to the personal and the academic began with the translation of rhetoric into English to meet the need for public education in a commercial society, and the new rhetoric served the need of teaching the reading public to concentrate on personal refinement as a means to social advancement within civil society. However, rhetoric may be on the verge of reassuming its traditional engagements with popular values and political controversies. While many composition courses have taken a rhetorical interest in public issues, a problem-posing approach to such issues politicizes them in ways that can be highly controversial, as is evident in the national debate that resulted from the reorientation of the composition course at the University of Texas to examine the conventions and purposes of antidiscrimination laws, a rather innocuous topic if approached in an appropriate academic manner (see Brodkey).[7]

The attention to political controversies within composition courses assumes transformative possibilities when it is made part of a programmatic effort to make bridge courses a two-way street that offers not just access to academic discourse but also opportunities to move back and forth from the academy to the communities who have not been represented there. Work on community literacy and "service" learning has the potential to transform academic work by blurring the distinctions between teaching, research, and service. When academic work is situated in a broader social context, it can be held accountable to the needs and purposes of groups who have had limited access to higher education.[8] The basic model of researchers as participant-observers has challenged the disinterested perspective of the impartial spectator in the classroom, and Shirley Brice Heath and other scholars have applied the methods of cultural ethnography to field research on community literacy. Some composition programs are beginning to adopt such models to help students learn how to work from the traditions and experiences that they bring to the classroom. Such efforts have the potential to transform learning in service courses, and also to transform research on cultural studies by integrating it into a broader service program that can alleviate the alienation of academic work from the practical experiences of the working classes.[9] Community literacy centers provide opportunities for students and faculty to develop more organic relations with broader communities through collaborations on political organizing, health problems, environmental racism, and a range of other public issues. Through such work, academics can develop an organic involvement with diverse communities. This involvement in civic life can benefit from and contribute to a critical reassessment of the traditional definition of rhetoric as a practical political art concerned with teaching people how to draw on the values of their tradition to resolve the problems that it faces.

American higher education is currently facing broad pressures to give more emphasis to teaching and less time to research, and such pressures are compounded by the fact that there are few "external" sources of support for research in the humanities. I believe that the most productive way to respond to such pressures is to question how the problem has been posed to limit academic work by removing it from community service, learning, and teaching. I have tried to provide a historical context for this project by situating the formation of college English at the borders of the dominant culture. I have documented how teaching and learning have been potential sites of social transformation, and I have valued a rhetorical perspective on the practical process of drawing on traditional beliefs to address controversial issues, and thereby showing that the modern construction of literature as a domain of study was neither disinterested nor productive. I would like to think that this account is consistent with the efforts of Giroux and others "to redefine the role of teachers as transformative intellectuals" or "engaged critics" who "understand the nature of their own self-formation" and are concerned with "education as a public discourse" (15). Giroux's "civic" philosophy of "border pedagogy" is concerned with "developing a democratic public philosophy that respects the notion of difference as part of a common struggle to extend the quality of public life" by challenging the boundaries of "culture, power, and knowledge" (16, 28). Giroux stresses that such a pedagogy "makes visible the historically and socially constructed strengths and limitations of those places and borders we inherit and that frame our discourses and social relations" (28).

My account has perhaps failed to make the borders we have inherited visible because I have tended to criticize them from within, concentrating too much on the theories of individuals such as Adam Smith and too little on the experiences of women and the working classes.[10] Working in Tucson, Arizona with Native Americans, large immigrant bilingual communities, and reactionary state administrators, I know that *border lands* are not just a trendy abstraction, that access needs to mean more than simply letting poorer students attend college, and that "the public" is often nothing more than a political fiction used to legitimize state control. However, I believe that such work needs to be included within our understanding of college English studies if teachers are to help students break through academic abstractions and gain access to the power needed to transform the public. Rhetoric can be an important part of this work if *rhetorician* is defined by an "active participation in practical life, as constructor, organizer, 'permanent persuader' and not just a simple orator." As Gramsci discussed in the passage quoted at the beginning of this conclusion, such a conception is grounded in a movement "from technique-as-work . . . to technique-as-science and to the humanistic conception of history, without which one remains 'specialized' and does not become 'directive' (specialized and political)" (*Prison Notebooks* 10). In this book, I have attempted to value the work done in the classrooms where English was first taught, to challenge efforts to demarcate science and literature as disinterested domains of study, and to contribute to a historical understanding of the humanities that has practical political significance. I hope to be able to continue this effort in a second volume that will examine how rhetorical theory and practice in the American colonies contributed not just to the formation of college English but also to the constitution of a system of government that both legitimized and contained public political debate.

Notes

Introduction: The Teaching of English in the British Cultural Provinces

1. William Riley Parker dates the beginnings of scholarship on English from the middle of the sixteenth century with the first serious research on Anglo-Saxon, lexical analyses of English, and textual studies of Chaucer. Michael's *The Teaching of English from the Sixteenth Century to 1870* (1987) provides a comprehensive survey of the texts that shaped the study of English at various levels of education, and like Parker, Michael concludes that English did not really become established as an object of formal study and teaching until the eighteenth century. According to Michael, "by the 1770s the teaching of English literature in school had become a matter of normal educational discussion" (160).

2. While it also shows a lack of awareness of rhetoric and composition, Crawford's *Devolving English Literature* (1992) did not simply reduce the history of English studies to current disciplinary priorities. Crawford acknowledged that "the subject of English Literature was, ironically, a Scottish Invention," and he examined how provincialism contributed to the anthropological concerns and heteroglossia of modernism, including the works of Joyce and Eliot that became established as the greatest works of modern English literature. Theories of postcolonial criticism have been used to broaden the history of English studies in Viswanathan's *Masks of Conquest: Literary Study and British Rule in India* (1989).

3. Almost without exception, eighteenth-century professors of poetry at Oxford lectured in Latin on classical literature. William Hawkins translated passages of Shakespeare into Latin verse in the lectures he delivered from 1751 to 1756. While some professors published significant works on English and its literature, lectures on English in English were first given by James Hurdis, who held the chair from 1793 to 1801. The lectures had little impact, historically or educationally, and the practice was not perpetuated (see Fairer).

4. Rhetoric has become reestablished as an area of scholarly study in the humanities only in the last few decades with the establishment of graduate programs and the hiring of faculty who do research in rhetoric and composition. As is documented by the job lists of the Modern Language Association, these positions are almost without exception in land-grant universities and other public and private colleges with broader missions than those elite institutions that are less accessible to the general public. If one were to look for scholarly work on rhetoric and composition at Harvard and Yale in the twentieth century, one would have to draw the same conclusions that historians of English studies have drawn

from looking at Oxford and Cambridge in the eighteenth century: the discipline does not exist.

5. Berlin and Vivion's *Cultural Studies in the English Classroom* documents how cultural studies has already transformed many courses and curricula, and collaborations with community literacy centers have the potential to redefine teaching, research, and service in ways that could dramatically change the work done by English departments. Both of these trends seem to be converging in the English Department at Carnegie Mellon University (see Alan Kennedy; Peck, Flower, and Higgins).

6. Within the civic humanist tradition of Aristotle and Cicero, moral philosophy concentrated on ethics and politics, but in the eighteenth century, Scottish moral philosophers such as Adam Smith broadened higher education to examine contemporary social relations, cultural assimilation, and modernization. Scottish moral philosophy courses, according to Bryson, commonly examined "human nature, social forces, progress, marriage and family relationships, economic processes, maintenance of government, religion, international relations, elementary jurisprudence, primitive customs, history of institutions, ethics [and] aesthetics" (*Man and Society* 4).

7. I will try to use *praxis* in a way that situates reflection and action in a dialectical relation with social conditions. Paolo Freire uses the term *praxis* to discuss his philosophy of critical literacy as a dialectic of situated reflection and purposeful action, and Antonio Gramsci uses it in a complementary way to relate intellection and intellectuals with broader social groups: "the philosophy of praxis does not tend to leave the 'simple' in their primitive philosophy of common sense, but rather to lead them to a higher conception of life" (*Prison Notebooks* 332). Such sources are the points of reference for my own use of the term, particularly in my criticisms of Scottish moral philosophers' efforts to make common sense into a natural faculty and use it to defend established conventions against the criticisms of Hume (see chapter 7; on commonsense realism, see also Berlin, *Writing Instruction*).

8. The term *belles lettres* was popularized by the translation in 1734 of Rollin's *Method of Teaching and Studying the Belles Lettres* (1726–1728). According to the *OED*, the term was used at some times as Rollin did to refer to all the humanities and at others in the "exact sense in which we now use 'literature'" (see also Howell 519–35). Blair requested that the term be added to the title of his proposed professorship to give it a "modern air," as is discussed in chapter 8, but by the nineteenth century *belles lettres* had become a term of derision associated with a superficial understanding of the humanities and a stylistic conception of literature, both of which Matthew Arnold accused Thomas Huxley of holding when they debated whether modern education should give priority to literature or science, as discussed in chapter 9. Scientism can be defined as the project of applying a quasi-experimental method to domains outside the natural sciences. In the eighteenth century, the project was often called "Newtonian," with Newton himself describing the method of "experimental philosophy" as proceeding by "the argument of induction" from particular "phenomena" to general laws (400; see also note 10 to chapter 7 below). As this methodology became formalized, the references to "Argument" were effaced, and according to Aronowitz, it came to be assumed "that exact knowledge is free of value orientations, of interest" (x). The scientific method gained authority from the power of technology and supplanted alternative ways of conceiving of practical reasoning about

ethics and politics according to Gadamer's *Truth and Method* (see also MacIntyre, *After Virtue*).

9. Gramsci treats the distinction between civil society and the state as a key principle of liberalism generally and liberal political economy in particular (*Prison Notebooks* 260–63; see also Salamini 137). This distinction has been discussed by scholars working from diverse perspectives, including Olson, who concludes that the tradition of liberal political economy from Hobbes through Smith is concerned "that this largely commercial domain of unrestricted—and therefore free—human activity remain as large as possible." Though he was a far more politically engaged advocate of liberal political economy than Smith, Joseph Priestley also commonly distinguished between "civil liberty" (freedom from political restrictions) and "political liberty" (freedom to act politically) (*Works* 24: 227). In contrast to civic humanists' vision of the public sphere as fulfilling the highest virtues of human nature, classical liberalism tends to identify the state as little more than "a vehicle for creating a secure setting for private-egoistical activity" (Olson, *Science* 57).

10. Salamini defines Gramsci's concept of "cosmopolitanism" as "the process by which a vertical relationship with the base" is replaced "by a horizontal one connecting intellectual elites among themselves on the national and international scale" (107; see also Gramsci, *Prison Notebooks* 17–18). As part of this process, intellectuals write histories and develop models of culture and political relations that justify their positions and their relations with other social groups and processes. The "science" of political economy, the first histories of "English literature," and the reduction of English to a logical system are all examples of this process.

11. I have appropriated the term *blurred genre* from Geertz's essay, "Blurred Genres: The Refiguration of Social Thought," which examined the blurring of the boundaries between the humanities and social sciences that has occurred with the waning of scientism in cultural anthropology and elsewhere in the study of culture (*Local Knowledge* 19–35).

12. According to an observer in 1746, "the main body of Dissenters are mostly found in cities & great towns among the trading part of the people & their ministers are chiefly of the middle rank of men, having neither poverty or riches" (qtd. Porter 195; see also Smith, *Birth of Modern Education*).

13. The growth of the elocutionary movement parallels the explosion of grammars, dictionaries, and rhetorics that began in the middle of the century. Elocutionary manuals began to appear at midcentury, and by the last decades of the century, "elocution" had become an established field of work and study, as I discuss in the section on Thomas Sheridan in chapter 4.

14. As discussed in my introduction to *The Selected Writings of John Witherspoon*, Witherspoon published the first work on rhetoric authored in America, and like other Scottish immigrants, he had an important impact on American education. After immigrating in 1768, Witherspoon spoke out for independence in regional and national assemblies, helped found the American Presbyterian Church, and signed the Declaration of Independence. As president of Princeton, he introduced Scottish moral philosophy and rhetoric to James Madison. Scottish conceptions of rhetoric, politics, and ethics were also introduced to Jefferson and Hamilton by teachers who were graduates of the Scottish universities (see Wills, *Inventing America* and *Explaining America*). Scottish influences can also be seen at the College of Philadelphia under another Scottish immigrant, William Smith. Smith had

witnessed efforts to reform the Aberdeen curriculum in the image of the logic of the sciences (see chapter 5). Franklin had cited leading Scottish reformers when he originally proposed founding a college to provide an alternative to the classical curriculum (see Sloan, *Scottish Enlightenment;* Hook; and Miller, "The Formation of College English").

15. Crawford has noted that because both cultural anthropology and English studies "were very much concerned with the process of 'improvement,' it comes as no surprise to find that the roots of the modern university disciplines of anthropology and of English Literature are mutually entwined, and that both are linked to the development of modern economics" (20).

16. This awareness is as much a fact of life in "basic" writing classes today as it was in provincial classrooms in the eighteenth century. According to the sociolinguist William Labov, the lower-middle classes commonly show a "hypersensitivity to stigmatized features which they themselves use" (12). Such "hypersensitivity" becomes overwhelming when teachers make stylistic proprieties more important than purposeful communication, as has been all too common since the first university courses on English.

17. Pratt defines "contact zones" as "social spaces where disparate cultures meet, clash, and grapple with each other, often in highly asymmetrical relations of domination and subordination" (4). I use the concept of *contact zones* to discuss English studies in Ireland's Anglican university, where the relations between the dominant culture and the provincial experience were most "highly asymmetrical."

1. The Expansion of the Reading Public, the Standardization of Educated Taste and Usage, and the Essay as Blurred Genre

1. Alston's *Bibliography of the English Language* (1965–1972) includes an index of English grammars, rhetorics, critical treatises, and related works that documents the explosion of such works around the middle of the eighteenth century.

2. As noted in the introduction, the first university professorships of rhetoric to concentrate on the teaching of English were established in the 1750s and 1760s. The popular interest in elocution is an important point of contact between the introduction of English into higher education and the standardization of the taste and usage of the educated public. At midcentury, *elocution* became distinguished from the classical art of delivery and established as a recognized movement with its own teachers, terminology, and canon, including such works as John Mason's *Essay on Elocution* (1748), James Burgh's *The Art of Speaking* (1761), Thomas Sheridan's *Lectures on Elocution* (1762), William Enfield's *The Speaker* (1774), William Scott's *Lessons in Elocution* (1779), and John Walker's *Elements of Elocution* (1781).

3. Reliable data on literacy is limited, and interpretations vary. Some of the best concrete data is supplied by Schofield's compilation of a random sample of 274 parish marriage registers, which dissenters as well as Anglicans were required to sign. Schofield concludes that adult male literacy remained relatively constant at around 60 percent from the middle of the eighteenth century to the middle of the nineteenth. Female literacy grew from around 35 to 50 percent, with a significant expansion in women's access to education apparently occurring in the last quarter of the eighteenth century ("Dimensions of Illiter-

acy" 207; see also Barnard; Lacquer; and Graff, *Legacies*). According to Stone, "the achieve-ment of the eighteenth century was to shift most of the lower middle classes from the ranks of the semi-literate, who could barely read, to those of the fully literate, who could both read and write with relative facility" ("Literacy" 130).

4. The reaction against the Puritans' emphasis on popular literacy, according to Altick, led to a pervasive "fear of teaching too much" that resulted in charity schools' assuming "an exclusively disciplinary motive" that stressed rote memorization and strict moral in-struction (33).

5. Elizabethan dramatists were the first class of professional writers of English literature, but in the eighteenth century more writers supported themselves by writing more diverse sorts of literature. Especially in the latter half of the century, "writers at home in the world of novels and magazines" could earn a comfortable living (Williams, *Long Revolution* 237).

6. McIntosh has gone beyond unsubstantiated generalizations about the simplification of English prose in the eighteenth century to examine the stylistic differences between sev-eral early and late eighteenth-century grammarians and other writers. His analysis is quite detailed, though the small sample yields only "provisional" conclusions. According to McIntosh, late eighteenth-century sentences are more likely to follow a direct "subject, auxilary, verb, and complement" pattern that is "more periodic and less loose." They are also less likely to have a series of nonrestrictive relative clauses "spliced onto the end of a sentence." "Colloquial expressions" are less common, as are "explicit connectives" of the sort common in oral discourse. McIntosh characterizes some of these differences as part of the "gentrification" of prose, including "a new fussiness" about proper word use and style (721, 727).

7. The expansion of print in the eighteenth century has been well documented. The printers of London numbered around sixty at the Restoration but grew to seventy-five in 1724, with one observer in 1757 estimating between one hundred and fifty and two hun-dred "constantly employed." Newspaper sales tripled from two and a quarter million in 1711 to seven million in 1753, and doubled again by 1780. In the last half of the century, the number of new books published annually almost quadrupled (growing from a rate of one hundred per year that had been stable for almost a century to an average of 372 annually from 1792 to 1802) (see Watt, *Rise* 36–37; Williams, *Long Revolution* 183; Altick 48).

8. Mandeville was condemned by at least ten books that restated the traditional view that conspicuous consumption was a sign of personal vanity and a threat to public virtue, including books by Francis Hutcheson and Isaac Watts, who are discussed in later chapters as advocates of polite self-improvement who helped institutionalize college English stud-ies. Mandeville did not intend to democratize consumption or unsettle the class system. In an "Essay on Charity and Charity Schools" added to the second edition of the *Fable of the Bees*, he argued that education is "very pernicious to the Poor" because "Men who are to remain and end their Days in a Laborious, Tiresome and Painful Station of Life, the sooner they are put upon it at first, the more patiently they'll submit to it for ever after" (*Fable* 288).

9. According to Plumb, as leisure activities became commercialized, efforts were made to make them more exclusive and to suppress or devalue the "vulgar" pastimes out of which they had emerged, for example by condemning the reading of popular romances, or by fencing off the commons where horse races and community fairs had taken place (282–83).

10. Swift's "Proposal" sought to flatter the Lord High Treasurer into establishing an English Academy with the queen as a patron, and Swift clearly intended to secure a pension for himself as a member of the academy or as court historian (see *Works* 11: 17). Swift enlisted in the "battle of the books" on the side of the classics against the moderns to support his patron, Sir William Temple, in a personal literary dispute.

11. Priestley and Campbell are commonly cited for having propounded the most liberal doctrines of usage in the eighteenth century. Priestley was the more consistent but less influential founder of the "scientific school" according to Leonard, who devotes a chapter, "The Appeal to Usage and Its Practical Repudiation," to examining how liberal doctrines were repudiated in practice by limitations on whose usage would be accepted (32, 139–65).

12. According to Michael, the eighteenth-century textbooks that began to anthologize English literature tended to "restrain" the "potential power of imaginative literature" within "a straitjacket of moral comment and interpretation" that was not loosened until literature began to emerge as a distinct subject of instruction late in the century (193).

13. According to many accounts, the essay is a freeform genre that is difficult to characterize because it favors an associational logic over formal reasoning, nuance over precision, nonsystematic explorations over well-defined generalizations, and the processes of its own development over an imitation of its predecessors (see, for example, Good, and Atkins). The essay is often distinguished from the article to set the genre off from more conventional forms (and from the commonplace "essays" that students are taught to write). Rather than getting into the general argument over whether the informality and subjectivity of the essay give individuals the freedom from conventions to express themselves, I focus in this section more precisely on the essay of taste and manners that was popularized by the *Spectator*. This genre was defined by the narrative voice of the critical observer who gains the authority to comment (often in an ironic tone) on popular social and moral conventions by displaying a refined taste that balances a sensitivity to human nature with an awareness of the modes of decorum appropriate to the situation or character—a balance between sympathy and propriety that Smith formalized in terms of the "impartial spectator."

14. The full title of John Hamilton Moore's popular work appealed to its audience by sketching out how belletristic essays could be used to mold character: *Young Gentleman and Lady's Monitor, and English Teacher's Assistant; Being a Collection of Select Pieces from our Best Modern Writers: Calculated to Eradicate Vulgar Prejudices and Rusticity of Manners; Improve the Understanding; Rectify the Will; Purify the Passions; Direct the Minds of Youth to the Pursuit of Proper Objects; and to Facilitate their Reading, Writing, and Speaking the English Language, with Elegance and Propriety. Particularly Adapted for the Use of Our Eminent Schools and Academies, as well as Private Persons, who have not an opportunity of Perusing the Works of those Celebrated Authors, From Whence this Collection is made . . .* (1789).

15. Phillipson and others have identified Adam Smith's *Theory of Moral Sentiments* with the Addisonian tendency to redefine the political values of civic humanism according to the civilities of polite society (see also Dwyer). Smith was influenced by the *Spectator*'s commentary on how individuals identify with others by feeling a sympathy for the sentiments expressed in their gestures and tones, and he may have taken the term *impartial spectator* directly from the journal (Raphael and Macfie 15 n). As discussed in chapter 6,

Smith studied how individuals internalize social and moral conventions because he feared that the expansion of commercial society was giving rise to an atomized individualism that threatened traditional values. Moral philosophers' examinations of moral sentiments influenced the trends in the "new" rhetoric toward belletrism and the "science of human nature."

16. Because they were marginalized not by cultural differences so much as by political restrictions, dissenters such as Priestley could not accept the distinction between "civil liberty" and "political liberty" as a justification for confining oneself to civil society (*Works* 24: 227). Priestley maintained that political action was necessary to secure and protect personal freedom, and he devoted less attention to the polite arts and human sciences than to his efforts as a practicing rhetorician.

2. *The Antiquarianism of the Centers of English Education*

1. In "History in the Service and Disservice of Life," Nietzsche explicates the potentials and limitations of "antiquarian," "monumentalist," and "critical" approaches to historical understanding as resources for action, concluding that "knowledge of the past in every age is desirable only insofar as it serves the future and the present" (103). Like a monumentalist veneration for ancient achievements, antiquarian scholarship treats historical studies as ends in themselves and divorces historical understanding from contemporary problems and priorities (see also Poulakos, "Nietzsche"). In the next chapter, I oppose the antiquarianism of the English universities with the critical stance that dissenters assumed on history, pedagogy, and politics.

2. Reasoning from the logic of a market economy, Smith concluded that "in general, the richest and best endowed universities have been the slowest in adopting" reforms, which "were more easily introduced into some of the poorer universities, in which the teachers . . . were obliged to pay more attention to the current opinion of the world" because they were paid by students and not endowments (*Wealth of Nations* 2: 772–73).

3. To refute the traditional view that the English universities were indifferent to experimental science in the early eighteenth century, Hans cited several professorships that were established by benefactors and noted that experimental studies were introduced by John Keill, who came from Edinburgh to teach at Cambridge before 1712. However, Hans agreed that scientific studies declined later in the century (47–51).

4. Further evidence for this conclusion is provided by educational guides and student correspondence from the time (see Waterland, Evans, and Gunning). Quarrie summarized another documentary source on what students read and wrote, "collection books" that recorded students' readings and compositions. From such records, one would conclude that virtually nothing worth studying had appeared since the ancients.

5. The continuities between "experimental religion" and the "science of man" are examined when I discuss how Scottish and dissenting moral philosophers drew on the methods of the natural sciences and the faith in the providential order of natural religion to formulate the "natural laws" that governed the balance of benevolence and self-interest within human nature and the political economy, as I will discuss in later chapters.

6. In 1880 the Merton Professorship of English Language and Literature was estab-

lished at Oxford. A debate raged in the *Times* about having Oxford teach English gentlemen English, and the position was finally given to a philologer who taught nothing later than Chaucer. In 1904 the chair was divided into two, and a student of Henry Morley's from the University of London took the professorship of literature (see McMurty 161–63). Morley and other early professors of English literature at the University of London are discussed in the last chapter. London University (which later became part of the University of London) was established by a group of dissenters and Utilitarians that included Scottish critics of the classicism of the English universities.

7. The definition of a "public" school evolved in conjunction with the evolution of the public sphere. The Latin *publica schola* was "public" in the sense of being both state funded and intended for civic purposes. Through the Renaissance "public" education was commonly defined in opposition to two sorts of private education: teachers working in private homes (as was common among the gentry) and schools that were run for personal profit (see *OED*). Schools like Eton, which today costs about twelve thousand pounds a year, were termed "public" not because they educated the public but because the upper classes were able to maintain the fiction that they represented the public, at least until the parliamentary reforms of the later nineteenth century, when Parliament had already designated Eton and other private boarding schools as "public" schools. In America this conception of "public" schools is unintelligible because the state has always represented the public in education in the form of local public school boards.

8. Stone has described the grammar school in anthropological terms: "It involved instruction of upper-class youths by a group of bachelors in the mysteries of the tribe and the wisdom of ancestors, expressed in a dead secret language, the mastery of which took years of diligent, dreary practice; sexual and peer-group segregation in an isolated compound, in association exclusively with other males of the same age; heroic (but quite futile) efforts to enforce total sexual abstinence; submission to deliberately inflicted cruelties, especially flogging on the buttocks; conformity to a series of severe and not easily comprehensible taboos. . . . So bizarre an institution, with its curious mixture of educational and sexual themes, only makes sense if one recognizes it for what it is: a prolonged male puberty rite with all the characteristics associated with such rites among primitive peoples" ("Literacy and Education" 72).

9. Vicesimus Knox considered instruction in English to be best left to English schools, with English literature only suitable in a grammar school as material for students' private reading. However, his popular anthologies of prose, poetry, and letters were widely used to teach English in various sorts of schools. One-third of Knox's *Elegant Extracts* (1783) of prose are taken from Hugh Blair's *Sermons,* and Knox's *Elegant Extracts* (1784) of poetry went through some fifteen editions by the first quarter of the next century (see Michael 188–90).

10. The Oxford professors of poetry in the eighteenth century were Joseph Trapp (1708–1718), Thomas Warton senior (1718–1728), Joseph Spence (1728–1738), John Whitfield (1738–1741), Robert Lowth (1741–1751), William Hawkins (1751–1756), Thomas Warton (1756–1766), Benjamin Wheeler (1766–1776), John Randolph (1776–1783), Robert Holmes (1783–1793), and James Hurdis (1793–1801). Matthew Arnold held the chair from 1857 to 1867, when he wrote some of his most important literary criticism.

11. Ironically, the translator's preface to Lowth's *Lectures* undercut his efforts to distinguish literature from the common idiom by arguing that literary studies should not be

confined to the "learned": "the greatest as well as the most useful works of taste and literature, are those, which . . . lie most level to the common sense of mankind" (vi).

3. Liberal Education in the Dissenting Academy Tradition

1. Histories of the dissenting academies include those of J. W. Smith, Irene Parker, and Herbert McLachlan. The academies have been recognized as colleges with a curriculum of "university standard" by educational and social historians (Barnard 29; see also Altick 42).

2. The *Compleat Gentleman*, like Defoe's *Complete Tradesman*, taught the public the sort of lessons that were learned in the academies. For example, Defoe criticizes the "bigots to the languages" and "the dead learning of the schools" because it lacked utilitarian value and stifled individuals' ability to learn from their own experience (215–17).

3. The general movement toward including more epistemology and less cosmology in pneumatology is evident in the lectures from several academies that are summarized in McLachlan (276).

4. According to one of Priestley's most accomplished private pupils, Anna Laetitia Barbauld, in the middle of the eighteenth century there was a "prejudice against any appearance of extraordinary cultivation in a woman," with women writers themselves objecting that words such as "*intellect*" and "*ethics*" are "too scholastic to proceed from the mouth of a female. What would some of these critics have said, could they have heard young ladies talking of gases, and nitrous oxide, and stimuli, and excitability, and all the terms of modern science" (Barbauld, *Correspondence of Samuel Richardson* [1804] 1: clxiii–iv).

5. Party politics were so well managed from 1754 to 1790 that twelve counties never voted at all, and local patrons had such unquestioned control of electors that in 1780 only two counties in all of England bothered to open the polls (Porter 126–27).

6. Turner reported on his own studies from 1777 to 1781 and those of John Simpson from 1760 to 1765 in *The Warrington Academy Monthly Repository* (8–10) from 1813 to 1815. The emphasis on free inquiry is evident, for example, in the teaching of John Taylor, the first divinity tutor. Taylor prefaced his lectures on works like Woolaston's *Religion of Nature Delineated* by advising students not to accept any doctrines that were taught in his course unless they appeared to be justified by reason (Turner 10–11; see also Taylor's *Sketch of Moral Philosophy*).

7. Priestley's approach to English studies was influenced by his interest in science, which he would have preferred to teach instead of rhetoric and belles lettres (*Works* 1.1: 47). Priestley published three works from his English courses at Warrington and at his own school at Nantwich from 1758 to 1761: *Rudiments of English Grammar* (1761), *Theory of Language* (1762), and *Course of Lectures on Oratory and Criticism* (1777). His most important contribution to liberal education was in the area of history, as discussed in the next section.

8. Priestley put forward such positions in the lecture notes he published in 1765 in *An Essay on a Course of Liberal Education for Civil and Active Life with Syllabuses of three courses of Lectures on "The Study of History," "The History of England," and "The Laws of England"*. In 1788 he expanded the work as *Lectures on History and General Policy. To which is prefixed, an Essay on a Course of Liberal Education for Civil and Active Life*, and in 1803 he published a revision with "An additional Lecture on the Constitution of the United

States." Smith's influence can be seen at numerous points in this last revision (see *Works* 24: 260, 308).

9. Priestley was active in the abolition groups like the "Committee of Correspondence for Abolishing the Slave-Trade" (see *Works* 15: 365). From the assumption that human nature was a tabula rasa, he rejected the common belief that Africans were innately inferior, arguing that they were in fact the race of the ancient Egyptians and had been degraded by the conditions of slavery (see *Works* 15: 379).

10. According to Hans, fifty-six dissenting teachers were awarded Scottish doctorates, and McLachlan records forty-seven heads of some twenty-five academies with Scottish degrees (Hans 247; McLachlan 188–91).

11. For example, front-page articles in the *Times* of November 8, 1792, included a condemnation of the "disorganizing plague" in France alongside an attack on Presbyterians for using books and schools to teach republican ideologies: "They have dispersed millions of artful books—they have established thousands of Republican Schools, for the purpose of training up the rising generation to a systematic plan of overturning our present Constitution."

4. The King's English and the Classical Tradition in Ireland

1. While visiting Ireland in the eighteenth century, Arthur Young noted that "hedge schools . . . are everywhere to be met with," though "they might as well be termed *ditch* ones, for I have seen many a ditch full of scholars" (202).

2. In *The College Examination* (1731), a pamphleteer describes the "*Fellow's* Labour, and the *Freshmen's* Curse" as including exams on logic, mechanics, astronomy, moral philosophy, and classical literature, with as much time given to the classics as all the rest combined (1).

3. From 1833 to 1852 no lectures were delivered by the professor of oratory, which was redefined in 1855 as professor of oratory and English literature. The professorship was held from 1857 to 1913 by Edward Dowden, an Anglican Unionist who was uncomfortable in Dublin and opposed literary nationalists such as Yeats as well as political liberals who favored expanding suffrage (see Maxwell; and Webb 230; Court 154).

4. Unfortunately, I do not have space to discuss Leland's translation of Demosthenes, the classical ideal for Leland as for Lawson. Leland's translation went through numerous editions and was reprinted in popular series like the Family Classical Library (1830), which quotes from some twenty reviews praising the taste for such cheap translations.

5. Leland also preached political quietism against revolutionary sentiments in the same way that Blair and Campbell did. In a sermon on December 13, 1776, Leland drew on the same Biblical precept that Campbell used to preach deference to established authorities: "Meddle not with them that are given to change" (Proverbs 24.21; Leland, *A Sermon* 16; see also *Sermons*). Like Blair and Campbell, Leland taught his audience to "habituate yourselves . . . to rational obedience, and submission." The dissenters preached quite different lessons.

6. *The Late Transactions between the Board of Senior Fellows and the Historical Society of Trinity College, Dublin* (1794) recounts the exile of the society to a public hall. The administration's determination to assert its authority over the society is evident in the uncompromising tone of the correspondence that is reprinted in the pamphlet.

7. An interesting example of how people taught themselves rhetoric is provided by *A Note-book of Edmund Burke*, which includes an entry on strategies for argumentation that draws on classical stasis theory as an aid for inventing political arguments (45–47). Classical rhetoricians had used stasis theory to locate the point at issue in a debate. As a practicing rhetorician, Burke recognized the crucial importance of being able to determine whether an argument turned on a matter of fact, definition, evaluation, or procedure. In contrast, the rhetorical theorists who translated the classical tradition into English generally deemphasized aids to invention and uniformly ignored stasis theory because they were less concerned with teaching students to situate conflicts in political debates than with instilling the perspective of the polite spectator who stands above such conflicts.

8. While he claimed to be the inheritor of classical rhetoricians, Sheridan was uninterested in classical moral philosophy—the "heathen morality" as he termed it—that provided the civic philosophy of classical rhetoric. Sheridan conceived of rhetoric itself as nothing more than the art of delivery, occasionally citing the very classical rhetoricians who had repudiated such limited conceptions and treated rhetoric as the art of putting civic virtue into social practice (*British Education* v, 13; see Howell 214–43). I examine the classical relationship between moral philosophy and rhetoric in the chapter on Adam Smith and the other rhetoricians and moral philosophers who reinterpreted civic humanism to adapt it to a "commercial society."

9. Such conceptions were common among Irish men of English letters. Swift referred to himself as "an Englishman born in Ireland," and Richard Steele, the Irish essayist who helped set the standards for English tastes with the *Tatler* and *Spectator*, described himself as "an Englishman born in the city of Dublin" (qtd. Beckett 431). Edmund Burke may be the most notable Irish man of English letters in the eighteenth century. As MacIntyre has discussed, Burke's success as a political and cultural commentator depended on his being able to speak as a representative Englishman, but it was his experience as an outsider who had consciously studied the conventions and history of the dominant culture that enabled him to defend it so successfully (*Whose Justice?* 217).

10. Speech gained greater academic legitimacy with James Rush's *Philosophy of the Human Voice* (1827), which founded principles of elocution on physiology. At the end of the nineteenth century, elocutionists turned to psychology to claim the authority of science, much as the "new" rhetoricians had a century earlier (see Benzie 44–51).

11. Writing on the works of James Joyce, Richard Ellmann concluded that "the Irish, condemned to express themselves in a language not their own, have stamped on it the mark of their own genius and compete for glory with the civilized nations. This is then called English Literature" (qtd. Crawford 263). Ellman's now jarring use of the term *civilized* highlights how views of colonial traditions have been transformed within college English studies in just the last two decades (see, for example, Viswanathan).

5. English Studies Enter the University Curriculum in Scotland

1. Crawford has argued that "the subject of English Literature was, ironically, a Scottish Invention" (15). Scholars who have reduced the study of English to the study of literature have treated the rhetoricians who introduced English as if they were literary critics (see Court).

2. Unlike more radical advocates of enlightenment in England and France, influential Scottish intellectuals tended to hold academic posts. Martin and others have argued that the positioning of intellectuals within established institutions was a distinguishing characteristic of "Moderate Enlightenment" (see also Sher). As educators, Scottish advocates of enlightenment were practically involved with the transmission of ideas through social institutions, and they tended to moderate the political implications of those ideas to avoid challenging the authority of their patrons and compromising their own positions.

3. The Society in Scotland for Promoting Christian Knowledge quoted this Act of the Privy Council in its *Account of the Society* in the assumption that its own efforts were but a continuation of the attempt to bring reformed religion and civility to the Highlands (2–3). According to Durkacz's *The Decline of the Celtic Languages* (1983), the SSPCK's proscriptions against the use of Gaelic in its schools "was the root of the language problem which dogged highland education thereafter" (39).

4. While Christison proudly identified popular literacy with social progress, the access of the lower classes to the Scottish universities was viewed quite differently by an English observer, Edward Topham (*Letters from Edinburgh* [1776], 8–11, 21). Topham admitted that the Scottish emphasis on lecturing was better than the tutorial method, but he felt that Scottish lectures would be better if they were not open to "almost every tradesman," even though he acknowledged that the universities had helped ensure that "the middle degree of people are not in such a state of ignorance as in England and in other countries" (209).

5. Sher's *Church and University* presents the most nuanced assessment of the Moderates' cultural philosophy and political practices, while Dwyer's *Virtuous Discourse* locates the polite sermonizing of the Moderates in the ideological context of the time (see also McCosh 15; Craig 66; Dickson 120; and my Introduction, *Witherspoon*).

6. As in the universities, moral philosophy was central to the expansion of Scottish letters. The writings of Hume and Hutcheson on moral philosophy in the 1740s were a common point of departure. Related works from the 1750s and 1760s include Hume's *Enquiry Concerning the Principles of Morals* (1751) and his *History of England* (1754–1762), Hutcheson's posthumous *System of Moral Philosophy* (1755), Smith's *Theory of Moral Sentiments* (1759), Robertson's histories of Scotland and Charles the Fifth (1759, 1769), Gerard's *Essay on Taste* (1759), Henry Home's *Elements of Criticism* (1762), Blair's *Critical Dissertation on the Poems of Ossian* (1763), and the first works on moral philosophy by Reid and Ferguson (1764, 1766).

7. Emerson's "The Social Composition of Enlightened Scotland: The Select Society of Edinburgh, 1754–1764" provides a richly detailed profile of the members of the group and their interests. By Emerson's count, forty of the sixty-eight questions debated by the group were on "economic-political-social" topics (298). In my assessment, such a conflation of topics blurs the distinction between practical discussions of political controversies and abstract moralizing about commonplace topics, but such distinctions are difficult to assess.

8. Sher views the Poker Club as an expression of the literati's patriotic feelings. He concludes that the failure of militia proposals encouraged Scots to redirect their ambitions from the political to the literary domain, where they were more successful (see *Church*).

9. During its existence, the group produced several works that directly contributed to the formation of college English studies: Alexander Gerard's *Essay on Taste* (1759), James Beattie's *Essay on the Nature and Immutability of Truth* (1770) and *The Ministrel; or the*

Progress of Genius (1771), and Reid's *Inquiry into the Human Mind, or the Principles of Common Sense,* published in 1764, the same year he moved to succeed Smith as professor of moral philosophy at Glasgow.

10. According to the analysis of Alasdair MacIntyre, Hume used a similar rhetorical ploy in the introduction to his *Treatise of Human Nature.* Hume used the fact that the work was published anonymously to imply that its author was not just English but an "Englishman curiously insensitive to the very existence of Scotland" (*Whose Justice?* 284). MacIntyre's analyses of Hutcheson and Hume parallel some of my concerns, as becomes evident in the next chapter.

11. With pride in a system that was being forced to conform to the centers of English education, J. S. Mill concluded in 1867 that "every Scottish University is not an University only, but a High School, to supply the deficiency of other schools. And if the English Universities do not do the same, it is not because the same need does not exist, but because it is disregarded. Youths come to the Scottish Universities ignorant, and are there taught. The majority of those who come to the English Universities come still more ignorant, and ignorant they go away" (136–37).

12. On the High School of Edinburgh that was attended by Blair and other literati, see Chalmers's *Life of Ruddiman* (1794).

13. The descriptions of Marischal and King's Colleges included in Sinclair's *Statistical Account* note that each offered about fifty scholarships to student populations that were between 100 and 130 for King's and 120 to 140 for Marischal (21: 111, 121 and 21: 89). Campbell and Skinner have estimated that the English universities cost three times as much as the Scottish universities (23).

14. Carstares's reforms were established at Glasgow University by a government commission in 1727, and the regenting system was also ended at St. Andrews in 1747, at Marischal College in 1753, and at King's in 1790.

15. According to Wood, "by promoting the ideals of polite learning" in a traditional center of Jacobite politics and Highland culture, "the curriculum reforms of 1753 can . . . be regarded as having furthered the ends of pacification, and as having thereby contributed to the consolidation of Hanoverian control in Scotland" (*Aberdeen* 162).

16. Ferguson seems to have been more committed to teaching than Blair, who taught for over twenty years without making many substantial revisions in his lectures. Ferguson published notes and several versions of his moral philosophy course so that students would not have to concentrate on copying down his words and could think about the ideas. Blair did not apparently devote much time to teaching writing, or oratory for that matter, but notes from Ferguson's lectures suggest that he emphasized composition. He had students write and submit "essays" and "exercises" argued inductively in order to teach "method," "Persuasion," and "Precision of Thought" and thus "cultivate . . . the Powers of Reason & of Elocution" (Edin. Univ. Mss. DC.1.84, 1: 14–15).

17. In 1758 Hume tried to lure Smith back to Edinburgh by reminding him that he had earned over a hundred pounds a year as a public lecturer and suggesting that an income of one hundred and fifty pounds (equal to Stevenson's, he notes) might be possible if Smith were established as a professor in the college (Smith, *Correspondence* 24).

18. Patriotic Scots were frequently advised to eradicate the characteristic idioms of their own country. In addition to Beattie's dictionary of proscribed terms, John Sinclair

published *Observations on the Scottish Dialect* (1782) to help Scots learn to speak like the English, and some editions of Hume's *Political Discourses* (1752) included a list of Scotticisms for readers to study along with his political theories (see Crawford 23–26).

19. According to his contemporary biographer, Home regularly refused to discuss politics because he felt that those who were not involved in state affairs were too ignorant to speak wisely of them and that political discussions only increased factionalism. For the same reasons, he also favored restrictions on the press (Tytler, *Memoirs* 2: 335–37).

20. According to Hamilton, Scotland's economic development can be divided into three periods. From midcentury to 1780, trade expanded, and improvements were made in agriculture and traditional industries like linen making (Scotland's main product). In 1755 imports and exports were 465,412 and 535,577 pounds sterling. In 1770 they had grown to 1,213,360 and 1,857,334. Exports to America grew from 82,669 pounds in 1755 to 2,118,936 in 1770, and linen rose from 2.1 million yards in 1728 to thirteen million yards in 1770 (Dickson 99). The second period, from 1780 to 1830, was "the first stage of the Industrial Revolution," and after 1830 Scotland became a center of heavy industry, including mining and shipbuilding (Hamilton 3).

21. The public debating societies of the last decades of the century were part of a different tradition than that of Bacon and learned societies. Their most famous predecessor was the Robin Hood Society, which was founded in London as a secret political society in 1613 but became a public group in 1667 and remained as such until the 1770s. Members included laborers, aristocrats, deists, and more practically engaged radicals like Peter Annet, one of the last people in England to be convicted of blasphemy because his penny pamphlets spread skepticism beyond the polite reading public. As in popular debating societies, a meeting of the Robin Hood Society included hundreds of people, rather than a dozen soft-spoken gentlemen correcting each other's English.

22. Reportedly referring to Millar, Smith, Ferguson, Hume, and Stewart, Marx wrote in a letter that he deserved no "credit" for "discovering the existence of classes in modern society nor yet the struggle between them. Long before me bourgeois historians had described the historical development of the class struggle and bourgeois economists the economic anatomy of the classes" (qtd. Perkins 27).

6. Adam Smith and the Rhetoric of a Commercial Society

1. According to Court, Smith was not "the first to attempt to include English literature in his course on rhetoric and belles lettres, but his efforts, the first of any historical consequence on the university level, posited a new classroom direction for English studies" (*Institutionalizing English Literature* 18). The "historical consequence" of Smith's lectures is questionable because they were not published until 1963. While Court attempts to sharply distinguish between the perspectives of Blair and Smith, the influence of Smith's lectures was exercised indirectly through Blair's popular *Lectures on Rhetoric and Belles Lettres*. While Court claims that Smith's lectures were "the first to be formally recognized and to be solely devoted to the subject," Smith was a professor of moral philosophy who lectured to his private class on rhetoric, with only passing references to "literature," in the modern sense of that term. To bring the rhetoricians who institutionalized English studies into his

history of literary studies, Court frequently equivocates between the modern definition of literature and the eighteenth-century conception of literature as all eloquent discourse. Ironically, the only notebook remaining from Smith's course does not even include the term *belles lettres* in the course title, and Howell has argued that what he taught was a course on rhetoric. While Blair had an international impact on the institutionalization of college English, Smith's remarks on "literature" in his unpublished lectures are far less important than his works on moral philosophy, which mapped out the political and cultural boundaries for the formation of college English.

2. Knud Haakonssen's wide-ranging works situate the Scottish Enlightenment between the natural law tradition and modern liberalism, though he is critical of any attempt to treat liberalism as a continuous development from Locke through Smith to Mill and the Utilitarians. The natural law tradition's contributions to the modern effort to reduce politics to a science are discussed in Habermas's *Theory and Practice*. On the other hand, Pocock, Phillipson, and Norton have treated civic humanism as the point of departure for Hutcheson, Hume, and Smith. For an important criticism of Pocock's sense of civic humanism, see Emerson's "Science and Moral Philosophy in the Scottish Enlightenment."

3. In *De Oratore* Cicero discusses how philosophy and rhetoric's shared concern for civic life was broken up by Platonic idealism (3: 19). Like other civic humanists such as Quintilian, Cicero distinguished speculative from moral philosophy by the latter's practical orientation. In fact, Cicero coined the term *moralis* (the predecessor of our terms *moral* and *moré*) to distinguish the study of *ethikos,* which like *moralis* has the double sense of customs and virtues (see Cicero, *De Fato; De Officiis* 1: 2; and *De Oratore* 1: 16; see also Quintilian 12: 2.10).

4. My understanding of civic humanism is indebted to Gadamer's treatment of *phronesis* as a paradigm for the situational nature of practical understanding. MacIntyre has also presented Aristotle's philosophy of practical wisdom as an important alternative to modern philosophies of practical understanding, particularly in the realm of values (see *After Virtue*). In *Whose Justice?* MacIntyre develops readings of Hutcheson and Smith that complement some of the points I make later in this chapter.

5. I have explored how Hutcheson's reinterpretation of civic humanism led to the subordination of rhetoric to belles lettres in my essay "Hutcheson and Civic Humanism." Hutcheson turns to "arbitration" rather than debate to mediate public conflicts (*Works* 6: 141). This legalistic frame of reference was due to his need to present the social contract as a consensual agreement rather than as the result of a few convincing the many through superior craft or power.

6. This development is consistent with Pocock's view that the natural law tradition had been "from its historic beginnings the fundamental expression of possessive individualism, in which the individual and his social and moral world are defined in terms of the property transactions in which he is engaged" ("Cambridge" 248).

7. Hume defended his view that the reason is a "slave" to the passions in *A Letter from a Gentleman* (1745) by claiming that he followed Hutcheson in assuming that morality rested not on reason, but on "the Feelings of our internal *Tastes* and *Sentiments*" (*Treatise* 2: 194–95; qtd. Jones, *Hume's Sentiments* 1). Smith concluded that his teacher was "the first who distinguished with any degree of precision in what respect all moral distinctions may said to arise from reason, and in what respect they are founded upon immediate sense and

feeling" (*Theory of Moral Sentiments* 320). On the "remarkable" continuities between Hutcheson's and Smith's positions on economic matters, see Campbell and Skinner (21).

8. As discussed later in this chapter, Smith attempts to make the disinterested spectator the voice of nature rather than convention, but even Hutcheson's arguments for a natural moral sense show that the deepening awareness of cultural differences and historical change had called human nature into question. As Eagleton discusses, the invocation of a "'moral sense' is equivalent to confessing that there is no longer any rationally demonstrable basis for value, even if we nevertheless continue to experience it. Morality, like aesthetic taste, becomes a *je ne sais quoi*: we just know what is right and wrong, as we know that Homer is superb or that someone is standing on our foot" (*Ideology* 64).

9. Hutcheson's chapter on "When it is that colonies may turn independent" was used to justify the American colonies' efforts to secure independence (6: 308; see also Norton, "Hutcheson"; Robbins; Wills; and Hamowy). The first of Hutcheson's writings to be printed in America was a series of excerpts from his *System* that were included in an antislavery tract by Anthony Benezet that was printed by Franklin in 1762. This was the first of several antislavery tracts to draw on Hutcheson's positions to argue against the Aristotelian assumption that slaves were naturally suited to servitude (see Fiering 128).

10. Smith stated the intentions of his revisions in a letter to a reader who criticized him for making the impartial spectator merely an internalization of convention. Smith wrote that he "intended both to confirm my Doctrine that our judgments concerning our own conduct have always a reference to the sentiments of some other being, and to shew that, notwithstanding this, real magnanimity and conscious virtue can support itselfe under the disapprobation of all mankind." Smith asked his reader to assess whether "I do not make Virtue sufficiently independent of popular opinion" (*Correspondence* 49).

11. Crowley's *Methodical Memory: Invention in Current-Traditional Rhetoric* has examined how the introspective orientation of the "new" rhetoric redefined the art of invention as the methodical review of mental experiences, with discourse functioning to reproduce those mental impressions in respondents. Crowley argues that this effort to discipline the individual authorial subject is generally characteristic of modernism. I return to Crowley's line of argument in the next chapter when I turn to the impact of the "science of human nature" on rhetoric.

12. Howell has lauded this expanding frame of reference, while composition specialists have generally decried the concentration of the "new" rhetoric on style. Charles Bazerman complicates such accounts by looking beyond changing theories of rhetoric to examine how Smith and Priestley attempted to put their theories of science into practice in their own writings. Bazerman's research provides an important counterpoint to my use of civic humanism as a point of reference. Bazerman values Smith's attention to the diversification of social and discursive conventions as a departure from the more narrow civic concerns of classical rhetoric.

13. Wordsworth called Smith "the worst critic, David Hume excepted, that Scotland, a soil to which this sort of weed seems natural, has produced" (qtd. Rae 34). Wordsworth may have read the posthumously published account of Smith's having pronounced that "it is the duty of a poet to write like a gentleman. I dislike that homely stile which some think fit to call the language of nature and simplicity." The comments were included in "Anecdotes tending to throw light on the character and opinions of the late Adam Smith. . . ,"

which was published in the journal the *Bee* and is reprinted in Bryce's edition of Smith's *Lectures on Rhetoric and Belles Lettres* 227–31.

14. The view that unintended outcomes shaped the progress of society was developed by Mandeville and advanced by Hume before Smith. On Hume, see Haakonssen, *Science of a Legislator* 21.

15. As can be seen from reviewing its history, *prudence* evolved from practical wisdom to the more modern sense of mere caution or frugality. According to MacIntyre, by Hutcheson's era little more than a "ghost" remained of the classical conception of practical wisdom, *phronesis* or *prudentia* (*Whose Justice* 276). Hobbes, for example, subordinated "prudence" to the more rigorously methodical approach to experience taken by "science" (35–36). While Hobbes associated prudence with inductive reasonings toward self-interest, a civic humanist like Harrington divided the history of political philosophy into "ancient" and "modern prudence," thus maintaining the civic association of prudence with shared practical wisdom or reasoned good sense (*Political Works* 161, 163). See also Cropsey, *Polity* 42, and Kahn's *Rhetoric, Prudence, and Skepticism in the Renaissance*.

16. Smith's conception of the impartial spectator has particularly close parallels with the religious conscience of Calvinism. Catholicism and Judaism have a strong sense that one is born into the shared traditions of the religious community, but constant introspection was required of Calvinists to assess whether they had experienced personal salvation. As Marshall discusses, biographies of Calvinists "reveal men and women who were intensely aware of themselves *as individuals*—sometimes tormented, sometimes ecstatic—but always individuals" (6–7).

17. As Gramsci emphasizes, for hegemony to be perpetuated, individuals must "voluntarily" identify themselves with dominant values and modes of behavior. Along the same lines, Marcuse discusses the dynamics of this psychological process in terms of "introjection," the process "in which the individual by himself reproduces and perpetuates the external controls exercised by his society." As Marcuse discusses, while the metaphor of internalization is problematic because it assumes that "a Self (Ego) transposes the 'outer' into the 'inner,'" the metaphor does provide a means to characterize how the "inner" sphere of the lived experience has been "invaded and whittled down by technological reality" (10).

7. Campbell's Philosophy of Rhetoric *and "The Science of Man"*

1. George Campbell (1719–1796) graduated from Marischal College in 1738. After completing his theological studies, he became a clergyman in 1746, principal of Marischal College in 1759, and professor of divinity in 1771, succeeding Gerard, who moved to King's College. The Aberdeen Philosophical Society before which Campbell read drafts of the *Philosophy of Rhetoric* was active from 1757 to around 1773 (see *Minutes of Aberdeen Philosophical Society*).

2. Turnbull's and Hume's efforts to claim the authority of the natural sciences may have had a common source, for both studied ethics and natural philosophy under Robert Steuart at Edinburgh (see Wood, *Aberdeen* 181).

3. According to Haakonssen, "from Turnbull Reid not only learned a providential nat-

uralism, with its methodological and pedagogical implications, but also acquired some idea of modern natural jurisprudence, a polite Shaftesburian Stoicism, and a humanism with 're-publican' or Commonwealth leanings, though one in which education in a more or less formal sense had become the primary means to full and active citizenship" (Introduction 8).

4. Fordyce provides a good example of how flexible the associations were between doctrines of "Sympathy" and "PUBLIC or COMMON SENSE" ("Elements" 2: 276). Van Holthoon and Olson's *Common Sense: the Foundations of Social Science* includes studies of the development of the concept in Cicero, the natural law tradition, the Enlightenment, and the modern human sciences, both normative and critical. Gadamer examines the complex history of common sense in *Truth and Method,* and Gramsci draws on historical concepts of common sense to establish a dialectic relationship among intellectuals, shared beliefs, and political action (*Prison Notebooks* 323–35).

5. Both Reid and Stewart did lecture on political topics, but their lectures were only published posthumously, in Stewart's case in his *Works* and in Reid's case in Haakonssen's edition of Reid's lectures at Glasgow. On the other hand, Hume published on practical morality, polite literature, and political history and theory. Norton's *David Hume: Common-Sense Moralist, Sceptical Metaphysician* (1982) treats Hume as a civic moralist along the same lines as Jone's *Hume's Sentiments: Their Ciceronian and French Context* (1982), which explicitly defines Hume as a "Ciceronian humanist" (4–5; see also Livingston).

6. Hume wrote Hutcheson in 1739 that he could not "agree to your Sense of Nature. Tis founded on final Causes; which is a Consideration, that appears to me pretty uncertain & unphilosophical. For pray, what is the End of Man? Is he created for Happiness or for Virtue? For this Life or for the next? For himself or for his Maker? Your Definition of *Natural* depends on solving these Questions, which are endless, & quite wide of my Purpose" (qtd. Norton, *Hume* 3). On the concept of "Providential Naturalism" in Turnbull and Reid, see Norton, *Hume* 171, and Haakonssen, Introduction 7.

7. Campbell responded to Priestley in *The Philosophy of Rhetoric,* noting that although "I use the term *common sense* in a more limited signification" than other common-sense philosophers, "there appears to be no real difference in our sentiments of the thing itself" (38).

8. Commonsense philosophers, along with Hutcheson and other Scottish moral philosophers, were widely influential in revolutionary America according to Garry Wills's analyses of the works of Jefferson and Madison, both of whom were taught rhetoric and moral philosophy by Scottish emigrés, in Madison's case by John Witherspoon, who introduced commonsense philosophy to America (see Witherspoon's *Selected Writings*).

9. Except for Beattie, who subordinated the study of rhetoric to logic in his *Elements of Moral Science* (1790–1793), Campbell was the only member of the commonsense school to publish on rhetoric. Reid, like his predecessor Smith, did lecture on rhetoric as professor of moral philosophy at Glasgow.

10. What came to be known as the "Newtonian Method" was laid out in Newton's "Rules of Reasoning in Philosophy," the third book of the *Principia*: a phenomenon is to be explained only by the causes sufficient to cause it; after generalizing to similar phenomena, one then formulates a governing principle, which is to be refined or refuted by further experimental inquiry (see Newton 398–400). See also note 8 of chapter 1, where I introduced the concept of *scientism.*

11. Campbell's terminology shows how formative the relationship between the new

logic and the sciences was at the time. Reserving the term *scientific reasoning* for mathematics, Campbell used "moral reasoning" for the modes of logic used in experimental studies, moral philosophy, and the "experience" of daily life (*Rhetoric* 35–61). Campbell stressed that "evidence from experience" includes "natural theology and psychology, which, in my opinion, have been most unnaturally disjoined by philosophers. Spirit, which here comprises only the Supreme Being and the human soul . . . is knowable to the philosopher purely in the same way, by observation and experience" (52–53). Campbell thus attempted to use pneumatology to reestablish the continuity between natural philosophy and natural religion that Turnbull had been able to assume.

12. Bain's *English Composition and Rhetoric* forms the direct point of contact with the nineteenth-century approach to rhetoric that defined the first recognized composition courses. Bain's theory is based on the view that "there are three principal ends in speaking,—to inform, to persuade, to please. They correspond to the three departments of the human mind, the Understanding, the Will, and the Feelings" (19; also chapter 9 below).

8. Hugh Blair and the Rhetoric of Belles Lettres

1. In "My Own Life," Hume recounted how he failed to gain the literary reputation he sought until he turned to the essays and histories that established his contemporary reputation (*Inquiry* 4). As he developed his own style of essay writing, he eliminated those essays that were most obviously modeled on the concerns and style of the *Spectator,* removing from subsequent editions such essays as "On Essay-Writing," "Of Moral Prejudices," "Of the Middle Station of Life," "Of Impudence and Modesty," and others that dealt with the sort of commonplaces that were favored by the many imitators of Addison's essays of taste and manners (see Hume, *Essays* xiin, xiiin).

2. Court's *Institutionalizing English Literature* strains to appropriate the theories of Adam Smith and distance the discipline from those of Blair, who has generally been seen as Smith's direct successor. According to Court, Smith took a practical and politically self-reflexive approach to English literature, while Blair narrowed English studies to "literary appreciation" and "perpetuated the proto-formalistic idea of the infinite progression of a unity of forms" (37). Blair's influence is well recognized by a wide range of rhetoricians, from James Berlin to W. S. Howell, but histories of English literary studies have deemphasized his importance in order to begin with the nineteenth-century origins of modern literary studies (see Gerald Graff; McMurty; Palmer; and William Riley Parker). Crawford's *Devolving English Literature* is a notable exception.

3. Blair made the request in a letter to Gilbert Elliot of March 1762 (NLS Mss. 11009: 111). The term *belles lettres* had been popularized by Rollin's *The Method of Teaching and Studying the Belles Lettres* (1726–1728; trans. 1734), which provided a broad survey of the "liberal Arts and Sciences" that included poetry, rhetoric, history, and moral philosophy.

4. Potkay's account of the death of eloquence in the age of Hume treats *eloquence* as a term of nostalgia for lost manly virtue and reduces orators from Thomas Jefferson to Martin Luther King to mere *topoi* of male angst marked by a "longing for a heroic father figure," an "infantile wish for Oedipal resolution," and "a plea for a masculine voice to unite us" (224).

5. The rejection of the classical art of invention was one of the distinctive features of the

"new" rhetoric. Beattie, for example, also concluded that "the art of Inventing" depends on genius, which "is an original Faculty & cannot be given by Instruction," let alone reduced "to a Science" (*Elements* 201). What is notable in such comments is how they place the creative capacities of discourse beyond the realm of logical analysis because they cannot be fit into the systematic methodology of the sciences.

6. Impromptu comments copied into lecture notes, records of the curriculum, and students' letters and diaries can provide only glimpses of what actually went on in the classroom, but Blair's pedagogy is more difficult to assess than most. For example, one would assume that he dictated his lectures for his students to copy, as was customary in the Scottish universities, but one set of notes includes the comment that "I shall allways discourage taking notes in the class, for this cause, that our reasoning is here [more] upon argument than fact" (Edinburgh Mss. DC.10.6: 13). This comment is difficult to reconcile with the numerous meticulously copied student notes of his lectures.

7. See Thomson's *The Gaelic Sources of Macpherson's "Ossian."* (1952). Though not using Pratt's term, recent scholarship has moved beyond questions about authenticity to treat the works as a rich site for examining the process of "transculturation" that develops when marginalized traditions interact with the dominant culture as it expands its sphere of influence and is transformed by its contact with groups that have not been inculcated into it (see Gaskill, deGategno, and Stafford).

8. Most of the sets of notes of Blair's lectures include references to the Ossianic poems as well as the thirty-seventh lecture that formed the basis for the *Critical Dissertation.* However, it is difficult if not impossible to use the manuscripts to examine how Blair responded to the sublimity of Ossian's natural genius because most of the sets of notes are undated, and one cannot be sure whether any set of notes was copied from Blair's lectures or from another copy. Notes from Blair's lectures were widely circulated and could even be bought from local booksellers.

9. Sinclair also published *A Dissertation on the Authenticity of the Poems of Ossian, in the Original Gaelic, with a Literal Translation into Latin* (1807). A fabricated Gaelic epic that had originally been composed in English was thus translated into the ancient language of the learned culture in an effort to prove the work's cultural authenticity. This is an especially striking example of the heteroglossia that is characteristic of the process of transculturation.

10. In "Blair, Witherspoon, and the Rhetoric of Civic Humanism," I have argued that Witherspoon put civic humanism into political practice to address the needs of pre-Revolutionary America, while Blair drew on classical ideals but ignored contemporary political rhetoric to adapt rhetoric to the social context of post-Union Scotland.

9. "'Rhetoric' in Modern Times Really Means 'Criticism'"

1. On the teaching of composition in British universities under the rubric of "English for academic purposes," see Muchiri, Mulamba, Myers, and Ndoloi.

2. Scottish and dissenting influences on Utilitarian educational reforms are clear in the most important reformer of the time, Robert Owen (1771–1858). After being educated at the dissenting academy at Manchester and joining in the Manchester Literary and Philo-

sophical Society with Warrington Academy's first student, Thomas Percival, Owen opened his famous school in his father-in-law's factory at New Lanark, Scotland. There he became friends with Smith's student, Professor George Jardine, who is discussed later in this chapter. Owen pioneered using student monitors to make instruction more efficient. He worked to adapt working-class education to a factory system where children as young as six worked from six in the morning to seven at night. With Owen's reforms, this regime was postponed until age ten, and two hours of class were added to the work day. Owen's efforts established the foundation for subsequent reforms (see Adamson; and Lawson and Silver).

3. Morley produced *English Writers* in eleven volumes (1864–1895), *A First Sketch of English Literature* (1873), a "sketch" of a thousand pages in subsequent editions, and several reprint series known as "libraries" because people subscribed to the whole series to reduce costs: *Morley's Universal Library* (1883–1988, sixty-four volumes), *Carisbrooke Library* (1889–1892), fourteen vols.), *Cassell's Library of English Literature* (1875–1881, five vols.), *Cassell's National Library* (1886–1891, about 220 vols.). Many of these encyclopedias of the educated culture were sold worldwide in excess of thirty, fifty, and even one hundred thousand copies (see McMurty 59).

4. If English was chosen as a subject for graduation examinations at University College, students were questioned in three areas: the history and structure of English, Anglo-Saxon, and special topics, which included specific periods and authors that had been announced in advance for the year. In his last year as a professor, 1890, Morley's students wrote about these topics: English literature from 1625 to 1800, *Hamlet,* and the first two books of *The Faerie Queene,* as well as Anglo-Saxon grammar and literature. Additional works of literature were included for those seeking honors (McMurty 51). McMurty has discussed the rising emphasis on examinations in higher education at the time, a response in part to the institution of civil service examinations in the imperial bureaucracy. These civil service exams helped to perpetuate the authority of Oxford and Cambridge by emphasizing classical languages.

5. According to Stone, the strengthening of "public" schools and traditional grammar schools brought classical education out of the decline of the eighteenth century, "and it then grew to such lush proportions that it obtained a strangle-hold on the English educational system which is only slowly being broken today" ("Literacy" 132).

6. Davie's *The Democratic Intellect: Scotland and Her Universities in the Nineteenth Century* devotes a chapter, "The Humanistic Bias of Scottish Science," to discussing how specialization undercut the generalist ethos of the curriculum.

7. One eighteenth-century trend that contributed to the introspective turn in moral philosophy was the view that moral philosophy was concerned with motivations rather than actions, as I discussed in chapter 6. Stewart also assumed that moral philosophy should not focus on purposeful action because we cannot know the effects of actions, but he questioned whether we could even know more than our own personal motivations: "the conjectures we form concerning the motives of others were liable to much uncertainty, that it is chiefly by attending to what passes in our own minds that we can reasonably hope to ascertain the general laws of our constitution as active and moral beings" (*Philosophy of the Active and Moral Powers of Man,* in *Works* 6: 124).

8. As discussed in chapters 2 and 3, Priestley and the dissenters were the first to develop

a more utilitarian understanding of "liberal" education. Dissenters rejected the traditional opposition of the "liberal arts" to the "mechanical" or "servile" arts suited to those who had to work for a living. Dissenters stressed instead the modern sense of "liberal" as opposed to traditional prejudices and conducive to enlightened reform.

Conclusion: Is the History of Classics a Model for the Future of English Departments?

1. For a comparative assessment of how academic writing is taught in universities in Britain, the United States, and several Commonwealth nations in Africa, see Muchiri, Mulamba, Myers, and Ndoloi. As the authors discuss, the discipline of rhetoric and composition is confined to North America, while in Britain and elsewhere the limited attention to teaching academic discourse tends to draw on linguistic theories. The history of college English has been expanded to include a postcolonial perspective in Viswanathan's *Masks of Conquest: Literary Study and British Rule in India* (1989).

2. Isocrates is held up as a model of efforts to use rhetoric to teach civic virtues not only by contemporary civic humanists such as James Kinneavy but also by proponents of critical pedagogy such as Patricia Bizzell (see 282–84).

3. Potkay has explicated the "masculinist political assumptions" of "the republican ideal of eloquence" in order to pose *the* rhetorical question: "why should any woman writer desire, even half-heartedly, a return to the rigidly communitarian assumptions of Demosthenes' Athens?" (1, 8).

4. Of course the social sciences have in the last several decades gone through an "interpretive turn" toward "participatory research" that repudiated the logic of disinterested observation (for a particularly relevant example, see Sullivan). Literary critics such as Eagleton have returned to rhetoric as an explicitly politicized mode of critical interpretation. The modern emphasis on critical interpretation has itself been contrasted with rhetoric's traditional involvement with practical action by Tompkins: "all modern criticism—whether response-oriented, psychological, structuralist, mythopoeic, thematic, or formalist—takes meaning to be the object of critical investigation, for unlike the ancients we equate language not with action but with signification" (203).

5. My understanding of rhetoric's centrality to a practical philosophy of the humanities has been greatly influenced by the writing and teaching of James Kinneavy. Kinneavy has argued that the modern "disinterested nature of humanistic education" contributed to the "exile" of rhetoric. As a result, the humanities lost the "practical orientation" that rhetoric had helped maintain by focusing on how to put traditional values into practical action in political life ("Restoring the Humanities: The Return of Rhetoric from Exile" 23; see also Kinneavy, *Theory of Discourse*).

6. While there are important exceptions such as the graduate program in rhetoric and composition at Carnegie Mellon University, Enos and Myers's survey shows that few graduate programs are found in either private universities or in the most prestigious English departments. The Modern Language Association's annual job lists document two basic facts about the discipline: there are more jobs in rhetoric and composition than any other specialization, and few if any of the tenure-track jobs in rhetoric and composition are in

elite institutions, ranging from Harvard and Yale to other private universities such as Vanderbilt, which in recent years invited applicants for a position in rhetoric and composition by specifying that no one with a scholarly background in the area should apply. Crowley has speculated from sales of textbooks that there are about thirty-three thousand teachers of composition and some one and a half million students taking composition each term in American colleges and universities (139). While the MLA has recognized it was ignoring the composition market, it recently published a survey of the discipline titled *Redrawing the Boundaries: The Transformation of English and American Literary Studies* that included diverse theories but maintained in its very title the boundaries imposed by defining college English studies as literary studies (see Greenblatt and Gunn). The chapter on rhetoric and composition basically concluded that the field does not exist as a scholarly discipline, but then the editors had chosen someone without a scholarly background in the area—a historian who directed the composition program at Harvard. At institutions such as Harvard, composition does not exist as part of the English department and is staffed by nontenured instructors hired on term contracts.

7. Linda Brodkey led the effort to transform English 306 at the University of Texas. Theories drawn from Kinneavy, Toulmin, and Perelman were used to examine how differences are constructed in federal antidiscrimination cases and related writings. The course was cited as an example of "political correctness" by George Will, the National Association of Scholars, and the *New York Times* (see Brodkey).

8. Like other institutions with undergraduate and graduate programs in rhetoric and composition, my colleagues and I at the University of Arizona have begun to develop ties with local community literacy initiatives, in our case the Pima County Adult Education programs that offer literacy courses oriented to refugees, workers, families on welfare, and others through community centers that also provide medical assistance, family counseling, and employment services to neighborhoods. Perhaps the most important example of such collaborations is the Community Literacy Center that has close ties with Carnegie Mellon's rhetoric and composition program (Community Literacy Center, 801 Union Avenue, Pittsburgh, PA 15212; see Peck, Flower, and Higgins).

9. Berlin and Vivion's *Cultural Studies in the English Classroom* includes diverse courses and programs in cultural studies that document the transformative potential of politically engaged pedagogy.

10. With Giroux, I maintain that "there are elements of a critical pedagogy in all traditions. The radical educator deals with tradition like anything else. It must be engaged and not simply received" (18). As I have tried to demonstrate, the dissenting academy tradition taught students to assume a critical perspective on received beliefs, while the Scots reformed the university curriculum against a critical reexamination of classicism, with both traditions documenting some of the historical possibilities and limitations of liberal reforms.

Works Cited

Aarsleff, Hans. *The Study of Language in England, 1780–1860.* Minneapolis: University of Minnesota Press, 1967.

Abrahms, M. H. *The Mirror and the Lamp: Romantic Theory and the Critical Tradition.* Oxford: Oxford University Press, 1953.

"Academical Repository." Daventry Academy, 1785–1797. Mss. 69.9–11. Dr. Williams Library, University of London.

Account of Society in Scotland for Propagating Christian Knowledge from its Commencement in 1709 . . . . Edinburgh, 1774.

Adamson, John William. *English Education, 1789–1902.* Cambridge: Cambridge University Press, 1964.

Alston, R. C. *A Bibliography of the English Language from the Invention of Printing to the Year 1800.* 20 vols. Menston: Scolar Press, 1965–1972.

Altick, Richard D. *The English Common Reader: A Social History of the Mass Reading Public.* Chicago: University of Chicago Press, 1957.

Amory, Hugh, ed. *Poets and Men of Letters.* Vol. 7, *Sale Catalogues of Libraries of Eminent Persons.* London: Mansell Information/Publishing Ltd., 1973.

Aristotle. *Basic Works.* Ed. Richard McKeon. New York: Random House, 1941.

Arnold, Matthew. *Complete Prose Works.* 10 vols. Ann Arbor: University of Michigan Press, 1960–1974.

Aronowitz, Stanley. *Science as Power: Discourse and Ideology in Modern Society.* Minneapolis: University of Minnesota Press, 1988.

Asquith, Ivon. "The Structure, Ownership and Control of the Press, 1780–1855." *Newspaper History from the Seventeenth Century to the Present Day.* Ed. George Boyce, James Curran, and Pauline Wingate. Beverly Hills: Sage Publications, 1978. 117–29.

Atkins, G. Douglas. *Estranging the Familiar: Toward a Revitalized Critical Writing.* Athens: University of Georgia Press, 1992.

Atkinson, Norman. *Irish Education: A History of Educational Institutions.* Dublin: Allen Figgs, 1969.

Auchmuty, James Johnston. *Irish Education: A Historical Survey.* Dublin: Hodges Figgs and Co., 1937.

Austin, Gilbert. *Chironomia, or a Treatise on Rhetorical Delivery.* 1806; Rpt., Carbondale: Southern Illinois University Press, 1966.

Bacon, Francis. *A Book of English Essays*. Ed. W. E. Williams. Middlesex: Penguin, 1952.

Bacon, Wallace A. "The Elocutionary Career of Thomas Sheridan (1719–1788)." *Speech Monographs* 31 (1964): 1–53.

Bain, Alexander. *Education as a Science*. New York: D. Appleton and Company, 1896.

———. *English Composition and Rhetoric*. American rev. ed., New York: D. Appleton and Company, 1866.

———. *Mental and Moral Science, A Compendium of Psychology and Ethics*. London: Longman & Company, 1868.

———. *On Teaching English*. London: Longmans and Co., 1887.

Bakhtin, Mikhail. *Dialogic Imagination*. Ed. Michael Holquist. Trans. Caryl Emerson and Michael Holquist. Austin: University of Texas Press, 1981.

Barbauld, Anna Laetitia, ed. *The Correspondence of Samuel Richardson*. 6 vols. 1804; New York: AMS Press, 1966.

Barnard, Howard Clive. *A History of English Education from 1760*. 2d ed. London: University of London Press, 1961.

Barrington, Jonah. *Personal Sketches of His Own Times*. 3 vols. London: Henry Colburn, 1827–1832.

Bartine, David. *Early English Reading Theory: Origins of Current Debates*. Columbia: University of South Carolina Press, 1992.

Bator, Paul. "The Formation of the Regius Chair of Rhetoric and Belles Lettres at the University of Edinburgh." *Quarterly Journal of Speech* 75 (1989): 40–64.

———. "The Unpublished Rhetoric Lectures of Robert Watson, Professor of Logic, Rhetoric, and Metaphysics at the University of St. Andrews, 1756–1778." *Rhetorica* 12 (1994): 67–240.

———. "The University of Edinburgh Belles Lettres Society (1759–64) and the Rhetoric of the Novel." *Rhetoric Review* 14 (1996): 280–98.

Baugh, Albert C., and Thomas Cable. *A History of the English Language*. 3d ed. Englewood Cliffs, N.J.: Prentice-Hall, Inc., 1978.

Bazerman, Charles. "How Natural Philosophers Can Cooperate: The Literary Technology of Coordinated Investigation in Joseph Priestley's *History and Present State of Electricity* (1767)." *Textual Dynamics of the Professions: Historical and Contemporary Studies of Writing in Professional Communities*. Ed. Charles Bazerman and James G. Paradis. Madison: University of Wisconsin Press, 1991. 13–44.

———. "Money Talks: The Rhetorical Project of *The Wealth of Nations*." *Constructing Experience*. Carbondale: Southern Illinois University Press, 1994. 215–44.

Bazerman, Charles, and David Russell. "The Rhetorical Tradition and Specialized Discourses." *Landmark Essays in Writing Across the Curriculum*. Davis, Calif.: Hermagoras Press, 1994. xii–xxxviii.

Beattie, James. *Elements of Moral Science*. 2 vols. 1790–1793; Delmar, N.Y.: Scholars' Facsimiles and Reprints, 1976.

———. *Scotticisms, Arranged in Alphabetical Order, Designed to Correct Improprieties of Speech and Writing*. Edinburgh, 1787.

Beckett, J. C. "Literature in English, 1691–1800." *A New History of Ireland*. Ed. F. X. Martin et al. Vol. 4, *Eighteenth-Century Ireland, 1691–1800.* Oxford: Oxford University Press, 1986. 424–70.

Bellot, H. Hale. *University College London, 1826–1926.* London: University of London Press, 1929.

Benjamin, Walter. "The Work of Art in the Age of Mechanical Reproduction." *Illuminations.* Ed. Hannah Arendt. Trans. Harry Zohn. New York: Schocken Books, 1969. 217–51.

Benzie, W. *The Dublin Orator: Thomas Sheridan's Influence on Eighteenth Century Rhetoric and Belles Lettres.* Leeds: University of Leeds, 1972.

Berlin, James A. "Revisionary History: The Dialectical Method." *Pretext* 8 (1987): 47–61.

———. *Writing Instruction in Nineteenth-Century American Colleges.* Carbondale: Southern Illinois University Press, 1984.

Berlin, James A., and Michael Vivion, eds. *Cultural Studies in the English Classroom.* Portsmouth, N.H.: Boynton/Cook Heinemann, 1992.

Bevilacqua, Vincent M. "Campbell, Priestley, and the Controversy Concerning Common Sense." *Southern Speech Journal* 30 (1964): 79–90.

———. "Philosophical Assumptions Underlying Hugh Blair's Lectures on Rhetoric and Belles Lettres." *Western Speech* 31 (1967): 150–64.

———. "Philosophical Origins of George Campbell's Philosophy of Rhetoric." *Speech Monographs* 32 (1965): 1–12.

Bitzer, Lloyd. Introduction. *The Philosophy of Rhetoric.* By George Campbell. Rev. ed. Carbondale: Southern Illinois University Press, 1988.

Bizzell, Patricia. *Academic Discourse and Critical Consciousness.* Pittsburgh: University of Pittsburgh Press, 1992.

Black, Jeremy. *English Press in the Eighteenth Century.* London: Croom Helm, 1987.

Blackwall, Anthony. *Introduction to the Classics.* 2d ed. London, 1719.

Blair, Hugh. *Critical Dissertation on the Poems of Ossian.* 2d. ed. 1765; New York: Garland Publishing Inc., 1970.

———. *Lectures on Rhetoric and Belles Lettres.* 1789; ed. Harold F. Harding. 2 vols. Carbondale: Southern Illinois University Press, 1965.

———. Letter to Sir Gilbert Elliot, Lord Minto. 4-3-1762. 3 pp. National Library of Scotland MS11009: 111.

———. *Observations Upon a Pamphlet Intitled "An Analysis of the Moral and Religious Sentiments contained in the Writings of Sopho, and David Hume, Esq.".* Edinburgh, 1755.

———. *Sermons.* 5 vols. Edinburgh, 1777–1801.

Bliss, Alan. "The English Language in Early Modern Ireland." *A New History of Ireland.* Ed. T. W. Moody, F. X. Martin, and F. J. Byrne. Vol. 3, *Early Modern Ireland.* Ed. F. X. Martin et al. Oxford: Clarendon Press, 1976. 546–60.

Bolton, Robert. *A Translation of the Charter and Statutes of Trinity College . . . .* Dublin, 1749.

Bond, Richmond P. Introduction. *Studies in the Early English Periodical.* Chapel Hill: University of North Carolina Press, 1957. 1–48.

"Book of Essays Written by Students in the Class of John Stevenson, Professor of Logic and Metaphysics, Edinburgh University, 1737–50." University of Edinburgh Mss. DC.4.54.

Bourdieu, Pierre. *Distinction: A Social Critique of the Judgement of Taste*. Cambridge: Harvard University Press, 1984.

Bowers, Claude G. *The Irish Orators*. Indianapolis: Bobbs-Merrill, 1906.

Brodkey, Linda. "Making a Federal Case Out of Difference: The Politics of Pedagogy, Publicity, and Postponement." *Writing Theory and Critical Theory*. Ed. John Clifford and John Schilb. New York: Modern Language Association, 1994. 236–61.

Brougham, Henry. *Practical Observations on the Education of the People*. London: Longman & Co., 1825.

Bryce, J. C., ed. Introduction. *Lectures on Rhetoric and Belles Lettres*. By Adam Smith. Oxford: Clarendon Press, 1980.

Bryson, Gladys. "The Emergence of the Social Sciences from Moral Philosophy." *International Journal of Ethics* 42 (1932): 304–23.

———. *Man and Society: The Scottish Inquiry of the Eighteenth Century*. Princeton: Princeton University Press, 1945.

Buchanan, James. *A Plan of an English Grammar-School Education*. Edinburgh, 1770.

Buchanon, George. "A Letter from a Member of the Easy Club to the Spectator." August 15, 1712. University of Edinburgh Mss. La II 212.3.

Buck, George. "The Third Universitie of England . . . ." *The Annales, or General Chronicle of England*. John Stow and Edmond Howes. London, 1615.

Bugter, S. E. W. "Sensus Communis in the Works of M. Tullius Cicero." *Common Sense: The Foundations for Social Science*. Ed. Frits van Holthoon and David R. Olson. Lanham: University Press of America, 1987. 83–97.

Burgon, John W. *Life & Times of Sir Thomas Gresham*. 2 vols. London: Robert Jennings, 1839.

Burke, Edmund. *A Note-book of Edmund Burke*. Ed. H. V. F. Somerset. Cambridge: Cambridge University Press, 1957.

Burke, Peter. *Popular Culture in Early Modern Europe*. London: Temple Smith, 1978.

Butler, S. *An Essay Upon Education*. London, 1753.

Campbell, George. *An Address to the People of Scotland Upon the Alarms That Have Been Raised in Regard to Popery*. Aberdeen, 1779.

———. *The Nature, Extent, and Importance of the Duty of Allegiance: A Sermon Preached at Aberdeen, December 12, 1776*. Aberdeen, 1777.

———. *The Philosophy of Rhetoric*. 1776; Rev. ed. Carbondale: Southern Illinois University Press, 1988.

Campbell, R. H., and A. S. Skinner. Introduction. *An Inquiry into the Nature and Causes of the Wealth of Nations*. By Adam Smith. Oxford: Clarendon Press, 1987.

Carlyle, Alexander. *The Autobiography of Dr. Alexander Carlyle of Inveresk, 1722–1805*. Ed. John Hill. London: T. N. Foulis, 1910.

Chalmers, George. *The Life of Thomas Ruddiman*. London, 1794.

Christison, Alexander. *The General Diffusion of Knowledge One Great Cause of the Prosperity of North Britain*. Edinburgh: John Brown, 1802.

Cicero. *De Officiis.* Loeb Classical Library. Cambridge: Harvard University Press, 1913.

———. *De Oratore, Books I–II.* Trans. E. W. Sutton and H. Rackham. Loeb Classical Library. Cambridge: Harvard University Press, 1942.

———. *De Oratore, Book III; De Fato; Paradoxoa Stoicorum; and De Partitione Oratoria.* Loeb Classical Library. Cambridge: Harvard University Press, 1952.

———. *On the Commonwealth.* Columbus: Ohio State University Press, 1929.

Clark, Ian D. L. "From Protest to Reaction: The Moderate Regime in the Church of Scotland, 1752–1805." *The Origins and Nature of the Scottish Enlightenment.* Ed. R. H. Campbell and Andrew S. Skinner. Edinburgh: John Donald Publishers Ltd., 1982. 200–224.

Clarke, John. *An Essay Upon Education.* 3d ed. London, 1740.

———. *An Essay Upon Study.* 2d ed. London, 1737.

Clarke, M. L. *Classical Education in Britain, 1500–1900.* Cambridge: Cambridge University Press, 1959.

———. "Classical Studies." *The History of the University of Oxford.* Vol. 5, *The Eighteenth Century.* Ed. L. S. Sutherland and L. G. Mitchell. Oxford: Clarendon Press, 1986. 513–33.

Claussen, E. Neal, and Karl R. Wallace. Introduction. *Lectures Concerning Oratory Delivered in Trinity College, Dublin.* By John Lawson. Carbondale: Southern Illinois University Press, 1972. ix–liii.

Clive, John, and Bernard Bailyn. "England's Cultural Provinces: Scotland and America." *William and Mary Quarterly* 11 (1954): 200–214.

Cohen, Murray. *Sensible Words: Linguistic Practice in England 1640–1785.* Baltimore: Johns Hopkins University Press, 1977.

The College Examination. Dublin, 1731.

Colley, Linda. "Whose Nation? Class and National Consciousness in Britain 1750–1830." *Past and Present* 113 (1986): 97–117.

Connors, Robert J. "The Rhetoric of Explanation: Explanatory Rhetoric from 1850 to the Present." *Written Communication* 2 (1985): 49–72.

Couper, William James. *The Edinburgh Periodical Press; Being a Bibliographical Account of the Newspapers, Journals, and Magazines Issued in Edinburgh from the Earliest Times to 1800.* 2 vols. Stirling: Eneas Mackay, 1908.

Court, Franklin E. *Institutionalizing English Literature: The Culture and Politics of Literary Study, 1750–1900.* Stanford: Stanford University Press, 1992.

Craig, David. *Scottish Literature and the Scottish People, 1680–1830.* Westport, Conn.: Greenwood, 1961.

Crawford, Robert. *Devolving English Literature.* Oxford: Clarendon Press, 1992.

Crook, Ronald E. *A Bibliography of Joseph Priestley, 1733–1804.* London: Library Association, 1966.

Cropsey, Joseph. *Polity and Economy: An Interpretation of the Principles of Adam Smith.* Westport, Conn.: Greenwood, 1977.

Crowley, Sharon. *The Methodical Memory: Invention in Current-Traditional Rhetoric.* Carbondale: Southern Illinois University Press, 1990.

Crowley, Tony. *The Politics of Discourse: The Standard Language Question in British Cultural Debates.* London: Macmillan Education Ltd., 1989.

Cullen, L. C., and T. C. Smout. *Comparative Aspects of Scottish and Irish Economic and Social History, 1600–1900.* Edinburgh: John Donald, 1977.

Curtis, S. J. *History of Education in Great Britain.* London: University Tutorial Press Ltd., 1961.

Dagg, Thomas Sidney Charles. *The College Historical Society, A History (1770–1920).* Tralee: privately printed, 1969.

Daiches, David. *The Paradox of Scottish Culture: The Eighteenth Century Experience.* London: Oxford University Press, 1964.

Dale, Thomas. *An Introductory Lecture Delivered in the University of London.* London: J. Taylor, 1829.

————., ed. *Lectures on Rhetoric and Belles Lettres.* By Hugh Blair. London: Thomas Tegg, 1845.

Davie, George Elder. *The Democratic Intellect: Scotland and Her Universities in the Nineteenth Century.* Edinburgh: Edinburgh University Press, 1961.

Davis, Arthur Paul. *Isaac Watts: His Life and Works.* New York: Dryden Press, 1943.

Davis, Lennard J. "A Social History of Fact and Fiction: Authorial Disavowal in the Early English Novel." *Literature and Society: Selected Papers from the English Institute, 1978.* Ed. Edward W. Said. Baltimore: Johns Hopkins University Press, 1980. 120–48.

Defoe, Daniel. *Compleat English Gentleman.* Ed. Karl D. Bülbring. Folcroft, Penn.: Folcroft Library Editions, 1972.

————. *More Short Ways with the Dissenters.* London, 1704.

————. *The Present State of the Parties in Great Britain: Particularly An Enquiry into the State of the Dissenters in England and the Presbyterians in Scotland . . . .* London, 1712.

DeGategno, Paul James. *James Macpherson.* Boston: G. K. Hall and Co., 1989.

Devine, T. M., and David Dickson, eds. *Ireland and Scotland 1600–1850: Parallels and Contrasts in Economic and Social Development.* Edinburgh: John Donald Publishers, 1983.

Dewey, John. *The Public and Its Problems.* Athens: Ohio University Press, 1985.

Dickson, Tony. *Capital and Class in Scotland.* Edinburgh: John Donald, 1982.

Doddridge, Phillip. *Correspondence and Diary of Phillip Doddridge.* Ed. J. D. 5 vols. London: Humphreys, 1829–1831.

————. *A Course of Lectures on the Principal Subjects in Pneumatology, Ethics, and Divinity; With References to the Most Considerable Authors on Each Subject.* 2 vols. London, 1763.

————. *Works.* 10 vols. Leeds: Edward Baines, 1803–1805.

Downey, Charlotte. Introduction. *English Grammar.* By Lindley Murray. 1824; Delmar, N.Y.: Scholar's Facsimiles and Reprints, 1981.

Durkacz, Victor Edward. *The Decline of the Celtic Languages: A Study of Linguistic and Cultural Conflict in Scotland, Wales and Ireland from the Reformation to the Twentieth Century.* Edinburgh: John Donald Pub., 1983.

Dwyer, John. *Virtuous Discourse: Sensibility and Community in Late Eighteenth-Century Scotland.* Edinburgh: John Donald Pub. Ltd., 1987.

Eagleton, Terry. *The Function of Criticism from the Spectator to Poststructuralism.* London: Verso, 1984.

———. *The Ideology of the Aesthetic*. Oxford: Blackwell, 1990.

Edinburgh Review. Ed. James MacKintosh. 1818; Rpt., *Economic Research* 55 (1975): 1–79.

Ehninger, Douglas. "George Campbell and the Revolution in Inventional Theory." *Southern Speech Bulletin* 15 (1950): 270–76.

———. "John Ward and His Rhetoric." *Speech Monographs* 18 (1951): 1–16.

Ehninger, Douglas, and James Golden. "The Intrinsic Sources of Blair's Popularity." *Southern Speech Journal* 21 (1955): 12–30.

Eisenstein, Elizabeth L. *The Printing Press as an Agent of Change: Communications and Cultural Transformations in Early-Modern Europe*. 2 vols. Cambridge: Cambridge University Press, 1979.

Elphinston, James. *A Plan of Education at Mr. Elphinston's Academy, Kensington*. London, 1760.

Emerson, Roger L. "Science and Moral Philosophy in the Scottish Enlightenment." *Studies in the Philosophy of the Scottish Enlightenment*. Ed. M. A. Stewart. Oxford: Clarendon Press, 1990. 11–36.

———. "Scottish Universities in the Eighteenth Century, 1690–1800." *Studies of Voltaire and the Eighteenth Century* 167 (1977): 453–74.

———. "The Social Composition of Enlightened Scotland: The Select Society of Edinburgh, 1754–1764." *Studies of Voltaire and the Eighteenth Century* 114 (1973): 291–329.

Enfield, William. *Essay on the Cultivation of Taste as a Proper Object of Attention in the Education of Youth*. Newcastle: n.p., 1818.

———. *Principles of Mental and Moral Philosophy. To which is prefixed, Elements of Logic.* . . . London: Thomas Tegg, 1809.

———. *The Speaker: or Miscellaneous Pieces, Selected from the Best English Writers,* . . . *To which is Prefixed an Essay on Elocution*. London, 1774.

Enos, Richard Leo. *Greek Rhetoric Before Aristotle*. Prospect Heights, Ill.: Waveland Press, 1993.

Enos, Theresa, and Paul Myer. "Directory of Graduate Programs in Rhetoric and Composition." *Rhetoric Review* 12 (1994): Special issue.

An Enquiry into the Plan and Pretensions of Mr. Sheridan. Dublin, 1758.

Evans, Margaret, ed. *Letters of Richard Radcliffe and John James of Queen's College, Oxford, 1755–83*. Oxford: Clarendon Press, 1888.

Fairer, David. "Oxford and the Literary World." *The History of the University of Oxford*. Vol. 5, *The Eighteenth Century*. Ed. L. S. Sutherland and L. G. Mitchell. Oxford: Clarendon Press, 1986. 779–805.

Febvre, Lucien, and Henri-Jean Martin. *The Coming of the Book: The Impact of Printing 1450–1800*. Trans. Davide Gerard. Ed. Geoffrey Nowell-Smith and David Wooten. London: NLB, 1976.

Ferguson, Adam. *An Essay on the History of Civil Society*. Ed. Duncan Forbes. Edinburgh: Edinburgh University Press, 1966.

———. "Lectures on Pneumatics and Moral Philosophy." 3 vols. Nov. 11, 1783. University of Edinburgh Mss. DC.1.84.

Ferguson, Delancey I. "Burns and Hugh Blair." *Modern Language Notes* 45 (1930): 440–46.

Ferguson, William. *Scotland 1689 to the Present*. New York: Fredrick A. Praeger, 1968.

Fiering, Norman. *Moral Philosophy at Seventeenth-Century Harvard: A Discipline in Transition*. Chapel Hill: University of North Carolina Press, 1981.

Finlayson, James. "A Short Account of the Life and Character of the Author." *Sermons*. By Hugh Blair. 5 vols. Edinburgh: Oliver and Boyd, 1815.

Forbes, William. *An Account of the Life and Writings of James Beattie, LL.D.* 3 vols. 2d ed. Edinburgh: Archibald Constable, 1807.

Fordyce, David. *Dialogues Concerning Education*. London, 1745.

———. *The Elements of Moral Philosophy*. In *The Preceptor*. Ed. Robert Dodsley. 6th ed. 2 vols. London, 1765.

Foucault, Michel. *The Archeology of Knowledge and the Discourse on Language*. New York: Pantheon Books, 1972.

———. *The Order of Things*. New York: Vintage Books, 1973.

Franklin, Benjamin. *Autobiography*. Ed. J. A. Leo Lemay and P. M. Zall. New York: Norton, 1986.

Freeman, Kathleen. *Ancilla to the Pre-socratic Philosophers*. Cambridge: Harvard University Press, 1957.

Freire, Paulo. *Pedagogy of the Oppressed*. New York: Continuum, 1970.

Fyfe, J. G., ed. *Scottish Diaries and Memoirs, 1746–1843*. Stirling, Scotland: Observer Press, 1942.

Gadamer, Hans-Georg. "Hermeneutics and Social Science." *Cultural Hermeneutics* 2 (1975): 307–16.

———. *Truth and Method*. Trans. G. Barden and J. Cumming. New York: Seabury Press, 1986.

Gaskill, Howard, ed. *Ossian Revisited*. Edinburgh: Edinburgh University Press, 1991.

Geertz, Clifford. *Local Knowledge: Further Essays in Interpretative Anthropology*. New York: Basic Books, 1983.

Gentleman's Magazine 1 (1731); 4th ed. London, 1732.

[Gerard, Alexander]. *A Plan of Education in the Marischal College and University of Aberdeen, with the Reasons of It*. Aberdeen, 1755.

Gibbon, Edward. *Memoirs of My Life*. Ed. Georges A. Bonnard. London: Thomas Nelson and Sons Ltd., 1966.

Gibbons, Thomas. *Memoirs of Dr. Isaac Watts*. London, 1780.

Gibbs, F. W. *Joseph Priestley: Adventurer in Science and Champion of Truth*. London: Thomas Nelson and Sons, Ltd., 1965.

Girdler, L. "Defoe's Education at Newington Green Academy." *Studies in Philology* 50 (1953): 573–91.

Giroux, Henry. *Border Crossings: Cultural Workers and the Politics of Education*. New York: Routledge, 1992.

Glau, Gregory R. "Mirroring Ourselves? The Pedagogy of Early Grammar Texts." *Rhetoric Review* 11 (1993): 418–35.

Godley, A. D. *Oxford in the Eighteenth Century*. London: Methuen, 1908.

Golden, James. "Hugh Blair: Minister of St. Giles." *Quarterly Journal of Speech* 38 (1952): 155–66.

Golden, James, and Edward P. J. Corbett, eds. *The Rhetoric of Blair, Campbell, and Whately.* New York: Holt, Rinehart, and Winston, Inc., 1968.

Golden, James, and Douglas Ehninger. "The Extrinsic Sources of Hugh Blair's Popularity." *Southern Speech Journal* 22 (1956): 16–32.

Goldsmith, Oliver. *An Enquiry Into the Present State of Polite Learning in Europe. Collected Works.* Ed. Arthur Friedman. 5 vols. Oxford: Clarendon Press, 1966. 1: 245–345.

Good, Graham. *The Observing Self: Rediscovering the Essay.* London: Routledge, 1988.

Graff, Gerald. *Professing English Literature: An Institutional History.* Chicago: University of Chicago Press, 1987.

Graff, Harvey J. *The Legacies of Literacy.* Bloomington: Indiana University Press, 1987.

Graham, H. G. *Scottish Men of Letters in the Eighteenth Century.* London: Adam and Charles Black, 1901.

Gramsci, Antonio. *Selections from Cultural Writings.* Ed. David Forgacs and Geoffrey Nowell-Smith. Trans. William Boelhower. London: Lawrence Wishart, 1985.

———. *Selections from the Prison Notebooks.* Ed. and trans. Quentin Hoare and Geoffrey Nowell-Smith. London: 1971.

Grant, Alexander. *The Story of the University of Edinburgh During Its First Three Hundred Years.* 2 vols. London: Longmans, Green, and Co., 1884.

Greaves, R. "Religion in the University 1715–1800." *The History of the University of Oxford.* Vol. 5, *The Eighteenth Century.* Ed. L. S. Sutherland and L. G. Mitchell. Oxford: Clarendon Press, 1986. 401–58.

Green, V. H. H. "The University and Social Life." *The History of the University of Oxford.* Vol. 5, *The Eighteenth Century.* Ed. L. S. Sutherland and L. G. Mitchell. Oxford: Clarendon Press, 1986. 309–58.

Greenblatt, Stephen, and Giles Gunn, eds. *Redrawing the Boundaries: The Transformation of English and American Literary Studies.* New York: Modern Language Association, 1992.

Grillo, R. D. *Dominant Languages: Language and Hierarchy in Britain and France.* Cambridge: Cambridge University Press, 1989.

Gunning, Henry. *Reminiscences of the University, Town, and Country of Cambridge From the Year 1780.* 2 vols. London: George Bell, 1854.

Haakonssen, Knud. "From Moral Philosophy to Political Economy: The Contribution of Dugald Stewart." *Philosophers of the Scottish Enlightenment.* Ed. V. M. Hope. Edinburgh: Edinburgh University Press, 1984. 211–32.

———, ed. Introduction. *Practical Ethics.* By Thomas Reid. Princeton: Princeton University Press, 1990.

———. *The Science of a Legislator: The Natural Jurisprudence of David Hume and Adam Smith.* Cambridge: Cambridge University Press, 1981.

Habermas, Jürgen. *The Structural Transformation of the Public Sphere: An Inquiry into a Category of Bourgeois Society.* Trans. Thomas Burger. Cambridge: MIT Press, 1989.

———. *Theory and Practice.* Trans. John Viertel. Boston: Beacon Press, 1973.

Hamilton, Henry. *The Economic Evolution of Scotland in the Eighteenth and Nineteenth Centuries.* London: G. Bell and Sons, Ltd., 1933.

Hans, Nicholas A. *New Trends in Education in the Eighteenth Century.* London: Routledge and Kegan Paul, 1951.

Harding, Harold F., ed. *Lectures on Rhetoric and Belles Lettres.* By Hugh Blair. 2 vols. 1783; Carbondale: Southern Illinois University Press, 1965.

Hardison, O. B., Jr. "Binding Proteus: An Essay on the Essay." *Essays on the Essay: Redefining the Genre.* Ed. Alexander J. Butrym. Athens: University of Georgia Press, 1989. 11–28.

Harrington, James. *Political Works.* Ed. J. G. A. Pocock. Cambridge: Cambridge University Press, 1977.

Harris, Michael. "The Structure, Ownership and Control of the Press, 1620–1780." *Newspaper History from the Seventeenth Century to the Present Day.* Ed. George Boyce, James Curran, and Pauline Wingate. Beverly Hills: Sage Publications, 1978.

Havelock, Eric A. *The Liberal Temper in Greek Politics.* New Haven: Yale University Press, 1957.

Heineccius, Jo. Got. *A Methodical System of Universal Law: Or, the Laws of Nature and Nations Deduced From Certain Principles, and Applied to Proper Cases.* Trans. George Turnbull. 2 vols. London, 1741.

Hely-Hutchinson, F. "Account of the State of the University of Ireland." Trinity College Mss., 1787.

[Henderson, Robert]. "A Short Account of the University of Edinburgh, the Present Professors in it, and the Several Parts of Learning Taught by Them." *Scots Magazine* 3 (1741): 371–74.

Hill, John. *An Account of the Life and Writings of Hugh Blair.* Edinburgh: J. Ballantyne and Co., 1807.

Hirsch, E. D., Jr. *Cultural Literacy, What Every American Needs to Know.* Boston: Houghton Mifflin Company, 1987.

"Historical Account of Students Educated in Warrington Academy." *The Monthly Repository of Theology and General Literature* 9 (1814): 201–5, 263–68, 385–90, 525–30, 594–99.

"Historical Society, Journals and Laws." 1770–1795. Trinity College, Dublin Mss. Mun/Soc/Hist.

The History of the Speculative Society 1764–1904. Edinburgh: T. and A. Constable, 1905.

Hobbes, Thomas. *Leviathan.* Ed. Richard Tuck. Cambridge: Cambridge University Press, 1991.

Home, Henry, Lord Kames. *Elements of Criticism.* 1762; Hildesheim: Georg Olms, 1970.

———. *Essays on the Principles of Morality and Natural Religion.* Edinburgh, 1751.

———. *Sketches of the History of Man.* 4 vols. Dublin, 1774–1775.

Hook, Andrew. *Scotland and America: A Study of Cultural Relations, 1750–1835.* Glasgow and London: Blackie, 1975.

Horkheimer, Max, and Theodor W. Adorno. *Dialectic of Enlightenment.* Trans. John Cumming. New York: Continuum, 1982.

Horner, Winifred Bryan. *Nineteenth-Century Scottish Rhetoric: The American Connection.* Carbondale: Southern Illinois University Press, 1993.

———. "Rhetoric in the Liberal Arts: Nineteenth-Century Scottish Universities." *The Rhetorical Tradition and Modern Writing.* Ed. James J. Murphy. New York: Modern Language Association, 1982. 85–94.

Houston, R. A. *Literacy in Early Modern Europe: Culture and Education 1500–1800.* London: Longman, 1988.

Howell, W. S. *Eighteenth-Century British Logic and Rhetoric.* Princeton: Princeton University Press, 1971.

Hume, David. *Essays Moral, Political, and Literary.* Ed. Eugene F. Miller. Indianapolis: Liberty Classics, 1985.

———. *An Inquiry Concerning Human Understanding.* Ed. Charles W. Hendel. Indianapolis: Bobbs-Merrill, 1955.

———. *Moral and Political Philosophy.* Ed. Henry D. Aiken. New York: Macmillan Publishing Co., Inc., 1948.

———. *A Treatise of Human Nature: Being An Attempt to introduce the experimental Method of Reasoning into Moral Subjects.* Ed. Ernest G. Mossner. London: Penguin Books, 1984.

Hurdis, James. *Lectures Shewing the Several Sources of that Pleasure Which the Human Mind Receives from Poetry.* 1797; New York: Garland Publishing, Inc., 1971.

Hutcheson, Francis. *Collected Works.* 7 vols. Hildesheim: Georg Olms, 1969–1971.

Huxley, Thomas. *Science and Education.* Vol. 3 of *Collected Essays.* 1898; New York: Greenwood Press, 1968.

Irvine, James R. "Rhetoric and Moral Philosophy: A Selected Inventory of Lecture Notes and Dictates in Scottish Archives, 1700–1900." *Rhetoric Society Quarterly* 8 (1978): 159–64.

Jackson, Ian. *The Provincial Press and the Community.* Manchester: University of Manchester, 1971.

Jaeger, Werner. *Paideia: The Ideals of Greek Culture.* Trans. Gilbert Highet. 3 vols. New York: Oxford University Press, 1945.

Jardine, George. *Outlines of Philosophical Education, Illustrated by the Method of Teaching the Logic Class in the University of Glasgow.* Glasgow: Glasgow University Press, 1825.

———. *Synopsis of Lectures on Logic and Belles Lettres; Read in the University of Glasgow.* Glasgow, 1797.

Jarratt, Susan. *Rereading the Sophists: Classical Rhetoric Refigured.* Carbondale: Southern Illinois University Press, 1991.

Jebb, John. *Remarks upon the Present Mode of Education in the University of Cambridge: to which is added a Proposal for its Improvement.* Cambridge, 1773.

Jennings, John. "An Account of the Revd. Mr. Jennings Method of Education." Mss. Dr. Williams Library, University of London.

Johnson, Nan. *Nineteenth-Century Rhetoric in North America.* Carbondale: Southern Illinois University Press, 1992.

Johnson, Samuel. *A Dictionary of the English Language.* 2 vols. Ed. H. J. Todd. London: Longman, Hurst, Rees, Orme, and Brown, 1818.

————. *Lives of the Poets.* 2 vols. New York: E. P. Dutton and Co., 1925.

————. *The Plan of a Dictionary of the English Language.* 1747; Menston: Scolar Press, 1970.

————. *Prefaces, Biographical and Critical, to the Works of the English Poets.* 10 vols. London, 1779–1781.

Johnston, Thomas. *The Working Classes in Scotland.* Glasgow: Forward Publishing Co., 1920.

Jones, Peter. *Hume's Sentiments: Their Ciceronian and French Context.* Edinburgh: Edinburgh University Press, 1982.

Jones, Peter. "The Polite Academy and the Presbyterians, 1720–1770." *New Perspectives on the Politics and Culture of Early Modern Scotland.* Ed. John Dwyer, Roger A. Mason, and Alexander Murdoch. Edinburgh: John Donald Publishers Ltd., 1982. 156–77.

Kahn, Victoria. *Rhetoric, Prudence, and Skepticism in the Renaissance.* Ithaca: Cornell University Press, 1985.

Kaminski, Thomas. *The Early Career of Samuel Johnson.* New York: Oxford University Press, 1987.

Kearney, Hugh F. *Scholars and Gentlemen: Universities and Society in Pre-Industrial Britain, 1500–1700.* London: Faber and Faber, 1970.

Keesey, Ray E. "John Lawson's Lectures Concerning Oratory." *Speech Monographs* 20 (1953): 49–57.

Kennedy, Alan. "Committing the Curriculum and Other Misdemeanors." *Cultural Studies in the English Classroom.* Portsmouth, N.H.: Boynton/Cook Heinemann, 1992. 24–45.

Kennedy, George A. *Classical Rhetoric and Its Christian and Secular Traditions from Ancient to Modern Times.* Chapel Hill: University of North Carolina Press, 1980.

Ker, W. P. "Thomas Warton." *The British Academy Warton Lecture on English Poetry, 1910.* Folcroft, Penn.: Folcroft Library Editions, 1971.

Kernan, Alvin. *Printing Technology, Letters, and Samuel Johnson.* Princeton: Princeton University Press, 1987.

Ketcham, Michael G. *Transparent Designs: Reading, Performance, and Form in the Spectator Papers.* Athens: University of Georgia Press, 1985.

Kingsley, Charles. *His Letters and Memories of His Life.* London: Macmillan and Co., 1895.

————. *Works.* 28 vols. 1880–1885; Hildesheim: Georg Olms, 1969.

Kinneavy, James. "Restoring the Humanities: The Return of Rhetoric from Exile." *The Rhetorical Tradition and Modern Writing.* Ed. James Murphy. New York: Modern Language Association, 1982. 19–28.

————. *A Theory of Discourse.* New York: W. W. Norton and Co., 1980.

Kippis, Andrew. "An Essay on the Variety and Harmony of the English Heroic Verse. . . . Notes taken by Joseph Cornish, New College, Hoxton." Dec. 21, 1769. Mss. Dr. Williams Library, University of London.

————. "Introductory Lectures to the Belles Lettres." New College, Hoxton, 1767. Mss. Dr. Williams Library, University of London.

————. "Notes on Professor Ward's System of Oratory By Andrew Kippis DD." 1769. Mss. Dr. Williams Library, University of London.

Kitzhaber, Albert Raymond. *Rhetoric in American Colleges, 1850–1900.* Dallas: Southern Methodist University Press, 1990.

Klancher, Jon. *The Making of English Reading Audiences, 1790–1832*. Madison: University of Wisconsin Press, 1986.

Knox, Vicesimus. *Essays, Moral and Literary*. 2 vols. 1778; New York: Garland Publishing, Inc., 1972.

———. *Liberal Education: or, a Practical Treatise on the Methods of Acquiring Useful and Polite Learning*. 2 vols. London, 1781.

Labov, William. "Hypercorrection by the Lower Middle Class as a Factor in Linguistic Change." *Sociolinguistic Patterns*. Philadelphia: University of Pennsylvania Press, 1972. 122–43.

Lacquer, Thomas. "The Cultural Origins of Popular Literacy in England 1500–1850." *Oxford Review of Education* 2 (1976): 255–75.

Landsman, Ned C. "Liberty, Piety and Patronage: The Social Context of Contested Clerical Calls in Eighteenth-Century Glasgow." *The Glasgow Enlightenment*. Ed. Andrew Hook and Richard B. Sher. East Lothian: Tuckwell Press Ltd., 1995. 214–26.

Lanham, Richard A. *The Electronic Word: Democracy, Technology, and the Arts*. Chicago: University of Chicago Press, 1993.

The Late Transactions Between the Board of Senior Fellows and the Historical Society of Trinity College, Dublin. Dublin, 1794.

Laudan, L. L. "Thomas Reid and the Newtonian Turn of British Methodological Thought." *The Methodological Heritage of Newton*. Ed. R. E. Butts and J. W. Davis. Oxford: Clarendon Press, 1970. 103–31.

Lawson, John. *Lectures Concerning Oratory*. Ed. Neal Claussen and Karl R. Wallace. 1758; Carbondale: Southern Illinois University Press, 1972.

———. *Occasional Sermons; With a Short Notice of the Author Prefixed*. Dublin, 1765.

Lawson, John, and Harold Silver. *A Social History of Education in England*. London: Methuen and Co. Ltd., 1973.

Lecky, W. E. H. *A History of Ireland in the Eighteenth Century*. 1892; Ed. L. P. Curtis. Chicago: Chicago University Press, 1972.

Leechman, William. "Lectures on Composition by the Reverend Mr Leechman, Professor of Divinity . . . . " University of Edinburgh Mss. DC.7.86.

———. "Some Account of the Life, Writings, and Character of the Author." *A System of Moral Philosophy*. Vol. 5, *Collected Works of Francis Hutcheson*. 1755; Hildesheim: Georg Olms, 1969. i–xlviii.

Leinster-Mackay, D. P. *The Educational World of Daniel Defoe*. Victoria: University of Victoria, 1981.

Leland, Thomas. *A Dissertation on the Principles of Human Eloquence . . . .* London, 1764.

———. *The History of Ireland, from the Invasion of Henry II*. 3 vols. London, 1773.

———. *Orations of Demosthenes*. 1756; 2 vols. London: A. J. Valpy, 1830.

———. *A Sermon Preached Before the University of Dublin, on Friday the 13th of December, 1776 . . .* London, 1777.

———. *Sermons on Various Subjects*. 3 vols. Dublin, 1788.

Leonard, Sterling Andrus. *Doctrines of Correctness in English Usage, 1700–1800*. New York: Russell and Russell, 1962.

A Letter to G—— W—— Esq. Concerning the Present Condition of the College of Dublin, and the Late Disturbances that Have Been Therein. Dublin, 1734.

A Letter to a School-Master in the Country, from his Friend in Town, Relative to Mr. Sheridan's Scheme of Education. Dublin, 1758.

A Letter to the Young Gentlemen of the University of Dublin on Occasion of their Late Disturbances. Dublin, 1734.

Liddell, Henry George, and Robert Scott. *Greek-English Lexicon.* Oxford: Clarendon Press, 1986.

Lincoln, A. *Some Political and Social Ideas of English Dissent, 1763–1800.* Cambridge: Cambridge University Press, 1938.

Lipking, Lawrence. *The Ordering of the Arts in Eighteenth-Century England.* Princeton: Princeton University Press, 1970.

Livingston, Donald W. *Hume's Philosophy of Common Life.* Chicago: University of Chicago Press, 1984.

Locke, John. *Some Thoughts On Education.* Ed. Peter Gay. New York: Columbia University, 1964.

Lowth, Robert. *Lectures on the Sacred Poetry of the Hebrews.* 1787; 2 vols. New York: Garland Publishing, Inc., 1971.

———. *A Short Introduction to English Grammar.* 1775; Delmar, New York: Scholar's Facsimiles and Reprints, 1979.

McCosh, James. *The Scottish Philosophy, Biographical, Expository, Critical, From Hutcheson to Hamilton.* New York: Robert Carter and Brothers, 1874.

McCracken, J. L. "The Social Structure and Social Life, 1714–60." In *A New History of Ireland.* Ed. T. W. Moody, F. X. Martin, and F. J. Byrne. Vol. 4, *Eighteenth-Century Ireland, 1691–1800.* Ed. F. X. Martin et al. Oxford: Oxford University Press, 1986. 31–56.

McDowell, R. B., and D. A. Webb. *Trinity College Dublin, 1592–1952: An Academic History.* Cambridge: Cambridge University Press, 1982.

McElroy, D. D. *Scotland's Age of Improvement: A Survey of Eighteenth-Century Clubs and Societies.* Pulman, Wash.: Washington State University Press, 1969.

McIntosh, Carey. "The Gentrification of English Prose, 1700–1800." *Language and Civilization.* Ed. Claudia Blank. Frankfurt-on-Main: Peter Lang, 1992. 720–35.

MacIntyre, Alasdair. *After Virtue: A Study in Moral Theory.* 2d ed. Notre Dame: University of Notre Dame Press, 1984.

———. *Whose Justice? Which Rationality?.* Notre Dame: University of Notre Dame Press, 1988.

Mackail, J. W. *Henry Birkhead and the Foundation of the Oxford Chair of Poetry.* Oxford: Clarendon Press, 1908.

McKendrick, Neil. "The Consumer Revolution of Eighteenth-Century England." *The Birth of a Consumer Society: The Commercialization of Eighteenth-Century England.* Bloomington: Indiana University Press, 1982.

McLachlan, Herbert. *English Education Under the Test Acts: Being the History of the Non-Conformist Academies 1662–1820.* Manchester: Manchester University Press, 1931.

Maclaurin, Colin. *An Account of Sir Isaac Newton's Philosophical Discoveries.* 1748; New York: Johnson Reprint Corporation, 1968.

McMurty, Jo. *English Language, English Literature: The Creation of an Academic Discipline.* Hamden, Conn.: Shoe String Press, 1985.

Macpherson, James. *The Works of Ossian, the Son of Fingal.* 2 vols. 3d ed. London, 1765.

Mandeville, Bernard. *The Fable of the Bees.* Ed. F. B. Kaye. 2 vols. Oxford: Clarendon Press, 1924.

Mant, Richard. "Memoirs." *The Poetical Works of the Late Thomas Warton.* 5th ed. 2 vols. Oxford: Oxford University Press, 1802.

Marcuse, Herbert. *One Dimensional Man.* Boston: Beacon Press, 1964.

Marrou, H. I. *A History of Education in Antiquity.* Trans. George Lamb. New York: New American Library, 1964.

Marshall, Gordon. *Presbyteries and Profits: Calvinism and the Development of Capitalism in Scotland, 1560–1707.* Oxford: Clarendon Press, 1980.

Martin, Terence. *The Instructed Vision.* Bloomington: Indiana University Press, 1961.

Maurice, F. D. *The Friendship of Books and Other Lectures.* Ed. T. Hughes. London: Macmillan and Co., 1874.

———. *Sketches of Contemporary Authors.* Ed. A. J. Harley. Hamden, Conn.: Archon Books, 1970.

Maxwell, Constantia. *A History of Trinity College Dublin, 1591–1892.* Dublin: University Press, 1946.

May, Henry F. *The Enlightenment in America.* Oxford: Oxford University Press, 1976.

Meikle, Henry W. "The Chair of Rhetoric and Belles Lettres." *University of Edinburgh Journal* 13 (1945): 89–113.

Michael, Ian. *The Teaching of English from the Sixteenth Century to 1870.* Cambridge: Cambridge University Press, 1987.

Mill, J. S. "Inaugural Address at St. Andrews." *James and John Stuart Mill on Education.* Ed. F. A. Cavenagh. Westport, Conn.: Greenwood Press, 1979. 132–98.

Millar, John. *Observations Concerning the Distinction of Ranks in Society.* 2d ed. London, 1773.

Miller, Thomas P. "Blair, Witherspoon and the Rhetoric of Civic Humanism." *Scotland and America in the Age of Enlightenment.* Ed. Richard Sher and Jeffrey Smitten. Edinburgh: Edinburgh University Press; Princeton: Princeton University Press, 1990. 100–114.

———. "The Formation of College English: A Survey of the Archives of Eighteenth-Century Rhetorical Theory and Practice." *Rhetoric Society Quarterly* 20 (1990): 261–86.

———. "Hutcheson and the Civic Humanist Tradition." *The Glasgow Enlightenment.* Ed. Andrew Hook and Richard B. Sher. East Lothian: Tuckwell Press, 1995. 40–55.

———. Introduction. *The Selected Writings of John Witherspoon.* Carbondale: Southern Illinois University Press, 1990.

———. "Reinventing Rhetorical Traditions." *Learning from the Rhetorics of History.* Ed. Theresa Enos. Carbondale: Southern Illinois University Press, 1993. 26–41.

The Minutes of the Aberdeen Philosophical Society, 1758–1773. Ed. H. Lewis Ulman. Aberdeen: Aberdeen University Press, 1990.

"Minutes of the Poker Club." University of Edinburgh Mss. DC.5.126.

Mitchison, Rosalind. "Ireland and Scotland: The Seventeenth-Century Legacies Compared." *Ireland and Scotland 1600–1850: Parallels and Contrasts in Economic and Social Development.* Ed. T. M. Devine and David Dickson. Edinburgh: John Donald Publishers, 1983. 2–11.

Mizuta, Hiroshi. "Moral Philosophy and Civil Society." *Essays on Adam Smith.* Ed. Andrew Skinner and Thomas Wilson. Oxford: Clarendon Press, 1975. 114–31.

Monk, Samuel H. *The Sublime: A Study of Critical Theories in Eighteenth-Century England.* Ann Arbor: University of Michigan Press, 1960.

Montaigne, Michel de. *The Essays.* London: Allen Lane, 1991.

Moore, James. "The Two Systems of Francis Hutcheson: On the Origins of the Scottish Enlightenment." *Studies in the Philosophy of the Scottish Enlightenment.* Oxford: Clarendon Press, 1990. 37–59.

Moore, James, and M. Silverthorne. "Natural Sociability and Natural Rights in the Moral Philosophy of Gershom Carmichael." *Philosophers of the Scottish Enlightenment.* Ed. V. M. Hope. Edinburgh: Edinburgh University Press, 1984. 1–12.

Moore, John Hamilton. *Young Gentleman and Lady's Monitor, and English Teacher's Assistant; Being a Collection of Select Pieces from our Best Modern Writers . . . .* London, 1789.

Moran, Michael G. "Joseph Priestley." *Eighteenth-Century British and American Rhetorics and Rhetoricians.* Ed. Michael G. Moran. Westport: Greenwood Press, 1994. 175–85.

Morgan, Alexander, and Robert Kerr Hannay, eds. *University of Edinburgh: Charters, Statutes, and Acts of the Town Council and the Senatus 1583–1858.* Edinburgh: Oliver and Boyd, 1937.

Morren, Nathaniel, ed. *Annals of the General Assembly of the Church of Scotland, 1739–1766.* 2 vols. Edinburgh: John Johnstone, 1838–1840.

Morrison, Samuel Eliot. *Three Centuries of Harvard, 1636–1936.* Cambridge: Belknap Press of Harvard University Press, 1936.

Morton, Charles. "Vindication drawn up when charged with breaking 'Stamford Oath.'" *A Continuation of the Account of the Ministers, Lecturers, Masters and Fellows of Colleges, and Schoolmasters who were Ejected and Silenced after the Restoration in 1660 . . . .* By Edmund Calamy. 2 vols. London, 1727. 1: 177–97.

Muchiri, Mary N., Nschindi G. Mulamba, Greg Myers, and Deosorous B. Ndoloi. "Importing Composition: Teaching and Researching Academic Writing Beyond North America." *College Composition and Communication* 46 (1995): 175–98.

Murray, Lindley. *English Grammar.* 1824; Delmar, N.Y.: Scholars' Facsimiles and Reprints, 1981.

Murray, Victor. "Doddridge and Education." *Phillip Doddridge, 1702–51, His Contribution to English Religion.* Ed. Geoffrey F. Nuttall. London: Independent Press, 1951.

Neuberg, Victor E. *Popular Education in Eighteenth Century England.* London: Woburn Press, 1971.

Nietzsche, Friedrich. "History in the Service and Disservice of Life." *Unmodern Observations.* Ed. William Arrowsmith. New Haven: Yale University Press, 1990. 87–145.

Norton, David Fate. *David Hume: Common-sense Moralist, Sceptical Metaphysician.* Princeton: Princeton University Press, 1982.

———. "Francis Hutcheson in America." *Studies on Voltaire and the Eighteenth Century* 154 (1976): 1547–68.

'O Cuív, Brian. "Irish Language and Literature, 1691–1845." *A New History of Ireland.* Ed. F. X. Martin et al. Vol. 4, *Eighteenth-Century Ireland, 1691–1800.* Oxford: Oxford University Press, 1986. 374–421.

O'Halloran, Clare. "Irish Re-Creation of the Gaelic Past: The Challenge of Macpherson's Ossian." *Past and Present* 124 (1989): 69–95.

Oldfield, Joshua. *An Essay Towards the Improvement of Reason.* London, 1707.

Oliver, Robert Tarbell. *The Influence of Rhetoric in the Shaping of Great Britain.* Newark: University of Delaware Press, 1986.

Olson, Richard. *Science Deified and Defied: The Historical Significance of Science in Western Culture.* Berkeley: University of California Press, 1982.

———. *Scottish Philosophy and British Physics, 1750–1880: A Study in the Foundations of the Victorian Scientific Style.* Princeton: Princeton University Press, 1975.

Ong, Walter, S. J. *Interfaces of the Word: Studies in the Evolution of Consciousness and Culture.* Ithaca: Cornell University Press, 1977.

———. Review of *Eighteenth-Century British Logic and Rhetoric.* By W. S. Howell. *William and Mary Quarterly* 29 (1972): 637–43.

———. *Rhetoric, Romance, and Technology.* Ithaca: Cornell University Press, 1971.

Orton, Job. *Memoirs of . . . Philip Doddridge, D.D. of Northampton.* London, 1766.

Oxford English Dictionary. 2 vols. Oxford: Oxford University Press, 1971.

Palmer, David J. *The Rise of English Studies: An Account of the Study of English Language and Literature from Its Origins to the Making of The Oxford English School.* Oxford: Oxford University Press, 1965.

Parker, Irene. *Dissenting Academies in England: Their Rise and Progress and Their Place Among the Educational Systems of the Country.* Cambridge: Cambridge University Press, 1914.

Parker, William Riley. "Where Do English Departments Come From?" *College English* 28 (1967): 339–51.

Peck, Wayne Campbell, Linda Flower, and Lorraine Higgins. "Community Literacy." *College Composition and Communication* 46 (1995): 199–222.

Percival, Thomas. *A Father's Advice to his Daughters.* 1777.

———. *Father's Instructions, Consisting of Moral Tales, Fables, and Reflections: Designed to Promote the Love of Virtue: A Taste for Knowledge: And an Early Acquaintance with the Works of Nature.* 8 vols. London, 1775–1800.

———. *Moral and Literary Dissertations: Chiefly Intended as the Sequel to A Father's Instructions . . . .* 2d ed. 1789; New York: Garland Publishing Inc., 1971.

Percy, Thomas. *Reliques of Ancient Poetry: Consisting of Old Heroic Ballads, Songs, and Other Pieces.* London, 1765.

Perkins, Harold. *The Origins of Modern English Society 1780–1880.* London: Routledge and Kegan Paul, 1969.

Peyton, V. J. *The History of the English Language; Deduced from Its Origin, and Traced through Its Different Stages and Revolutions.* London, 1771.

Phillipson, Nicholas. "Adam Smith as Civic Moralist." *Wealth and Virtue: The Shaping of*

Political Economy in the Scottish Enlightenment. Ed. Istvan Hont and Michael Ignatieff. Cambridge: Cambridge University Press, 1983. 179–202.

———. "Culture and Society in the Eighteenth-Century Province: The Case of Edinburgh and the Scottish Enlightenment." *The University in Society.* 2 vols. Ed. Lawrence Stone. Princeton: Princeton University Press, 1974. 2: 407–48.

———. "Public Opinion and the Union in the Age of Association." *Scotland in the Age of Improvement: Essays in Scottish History in the Eighteenth Century.* Ed. N. T. Phillipson and Rosalind Mitchison. Edinburgh: Edinburgh University Press, 1970.

———. "The Pursuit of Virtue in Scottish University Education: Dugald Stewart and Scottish Moral Philosophy in the Enlightenment." In *Universities, Society, and the Future.* Ed. Nicholas Phillipson. Edinburgh: Edinburgh University Press, 1983. 82–101.

Pittock, Joan. "Thomas Warton and the Oxford Chair of Poetry." *English Studies* 62 (1981): 14–33.

Plowden, Francis. *An Historical Review of the State of Ireland . . . to its Union with Great Britain.* 2 vols. London: C. Roworth, 1803.

Plumb, J. H. "The Commercialization of Leisure in Eighteenth-Century England." *The Birth of a Consumer Society: The Commercialization of Eighteenth-Century England.* London: Europa Pub. Ltd., 1982.

Pocock, J. G. A. "Cambridge Paradigms and Scotch Philosophers: A Study of the Relations between Civic Humanist and the Civil Jurisprudential Interpretations of Eighteenth-Century Social Thought." *Wealth and Virtue: The Shaping of Political Economy in the Scottish Enlightenment.* Ed. Istvan Hont and Michael Ignatieff. Cambridge: Cambridge University Press, 1983.

———. *Politics, Language, and Time: Essays on Political Thought and History.* New York: Atheneum, 1971.

Porter, Roy. *English Society in the Eighteenth Century.* London: Penguin, 1982.

Post, Robert M. "Forensic Activities at Trinity College, Dublin in the Eighteenth Century." *Central States Speech Journal* 19 (1968): 19–25.

Potkay, Adam. *The Fate of Eloquence in the Age of Hume.* Ithaca: Cornell University Press, 1994.

Potter, David. *Debating in the Colonial Chartered College.* New York: Teachers College, Columbia University, 1944.

Poulakos, John. "Nietzsche and Histories of Rhetoric." *Writing Histories of Rhetoric.* Ed. Victor J. Vitanza. Carbondale: Southern Illinois University Press, 1994. 8–97.

Poulakos, Takis. "Isocratean Rhetorical Education: A Structural Precedent for Cultural Studies." *Rhetoric in the Vortex of Cultural Studies.* Ed. Arthur Walzer. Minneapolis: Burgess Pub., 1993. 42–50.

Pratt, Mary Louise. *Imperial Eyes: Travel Writing and Transculturation.* London: Routledge, 1992.

Price, Richard. *A Review of the Principal Questions in Morals.* 1758; Ed. D. D. Raphael. Oxford: Clarendon Press, 1948.

Priestley, Joseph. *A Course of Lectures on Oratory and Criticism.* 1777; Ed. Vincent M. Bevilacqua and Richard Murphy. Carbondale: Southern Illinois University Press, 1965.

———. *A Course of Lectures on the Theory of Language, and Universal Grammar.* Warrington, 1762.

———. *An Examination of Dr. Reid's "Inquiry into the Human Mind on the Principles of Common Sense," Dr. Beattie's "Essay on the Nature and Immutability of Truth," and Dr. Oswald's "Appeal to Common Sense in Behalf of Religion".* London, 1774.

———. *The Rudiments of English Grammar; Adapted to the Use of Schools.* 1761; Menston: Scolar Press, 1969.

———. *Theological and Miscellaneous Works.* 25 vols. Ed. John Towill Rutt. London: 1817–1831.

Prior, James. *Memoir of the Life and Character of the Right Hon. Edmund Burke.* 2d ed. London: Baldwin, Cradock, and Jay, 1826.

"Proceedings of the Belles Lettres Society." January 12, 1759 to May 5, 1761. National Library of Scotland Mss. 23.3.4.

Quarrie, P. "The Christ Church Collections Books." *The History of the University of Oxford.* Vol. 5, *The Eighteenth Century.* Ed. L. S. Sutherland and L. G. Mitchell. Oxford: Clarendon Press, 1986. 493–511.

Quintilian. *Institutio Oratoria.* Trans. H. E. Butler. 4 vols. Loeb Classical Library. Cambridge: Harvard University Press, 1936.

Rae, John. *Life of Adam Smith.* 1895; New York: August M. Kelley, 1965.

Ramsay, Allan. *Works.* Ed. Burns Martin, John W. Oliver, Alexander Law, and Alexander Kinghorn. 6 vols. Edinburgh: Scottish Text Society, 1951–1974.

Raphael, D. D. "The Impartial Spectator." *Essays on Adam Smith.* Ed. Andrew Skinner and Thomas Wilson. Oxford: Clarendon Press, 1975. 83–99.

Raphael, D. D., and A. L. Macfie. Introduction. *The Theory of Moral Sentiments.* By Adam Smith. Oxford: Clarendon Press, 1987.

Reid, H. M. B. *The Divinity Professors in the University of Glasgow, 1640–1903.* Glasgow: Maclehose, Jackson and Co., 1923.

Reid, Thomas. *Abstract of Some Statutes and Orders of King's College in Old Aberdeen.* Aberdeen, 1754.

———. *Philosophical Works.* Ed. William Hamilton. 1895; Hildesheim: Georg Olms, 1967.

———. "Statistical Account of the University of Glasgow." *The Statistical Account of Scotland.* 21 vols. Ed. John Sinclair. Edinburgh, 1791–1799.

A Reply to the Calumnies of the Edinburgh Review Against Oxford Containing an Account of Studies Pursued in that University. 2d ed. London: J. Cooke, J. Parker, and J. Mackinlay, 1810.

Reyner, Edward. *Treatise of the Necessity of Humane Learning for a Gospel-Preacher.* London, 1663.

Rinaker, Clarissa. *Thomas Warton: A Biographical and Critical Study.* Urbana: University of Illinois Press, 1916.

Robbins, Caroline. *The Eighteenth-Century Commonwealthman: Studies in the Transmission, Development and Circumstances of English Liberal Thought from the Restoration of Charles II Until the War with the Thirteen Colonies.* Cambridge: Harvard University Press, 1961.

Robertson, John. "The Scottish Enlightenment at the Limits of the Civic Tradition." *Wealth and Virtue: The Shaping of Political Economy in the Scottish Enlightenment*. Ed. Istvan Hont and Michael Ignatieff. Cambridge: Cambridge University Press, 1983. 137–78.

[Robertson, William, et al.] "Reasons of Dissent from the Judgment and Resolution of the Commission, March 11, 1752, Resolving to Inflict No Censure on the Presbytery of Dunfermline . . . ." *Annals of the General Assembly of the Church of Scotland, 1739–1766*. Ed. Nathaniel Morren. Edinburgh: John Johnstone, 1838–1840. 1: 231–42.

Rogers, Charles. *Social Life in Scotland From Early to Recent Times*. 2 vols. Edinburgh: William Paterson, 1886.

Rogers, Pat. *Literature and Popular Culture in Eighteenth-Century England*. New Jersey: Barnes and Noble Books, 1985.

Rollin, Charles. *The Method of Teaching and Studying the Belles Lettres: or, an Introduction to Languages, Poetry, Rhetoric, History, Moral Philosophy, Physics, & c. with Reflections on Taste and Instructions with regard to the Eloquence of the Pulpit, the Bar, and the Stage . . . Designed more particularly for Students in the Universities*. 4 vols. 10th ed. Edinburgh, 1778.

Rothblatt, Sheldon. *Tradition and Change in English Liberal Culture*. London: Faber and Faber, 1976.

"Rules and Minutes of the Select or St. Giles Society." May 2, 1754 to 1762–1763. National Library of Scotland Mss. 23.1.1.

Rush, Benjamin. "Thoughts on Common Sense." *Essays Literary, Moral, and Philosophical*. Schenectady, N.Y.: Union College Press, 1988. 147–50.

Saintsbury, George. *A History of Criticism and Literary Taste in Europe*. 3 vols. London: William Blackwood and Sons, 1902.

Salamini, Leonardo. *The Sociology of Political Praxis: An Introduction to Gramsci's Theory*. London: Routledge and Kegan Paul, 1981.

Sanders, Scott Russell. "The Singular First Person." *Essays on the Essay: Redefining the Genre*. Ed. Alexander J. Butrym. Athens: University of Georgia Press, 1989. 31–42.

Samuels, Arthur P. I. *The Early Life, Correspondence and Writings of the Rt. Hon. Edmund Burke, LL.D. With a Transcript of The Minute Book of the Debating "Club" founded by him in Trinity College Dublin*. Cambridge: Cambridge University Press, 1923.

Schmitz, Robert Morell. *Hugh Blair*. Morningside Heights, N.Y.: King's Crown Press, 1948.

Schofield, R. S. "Dimensions of Illiteracy, 1750–1850." *Explorations in Economic History* 10 (1973):437–54.

———. "The Measurement of Literacy in Pre-Industrial England." *Literacy in Traditional Societies*. Ed. Jack Goody. Cambridge: Cambridge University Press, 1968. 311–25.

Scott, William Robert. *Francis Hutcheson: His Life, Teaching and Position in the History of Philosophy*. 1900; Cambridge: Cambridge University Press, 1966.

Second Letter to G—— W——, esq. Concerning the Present Condition of the <Trinity> College. Dublin, 1734.

Seddon, John. "Lectures on Oratory." 2 vols. ND. Manchester College, University of Oxford Mss.

———. "Lectures on Philosophy of Language and Grammar." 2 vols. 1767. Manchester College, University of Oxford Mss.

Selfe, Lois S. "Rhetoric and *Phronesis*: The Aristotelian Ideal." *Philosophy and Rhetoric* 12 (1979): 130–45.

Shaftesbury, Anthony. *Characteristics of Men, Manners, Opinions, Times*. 2 vols. Ed. John M. Robertson. Indianapolis: Bobbs-Merrill Company, Inc., 1964.

Shaw, John Stuart. *The Management of Scottish Society, 1707–1764: Power, Nobles, Lawyers, Edinburgh Agents and English Influences*. Edinburgh: John Donald Pub., 1983.

Sheldon, Esther K. *Thomas Sheridan of Smock Alley*. Princeton: Princeton University Press, 1967.

Shepherd, Christine M. "The Arts Curriculum at Aberdeen at the Beginning of the Eighteenth Century." *Aberdeen and the Enlightenment*. Ed. J. J. Carter and J. H. Pittock. Aberdeen: Aberdeen University Press, 1988. 146–54.

———. "Newtonianism in the Scottish Universities in the Seventeenth Century." *The Origins and Nature of the Scottish Enlightenment*. Ed. R. H. Campbell and A. Skinner. Edinburgh: John Donald Pub., 1982. 65–85.

Sher, Richard. *Church and University in the Scottish Enlightenment: The Moderate Literati of Edinburgh*. Edinburgh: Edinburgh University Press; Princeton: Princeton University Press, 1985.

———. "Moderates, Managers and Popular Politics in Mid-Eighteenth Century Edinburgh: The Drysdale 'Bustle' of the 1760s." *New Perspectives on the Politics and Culture of Early Modern Scotland*. Ed. John Dwyer, Roger A. Mason, and Alexander Murdoch. Edinburgh: John Donald Pub., 1982. 179–209.

———. "Professors of Virtue: The Social History of the Edinburgh Moral Philosophy Chair in the Eighteenth Century." *Studies in the Philosophy of the Scottish Enlightenment*. Ed. M. A. Stewart. Oxford: Clarendon Press, 1990. 87–126.

Sher, Richard, and Alexander Murdoch. "Patronage and Party in the Church of Scotland." *Church, Politics and Society: Scotland 1400–1929*. Ed. N. Macdougall. Edinburgh: John Donald Pub., 1983. 197–220.

Sheridan, Thomas. *British Education: Or The Source of the Disorders of Great Britain; Being an Essay towards Proving, that the Immortality, Ignorance, and False Taste, which so Generally prevail, are the Natural and Necessary Consequence of the Present Defective System of Education*. 1756. Menston: Scolar Press, 1971.

———. *Complete Dictionary of the English Language, Both with Regard to Sound and Meaning. One Main Object of which is to Establish a Plain and Permanent Standard of Pronunciation*. 2 vols. 4th ed. London, 1797.

———. *A Course of Lectures on Elocution*. 1762; Menston: Scolar Press, 1968.

———. *A Discourse . . . being Introductory to his Course of Lectures on Elocution and the English Language*. 1759; Los Angeles: William Clark Memorial Library, 1969.

———. *A Dissertation on the Causes of the Difficulties which Occur in Learning the English Tongue; with a Scheme of publishing an English Grammar and Dictionary . . . .* 1762; Rpt., Ann Arbor: University Microfilms International, 1980.

———. *Elements of English*. 1786; Menston: Scolar Press, 1968.

———. *Lectures on the Art of Reading.* London, 1775.

———. *An Oration Pronounced Before a Numerous Body of the Nobility and Gentry, Assembled at the Musick-Hall . . . .* 2d ed. Dublin, 1757.

———. *A Plan of Education for the Young Nobility and Gentry of Great Britain.* Dublin, 1769.

———. *A Rhetorical Grammar of the English Language.* 1781; Menston: Scolar Press, 1969.

Shor, Ira. *Empowering Education: Critical Teaching for Social Change.* Chicago: University of Chicago Press, 1992.

Silver, Harold. *English Education and the Radicals 1780–1850.* London: Routledge and Kegan Paul, 1975.

Simms, J. G. "The Establishment of Protestant Ascendancy, 1691–1714." *A New History of Ireland.* Eds. T. W. Moody, F. X. Martin, and F. J. Byrne. Vol. 4, *Eighteenth-Century Ireland, 1691–1800.* Ed. F. X. Martin et al. Oxford: Oxford University Press, 1986. 1–30.

Sinclair, John. *Analysis of the Statistical Account of Scotland; with a General View of the History of that Country and Discussions on Some Important Branches of Political Economy.* Edinburgh: Arch. Constable and Co., 1825.

———. *A Dissertation on the Authenticity of the Poems of Ossian, in the Original Gaelic, with a Literal Translation into Latin.* 3 vols. London, 1806.

Sloan, Douglas. *The Scottish Enlightenment and the American College Ideal.* New York: Teachers College Press, 1971.

———. "The Teaching of Ethics in the American Undergraduate Curriculum, 1876–1976." *Ethics Teaching in Higher Education.* Ed. Daniel Callahan and Sissela Bok. New York: Plenum Press, 1980.

Smith, Adam. *Correspondence.* Ed. Ernest Campbell Mossner and Ian Simpson Ross. Oxford: Clarendon Press, 1987.

———. *An Inquiry into the Nature and Causes of the Wealth of Nations.* Oxford: Clarendon Press, 1987.

———. *Lectures on Jurisprudence.* Ed. R. L. Meek, D. D. Raphael, and P. G. Stein. Oxford: Clarendon Press, 1978.

———. *Lectures on Rhetoric and Belles Lettres.* Ed. John Lothian. Carbondale: Southern Illinois University Press, 1963.

———. *The Theory of Moral Sentiments.* Ed. D. D. Raphael and A. L. Macfie. Oxford: Clarendon Press, 1987.

Smith, Janet Adam. "Some Eighteenth-Century Ideas of Scotland." *Scotland in the Age of Improvement.* Ed. N. T. Phillipson and Rosalind Mitchison. Edinburgh: Edinburgh University Press, 1970. 107–24.

Smith, J. W. Ashley. *The Birth of Modern Education: The Contribution of the Dissenting Academies, 1660–1800.* London: Independent Press Ltd., 1954.

Smith, Olivia. *The Politics of Language, 1791–1819.* Oxford: Oxford University Press, 1984.

Smout, T. C. *A History of the Scottish People.* New York: Charles Scribner's Sons, 1969.

Snow, C. P. *The Two Cultures: And a Second Look.* New York: New American Library, 1964.

Somerset Fry, Plantagenet, and Fiona Somerset Fry. *A History of Ireland.* London: Routledge, 1988.

Sommerville, Thomas. *My Own Life and Times 1741–1814*. Edinburgh: Edmonston and Douglas, 1861.

The Spectator. 5 vols. Ed. Donald F. Bond. Oxford: Clarendon Press, 1965.

Sprat, Thomas. *History of the Royal Society*. Ed. Jackson I. Cope and Harold Whitmore Jones. Saint Louis: Washington University Press, 1958.

Spellmeyer, Kurt. *Common Ground: Dialogue, Understanding, and the Teaching of Composition*. Englewood Cliffs, N.J.: Prentice Hall, 1993.

Spender, Dale. *The Mothers of the Novel: 100 Good Women Writers Before Jane Austen*. New York: Pandora, 1986.

Stafford, Fiona. *The Sublime Savage: A Study of James Macpherson and the Poems of Ossian*. Edinburgh: Edinburgh University Press, 1988.

"Statistical Account of Marischal College." *The Statistical Account of Scotland*. Ed. Sir John Sinclair. 21 vols. Edinburgh, 1791–1799.

Stevenson, John. "Notes from Lectures on Logic." 1775. "Observations on Logic by Several Professors." 1775. University of Edinburgh Mss.

Stewart, Donald. "The Nineteenth Century." *The Present State of Scholarship in Historical and Contemporary Rhetoric*. Rev. ed. Ed. Winifred Bryan Horner. Columbia: University of Missouri Press, 1990.

Stewart, Dugald. "Account of the Life and Writings of William Robertson, D.D." *The Works of William Robertson, D.D.* 2 vols. Edinburgh: Edinburgh University Press, 1830.

———. *Collected Works*. 11 vols. Ed. William Hamilton. Edinburgh: Thomas Constable and Co., 1854–1860.

Stone, Lawrence. "Literacy and Education in England, 1640–1900." *Past and Present* 42 (1969): 69–139.

———. "The Size and Composition of the Oxford Student Body 1580–1909." In *The University in Society*. Ed. Lawrence Stone. Princeton: Princeton University Press, 1974. 1: 3–110.

Stubbs, John William. *The History of the University of Dublin from its Foundation to the End of the Eighteenth Century*. Dublin: Dublin University, 1889.

Sullivan, William M. *Reconstructing Public Philosophy*. Berkeley: University of California Press, 1986.

Sutherland, Lucy. "The Curriculum." *The History of the University of Oxford*. Vol. 5, *The Eighteenth Century*. Ed. L. S. Sutherland and L. G. Mitchell. Oxford: Clarendon Press, 1986. 469–91.

———. *The University of Oxford in the Eighteenth Century, A Reconsideration*. Oxford: Oxford University Press, 1973.

Swift, Jonathan. *Prose Works*. 12 vols. Ed. Temple Scott. London: George Bell and Sons, 1900–1907.

Taylor, John. *Sketch of Moral Philosophy*. London, 1760.

Terry Richard. "The Eighteenth Century Invention of English Literature: A Truism Revisited." *British Journal of Eighteenth Century Studies* 19 (1996): 47–62.

Thom, William. *Works*. Glasgow: James Dymock, 1799.

Thomas, D. O. *The Honest Mind: The Thought and Work of Richard Price*. Oxford: Clarendon Press, 1977.

Thompson, E. P. *The Making of the English Working Class*. New York: Random House, 1964.

Thomson, Derick. *The Gaelic Sources of Macpherson's "Ossian."* Edinburgh: University of Aberdeen Press, 1952.

Tompkins, Jane P. *Reader Response Criticism: From Formalism to Post-Structuralism*. Baltimore: Johns Hopkins University Press, 1980.

Tompson, Richard S. *Classics and Charity?: The Dilemma of Eighteenth-Century Grammar Schools*. Manchester: Manchester University Press, 1971.

———. "English and English Education in the Eighteenth Century." *Studies on Voltaire and the Eighteenth Century* 167 (1977): 65–84.

Topham, Edward. *Letters from Edinburgh Written in the Years 1774 and 1775*. London, 1776.

Trapp, Joseph. *The Character and Principles of the Present Set of Whigs*. London, 1711.

———. *Lectures on Poetry Read in the Schools of Natural Philosophy at Oxford*. 1742; New York: Garland Pub. Inc., 1970.

Trimbur, John. "Essayist Literacy and the Rhetoric of Deproduction." *Rhetoric Review* 9 (1990): 72–86.

Turnbull, George. *Observations Upon Liberal Education*. London, 1742.

———. *The Principles of Moral Philosophy*. 2 vols. 1740; Hindesheim: George Olms, 1976.

Turner, William. *The Warrington Academy Monthly Repository* 8, 9, 10 (1813–1815). Rpt., Warrington: Library and Museum Committee, 1957.

Tytler, Alexander. "The History of the Society." *Transactions of the Royal Society of Edinburgh*. Edinburgh: Neill and Company, Printers, 1890.

———. *Memoirs of the Life and Writings of the Honourable Henry Home of Kames*. 3 vols. 2d ed. Edinburgh: T. Cadell and W. Davies, 1814.

Ulman, H. Lewis. *Things, Thoughts, Words & Actions, The Problem of Language in Late Eighteenth-Century British Rhetorical Theory*. Carbondale: Southern Illinois University Press, 1994.

Van Holthoon, Frits. "Common Sense and Natural Law: From Thomas Aquinas to Thomas Reid." *Common Sense: The Foundations for Social Science*. Ed. Frits van Holthoon and David R. Olson. Lanham: University Press of America, 1987. 99–114.

Van Holthoon, Frits, and David R. Olson, eds. *Common Sense: The Foundations for Social Science*. Lanham: University Press of America, 1987.

Viswanathan, Gauri. *Masks of Conquest: Literary Study and British Rule in India*. New York: Columbia University Press, 1989.

Walker, Obdiah. *Of Education, Especially of Young Gentlemen*. Oxford, 1673.

Ward, John. *The Lives of the Professors of Gresham College . . . .* 2 vols. London, 1740.

———. *A System of Oratory, Delivered in a Course of Lectures Publicly Read at Gresham College . . . .* 2 vols. London, 1759.

Warton, Thomas. *History of English Poetry from the Twelfth to the Close of the Sixteenth Century*. 4 vols. Ed. W. Carew Hazlitt. 1871; Hildesheim: Georg Olms, 1968.

Waterland, Daniel. *Advice to a Young Student, with a Method of Study for the Four First Years*. London, 1730.

Watt, Ian. *The Rise of the Novel*. Berkeley: University of California Press, 1965.

Watts, Isaac. *Works*. 6 vols. London, 1753.

Webb, Robert K. *The British Working Class Reader*. London: Allen and Unwin, Ltd., 1955.

Webster, Noah. Preface. *A Grammatical Institute of the English Language*. 1789; Rpt. in *The Native Muse: Theories of American Literature*. Ed. Richard Ruland. New York: E. P. Dutton and Co., 1976.

Wellek, Rene. *The Rise of English Literary History*. Chapel Hill: University of North Carolina Press, 1941.

Wesley, Samuel. *A Letter from a Country Divine to his Friend in London Concerning the Education of Dissenters . . . .* London, 1703.

Williams, Raymond. *Culture and Society 1780–1950*. London: Chatto and Windus, 1958.

———. *The Long Revolution*. London: Chatto and Windus, 1961.

Wills, Garry. *Explaining America: The Federalist*. Garden City, New York: Doubleday, 1981.

———. *Inventing America: Jefferson's Declaration of Independence*. Garden City, New York: Doubleday, 1978.

Winstanley, D. A. *The University of Cambridge in the Eighteenth Century*. Cambridge: Cambridge University Press, 1922.

Winterowd, Ross W., with Jack Blum. *A Teacher's Introduction to Composition in the Rhetorical Tradition*. Urbana, Ill.: National Council of Teachers of English, 1994.

Winton, Calhoun. "Richard Steele, Journalist and Journalism." *Newsletters to Newspapers: Eighteenth-Century Journalism*. Ed. Donovan H. Bond and W. Reynolds McLeod. Morgantown: West Virginia University Press, 1990.

Wishart, William. Letter to John Ward. 1747. British Library 6211.f.161.

Witherspoon, John. *Selected Writings*. Ed. Thomas P. Miller. Carbondale: Southern Illinois University Press, 1990.

Withrington, Donald J. "Education and Society in the Eighteenth Century." *Scotland in the Age of Improvement: Essays in Scottish History in the Eighteenth Century*. Ed. N. T. Phillipson and Rosalind Mitchison. Edinburgh: Edinburgh University Press, 1970. 169–99.

Wood, Paul. *The Aberdeen Enlightenment: The Arts Curriculum in the Eighteenth Century*. Aberdeen: Aberdeen University Press, 1993.

———. "Science and the Aberdeen Enlightenment." *Philosophy and Science in the Scottish Enlightenment*. Ed. Peter Jones. Edinburgh: John Donald Publishers Ltd., 1988. 39–66.

———. "Science and the Pursuit of Virtue in the Aberdeen Enlightenment." *Studies in the Philosophy of the Scottish Enlightenment*. Ed. M. A. Stewart. Oxford: Clarendon Press, 1990. 127–50.

Yolton, J. "Schoolmen, Logic, and Philosophy." *The History of the University of Oxford*. Vol. 5, *The Eighteenth Century*. Ed. L. S. Sutherland and L. G. Mitchell. Oxford: Clarendon Press, 1986. 565–91.

Young, Arthur. *A Tour in Ireland with General Observations on the Present State of that Kingdom Made in the Years 1776, 1777 and 1778*. Ed. Constantia Maxwell. 1780; Cambridge: Cambridge University Press, 1925.

Index

Academy of Belles Lettres, 132–33

Academy to establish standards for English language, 38–39, 296

Addison, Joseph, 16–17, 47

Aikin, John, 99

Anti-slavery sentiment, 300, 306

Antiquarianism, 63, 67, 73–74, 76, 79, 81, 128, 158, 278, 281–2; source of term in Nietzsche, 62, 297

Aristotle, 8, 183–84

Arnold, Matthew, 24–25, 39, 268–73, 275

Ashworth, Caleb, 98

Bacon, Francis, 44–45

Bain, Alexander, 265–67

Beattie, James, 154–55

Belles Lettres Society, 171

Belletrism, 9–10, 110–11, 166–67, 187, 192–96, 230–52, 266, 273. *See also* Two cultures

Blair, Hugh, 12, 14, 52, 114; appointed to teach English, 169–70; criticism of public debating societies by, 173; defense of personal freedoms by, 245; focus of on style, not content, 237–40; gains power, 145; and *Lectures,* 2, 227–28; overview of lectures, 230–36; political agenda of, 237, 246–48; and *Sermons,* 229, 243–45

British cultural provinces, 18. *See also* Provincialism

Brougham, Henry, 260–61

Burke, Edmund, 132–33, 301

Burns, Robert, 250

Calvinism, 96–97, 307

Cambridge University, 62–70

Campbell, George, 15, 39, 41–42, 206, 227–28; career of, 307; opposition of to Hume's scepticism, 213–14; defense of personal freedoms by, 245; reformulation of language arts by, 216–24

Catholics, Irish, 117, 119, 121

Censorship, 57–58

Centripetal and centrifugal trends: in discourse, 13, 30–31, 37–38, 55–56; in education, 71–72, 175–76, 221–22, 281, 284–85, 286

Cicero, 8, 51, 185

Ciceronianism, 67–68

Civic humanism, 8, 113, 176–77, 179–86, 189, 196–97, 201, 203, 230, 310, 312; and Addison, 182, 185–86, 189, 203; and Commonwealthman tradition, 184–85, 308; emphasis of on rhetoric, 183; and ideal of "good man speaking well," 183, 202; and natural rights tradition, 182, 185, 305; political limitations of, 181, 183–85, 312; as tradition of philosophies of *praxis,* 182, 198, 202–03, 210, 211–12, 278–79, 288

Civil society, 54–55, 152, 155–56, 167, 172, 173–77, 283–84, 293; and essay of taste and manners, 53–54. *See also* Commercial society

Clarke, John, 71–72

Class consciousness, 56–57

Classicism, 4, 20, 65–66, 68–69, 88–89, 105–06, 123, 126–27, 129, 136, 157–62, 164, 174–75, 261–62, 267, 272, 273, 277, 311. *See also* Antiquarianism

Cole, Thomas, 88–89

College Historical Society, 133–34, 135

Commercial society, 11, 177, 196, 199–200, 203; and consumption, 32

Commercialization: of authorship, 34–35; of leisure, 36, 295

Common sense, 206–08; and collective action, 207, 212, 224–25; criticisms of, 99, 113, 214–15; history of, 211–12, 308; school of moral philosophy of, 154–55, 206, 207, 212, 214–16, 223, 225, 232, 251, 308

Comparative method of instruction, 22, 86, 87, 98, 282; as critical pedagogy, 94–95, 113, 114

Composition, 312–13

Contact zones, 6, 29, 141–43, 286–89, 294. *See*